EXPANDING PROCESS

SUNY series in Chinese Philosophy and Culture

Roger T. Ames, *editor*

EXPANDING PROCESS

Exploring Philosophical and Theological Transformations in China and the West

JOHN H. BERTHRONG

STATE UNIVERSITY OF NEW YORK PRESS

The cover illustration is a *Catherine Wheel of Ideas and Ideals* by E. N. Berthrong © 2008.

Published by
STATE UNIVERSITY OF NEW YORK PRESS
ALBANY

Printed in the United States of America

For information, contact State University of New York Press, Albany, NY
www.sunypress.edu

Production by Diane Ganeles
Marketing by Michael Campochiaro

Library of Congress Cataloging-in-Publication Data

Berthrong, John H.
Expanding process : exploring philosophical and theological transformations in China and the West / John H. Berthrong.
p. cm.
Includes bibliographical references and index.
ISBN-13: 978-0-7914-7515-7 (alk. paper)
ISBN 13: 978-0-7914-7516-4 (pbk. alk. paper)
1. Philosophy, Chinese. 2. Philosophy. 3. Philosophy and religion—China. 4. Philosophy and religion. I. Title. II. Title: Exploring philosophical and theological transformations in China and the West.

B126.B42 2008
109—dc22 2007037591

10 9 8 7 6 5 4 3 2 1

CONTENTS

PREFACE

Anyone fascinated by the *Daodejing*, the *Zhuangzi*, and the *Liezi*, classical Confucian thought and later Song neo-Confucian revivals, as well as pragmatism, naturalism, and the process movement in philosophy and theology inspired by Alfred North Whitehead is bound to have a strong fascination with the topic of process, change, and transformation. Though I did not consciously plan it thus when I began the project, *Expanding Process* has become the last of a trilogy of works, proceeded by *All under Heaven* and *Concerning Creativity* (both published previously by the State University of New York Press) about how themes of process philosophy in both Asia and the West are becoming increasingly great parts of the growing world of global philosophy in the twenty-first century.

The first inspiration for the book was the recognition that the concept of process, change, transformation, or creativity is one of those wonderfully protean ideas that drive philosophers and intellectual historians crazy because it is so hard to define—both in the West and in China. While "process" might not a hero with a thousand faces, it is a term that has diverse and changing manifestations in different cultural settings. In this book I will explore only a limited way how the notion of process is framed in one broadly defined lineage of modern American thought and in the Chinese Confucian and Daoist traditions. Dorothy Emmet perfectly caught the nature of the problem in writing:

> "When I remarked to a philosopher friend that I was wanting to think about processes, he rejoined 'A process is just one damn event after another.' I didn't think it was; indeed it was the difference between processes, facts, and events or just things changing that interested me" (Emmet 1992, 1).

The first chapter explains the broad outlines of the project and sets up the parameters of the cross-cultural comparison of Chinese and Western philosophical works. It also begins reflecting on how to conduct such a comparative project as well as suggests why such a event is both possible and rewarding.

As we shall see, the concept of process is a perfect example of a middle-range philosophical concept. This is quite clear when we review the Chinese thinkers in chapters 2, 3 and 4. There are the grand ideas of Chinese Confucian and Daoist philosophy such as the Dao 道 or *tian* 天 that govern the ontological and cosmological visions of these traditions. In the West they would be comparable to the notion of God, the cosmos, nature, the way things are, or, for someone like Buchler in the naturalist tradition, a natural complex. Then there are the concepts that govern the opposite end of the cosmological and ontological spectrum—such as things, events, or the stuff of mundane life, the cabbages and kings of the lifeworld of persons in all kinds of cultures. These are the wonderfully variegated superfluous things that give our quotidian lives such a rich and concrete texture. Between the cosmic and the quotidian dwell notions such as process, change, transformation, and creativity. In *Key Concepts in Chinese Philosophy* (2002) Zhang Dainian demonstrates how this is the case in Chinese philosophy by showing the place of concepts such as numinous transformation and the various forms of change that play an important role in Chinese intellectual history.

The second inspiration of the study was Nicholas Rescher's *Process Metaphysics* (1996). In this succinct historical and philosophical appreciation of the notion of process in the history of Western philosophy, Rescher makes the point that themes of process, change, and creativity are found beyond the confines of the mature process thought of A. N. Whitehead and the philosophical and theological schools he helped to found. It struck me, accepting Rescher's irenic challenge, that it would make a great deal of sense to add another set of voices to the discussion of the concept of process by engaging Confucian and Daoist philosophers and texts. What would "process metaphysics" look like if we added, as we should at the beginning of the twenty-first century, dialogue partners from the two great philosophical and religious traditions of China: the broad paths of Confucian and Daoist thought. To use a common metaphor these days, what is on the Chinese radar that is off the North American screen, and vice versa?

I choose to focus on the Confucian tradition by examining key thinkers during the two of the most creative and novel periods in the history of Chinese thought,—namely, the work of Xunzi 荀子 at the end of the Warring States period (480–221 BCE), and Zhu Xi 朱 熹 (1130–1200) and his students during the Southern Song (1127–1279). Although these two moments in Confucian philosophy are divided by more than a millennium, both Xunzi and Zhu Xi are recognized as paradigmatic Confucian philosophers. In order to balance this double dose of Confucian discourse, I added the great Daoist classic, the *Liezi* 列子, to the mix. Not only is the *Liezi* acknowledged as an equally paradigmatic text, but in its present form it represents a final redaction in a philosophically creative period between the Warring States period and the Southern Song. The Wei-Jin (220–420) era is yet another of those brilliantly creative philosophical epochs in Chinese intellectual history, especially for Daoists of all stripes. The second chapter charts the notion of process in the *Xunzi*, the third chapter does the same for the *Liezi*, and the fourth chapter concludes the Chinese section of the study by looking carefully at the work of Zhu Xi and his *daoxue* 道學 school and how they inherited classical and medieval notions of process and forged them into a new synthesis that dominated Chinese intellectual life for the next eight hundred years.

In order to give some specificity in terms of Western philosophy to my three Chinese dialogue partners, I choose the closely related American schools of pragmatism, naturalism, and process thought as conversation allies. I fully recognize that Whitehead was quintessentially English, but his period of constructive speculative philosophy was conducted while he was teaching at Harvard and proved to be highly stimulating to his American colleagues. Whitehead also recognized the close links between his philosophy and that of the pragmatists. I have merely linked pragmatists, process thinkers, and the American naturalists—all first cousins—to forge my North American bricolage in order to balance my three Chinese dialogue partners. Moreover, I hope to demonstrate that the naturalists, the least known of the American threesome, have a contribution to make to the now global discussion of the concept of process along with process philosophers and pragmatists of all persuasions. The fifth and concluding chapter returns to the North American present and looks at how the three forms of contemporary Western philosophy can dialogue with Chinese philosophers and texts from various periods in Chinese intellectual history.

At the end of the work I have also added an appendix entitled "The Alchemy of Process." At one point I was planning to explore the completely alternative universe of discourse, of the Western occult and esoteric tradition going—and so back at least as far back as the Majorcan theologian, philosopher, and mystic Ramon Llull (1232–1316)—as a counterpoint to the more sober Chinese and Western philosophers I was studying and as a colleague for the author of the *Liezi*. While I found this a fascinating arena in which to explore the notions of process, I quickly discovered that it was historically, religiously, and philosophically too complex and obscure for me to compose a companion chapter to the other five. Nonetheless, as an appendix I want to offer these first investigations as an indication that the study of process and change in the Western occult and esoteric tradition probably would more than repay any effort expended on it in terms of the richness of its novel insights into the transforming world of the Western magus.

Comparative philosophy can mean many things. Here it means comparing notions of process from various Confucian and Daoist philosophical texts and analogous ideas generated by the American naturalist, pragmatist, and process philosophical schools. As I noted above, I have linked American naturalism, pragmatism and process thought because I hold them to be first cousins (or perhaps even siblings) when it comes to the appreciation and understanding of notions of process broadly conceived. With the revival of all forms of Chinese Confucian, Daoist, and Buddhist thought these days in China and the Chinese diaspora, we are at one of those moments when philosophers from vastly different cultural backgrounds are beginning to talk to each other. I truly believe that Confucians and Daoists do have something worthwhile to share with contemporary American philosophers and theologians. The conversation is already rich on the Chinese side of the Pacific, and there is every indication that it is becoming more fruitful on the North American side as well. It is a time of change, and hence the concept of process is a worthy topic of discussion, reflection, analysis, and debate.

ACKNOWLEDGMENTS

Writing the acknowledgments for a book is always the most pleasant part of the composition process. Not only can you reflect back on the twists and turns of the arguments of your work, you can remember and thank all the good friends who helped you along the way. Given that one of the main reoccurring topics of this book about process, change, and transformation is the Confucian and Daoist conception of the Dao, the metaphor of a changing and twisting path walked together with a host of family, friends, and colleagues, it is entirely apt to list those who have been an inspiration on the journey.

I first want to thank a group of wonderful colleagues in the maturing study of Confucianism over the last four decades. I first encountered the Confucian Way as an exchange student at the University of Hong Kong in 1964. At that time wonderful teachers and friends such as Professor William Wong took the time to introduce a young man from Oklahoma to a much wider world, a world that included Kongxi. Later, when I as an undergraduate back in Kansas, Professors John Dardess and Alfonso Verdu of the University of Kansas provided me with solid training in the history of China, and the devoted staff in East Asian studies labored to try to teach me to read the *Analects*. During my graduate studies at the University of Chicago, Professor Edwin Kracke introduced me to Zhu Xi, because he knew of my growing interest in the history of Chinese philosophy. Professor Anthony C. Yu and Professor David Roy then taught me as much as I could learn about the art of sinology as the dedicated, engaged, committed, and passionate study of Chinese history, culture, philosophy, literature, and religion. At the end of the process of writing my dissertation, Professor Edward T. Ch'ien was extremely gracious with his time and good advice. Through the good offices of my teachers at Chicago I even had the rare and precious chance to meet with Professor Mou Zongsan of the Chinese University of Hong Kong in the summer of 1975. Professor Mou spent a whole illuminating afternoon talking with a young North American graduate student about Zhu Xi's grand philosophical synthesis and encouraged me to continue my studies of Song thought.

While I was finishing my dissertation, I had the opportunity to study with Professor Tu Weiming, then teaching at the University of California, Berkeley. Later I had the privilege of meeting a host of fine Chinese scholars such as Professors Liu Hsu-hsien, Peter Lee, Julia Ching, Thomas H. C. Lee, Huang Chun-cheih, Lee Ming-hui, Chen Lai, On-cho Ng, Yang Guorong, Peng Guoxiang, and Fu Youde—just to mention a few of my Chinese friends and colleagues who have encouraged my fascination with Confucian discourse over the decades and who have gently tried to correct my misunderstandings and oversights. Along with my Chinese friends and colleagues I must also acknowledge a group of North American scholars such as Professors Mary Evelyn Tucker, Robert C. Neville, Rodney Taylor, David Hall, Roger Ames, Peter Nosco, Peter Bol, Michael Puett, P. J. Ivanhoe, Joseph Adler, and Stephen Angle who have been constant conversation partners about the study of the varied aspects of Confucian scholarship. Along with all of these friends, I must confess a special debt, as does everyone in Confucian studies, to Professor Wm. Theodore de Bary for his meritorious leadership for more than five decades of the Neo-Confucian Seminar at Columbia University, where he still continues to mentor and advise today. If there were ever a scholar who taught, as Kongzi advised so long ago, with an open hand, it is Professor de Bary. My last group of colleagues in need of thanks are the hard-working members of the Confucian Studies group of the American Academy of Religion—an important forum for showcasing the contemporary study of Confucianism in Asia and North America.

I also want to thank my editors, such as Ms. Nancy Ellegate, and friends at the State University of New York Press for their continued support of my projects over the years. Further, I owe a deep debt of gratitude to the two anonymous reviewers of this book for extremely valuable advice in how to improve, clarify, prune, and sharpen the overall argument of *Expanding Process*.

Of course, any Confucian knows that all life and thought begins within the family. I have been supported by my parents, who first took me to Hong Kong as an undergraduate, and then by my wife, Evelyn, and my son, Sean. I have even had the rare privilege and pleasure of coauthoring a basic text on the history of the Confucian Way with Evelyn,—namely, *Confucianism: A Short Introduction*. Along with my human family I have been accompanied along the way with a wonderful pack of three poodles: Fafner, Yoyo, and Diva. There is nothing like an affectionate cold nose to help academic writing move along when writer's cramp threatens what Whitehead called the creative advance into novelty. Whatever good is to be found in this book comes from this host of family, friends, companions, and colleagues—the errors come entirely from my own stubborn nature that has failed to learn from these wonderful teachers.

1

Introduction

PROLOGUE

That everything changes is a commonplace in diverse religious and philosophical cultures spread across time and space. But even if we accept this adage for the moment, the really interesting question then becomes, what is the nature of the process of change? How are things transformed? What remains the same even within such general transformations, if anything at all? This concern with change and its process is not a new philosophical insight. At the beginning of the Greek adventure in philosophy, Heraclitus made his famous observation about not being able to step into the same river twice—"Everything flows and nothing abides; everything gives way and nothing stays fixed. You cannot step into the same river, for other waters and yet others go flowing on" (Lakoff and Johnson 1999, 359). Whitehead once quipped that you probably could not step into the same river even once. Whitehead's particular contribution to the discussion of the universal reach of process is partially defined in the famous category of ultimate as creativity: "'Creativity' is the universal of universals characterizing matter of fact" (Whitehead 1978, 21). A moment later Whitehead glosses creativity as "the principle of *novelty*" (21). Commenting on the vast range of opinion about change or process, Nicholas Rescher writes in his short introduction to the history and praxis of process metaphysics: "Process metaphysics as a general line of approach holds that physical existence is at bottom processual; that processes rather than things best represent the phenomena that we encounter in the natural world about us" (Rescher 1996, 2). Gordon Kaufman, from a theological perspective that would have been appreciated by Mou Zongsan (1909–95), writes, "We do not know why or how creativity comes about: it is a profound *mystery*. The mark that identifies the occurrence of creativity is its *consequence*: something strikingly *new*, something *transformative* has come into being, has become a significant feature of the ongoing world" (Kaufman 2006, xiv). Like so many other primordial philosophical insights, the concept of creativity is a perfect example of a vague general category that is specified in many different fashions. Yet one thing is clear: something new, novel, transformative, and transforming marks the mystery of creativity.

Nonetheless, Dorothy Emmet's conversation with a philosopher friend captures the difficulty to specifying just what "process" can possibly mean (remember that Emmet was one of Whitehead's first and foremost students). "When I remarked to a philosopher friend that I was wanting to think about processes, he rejoined 'A process is just one damn event after another.' I didn't think it was; indeed it was the difference between processes, facts and events or just things changing that interested me" (Emmet 1992, 1).

At the other end of the Eurasian landmass, Kongzi Confucius 孔子 also opined that a river runs on constantly and later exegetes took the master to be observing by his cryptic remark the constant passage of nature as a form of process. "The Master was standing on the riverbank, and observed, 'Isn't life passing just like this, never ceasing day or night?'" (*Analects* 9.17).[1] Of course, it is a stretch to relocate from Kongzi's Zhou dynasty Shandong riverbank to Whitehead's Charles River in the contemporary American city of Cambridge.

The point that Heraclitus sought to make (we think) was that there is a pattern of change that governs the flux of the world. "All things come to pass in accordance with the Logos" (Lakoff and Johnson 1999, 360). In their commentary on the pre-Socratics, Lakoff and Johnson note that we find three great metaphors for the essence of philosophy in this early period that endure throughout the history of Western philosophy. These are: essence is matter; essence is form; and essence is patterns of change. They give rise, à la Stephen Pepper's theory of root metaphors (Pepper 1942), to classical materialist, formalist, and process metaphysics (Lakoff and Johnson 1999, 363). In some respects, Kongzi may be even more process-oriented than Heraclitus, because he does not seek the logos of change amid the other structures of life, but merely notes that life and the river are in constant flux. However, it is as difficult to know precisely what Kongzi intended to teach as it is to explain the cryptic saying of Heraclitus. One could also argue that the Buddha even founded a whole religious reform movement on the fact that nothing ever stays the same.[2]

However difficult comparative philosophy is, we are driven to make comparisons between currency exchange rates when we travel and different ideas when we encounter them.[3] Second-generation cognitive science scholars such as George Lakoff and Mark Johnson argue that all human thought is based on the use of metaphor. Metaphors are engines of comparison; hence, we are caught in a double bind. Postmodernists and critical theorists are worried about all the potential problems of comparison done in blissful ignorance or bad faith, and yet we cannot escape the act of comparison. This is a delicious irony for postmodernism when one stops to think about it for a moment. Notwithstanding his qualms about the magical shortcomings of comparison, Jonathan Z. Smith considers that comparison is essential to the study of the history of religion; what Smith asserts is that we need to use comparison responsibly and with as much critical self-awareness as we can muster.[4] We all compare, and we all want to make our comparisons as accurate or correct or interesting as possible. These days we also do not want the domination of taxonomies wherein we force our own prejudices willy-nilly on the philosophical categories and religious ideals of other people. Our global city is a place, we hope, of informed and compassionate dialogue at the very least. We might not practice the perfect art of comparison, but we do not want to be caught out being naive about what a good comparison might look like.

In the philosophical and theological arts, Japanese, Korean, Vietnamese, and Chinese intellectuals and educated professionals already have appropriated or are appropriating the best of the Western philosophical traditions. On the other side of the Pacific, Western intellectuals have lagged behind this kind of intercultural exchange, though this is gradually beginning to change as more and more philosophers and theologians become fascinated by the revival of various Asian cultures and philosophical and theological traditions. Although I will confine myself to examples drawn from the rich scope of Chinese thought, the same argument holds for engagement with the worlds of South Asia (Hindu, Muslim, Buddhist, Jain, and Sikh) and the Middle East—not to mention the riches of what has been labeled "traditional wisdom" in Africa, the Americas, Asia, and Oceania. Actually, what is really needed is an awareness of what Ninian Smart calls "world philosophies" (1999) as inclusive of the best of human thinking from any continent and many islands. It is time that Western philosophers and theologians engage "other worlds" so that such new intellectual suppleness might, in the end, make them more effective "game players" in the pluralistic matrix of the modern world.[5]

COMPARATIVE NARRATIVES: THE PARITY OF NATURAL COMPLEXES

The simplest comparative way forward would be to compare and contrast these classical, early modern, and modern Chinese and Western expositions of the trait of process to find out their similarities and differences.[6] However, chastened by criticism by scholars such as Jonathan Z. Smith and Lloyd and Sivin (2002) that such unreflective comparison, however interesting it might be, is methodologically unsound, some account of why such a comparison of significant traits is possible is in order. If we accept Whitehead's argument about the importance of the analysis of the trait of process within any adequate speculative philosophy as a working comparative hypothesis, then there is a warrant for proceeding with a cross-cultural comparison of selected Chinese and Western texts and traditions.

Prudence suggests that when comparison is made across cultures, a vague general category, following Neville's (2001a, 2001b, 2001c) discussion of vagueness based on Peirce, is a useful intermediary step before the specifics of the comparison are investigated. The examples will be selected texts from the Chinese Confucian and Daoist traditions and the American naturalist tradition, of which Whitehead's process philosophy is a stellar example. Moreover, I have decided to choose a specific philosophical notion from the work of Justus Buchler to serve as a vague general comparative category. I announce my choice for a pragmatically useful comparison, but I will not mount a full defense of the choice until the final chapter. My reticence is based on a pragmatic consideration. The proof the value of the choice of Buchler's category of a *natural complex* will become clear if and only if the choice of the concept of natural complexes is shown to have worked to evoke a successful comparison of the role of the trait of process in philosophies as diverse as Whitehead's speculative cosmology and Liezi's romp through the various orders of the Dao 道. Both the Dao and Whitehead's cosmological notion of creativity would be examples of natural complexes qua vague general terms in Chinese and Western philosophical discourse.[7]

Buchler opens his essay on metaphysics with the following lines: "Whatever is, in whatever way, is a natural complex. The entire sequel, in a sense, amplifies the statement" (Buchler 1990, 1). The two phrases, "in whatever way" and "in a sense" ironically even parallel the double negations of the *Daodejing*'s reflections on the Dao and name(s). As we shall see in chapter 4, Chen Chun (1159–1223) defines the Dao in the following manner: "Tao is the way. Originally the meaning of the word was a path, and path means a common road for people to walk on. If it is meant for only one person, it cannot be called a road" (Chen Chun 1986, 105). Slightly later Chen adds, "Tao is not external to things and affairs as something empty. In reality Tao is not separate from things" (107). Hence, whatever is, is a natural complex, or, as Chen would say, affairs and things (*shi wu* 事物) that need to be endlessly connected to other things and affairs and that can be endlessly ramified by walking along the path of the Dao. But my comparative rhetoric is getting ahead of the path as a natural complex we will traverse together.

Another reason I have chosen Buchler's notion of a natural complex as the vague general comparative concept is that, at least according to Buchler's own account, a natural complex has both ontological and cosmological implications. Neville (1992, 1995b, 1995c), for one, has been highly critical of Whitehead's version of process philosophy because it lacks an ontological dimension. According to Neville, Whitehead has provided us with a brilliant cosmology, but this is only half of what counts for an adequate speculative philosophy in the Western tradition (Berthrong 1998b). Neville maintains that an adequate speculative philosophy must embrace both cosmology and ontology. If Buchler's notion of a natural complex helps to show how philosophies of process as diverse as Xunzi's classical Confucian discourses, Liezi's

Daoist speculations, Zhu Xi's and Chen Chun's *daoxue* 道學 (Study of the Way), and Whitehead's system can generate an ontological trait to parallel their processive cosmologies, then the notion of a natural complex will have played a very important comparative role between classical Confucianism, Wei-Jin (220–316 CE) Daoism, Song *daoxue*, and modern American naturalism. We will return to the ontological question in chapter 5.

At present all I can do is anticipate the arguments that will follow about how the notion of a natural complex helps to tease out both the cosmological and ontological traits implicit in Song and contemporary Anglo-American process thought. I will return to a dialogue among the three forms of Chinese philosophy and contemporary American naturalism in chapter 5.

TEXTUAL CONTENTS

As the twentieth century turned into the twenty-first, many other scholars, following the lead of Joseph Needham, began to notice and explore the processive nature of Chinese thought.[8] The notion of process, postulated as a secondary concern in Western philosophy and philosophical theology—a thesis that will be tested in the following chapters—was discovered to be a major theme of Chinese thought. By any fair descriptive measure, certain Chinese philosophers, separated in time and divided by genealogical loyalties in the Daoist and Confucian wings of Chinese culture, did have a place for process in their philosophies and worldviews.[9] Moreover, I was delighted to discover that Mou Zongsan asserted that process or "creativity itself," as he would define it, was a foundational trait informing all of Confucian thought (Mou Zongshen 1994, 31–32, 53–54). Because Mou has been recognized not only as one of the founders of the New Confucian movement but also as perhaps its most important systematic philosopher in the twentieth century, I felt confirmed in my search for process themes in Confucian discourse.

So after having discovered that Mou Zongsan postulated a vital role for process as creativity itself in Confucian thought, I formulated the following problem: How do we go about explaining its functions both in Chinese philosophy and in traditions of Western Modernity[10] such as the philosophical and theological school of thought inspired by Whitehead? And what would this Chinese version of process possibly mean for modern Western philosophical understandings of creativity and process philosophy and theology? I am challenged by Nicholas Rescher's (1996) hypothesis that process is indeed a part of a great deal of Western thought and did not have to wait for Whitehead to explain it to us.[11] If I am correct, Whitehead's firm enunciation of the role of process in the cosmos would have been both comprehensible and appreciated by many Chinese intellectuals, ranging from classical thinkers of the Zhou dynasty, Wei-Jin savants, and Confucian revivalists of the Song, Yuan, Ming, and Qing periods, to modern New Confucians—as well as to assorted Daoist and Buddhist intellectuals.

Of course, the Chinese Confucian or Ruist tradition 儒學[12] is as diverse as the Western philosophical tradition. In order to escape vacuity of reference, I will focus my attention on three specific Confucian and Daoist thinkers and spend most of my time on the Confucians. My major Confucian interlocutors are drawn from the classical and the neo-Confucian periods—namely, Xunzi, at the end of the Warring States period, Zhu Xi, and Zhu Xi's student Chen Chun in the Southern Song. However, in order to avoid the unwarranted hegemony of the Confucian voice, I will also devote a chapter to the Wei-Jin period text of the *Liezi*.[13] I will, of course, defend these choices in later chapters.[14]

Moving forward to the contemporary scene, one of the particularities of the modern world has been the explosion of information, of which comparative philosophy is only one protodiscipline seeking to find a place among the voices of a contested postmodernity. If we cannot even understand the complexities of the canonical Western tradition, what hope is there for comprehending something as strange as Confucian, Daoist, or neo-Confucian ontology, cosmology or axiology? It is scant support to remember that Montaigne (Toulmin 1990), at the very beginning of Western Modernity, was excited by the discovery of peoples and forms of thought from around the expanding world of the sixteenth century. Nonetheless, timidity has never been a great virtue in philosophical discourse. Prudence might make us hesitate before launching into new oceans of thought before we have even plumbed the depths of the Western heritage, but faintness of vision has never been one of the characteristics of the modern Western world. The positive caution is, again, the legitimate concern for scholarly rigor, the persistent desideratum to compare apples to apples and oranges to oranges and only compare them as exemplars of fruit.

I will defend the claim that it is more and more pressing to develop responsible methodologies for comparison among worldviews from different philosophical and religious cultures in the modern world. This has a pragmatic component: like mountain climbers taking on the Himalayas and the Alps, philosophers compare and contrast rival visions of intellectual structures of human cultural creativity because they are there. Intellectuals indulge in comparative praxis sometimes for nothing more than the pure joy of comparing Xunzi with Aristotle or Augustine (Stalnaker 2006), or Laozi and Zhuangzi with the skeptics, or Zhu Xi with Whitehead (Berthrong 1998b). The permutations are legion and governed both by taste and the magic of an illuminating comparison, which can have the same impact as a really lively metaphor. But as with all the arts, some comparisons make more sense than others, and some comparative methodologies help to make for better, more rigorous, and more responsible comparative acts. Finally, in the pragmatic mode, given the shrinking nature of our ecumenical world, we had better learn to compare, contrast, and appreciate our different philosophies and religions if we have any hope of living in a peaceful world. Although good comparison will not end international and intercultural conflict, it is hard to envision any reduction of tension without better understanding based on responsible comparisons.

WORLD PROCESS

One of the new insights of global scholarship in history and economics is that history and economics must be truly global in scope. For instance, André Gunder Frank (1998) urges the writing of a truly ecumenical or universal economic history. Frank makes the case for a unified world, or at least a unified Afro-Eurasian economy, long before the "rise of the West." He contends that, in fact, the rise of the West to economic dominance was only made possible by two other ecumenical conditions. First was the European conquest of the Americas and the concomitant discovery of vast amounts of silver and gold. Franks notes that the plundered silver reserves of the New World were the price of admission of the West into the flourishing economy of the East. Second was the fact that the East—that is to say, primarily India and China—had created a huge interregional world of trade that allowed for the rise of the West economically. Moreover, Frank notes that the West only became a dominant partner in this Afro-Eurasian trading world in the early nineteenth century. By the beginning of the twenty-first century, the traditional dominance of Asia, and most specifically China and the wider East Asian world, began to assert itself yet again. If Napoleon was correct that China is a sleeping giant dragon awakened only at risk to Western notions of the self and society, then the transformations could be as great and dangerous in the intellectual world as they already are in the economic domain. Buddhism, for instance, is the most rapidly growing religion in North America. Does this mean that the importation of Nissans, Subarus, and Toyotas signal the arrival of Buddhism, Vedanta, Daoism, Shinto, and Song-style neo-Confucianism into the mind of the West? No one really knows, but if silver and gold flowed east along with theoretical baggage, then perhaps ideas will now flow west along with tangible goods.

On a deeper level, some kind of comparative methodology is necessitated by the very act of cross-cultural comparison. Just as with all other cultural domains, there are good comparisons and bad comparisons, magical or dull in their turn. Ultimately what makes for a good comparison is the new light that it throws on one or both of the parties being compared. Good comparison can lead to an increase of human knowledge. It can also lead to the reduction of intercultural social gaffes. We can all learn what color flowers to send to weddings and funerals after having learned that American and East Asian understandings of appropriate colors for joy and sorrow are different. For instance, white is sign of bereavement and should definitely not be sent along to a joyous Chinese wedding.

The art of comparison requires sensitivity to the creation and management of comparative categories. Even though we are all human beings, and equal in that respect, it is not likewise clear that we are all theists or atheists in our own ways. What counts as a good work in Confucian thought needs to be compared meticulously to what would count as a good work in Christian theology. Sometimes we will find a convergence, but in other cases we will find divergence and diversity. The diversity of what counts for human flourishing among different cultures should cause us to pause and ask if the comparative categories we are using to illumine the contrasts are good ones—that is, whether they work to bring clarity rather than further darkness and confusion.

Of course, the range of traditions that pay careful philosophical attention to the root metaphor, prototype, hypothesis, trait, or motif of process in what is loosely called "Asian" thought could be expanded greatly beyond even our test cases of Xunzi, Liezi, and Zhu Xi and his disciple Chen Chun. For instance, within the Chinese cultural world, the diverse set of traditions collectively known as Daoism are prime candidates for honorable mention as foundational texts and schools of process thought along with Confucianism. In fact, when talking about the early classical Chinese world that gave birth to the Confucian tradition, it is impossible not to mention its dialectical twin, Daoism. In the later periods of the development of Confucian thought in the Northern and Southern Song, the massive influence of Buddhism on the neo-Confucian revival makes it is impossible to consider the neo-Confucians without a sidelong glance at their Buddhist cousins. The only excuse for not discussing neo-Confucianism, Daoism, and Buddhism together is that such a comparison is pragmatically unfeasible, given the question of scope (and that publishers are nervous about printing books too large to sell).

In an appendix, "The Alchemy of Process," I will explore another neglected pathway of process thought within the Western world. This is the world of Western esoteric, occult, theosophical, or magical religion. This esoteric tradition, albeit often unnoticed, ignored, scorned, and repressed, extends from thinking in the ancient Near East to the modern New Age movement. While many other students of process thought have already shown its extensive roots in the mainline history of Western philosophy and theology, I want to explore the world of what Dame Frances Yates (1979, 1986) has called the history of occult philosophy and theosophy. There was and is always something worrisome about looking into those subjects; nonetheless, there are certain features of the history of occult philosophy, especially beginning with Ramon Llull in the thirteenth century, that merit our attention. Llull, who lived and was inspired by the religious and philosophical pluralism of the Spain of his day, helped to introduce the Cabala into Christian theology.[15] His style of thinking had a great impact, as we shall see, on various Renaissance thinkers and through that tree of learning, down to the world of contemporary New Age religion. While these connections with the Western esoteric tradition may not endear process thought to orthodox Christian theologians, it is an interesting and perhaps not-so-minor footnote to the expansion of our understanding of the interest in process themes in Europe and beyond.

One fascinating feature of the occult and esoteric philosophers of early modern Europe is their ecumenical openness to other philosophical and religious traditions. Although many of these thinkers remained, at least according to their own lights, Christians, they demonstrated a marked willingness to consider dialogue with the Jewish and Islamic worlds. For instance, one of the main features of the early modern occult movement was the creation of a Christian Cabala in which there was always an element of spiritual practice. The more orthodox Christian authorities were always worried that these occult philosophers were too much interested in magic—especially evil ritual magic—but this element of praxis would have been perfectly comprehensible to various strains of the Chinese tradition. But then, Confucians were used to dealing with their Daoist cousins, the occult masters of the Chinese world.

THE PROTOTYPE OF PROCESS

The cooperative duo of George Lakoff and Mark Johnson, with Lakoff representing linguistics and cultural analysis and Johnson philosophy, have written a number of influential studies focusing on the topic of metaphor (1980, 1999). Edward Slingerland (2003) has creatively applied the Lakoff-and-Johnson method of metaphor analysis or "philosophy in the flesh" to a set of early Chinese philosophical texts. Of course, the study of metaphor has a storied history in the development of Western thought; Aristotle would hardly be surprised by the perennial fascination shown by philosophers, literary critics, and even theologians with the supple and pervasive role that metaphors, living and dead, play in our collective cultural sensitivities. Stephen Pepper (1942) wrote about the "root metaphors" that govern all philosophical systems whether or not the metaphors are recognized as the roots to alternative worldviews as such.

While philosophers and theologians have acknowledged more than a passing interest in the role or rule of metaphor in thought and life, there has also been a countervailing opinion about metaphoric influence. As Plato portrays him, Socrates fought a long battle against the sophistic tradition and rhetoric in general in his constant search for a strict definition of virtue and true knowledge. The dialectical argument of Plato is that merely giving a facile account of a virtue or a cracking good metaphor will not do. What we really need is the clear articulation of principles to order thought, action, and passion. This is also a story told by David Hall and Roger Ames, as well, in terms of what they call first- and second-order philosophical sensibilities.[16] According to Lakoff and Johnson (1980), there are literally "metaphors we live by"; hence, I can assume that Whitehead's system is a prototype *sensu stricto* that can be used to focus attention on what constitutes an ecumenical global family of process philosophies *sensu lato*. I will demonstrate how reflection on the Chinese Confucian and Daoist material helps us move from a strict to a wide sense of process thought, and how the Chinese discourse can interact creatively with modern Western philosophy and theology.

The collaborative and individual work of Lakoff and Johnson is attractive for the investigation of Chinese thought because of reasons intrinsic to its own form and because of the way it throws new light on certain features of Chinese thought (Slingerland 2003). The first reason is that metaphoric analysis takes us to a vague and yet specific level; metaphors are general enough that they sometimes make sense across cultures, and when they are too culturally specific to be readily understood beyond the culture of origin, they provoke in us the desire to perform acts of multicultural hermeneutic. Secondly, the study of metaphor does not claim logical universality, yet it does point to very concrete human proclivities for action and reflection in the lifeworlds of individuals and communities. Moreover, many generations of modern critical students of Chinese thought in general and the Confucian and Daoist traditions in particular have noticed the extensive use of metaphors as a basis for philosophical argumentation. I will argue that metaphoric analysis (my label for the philosophical work of Lakoff and Johnson) provides an intriguing segue into the cross-cultural study of ecumenical process thought. Of course, the proof for this assertion, as with other such hypotheses announced in the introduction, will only become evident over the course of the book.

Because some younger scholars are only now attempting the specific link between Lakoff and Johnson's metaphoric analysis and the Chinese traditions in any systematic way,[17] I would like to outline the reasons for this methodological approach to cross-cultural hermeneutic. First, metaphors, although often specifically culturally and historically located, are, if Lakoff and Johnson are correct, about as foundational to human language and culture as any item in the human communicative repertoire. Metaphoric analysis holds that metaphors literally structure the way we feel, think, and act—we really do need to walk the road of the Way, as the Daoists and Confucians would say. Second, building on this initial premise of the role of metaphor in all human interactions, is the oft-noticed proclivity for Chinese philosophers to use stories and metaphors to make their intellectual points.

I will argue that the Lakoff-and-Johnson theory of metaphors and its application to the use of metaphors in Chinese thought is not related to the old theory that Chinese thinkers do not have anything resembling Western general theories. This old bromide stated that Chinese philosophers had recourse to metaphors as rhetorical devices because Sinitic traditions lacked any sustained theory of the rational articulation of thought in the way the West had Aristotle's theory. Of course, as scholars have continued to analyze and even discover more and more texts from the Zhou period, it has become clear that some Chinese philosophers, most notably those associated with the lineage of Mozi and the later Confucians and Legalists, were perfectly capable of articulate reasoning and the logical presentation of their various cases. In the Confucian tradition, Xunzi adapted the Moist logic for his own Confucian purposes.

Truth be told, most Confucians, following Mengzi (Mencius), did not like to enter into the logical world of Mozi but were forced to do so in order to defend "this culture of ours." Notwithstanding the general lack of interest in following either the Moist school or Xunzi's style of carefully reasoned essays, clarity of thought was as highly prized in China as anywhere else, as we shall see in the work of Zhu Xi and Chen Chun.

My thesis is that although there is plenty of vagueness and lack of precision in Chinese intellectual life, there is nothing in the manner that Confucians or Daoists articulate their worldview that is less coherent than the discourses of any other great culture if we understand the Confucian Way as a vast tradition spanning time and even as an international movement with significant outposts in Korea and Japan.[18] It is simply vastly different from the forms of respectable discourse developed in the European, Islamic, Buddhist, and South Asian cultural worlds. Chinese thought is an intricate interlocking array of natural complexes and root metaphors to live by.

One of the reasons why Western scholars have had difficulty in recognizing the typical Confucian patterns of reasoning is that so much of the best Confucian thought has been devoted to the writing of commentaries ever since the founding of the Han dynasty in the second century BCE. Lloyd and Sivin (2002) have also given some cogent thought to the social location of the famous early Chinese thinkers and to the question of why they used certain genres in explaining their insights into the world. Perhaps this is why many modern Western intellectuals also overlook the rich resources of medieval Western theologians who also often did their work in the commentary mode. Moreover, very little of this vast East Asian commentarial tradition has been translated into any European languages and remains locked away in the records of the voluminous battles between Chinese, Vietnamese, Korean, and Japanese scholars about the various levels of meaning to be found in the Confucian canon. I have always felt that it was regrettable that someone like Zhu Xi did not follow Xunzi's example in writing topical essays explaining contested points of theory and practice; but this is just a perfect example of my modern Western proclivity for a certain format in philosophical presentation.

When Confucians seek clarity about some matter—say, for instance, the proper form of a family ritual—they can do so with a precision that would make Emily Post proud. Zhu Xi was as famous for his easy-to-understand compendium of rituals (Chu 1991) as for his philosophy; surely, more people made use of his rituals for family life than of the intricacies of his philosophical speculations. No, it is not that the Confucians lacked the tools of intellectual precision or logic; rather, Confucians were concerned with topics different from those often thought to be fundamental to any serious Western philosophy. Some Chinese thinkers, such as the medieval Buddhist theoreticians of the Tiantai and Huayan schools, could be as metaphysical as any systematician anywhere in the world (Ziporyn 2000). As we shall see, Xunzi and the great Song neo-Confucian Zhu Xi also had systematic inclinations when they thought it was necessary.

The Daoists provide a counterpoint to the Confucian view of a well-ordered world of sages and their commanding rituals. The Daoists will have none of this Confucian pomposity. Because of their rejection of Confucian orderliness, some scholars have argued that the classic Daoist texts of the late Zhou period are irrationalist in nature. However, I will argue, based on the work of scholars such as A. C. Graham (1992b) and others, that what we find in the best of Daoist writing is not irrationalism, but rather an antirationalist sensibility. Irrationalism and antirationalism might look alike but are decidedly different beasts. Our excursion into the *Liezi* will show this side of Chinese thought.

MOTIFS OF GLOBALLY ECUMENICAL PROCESS THOUGHT

It is now proper to ask a basic question: What do we mean by process thought? What does a process prototype look like? The first reason for not attempting a concise or strict definition of the term or tradition(s) should be obvious by now. Whitehead often made the point that in complex matters we should distrust the simple and seek the obscure or complex for the simple reason that the obscure might be shadowy but more congruent with the reality being described. The great Wei-Jin *xuanxue* 玄學 Dark Learning masters would have agreed (Ziporyn 2003). The second reason is that I have been convinced by the work of Lakoff and Johnson that it makes more sense to begin the process of definition by providing a set of metaphors than a strictly logical and exhaustive definition of process thought. The third reason derives from the second. If one expressed aim of this book is to expand the ecumenical global reach of an extensive definition of process thought, then we would expect that something new might be added to the definitional mixture by the inclusion of Chinese material. Of course, nothing might be added by that addition, but the outcome will be obvious only after the attempt has been made.

In Western philosophy, Nicholas Rescher has provided us with a starting place for constructing a prototype in *Process Metaphysics: An Introduction to Process Philosophy* (1996). Rescher, while deeply appreciative of Whitehead's achievement, argues that process philosophy is a phenomenon wider than just the movement begun by Whitehead. Rather, Rescher notes that we can find motifs anticipating modern process thought beginning among the classical Greek philosophers. As Rescher moves into the modern period, he lists pragmatic theorists such as Peirce, James, Bergson, and Dewey as major process thinkers alongside Whitehead.

After his historical review, Rescher provides a list of six basic themes and ideas of process thought *sensu lato*. In framing his synopsis of process traits, Rescher states: "*The characteristic feature of process philosophy is its stress on the primacy of activity—and on the range of associated factors such as time, change, innovation, and so forth. It maintains that these conceptions are not just necessary but even basic to our understanding of the world*" (1996, 27; italics in the original). Along with these fundamental two motifs—the primacy of activity and the concomitant need for themes such as change and innovation—Rescher (27–49) lists four other key traits for any process philosophy *sensu lato.* I will list all six motifs in bullet form because they provide us with a starting point for identifying the range of what counts as process thought.

Rescher's List

- primacy of activity
- necessity of change and innovation and so forth
- the internal complexity of change and development
- the idea of process entails various characteristic distinctions concerning change and development over time
- substance is subordinate to process
- the real is processual and things are what they do

Additional Themes and Motifs

- pluralism
- relationality

I add two more basic traits to Rescher's list in anticipation of the expansion of process thought beyond the European cultural world—namely, the themes of pluralism and relationality. Most process philosophy *sensu stricto* and *sensu lato* is pluralistic and hence also interested in the relationships of natural complexes. The patron saint of the seventh trait of pluralism within process thought is William James. It is hard to have process without a plurality of occurrences and things, to use Rescher's formulation of process pluralism. According to Rescher, "[T]he overarching neutral category of *existent item* or *entity* or *individual* branches out into two realizations: *things* (substances) and *processes* (activities)" (1996, 34). However, the inclusion of pluralism as a seventh basic idea of process thought will need to be defended during the rest of the book.

The eighth basic theme is relationality or the connections of the various natural complexes. I have added this in deference to the Confucian and neo-Confucian traditions. The modern New Confucian philosopher Mou Zongsan has suggested that a prime characteristic of all Confucian thought is what he calls "concern consciousness"—a profoundly pluralistic form of connectional axiology (1994, 19). Moreover, Rescher details how important various doctrines of relationality are to diverse Western process philosophers. I think that Whitehead would have appreciated the addition of the theme of relationality. In *Modes of Thought* (1938, 229–30) he reminds us of the Quaker admonition to have a care or concern for each other and for the created order. This is a statement of the profound relational and axiological nature of process thought. For instance, if we affirm a pluralistic universe, it stands to reason that we will have to explore the relations between the creatures of a pluralistic cosmos, even if these relationships are judged to be trivial in nature, or as profound as they often are for *daoxue* thinkers such as Zhu Xi and Chen Chun. Furthermore, it is hard to see how concern consciousness for self and others does not imply pluralism. If there is not something or someone to be concerned about, why bother?

In the spirit of the project of expanding Rescher's discussions beyond the examination of process in the various Western traditions, what are the kinds of semantic terms common the Confucian and Daoist texts and contexts? Ames and Rosemont (1998, 281) have a very useful discussion of five key Chinese terms for change. These five are:

gai 改 (to change, alter, correct, amend, or reform)
bian 變 (to manifest gradual change over time)
hua 化 (the trait of transformation such that one thing becomes something else)
qian 遷 (to change from one place or aspect to another)
yi 易 (to exchange one thing for another); also, part of the title of the essential text, the *Yijing* 易經 (*Book of Changes*)

To this list I would also add terms such as:

ziran 自然 (the primal trait of spontaneity)
sheng 生 (birth or generativity); often quoted from the *Yijing*'s famous formulation *shengsheng buxi* 生生不息 (ceaseless generativity)
shi 勢 (the transformative efficacy of things and events)
wei 僞 (the active art of contrivance); especially important for Xunzi

Ziran is extremely important as a marker for change or transformation in the tradition of the *Zhuangzi* and the *Liezi*—and actually for all elite Chinese intellectuals, including the Song *daoxue* scholars. *Sheng*, as Mou Zongsan has argued over and over again, represents the key notion of fundamental change as a critical trait of the cosmos in the whole Confucian tradition.[19] François Jullien (1995) has devoted a whole monograph to the philosophical exposition of the notion of *shi* as the dynamic power of efficacy, yet another important demonstration of the role of the trait of process in the Chinese cultural world. And as we shall see, *wei* as artful human contrivance is a critical notion for Xunzi.

Rescher goes on to provide an interpretation of the basic motif of process. "A process is a coordinated group of changes in the complexion of reality, an organized family of occurrences that are systematically linked to one another either casually or functionally" (1996, 38). Moreover, processes develop over and in time, according to Rescher. Process has a "developmental, forward-looking aspect" (39). Rescher also has a good method of distinguishing two major modes of process—namely, those that produce "things" and those that produce transformation among things or events. There are "*product-productive processes*" that create the kinds of things that we call concrete objects or substances. The other modality is "*state-transformative processes*" such that what are changed are the various present configurations of reality in order that further processes can occur. Here Rescher gives examples such as windstorms and earthquakes. The great Southern Sung neo-Confucian Zhu Xi adds, as we shall see, another set to the state-transformative processes—namely, the inclusion of events such as refined ethical rituals. According to Zhu, an appropriate ethical response to a complicated personal situation has as much claim to concrete reality as a bowl of steaming rice.

Rescher adds another key motif for process thought *sensu lato* by differentiating *owned* and *unowned* processes. Owned processes "are those that represent the activity of agents: the chirping of birds, the flowering of a bush, the rotting of a fallen tree" (1996, 42). Unowned processes, in contrast, do not represent the actions of any specific actor. Rescher's examples of unowned processes are "the cooling of the temperature, the change in climate, the flashing of lightning, the fluctuation of a magnetic field" (42). The Chinese tradition, as well as others, may have some problems with the notion of unowned processes. From Zhu's vantage point, the Dao as the Way of Heaven owns all processes—or better, all processes are integrally related as manifested in the Dao. Perhaps Rescher's point is better expressed when he notes: "Not every [unowned] process can be seen as consisting, in the final analysis, in the activities of one or more things" (43). As we shall see, individual principles or *li* for Zhu are representative of the Supreme Ultimate as the highest expression of all coherent principle in general.[20]

Rescher continues his discussion of basic ideas of process thought, but for our purposes, the present list, as expanded to include various Chinese terms, provides us with a prototype of what process philosophy is in its modern European (and Chinese) guise. Rescher's work, to borrow from ethnography, is both emic (internal to the tradition) and etic (external to the tradition). It is an emic account because Rescher approves of many of the original themes of process philosophy and commends them to other modern philosophers. It is etic because it is not biased toward any one version of the process tradition; for instance, Rescher does not privilege Whitehead as the sole prototype of process philosophy. In short, Rescher provides a benchmark against which other philosophies can be measured in order to decide if they are part of the process family or merely close relatives. Of course, it may also be necessary, from time to time, to add additional motifs to Rescher's list when we move into the worlds of classical Confucian, Daoist, and neo-Confucian discourses. But before we deal with the three specific Chinese thinkers and movements, we need to reflect more on the nature and scope of comparative nomenclatures and methods.

THE QUESTION OF NOMENCLATURE

Before we launch into our investigation of the trait of process in Xunzi, Liezi, Zhu, and Chen's thought in the following three chapters, we need to examine the question of nomenclature for describing the Confucian and Daoist traditions. This may seem somewhat pedantic, but it is not, especially because of a recent spate of discussions about the status of Western categoreal constructs such as Confucianism and Daoism when compared to the Chinese materials in question. The crux of the matter is that some quite reputable scholars have now argued that there are no such things as Confucianism or Daoism to be found in East Asia—these are pure categorical fictions conjured up by the Western imagination. The argument is, not to put too fine a point on it, that these are traditions invented by Western scholars in the nineteenth century. And if these are mere Western inventions, we cannot pretend that these terms can pick out anything that has coherence within traditional Asian cultures.

The intellectual and social historian of Japan Harry Harootunian, has extended the argument beyond the invention of specific world religions such as Buddhism, Hinduism, Confucianism, Daoism, and Shinto to the very notion of Asia itself. "It has been one of the enduring ironies of the study of Asia that Asia itself, as an object, simply doesn't exist. While geographers and mapmakers once confidently named a sector on maps, noting even its coordinates as if in fact it existed, this enmapped place has never been more than a simulacrum of a substanceless something. . . . I have always felt that the Association of Asian Studies periodically brought specialists together in order to reaffirm the existence of what clearly is a phantom" (Harootunian 2000, 25).

Harootunian is making the same kind of point that Zhang Longxi (1998) has made about markers such as Confucianism and Daoism. We need to be careful about mistaking our terminology concerning philosophical and religious traditions for something of ontological or cosmological reality.

The problem is that we have become accustomed to these terms, rather like the way Professor Henry Higgins becomes accustomed to faces. When I talk about Buddhism, Daoism, and Confucianism with my Chinese colleagues, they know what I am talking about, either using Modern Chinese or English. Modern Chinese intellectuals have developed perfectly good neologisms or have refurbished older terminology to match what Western scholars call Confucianism or Daoism; words such as *rujiao* 儒教 or *rujia* 儒家, for instance, are used in the case of Confucianism. What in the West is designated "neo-Confucianism" is now simply called *xin* 新 *rujiao* or (neo-Confucianism) to distinguish the Song revival from the classical thinkers of the Warring States period. This does not mean that my Chinese colleagues are not sensitive to the kinds of definitional questions I am raising. They are concerned, but they are ecumenical comparative scholars who are as steeped in the Western study of philosophy and religion as they are in the study of Chinese intellectual history.

I will return to a longer examination of the Daoist side of things in the chapter on the *Liezi*. Besides, scholarly concerns about the nature and history of texts and the definition of traditions and religions would strike the Daoist sages like Liezi as a very Confucian conceit. Texts, just like everything else in the world, are self-creative or autotelic when you come right down to it. Whatever order we find, we humans impose it from our limited personal perspectives, like frogs looking at the sky from the bottom of a well and defining the sky as a very small blue ball. Zhuangzi made the point once that when you use a finger to point at the moon, you should not keep looking at the finger once you have sighted the moon. The moon and finger have other uses. Who cares who wrote the texts? The point is the point, maybe—if you can figure out if there is a point to be made in any case.

No one is arguing that there is nothing in East Asia that resembles the common understanding of "Confucianism" as the term is now commonly understood in scholarly circles in the Euro-American world and in China, Korea, Japan, and Vietnam. Whole libraries are full of works that deal with Kongzi, Mengzi, Xunzi, Dong Zonghu, and all the Song, Ming, Yuan, and Qing revivalists—as well as the writings of generations of Korean, Japanese, and Vietnamese followers of the Confucian Way (Berthrong 1998a; Yao 2003). What is at stake is the scholarly definition of the term "Confucian" or "Confucianism." Another variant of the problem with finding proper names is the already lengthy debate about whether or not Confucianism (or Daoism) is a religion.[21] There are those who maintain one side of the contest with great vigor. The crux of the matter is how one defines religion. If we take the model for religion to be that of Western Asia in general and Christianity in particular, then it is hard to see how Confucianism can be called a religion. It lacks so many of the marks of a true Christian church that it is hard to see how the name "religion" can be applied to it. However, most historians of religion have now learned to move beyond the strict confines of Western Christian history in order to define religion.

Mark Edward Lewis (1990) provides one of the most original and persuasive accounts of the rise of the "Confucian" school. In a brilliant reexamination of the development of Chinese intellectual culture from the Shang to the end of the Han dynasty, Lewis alternates between using the Chinese term *ru* 儒 and the English form of "Confucian" or "Confucianism" (see also Puett 2001, 2002). Lewis is well aware that there is nothing quite like what modern Western and Chinese scholars take to be Confucianism in early China. The term that comes closest to Confucianism is *ru*. However, Lewis further demonstrates that there is not a perfect fit between the Chinese notion of *ru* and the English term "Confucian." "Confucian" would actually be a specialized subset of the *ru*—that is, scholars who see themselves following in the steps of Kongzi in contradistinction to other scholars following teachers such as Laozi, Zhuangzi, or Mozi, for instance. Even the definition of *ru* is contested; suffice it to say that it came to identify a rather ill-defined group of ritual specialists and scholars during the long development of the Zhou dynasty. Later it became more and more a term for disciples of Kongzi, Mengzi, and Xunzi. I commend Lewis's meticulous account of this story for the details of the vicissitudes of the history of the development of *ru* as a marker for a group of scholars with a particular pedigree.[22]

A direct descendant of Kongzi, Kong Zigao (312–262 BCE), responded with the following definition of what it means to be a Confucian: "Prince P'ing-yüan said: 'From where is the term "Confucian" derived?' Tzu-kao (Zigao) answered: 'It is derived from the idea of the combination of the various exquisite virtues, and the conjoining of the six arts, such that whether in action or repose he never loses the core of the Way'"(Ariel 1989, 135). This definition comes from a text at least as early as the *Liezi* and shows that a descendant to the master had a pretty good idea of what it takes to be a *ru* or Confucian.

However this might be in terms of the history of the English terms "Confucian" and "Confucianism," it is good to remember the sensible words of Xinzhong Yao, the editor of the newly published multivolume encyclopedia of Confucianism, He writes that

> "Confucianism" is never a clear-cut notion that can be defined in terms of one or another western discipline. Like all other Eastern traditions Confucianism contains within itself multidimensional ideas and ideals, ethical, political, religious, philosophical, educational, etc. These values are intertwined with each other, and are explored and manifested in Confucian doctrines concerning human nature and destiny, familial relationships and virtues, community norms and disciplines, social structure and political cohesion, and religious beliefs and spiritual practices. In history, Confucian ideas and ideals were the basic way of life in China and other East Asian countries, and to some extent they continue to function as such in modern times. (Yao 2003, 1:5)

Although the term "Confucianism" does lack a specific and clearly defined Chinese counterpart, generations of Chinese, Korean, and Japanese scholars have had a sufficiently accurate sense of intellectual self-identity that they have been able to distinguish their teachings from those of Moists, Daoists, Legalists, and Buddhists with clarity. Whatever else they were, they were *ru* scholars.[23]

PROCESS, SCEPTICISM, AND NATURALISM

The more I reflected on the text of the *Liezi*, the more I became convinced that two other philosophical themes or traits are linked to the cross-cultural expansion of the comparative history of process thought—especially in its Daoist manifestation as a decidedly skeptical turn of mind. These two are skepticism per se and its close cousin, relativism. Although it is hard to think of Zhu Xi or Whitehead as skeptics, in highly circumscribed epistemological terms Whitehead, at least, actually is one. "But, putting aside the difficulties of language, deficiency in imaginative penetration forbids progress in any form than that of an asymptotic approach to a scheme of principles, only definable in terms of the ideal which they should satisfy" (Whitehead 1978, 4). In short, we must be skeptical about any final claims of dogmatic certainty. "There remains the final reflection, how shallow, how puny, and imperfect are efforts to sound the depths in the nature of things. In philosophical discussion, the merest hint of dogmatic certainty as to finality of statement is an exhibition of folly" (xiv). This kind of epistemological modesty is not a flaming skepticism that denies we can know anything with precision, but rather a warning about thinking too highly of the mind-heart's ability to provide us with a perfect philosophical dictionary. Whitehead never denies that we cannot know all sorts of things about the world, and that some of these conclusions are much more accurate than others. Nor does Whitehead ever suggest that we suspend all judgment about the world. Rather, Whitehead pleads for humility about the range and scope of human cognition and about any claims to finality in terms of metaphysical insight. And while Zhu Xi thought a sage could comprehend the principles of the myriad things and events of the world, he was also aware of how difficult such comprehension was and that the world was an endlessly complex, growing, and changing array of the ceaseless interplay of the generativity of the yin and yang forces. Sages can also make mistakes; but what makes a sage a sage is that the sage then tries to correct her or his mistakes.

In the Chinese philosophical tradition, skepticism and Xunzi and Zhu Xi are not often linked. Being "Ruist" philosophers, both are probably mild skeptics at most; their skepticism is somewhat like that of Whitehead, although different in important respects, as we shall see. They believed that we can learn a great deal about the world, and what we can learn is more than enough to cultivate personal and social morality. They simply were not interested in the kinds of epistemological questions that gave rise to the skeptical tradition in the West. For instance, Zhu Xi may not want to be a skeptic, but this does not mean that the burden of his reflections on human knowledge do not conduce, at least in modern terms, to a skeptical or restrained epistemology when compared to other Song, Yuan, and Ming thinkers such as Wang Yangming and his followers. Zhu Xi knew a lot but also realized that the world was a vast place and that there were always new things to investigate. If investigation never really stops, then a certain mild skepticism is in order. Nonetheless, Xunzi and Zhu Xi, when compared to the author of the *Liezi* and Whitehead, are hardly skeptical of their world at all. To claim perfection in terms of their own cultivation would have offended against Confucian humility and deference, but it was clear nonetheless that if they were skeptics at all, they were mild ones.

The second theme that trails along after skepticism is relativism. Here again, there is nothing strange about noting the relativistic tendencies of the classical Daoist texts such as the *Liezi*. Moreover, Ruist scholars likewise have always recognized the need for sensitivity to context and perspective, and this lends their thought a mild relativist cast in the sense of awareness that judgment must always allow for sensitivity to the context of a situation or the perspective of the witness. Whether this Ruist relativism is merely the recognition that all things are related to all other things and events or is expressive of a more robust relativism such as found in Protagoras is something that we will explore in later parts of the book. This realism expresses itself in terms of what Justus Buchler calls ordinal naturalism in the sense that each thing is related to other things or events via its position in the various orders of nature.[24]

Although Zhu Xi defines the world in terms of a realistic pluralism based on and nourished by an ethical axiology that can be defined as an ordinal (relational) naturalism (Kim 2000), it is much harder to see how Zhu Xi can then move to a strong form of epistemological skepticism as some kind of logical entailment. As Joseph Margolis (1991) has argued at length, a philosopher can defend a robust version of relativism and yet not succumb to epistemological skepticism. According to Margolis there is no automatic logical path leading from Protagoras and the other Sophists to the teachings of Sextus Empiricus.

While Margolis is correct in warning the unwary about jumping from relativism as a mild form of skeptical cognition to a complete suspension of any opinion, Scharfstein is also equally prescient in noting that such jumps from philosophical position to philosophical position do happen with enough frequency to warrant curiosity about why this categorical drift takes place. Scharfstien buttresses his argument (1989, 1998) by carrying out his research in the history of philosophy in a comparative fashion, noting that these kinds of connections between process and the other traits do exist in India and China as well as in the West. Of course, merely piling up examples drawn from different cultures over the last three thousand years does not make a conclusive philosophical case. As Jonathan Z. Smith has repeatedly warned (Patton and Ray 2000), it could be just another example of the magic of comparison. It does, nonetheless, provide material for examining why certain ideas are affined to others, even cross-culturally. As the Indian philosophers are fond of saying, when we see smoke, can fire be far behind? There is perhaps no necessary connection between seeing smoke and finding a fire, but more times than not, there will be a fire somewhere.[25]

My initial hypothesis is that realistic pluralism is one key categorical natural complex or root metaphor, aided and abetted by an emphasis on the role of process for my Chinese and Western exemplars. The point is not hard to fathom. If there are many things or events, then they will stand in various relations one to another. They will be "relative" to each other for no more astounding reason than that they are plural and hence in some kind of relation to each other (Emmet 1992). This was the basis for Whitehead's own version of relativism. Buchler (1990) also grounds his metaphysics of natural complexes on the notion that natural complexes are plural and always related to other natural complexes. As we shall see in chapter 4, Zhu Xi believed that while principle was one, its manifestations were many. Zhu's vision of the world was relentlessly pluralistic in terms of the range of objects and events he believed needed to be examined on the way to the cultivation of sage wisdom. The kinds of relations and the natures of the objects and events need not be immediately defined. The objects and events could be featureless monadic billiard balls or complicated emotional creatures such as standard poodles or human beings living in complex packs. Yet the main point stands: these objects and events are related to each other because they are separate, realistic objects or events.

My second hypothesis is that there is an even stronger tendency toward a more robust relativism if the objects and events are interpreted as processive in nature. The classic modern Western example is Whitehead's exposition of actual entities—the famous reformed-subjectivist cognitive principle that helps these actual entities share a common epistemological and causal world. Daoist figures such as Zhuangzi and Liezi, the stipulated authors of the texts that bear their names, also demonstrate pluralist, processive, relativist, and skeptical sensibilities. Although more restrained by Ruist ethical decorum, Xunzi and Zhu Xi also have a world comprised of pluralistic and processive objects and events. Yet, as we shall see, Xunzi borrows a great deal of Zhuangzi-like theories of the mind-heart.

Mou Zongsan, certainly no great fan of Zhu's specific *lixue* 理學 (Study of Coherent Principle) version of the Confucian Way, affirms the pluralistic sensibility of the Confucian tradition, including that of Zhu Xi. Mou (1990, 1994) argues that Confucians constitute their lifeworlds by a method of intersubjectivity. No person is a person without interaction or "transaction"—to use Dewey's phrase (or query, à la Buchler)—with other persons. This is the Confucian version of the social construction of the world. It is realistic in that there is a world outside of the skin of any particular person, but as in Whitehead, each person is coconstituted by others. Typically the Confucians focus on the interaction and transactions of one person with another, and do not speculate, as does Whitehead, on the broader issues of panpsychicalism or panexperientialism (Griffin 2001). Mou deems Zhu a fellow Confucian in terms of the intersubjective and pluralistic nature of reality. Moreover, Mou also defines the Confucian Dao in terms of the process of the ceaseless productivity of the Dao. Zhu certainly fits the generalized Confucian profile. Mou's strong critique Zhu has more to do with Zhu's epistemology and methods of self-cultivation than with Zhu's fervent Confucian sensibilities.[26]

My third hypothesis is that the thought of Liezi, as a devoted follower of Zhuangzi with a Wei-Jin twist, is an exemplary bricolage of musings about pluralism, relativism as context, relativism as suspension of judgment, and process as key philosophical trait—all mixed with a healthy dose of skepticism about how well we can describe, explain, understand, and commend this mélange of objects and events via philosophical ruminations. If the classical Greek skeptics had discovered the *Liezi* as good skeptical philosophy, Montaigne would have found in its thought a kindred soul. Confucians generally stay away from some of the excesses of their Daoist cousins, because they remain focused on ethical matters of personal and social efficacy. The Confucians really want society to work, and they believe that the Confucian Way will contribute to the achievement of human flourishing for one and all. Daoism might be a wonderful teaching for a few isolated hermits, but Confucianism is needed for people living within the confines of complicated social orders. This kind of Confucian argument is forcefully made, as we shall see, by Xunzi, among others.

My fourth hypothesis is that axiology as a concern for method and judgment is a bridge between the other elements of expanded, global process philosophy and natural theology. Although there may be such a beast, I have still to find any historically recognizable process philosophy or theology that does not take axiology seriously either in terms of aesthetics or ethics. In fact, it might just be that the skeptical and contextual traits of a robust process thought conduce to reflecting on the role of values qua the relations between realistic pluralistic objects, persons, and events. As odd a thought as it might seem at first blush, when one realizes that one lacks perfect knowledge, and moreover, one is ipso facto not likely to achieve perfect knowledge or moral certainty anytime soon, then the questions of value become pressing. For instance, how does a Daoist like the author of the *Liezi* tell us we should act? Naturally, of course. How does a skeptical relativist in the middle of complex events and contexts distinguish, if at all, between good and evil, the better or the worse, or any other kind of relevant guide to moral action? In short, even Daoist philosophers as skeptics and relativists are axiological in their desire to help us live well in a complex, dangerous world.

As a fifth hypothesis I hold that, in terms of contemporary American philosophy, the Confucian tradition, along with its emphasis on the process trait, is likewise a form of naturalism. Of course, there is nothing revolutionary about defining the Confucian tradition as a form of naturalism. Scholars have argued for generations that Xunzi, for instance, helped to naturalize the classical Confucian tradition, moving it away from its distinct roots in a worship of *shangdi* 上帝(Lord on High) or *tian* 天. In fact, the Confucians themselves often made just such a claim for their tradition in contradistinction to Daoists and Buddhists, whom they believed to be hopelessly superstitious about matters religious.

The specific Confucian claim was that they themselves were realistic—that is to say, that they affirmed the reality of the world of mundane things and events. The Confucians argued that this affirmation of a pluralistic realism differentiated them from the Buddhists, who sought nirvana as emptiness, and from the Daoists, who believed in *wu* 無 (non being). In this regard, I will deem Justus Buchler's natural complexes to be philosophical cousins of the classical and neo-Confucian Dao. According to Buchler, Xunzi, and Zhu Xi, we encounter a world wherein we find complex upon complex that we deem to be real in a fundamental ontological sense; all complexes are natural parts of the *ars contextualis,* to borrow the nomenclature of Hall and Ames. There is no supernatural order, though there is often a clearly discernable religious dimension to the Confucian Way. There is just this world, and everything in it is real in one sense or another, providing a kind of ontological parity. In modern American philosophical terminology, this is a form of naturalism. I will return to a more extended discussion of this point when we reach the modern West at the end of the book in chapter 5.

2

Xunzi

Acting in the Dao

THE ENIGMA OF XUNZI

Whatever the precise dates, which may never be established beyond a doubt, it is clear that Xunzi 荀子 (ca. 310–210 BCE) played a role as a public intellectual in the last stages of what Chinese historians have called the Warring States period; he may have lived to see the founding of the victorious Qin 秦 empire.[1] This was truly the classical and foundational era of Chinese philosophy. If Xunzi himself did not see the founding of the Qin, some of his students assumed important roles in the establishment of the first of China's great imperial dynasties, which would rule China until 1911. Moreover, there is equally little doubt that Xunzi was the greatest scholar the classical Confucian tradition has produced in terms of the articulate and organized sophistication of his philosophical essays.

But it is not the problem with dating Xunzi's life that makes him such an enigma for the study of the development of the Confucian tradition in classical China. The presenting problem is that Xunzi had the audacity, according to the great Zhu Xi (1130–1200) and the other Song dynasty masters, to contravene unambiguously one of the central teachings of Mengzi 孟子, whom they reverently considered as the second sage after Kongzi 孔子. Mengzi taught that *xing* 性 (human nature) was inherently good, whereas Xunzi argued that it was odious or evil, or at least odious without proper self-cultivation. It has only been in the last few decades that contemporary Confucians have begun to reverse this historical judgment on Xunzi's place in the evolving philosophy of the Confucian Way. Xunzi, they now claim, only misunderstood Mengzi when he had the temerity to say that Mengzi was incorrect on a point of philosophy critical to the Song renovation of the classical Warring States tradition and the accurate transmission of the Way.

There was something else that the Song scholars held against Xunzi, though this was a flaw from almost any Confucian perspective and not peculiar to developments of Confucian thought in Northern and Southern Song. Xunzi, as we shall see, was a famous teacher and, as such, unleashed some equally famous—or rather, infamous—students. The teacher sets an example by formal teachings and conduct of life; the student is supposed to follow both, and in doing so, to cultivate the mind-heart in such a way as to become both a fine scholar and a good person. This is a chilling demand for any teacher, especially if some of the students turn out to be villains famous in the history of imperial China.

Xunzi had two famous students—Li Si 李斯 and Hanfeizi 韓非子—who fitted the bill as classic villains in the historiography and cultural memory of Chinese intellectuals ever since the Han dynasty put the imperial system on a solid footing after replacing the disgraced Qin regime. Both Li and Han, in rejecting the Confucian philosophy of Xunzi, became leading theorists for a great alternative philosophy, Legalism (K. Smith 2003). The Legalists rejected the Confucian emphasis on moral cultivation as the basis for good government and devised a political theory based on calculations of power and the formulation of a strict set of penal and administrative laws designed to regulate every aspect of human life in service to an all-powerful state. Moreover, the Legalists were highly successful in furnishing the intellectual ideology for the Qin unification of the Warring States into an empire that the Qin hoped would become eternal.[2] Save for a few moments during the reign of Mao, it has always been a terrible thing to be called a Legalist by Chinese intellectuals. The larger Chinese public remains dubious about the claims that the rule of law will solve everything wrong with a social system. And because he was the teacher of two of the most famous Legalists, a whiff of suspicion lingers around Xunzi as well. Ultimately, the rejection of Xunzi by the Song philosophers was a double tragedy for the flourishing of the Confucian Way. First, it deprived the Song masters of an easy recourse to the most philosophically sophisticated of the Warring States Confucians. It has only been very recently that the tide has turned toward a more positive reception of Xunzi's contribution to the contemporary renewal of the Confucian Way. For instance, the great modern New Confucian, Mou Zongsan, stated in his last lecture that this post-Song shunning of Xunzi no longer makes any sense. Mou was firmly convinced that the modern reconstruction of Confucianism needed to make use of all the resources of the cumulative tradition. Not to make use of the most capable of the Warring States masters was ill-conceived.

Second, the abandonment of Xunzi by post-Song Confucian thinkers has had an unanticipated consequence for the reception of Confucian philosophy in the West. Without putting too fine a point on it, Xunzi was by far and away the most systematic of the early Confucian masters. As Knoblock noticed, there is good reason to make the analogy between the placement of Xunzi and Aristotle in their respective philosophical traditions. Aristotle and Xunzi parallel each other insofar as both masters summarize what has come before them, and both are remembered as the most coherent philosophers of their generation. This does not mean that everyone agrees with them, but no one has doubted their ability to write systematically coherent philosophical essays.

It is shame that scholars of Confucian philosophy cannot simply introduce Western friends to Xunzi. Xunzi writes, among other things, perfectly orderly essays on a variety of topics that are of perennial interest to any student of philosophy. Xunzi is interested in poetry, and even writes some credible verse himself. He also discourses about history, interpretations of other philosophers, philosophy of the mind-heart, theories of ritual action, the economy, epistemology, warfare, and logic, among other topics. Xunzi, borrowing from A. C. Graham's memorable characterization (1989), was one of the true master disputers of the Dao in classical China.

ROOT METAPHORS OF XUNZI'S CONFUCIAN WORLDVIEW

Joseph Needham suggests that whereas the typical Western philosopher seeks to find substances or essential features of reality, the Chinese philosopher seeks a relation as the major modality for explaining how the world works (Ronan 1978, 78). As we shall see, the trait of relationship or relations is often affined to those of process in both the Confucian and Western traditions when process is taken seriously as an aspect of the working of the world. Later scholars such as Hall and Ames (1987, 1995, 1998), themselves writing from a comparative view emphasizing the trait of process, name this contrast as the difference between a substance view of reality and a relational view of reality. Or to use a slightly different root metaphor drawn from the respected modern New Confucian philosopher and intellectual historian Xu Fuguan (1902–92) 徐復觀, the essence of the early Chinese worldview was a profound sense of shared concern as a deepened intersubjectivity between all persons (Xu Fuguan 1975, 20–24).

This profound sense of concern for self and other, which Xu's New Confucian colleague Mou Zongsan contrasts to a sense of wonder as intellectual query in Greece and the religious sense of awe or homage in Israel and India, means that the relational side of reality is heavily stressed in all classical Confucian thought (Mou Zongsan 1983, 1994). This assertion of the root metaphor of concern consciousness, as Mou calls it, is the basis for the common affirmation that all Confucian thought is fundamentally ethical or axiological, and more specifically, a form of social ethics with a strong pragmatic and realist sensibility. The premise of Xu and Mou[3] rests on the presupposition that ethics and general social action would be ideationally meaningless if they did not refer in the first place to relations between creatures (Berthrong 1994).

In summary, it is clear that Xunzi lived at the end of the most creative period of Chinese intellectual and philosophical history (Collins 1998).[4] Because of this, Master Xun inherited, either positively or negatively, the assumptions, problems, sensibilities, perplexities, and answers of those who came before him—primarily those of his beloved Confucian ancestral sages and later masters such as Kongzi. He directly systematized the emerging Confucian heritage, and he most definitely believed that there was such a lineage, plus a somewhat uneasy load of heavy debts owed to the Daoists, Moists, Legalists, and others as well. Although we cannot always be sure about his sources (careful citation of sources was not a virtue in this period), Xunzi emerges as one of the most cogent, penetrating, passionate, and systematic intellectuals of his or any other age. As Whitehead wrote of both Plato and Locke, Xunzi combined a powerful mind with a breadth of learning and experience and had the luck to live at the end of a great era of innovative speculation and was hence able to produce a summary of some of the best philosophical insights of classical China. Whitehead should have added Aristotle, whom Xunzi rivals as a Confucian paladin of comprehensive and organized learning.

While Xunzi manifests a strong sense of "vertical transcendence", it is equally true to say that Xunzi was the great naturalizer of the Confucian tradition, with the secular here a signifier for a naturalist philosophical vision.[5] Actually, it is through his naturalization of the Dao that many scholars have defined Xunzi when his philosophy is placed in the Western taxonomy of the secular versus the sacred. Mou, for instance, characterizes the Confucian Way as a religious path, or at least a tradition that embraces a major religious or spiritual dimension. Confucians have a sense of what Mou calls vertical transcendence as well as an appreciation of the ritual life of horizontal social connections between people. Mou notes that every great religion, even those such as Confucianism that do not resemble the theistic traditions of Judaism, Christianity, and Islam, must have a vertical dimension of transcendence and a horizontal dimension of social ethics and rubrics for self-cultivation. Confucian scholars are not secularist naturalists in the same sense in which Western intellectuals use the term for post-Enlightenment public intellectuals hostile to the Christian churches in the Euro-American scene. In many ways this vision of the Confucian Dao echoes Charles Hartshorne's notion of dual transcendence in process thought (Berthrong 1994; Bresciani 2001; Liu 2003).

What Xunzi and the American naturalists like Buchler and Corrington reject is the contrast of the natural with something called the supernatural. For Xunzi there is nothing beyond the agency of the nature forces of the created order even when considered as *tian* 天; for Buchler and Corrington, there is nothing beyond natural complexes that ramify infinitely. For Xunzi the old religious concept of *tian* (heaven) clearly becomes a name for a natural process or set of natural processive complexes. In Buchler's language, Xunzi's concept of the Dao is the concept of a natural complex as the infinite ramifying order of order upon order. It is just ordinal location all the way down for the ten thousand things and events as William James always claimed for concrete things.

On the one hand, Xunzi believed that all the things and events of the world were created though the agency of the yin-yang forces of the primal *qi* 氣 (vital force). Further, he was quite definite that there was no theistic intention, plan, or will behind the natural order of the world. As Xunzi noted, "Heaven has the constant way; earth has the constant categories" (Ren 1979, 1:210).[6] In *Discourse on Nature* he observes, "Heaven possesses a constant Way; Earth has an invariable size; the gentleman has a constancy of deportment" (Knoblock 1988–94, 3:17). Xunzi is often interpreted, when teaching about social relations, language, and ritual actions, to be a conventionalist in terms of the orders of human life. However, he also recognized relatively objective rules, regulations, and agencies beyond the power of social convention. Xunzi's point, however, was that these are also natural orders that are not subject to the whims of a god or other theo-volitional spirits inside or outside of the world. Moreover, it was not the case that Xunzi was unfamiliar with the theistic option. Mozi, the great opponent of naturalist Confucians such as Xunzi, had a robust theistic natural theology that had *tian* 天(heaven) very much intentionally in control of the cosmos. But for Xunzi, human beings are very much part of the natural order and are not subject to agencies from outside of the natural complex of the yin-yang forces and other natural categories. It is true that human beings have certain complex functions, such as the ability to create intelligent ritual patterns, yet these patterns or orders of human life emerge out of the basic *qi* of the cosmos (see Ren 1979, 1:221).

On the other hand, Xunzi was not a thoroughgoing mechanistic or strict determinist. For Xun, both our successes and failures come from human effort; there is no realm beyond nature, no supernatural realm from which strange forces operate. He rejects the notion that one can read the heavens for omens or interpret strange natural events as portents for future human outcomes. Further, he also rejects some of the pseudosciences or technologies of his day, such as physiognomy. Social decay, he contends, comes from a trio of human errors: (1) the decline of agricultural production, (2) governmental interference in the economy, and (3) social disharmony or imbalance. There is nothing that needs supernatural or even spiritual intervention here—just hard human work, though there is a distinctive Confucian note registered. The emphasis on social harmony is something that Confucians would always be concerned to express. In fact, a great deal of Confucian thought and praxis is given to bringing a sense of harmony to self, family, the larger society, and even the cosmos of the ten thousand things. As Xunzi put it, humanity must "regulate the decree of *tian* in order to make use of it" (Ren 1979, 1:221–13). *Tian* has its seasons, the earth has its material abundance, and human beings have, in a limited manner, the capacity to control the natural forces, or at least to understand their ceaseless ordering functions. The perfect person, the sage, is one who knows what can and cannot be done within society based on the prudent manipulation of natural resources.

In the human social sphere, just as with the naturalistic doctrine of *tian*, Xunzi offers a new interpretation of ritual action as an essential praxis for returning harmony to persons and society. If Xunzi is not awed by the kind of strange natural events that impressed other Warring States intellectuals, he could wax rhapsodic about the role of ritual in human life. He became the most important theorist of ritual in early China, and in fact set the standard for all future work even when later thinkers, such as the Song masters, could not openly acknowledge his contribution. It is impossible to think of the Confucian Way without calling to mind the holy and quotidian rites; in fact, if people today have any memory of the Confucian Way it is that of ritual practice, both as the creative seeking of civility or as the dead hand of the past constraining the emergence of modern societies in East Asia. Women especially have an inscribed cultural memory of the heavy hand of Confucian ritual modeled on the complete control of the family by the father. It is this patriarchal imposition of authoritarian control, some feel, that enslaved the women of Confucian Asia for over two millennia.

Xunzi's epistemological stance is of a piece with his view of the cosmos and humanity's place within it as one natural complex nested within many other natural orders. For him, what one knows about human nature is the natural desires for food and shelter, and what one knows by extension or analogy is the pattern of things in the natural order. Although the later Song Confucians were not, because of ideological reasons, able to emphasize this fact, it was Xunzi among the classical Confucians who had a place for the trait of coherent principle, pattern, or order—the notion of *li* 理—that was so central to the thought of the Cheng brothers and Zhu Xi. In his analysis of the human cognitive process, Xunzi starts with sensation and then moves on to an analysis of the features and functions of the mind-heart. Xunzi maintains that the cognitive or discriminative capacities of the mind-heart revolve around the ability to discriminate or to notice differences between things and events. For him the greatest obstacle on the road to genuine knowledge of the patterns of the natural order is "one-sidedness," an improper fixation with this or that aspect of life. We become fascinated with one feature of an object or event and forget to sense its other ramifications and connections to the broader world. As Needham noted, there is a persistent habit of looking for relationships between things, and Xunzi is no exception. His essay "Dispelling Blindness" spends a great deal of effort providing possible cures for this persistent human inclination toward unwarranted fixation on just one aspect of any situation.

Xunzi writes, "One who concentrates on things will treat each thing as a particular thing. One who concentrates on the Way will treat things in all their combinations as things. Thus, the gentleman is one with the Way and uses it to further his testing of things" (Knoblock 1988–94, 3:106). What Xunzi wants to cultivate is a mind-heart that can take in all the relevant data via the broadest possible use of the human cognitive sensorium. A. C. Graham has argued that Xunzi (and this is typical of the Daoists as well) counsel the wise person to take in as much sensory data as possible and to think seriously about all the relations these data display and then act according to this broadness of vision (Graham 1989). If we do not follow this path of broadness, then "if the mind goes astray, it will lack knowledge. If it is deflected, it will not have unity of purpose. If it is divided in purpose, it will be filled with doubts and delusions" (Knoblock 1988–94, 3:106). Xunzi, citing Kongzi as his source, says, "Those who are called sages are persons who have an awareness that extends to the Great Way, who are limitlessly responsive to every transformation, and who discriminate between the essential and inborn natures of each of the myriad things" (3:261). These kinds of passages, besides demonstrating Xunzi's faith in the superlative cognitive powers of the sage mind-heart, also demonstrate why Xunzi is always considered part of the cumulative Confucian tradition. He might have held that *xing*, the natural human tendencies, are corrupt or inclined to evil, contrary to Mengzi's optimistic view of *xing*, but he is lucidly clear that the properly cultivated mind-heart of the sage is anything but deluded or prone to error or evil actions. The mind-heart of the sage is, to the contrary, supremely good.

Xunzi provides the following description of the perfected actions of the sage: "The Great Way is what is employed to alter and transmute and then in consequence to perfect the myriad things. The essential and inborn nature of things provides the natural principles of order whereby one determines what is so and what is not so of them and whether one should select or reject them" (3:261).

Xunzi concludes this encomium of the sages with the following statement: "With their formless majesty and their profound and pure mystery, their activities cannot be grasped. It is as though they were the successor of Heaven whose undertakings cannot be recognized" (3:261). Such indeed are the persons who can be called the Great Sages. Moreover, it should be noted that alternation and transmutation, certainly traits of process, are part of Xunzi's vision of the sages' profound wisdom.[7]

Xunzi in his essay "Dispelling Blindness" argues that

> in the past, when Shun put the world in order, he did not issue instructions
> about each task, yet the myriad things were brought to completion.
> Abide in unity, being anxiously on guard about it,
> and its flowering will fill every side.
> Nurture unity, being attentive to its subtlest manifestations,
> and its flowering will never be recognized.

Thus, the *Classic of the Way* says:

> The mind of man is anxiously on guard; the mind of the Way is attentive to these subtle manifestations.
> Only the gentleman who is already bright and clear is able to know the first hints of being anxiously on guard or of attentiveness to subtle manifestations.
> (3:106–7)

Or again, in discussing the reasoning capacity of the mind-heart, he says, "Thus, if you lead it with rational principles, nurture it with purity, and not allow mere things to 'tilt' it, then it will be adequate to determine right and wrong and to resolve any doubtful points" (106–7). As we shall see, Xunzi's vision of the role of the mind-heart of the sage is distinctively different, and perhaps even more activist, than that of his Daoist counterparts. The sage acts naturally but makes use of all the various human talents, including the ability to use rational principles in order to enhance human flourishing. This human flourishing, as the later Han Confucian doyen Dong Zhongshu proclaimed, complements and completes the holistic functioning of the cosmos (Berthrong 1998a, 42–46).

Xunzi also provides an account of the cognitive/epistemological functioning of the mind-heart. This is his famous theory of the mind-heart as "empty, unified, and still." I will cite this text at length because it is such an important passage.

> What do men use to know the Way? I say that it is the mind. How does the mind know? I say by its emptiness, unity, and stillness. The mind never stops storing; nonetheless it possesses what is called emptiness. The mind never lacks duality; nonetheless it possesses what is called unity. The mind never stops moving; nonetheless it possesses what is called stillness. Men from birth have awareness. Having awareness, there is memory. Memories are what is stored, yet the mind has the property called emptiness. Not allowing what has previously been stored to interfere with what is being received is called emptiness. The mind from birth has awareness. Having awareness, there is perception of difference. Perception of difference consists in awareness of two aspects of things at the same time. Awareness of two aspects of things all at the same time entails duality; nonetheless the mind has the quality called unity. Not allowing the one thing to interfere with the other is called unity. When the mind is asleep, it dreams. When it relaxes, it plans. This mind never stops moving; nonetheless it possesses the quality called stillness. Not allowing dreams and fantasies to bring disorder to awareness is called stillness. (Knoblock 1988–94, 3:104)

The mind-heart is empty of unwarranted preconceptions and therefore is able to entertain both new theories and new sensory data while retaining that wonderful quality of seeming empty. Who has not had the experience of emptiness at the moment when taking in vast amounts of new sensory data or when struck by an astounding new theory? Being unified or having the quality of unity of cognition means to be able to compare things without mentally confusing their traits. And finally, stillness or quietude means to be calm, dispassionate, and undeluded by the new data, whether they are internal to the workings of the dreaming mind-heart or represent new external sense data.

Although this is opaque to anyone not familiar with the history of Chinese philosophy, Xunzi here is making use of terminology that would have seemed quite like what the great Zhuangzi would have used in talking about the functioning of the mind-heart. But as was his wont, Xunzi gives all of these terms a distinctive Confucian twist. This copious borrowing from other philosophers was quite common to Xunzi (and probably all other Chinese thinkers of this period). If an idea were useful and not completely bolted down, it would be borrowed and then interpreted for new purposes. For instance, the notion of stillness or quiet nature of the cognitive abilities of the mind-heart is surely reminiscent of the writing of Zhuangzi and Laozi. However, notice how Xunzi takes the idea of stillness and translates it into the new key of sage action in the world.[8] But I confess that it would still be pleasant to find some early Confucian sources with a full set of source notes and comments on what the author thought he or she was doing with the texts of the other thinkers of the classical period.[9]

For a Confucian, Xunzi was also inordinately, interested in disputation, logic, and the role of language as a philosophical topic. However, before we examine Xunzi's own exposition of the arts of disputation, we need to practice the hermeneutic of suspicion. Confucians as far back as Kongzi, but especially Mengzi, professed not to want to take part in logic chopping. The standard Confucian trope is "Someone else makes me do it." The not-so-suppressed premise is that, left to its own devices, really authentic Confucian discourse would be about things like cultivating the vast, flowing *qi* for ethical purposes, exegesis of *The Book of Odes*, divination with the *Yijing*, and finding the historical precedents for various rites. The story continues that Confucians, alas, do not have the luxury of going about their business because of all the mistaken views that have become current in Warring States China, beginning with the rise of the Mozi and Yang Zhu. There are moments in reading even Mengzi when it seems he doth protest too strongly about his disdain for the arts of disputation. All the classical Confucians, even if we grant that they were not inclined to teach the arts of disputation, were accomplished rhetoricians and debaters.

Actually, this is part of a larger discussion about the role of the arts of disputation—and, by extension, logic—in traditional China (Graham 1989; Harbsmeier 1998). It was granted that traditional Chinese philosophers might indeed have mastered rhetoric in an informal albeit highly refined sense, but they did not generally show an inclination to pursue the study of either informal or formal logic as part of their rhetorical techniques in debate with other thinkers. For the most part, Chinese scholars, when they began to study philosophy in the West over a century ago, came to the preliminary conclusion that Chinese philosophy lacked anything like the Western preoccupation, with the development of informal and formal logics. Hu Shi, who studied with Dewey at Columbia and wrote his doctoral dissertation on the development of the logical method in classical China, bemoaned the fact that China had done little to develop the formal study of and practice of logic after the promising beginnings of the Moist school during the Warring States period. One of the reasons that Hu Shi became a critic of all aspects of the Confucian Way was that he believed that Confucians did not merely ignore logic; rather, Hu deemed that Confucians were positively hostile to the development of logic as a form of human discourse. Because modern China needed to develop the intellectual habits of logical thinking, the hold of Confucianism had to be broken before China could become a modern country.[10]

Even if we will never know from where Xunzi derived all of his material on the art of disputation—or it may even have been the outcome of his own fertile imagination—he was very concerned to correctly understand the proper role of general ideas, the nature of cognitive discrimination, and the function of inference (Ren 1979, 1:219–20). For him, concept formation arose from the labeling of things or events in order to fit reality as conventionally defined by human discourse. There was nothing supernatural about how we derive the names of things and events. How do we know that the reality we perceive and the name we give it will fit? We make use of empirical observation of the nature of the objects named. Therefore, even if names are conventional, they are based on empirical observation and noted similarities and differences. He clearly recognizes that names represent family types that are the same even if the individuals are actually unique. For example, the greatest common name (*dakongming* 大公名)would be "thing" (*wu* 物) or, as Knoblock renders Xunzi's definition, "'Thing' is the name of greatest generality" (Ren 1979, 1:221; Knoblock 1988–94, 3:130). This common name of "thing" indicated the most general object or entity we could name by the method of difference. Yet why do we use certain names and not others? Xunzi notes that we use names because of general social agreement about their particulars over a long period of time.

It is of passing interest to Xunzi why we argue about names in the first place. His theory of names fits his general theory about the generation of human society and the cultivation of human nature as well. We will return to the contested ground of the second issue. The locus of the first problem is that since the sage-kings are no more, and because it is only the sage kings who really had perfected mind-hearts capable of knowing the patterns of the world, we have lost our ability to manipulate language in an effective manner without recourse to the teachings of the sage kind. This loss of ability is nowhere more evident than in the fact that strange propositions have sprung up (here Xunzi is no doubt considering thinkers such as Mozi, Zhuangzi, and even Mengzi and other Confucians). He says, "The preservation of names is neglected, strange propositions have sprung up, names and their realities have become confused, and the boundary between right and wrong has become unclear" (Knoblock 1988–94, 3:128). As is almost always the case, Xunzi, as a Confucian, brings the conversation back to ethical implications of bad nomenclature. It is not that bad logic is bad in and of itself but that it leads to perverse social actions.

But all hope is not lost, according to Xunzi. It is always possible that a new true king will arise and be able to correct names yet again. "That being so, it is indispensable that he investigate (1) the purpose of having names together with (2) what is the basis for distinguishing the similar from the different and (3) the crucial considerations for instituting names" (128). After suggesting his method for healing the wounds of bad names, Xunzi points out that our very ability to act with reasoned intentions is at stake unless we are able to institute a better way to institute correct names. "When the noble and base are clear and the same and different are kept apart, conveying intentions is no longer frustrated through a failure to explain, and carrying out duties no longer suffers from being hampered and obstructed. This is the purpose of having names" (129).

How do we begin the process of correct naming? "This being so [the problem with the lack of proper methods for correct naming], what is the basis of deeming something the same or different? I say it is based on the sense organs given us by nature" (129). On the surface, this is a statement to warm the mind-heart of a robust philosophical naturalist. Xunzi goes on to note that, generally speaking, the various things and events of the world will be presented to each person by the senses in a similar fashion, all things being equal. This is why convention works so well in the process of naming. As we shall see, this kind of rough parity of the sense apparatus is affirmed by the cognitive, metaphoric, and embodied philosophy of Lakoff and Johnson. For Lakoff and Johnson the fact that a healthy and sober person will perceive the objects of the world in roughly the same fashion is the basis for the metaphoric imagination that lies at the basis of the generation of human philosophizing based on metaphor. Xunzi notes, "Pain and itching, cold and heat, smoothness and roughness, and lightness and heaviness are differentiated by the body. (Speech and phenomena,) pleasure and anger, sorrow and joy, love and hate, and desire are differentiated by the mind" (129).

It is easy to see why Xunzi is considered the defining naturalistic thinker of the classical period. He goes on to ask the pertinent question about how the mind-heart, when based on the evidence of the senses, can make the distinctions proper to cognition and hence to support the higher aspects of human life, most specifically moral judgments. Discriminating cognition functions via "the awareness that the mind has of defining characteristics that distinguish things. Only when it rests on evidence provided by the ear is it possible for this awareness of the defining characteristics to know sound," and so forth for the other sense organs. "If the five senses come into contact with a thing and you do not become aware of it, or if the mind notes its defining characteristics and you can offer no explanation, then everyone will agree that there is 'no knowing'" (129–30). After we have gotten clear about these basic acts, Xunzi says, we can go on to name things according to the sensory awareness of the things and our common deliberation about what their defining characteristics are.

It is at this point that Xunzi shows how we work from what he calls single names, which are the individual names for specific things or events, up to the name of greatest generality, which is simply the designation of "thing". We have a whole range of possibilities from specific titles to the greatest general term. "By extending the process, one draws distinctions within these groups, and within these distinctions one draws further distinctions until there are no further distinctions to be made, and only then does it stop" (130).

Xunzi then explains that all naming is conventional. "Names have no intrinsic appropriateness. They are bound to something by agreement in order to name it" (130). What fixes the use of a name is the habit of agreement over time. Moreover, names "have no intrinsic object. They are bound to some reality by agreement in order to name the object. The object becomes fixed, the custom is established, and it is called the name of the object" (130–31).

This technical discussion of the art of naming, as with so much of Xunzi's philosophy, drives us to ask him to answer another fundamental question. Even if we grant for a moment that his analysis of the correct use of names is persuasive intrinsically as a philosophical argument and cogent within the larger context of the history of early Chinese philosophy, we are still left with the question: How do we generate what Xunzi deems "good" conventions? Xunzi makes a very strong claim about how the mind-heart of the sage can achieve its cognitive activities. "When the mind conforms to the Way, explanations conform to the mind, propositions conform to the explanations, and when names are used correctly and according to definition, the real and true qualities of things are clearly conveyed" (133). Of course, the sages ultimately base this function of correct naming on the arts of disputation and dialectic as practices. "Defining and explanation are the function of dialectics and explanation. Dialects and explanation are the mind's representation of the Way. The mind is the artisan and the manager of the Way. The Way is the classical standard principle of order" (132). Again, all well and good, but the question still remains, who is the artisan of the principle of order? The answer, of course, is the correctly cultivated mind-heart of the sage.

Xunzi actually begins the essay "On the Correct Use of Names" with a cryptic explanation of where established names come from. "They [that is, the later kings] followed the Shang dynasty in the terminology of criminal law, the Zhou dynasty in the names of titles of rank and dignity, and the *Rituals* in the names of forms of culture. In applying the various names to the myriad things, they followed the established custom and general definitions of the central Xia states" (127). In short, Xunzi can track the correct use of names back to the three historical dynasties of classical China: the Xia, Shang, and Zhou. In the opening passage of "Dispelling Blindness" Xunzi gives us an explanation of why we need the sages in order to correct the use of names. "It is the common flaw of men to be blinded by some small point of the truth and to shut their minds to the Great Ordering Principle. If cured of this flaw, they can return to the classical standard, but if they remain with double principles, they will stay suspicious and deluded. The world does not have two Ways, and the sage is not of two minds" (100). This was the problem with someone like Zhuangzi, for instance. According to Xunzi, Zhuangzi, brilliant though he often was, was blinded by his own inability to understand how human beings properly fit into the wonderful spontaneity of the natural world of the Dao.

HUMAN TENDENCIES

What Xunzi has done is to back us into a discussion of the origin of the cultivated mind-hearts of the sage—the point of the emergence of both wisdom and things, the foundational pivot of his Confucian naturalism. At some point we have to ask the question, how were the predynastic and early dynastic sages able to cultivate their mind-hearts in order to understand the Great Ordering Principle? What is the source of their cultural creativity upon which the Confucian masters stand? But before we can answer this question of the origin of creativity in Xunzi's philosophy, we must attend to Xunzi's theory of human tendencies or nature, the most contested area of his thought because of his vehement disagreement with Mengzi about human nature.[11]

The basis of human nature lies, as we have seen in Xunzi's discussion of mind-heart, in our responsiveness to the world as mediated through our senses. "We are hungry and want to eat, cold and desire warmth, tired and desire rest, love profit and hate injury" (Ren 1979, 1:225). But as we shall see, what really makes us human beings is not our *xing* 性(human nature) per se, but how the *xing* acts in concert with the mind-heart. We shall see that Xunzi does have a quarrel with Mengzi, although it is not quite the simple dispute over the goodness or evil of *xing* that he is supposed to have had with the Second Sage.

ON RITUAL ACTION OR CIVILITY

Xunzi argued that he developed his philosophy not because he loved to dispute but rather because he sought to provide a clear understanding of the world such that proper social order would obtain. Key to the smooth functioning of society was the promulgation of the rites or *li* 禮. *Li*, like most complex concepts, is difficult to define because the diverse range of meaning assigned to rites even within the work of Xunzi is great, let alone within whole history of ritual theory and practice in traditional China (Chow 1995; Nylan 2001;

Wilson 2002). Moreover, because the Confucian tradition was so committed to the genre of commentary on canonical texts, terms having once become important hardly ever disappear from the philosophical vocabulary (Chen Chun 1986). However, the terms grow new meanings from period to period and even from thinker to thinker. *Li* is definitely one of those archaic yet ever present protean terms that inhabit the Confucian historical, religious, social, and philosophical sensibility.

Li qua ritual civility also illustrates another characteristic feature of early Chinese philosophy. As Justus Buchler has ceaselessly argued, philosophical discourse is not just the domain of assertive or prepositional statements. Human inquery, according to Buchler, is also carried out via exhibitive and active modes of query. In the development of Chinese philosophy, the rites as ritual action and the basis for much second-order cognitive speculation make Buchler's case for him. Philosophers such as Xunzi are concerned to define the nature and role of the rites, and hence develop an assertive, exhibitive, and active discourse about a philosophy of ritual action and personal self-cultivation. Along with this drive to define the nature and structure of ritual action, it was equally important that these rites exhibit true civilized conduct and display publicly the cultivated disposition of the ritual master. Rites, by their very nature and role in social interaction, are also active modes of query; or to use a different vocabulary, the *li* are performative utterances and actions that make a difference to those who take part in the carefully choreographed dance of ritual action. This can range from the marriage ceremony of an emperor to the proper deportment of a scholar in his or her private study (Fehl 1971).

No doubt *li* was first commonly used to describe a particular code of aristocratic ethics, types of behavior only appropriate for the cultured elite of the Xia, Shang, and Zhou cultures. For practical purposes, most of the ritual texts the classical Confucians would have studied were doubtlessly of Zhou origin; we will probably never know how far back some of these rituals actually go. The old maxim that laws do not extend to the gentleman or ritual to the common people makes this point about the elite origins of the rites. However, once the classical Confucian thinkers, beginning with Confucius, got their hands on the rites, these codes of elite conduct became much more; the rites became the glue that was to hold society together and, to make this society not just a conglomeration of people but a civilized order.

Of all the early philosophers, none was more interested in defending the rites than Xunzi. If fact, if he is remembered and honored today for only one thing—beyond the infamous doctrine of that human nature is evil/bad or odious—it is for his philosophy of *li* as the symphony of rites or ritual actions that constitute civilized society, from the cultivation of the person to the harmony of heaven, earth, and humanity. In his subtle theory, the old concept of aristocratic action and deportment becomes the supple backbone for future Confucian social life (Dubs 1966, 88–103, 111–54, Fehl 1971, 151–212). As we shall see, ironically, Zhu Xi was as great a master and scholar of the rites as Xunzi. Zhu Xi's famous *Family Rituals* is a handbook still in use today throughout China to help with all kinds of important family ceremonies, such as those of birth, marriage, and death (Ebery 1991; Chu Hsi 1991).

Xunzi, however, did more than simply preserve the old aristocratic codes of conduct and ritual civility. He innovated by universalizing aristocratic ritual, and in this he was simply continuing the pattern already established by Kongzi and Mengzi. One of the striking features of the early Confucians was that through their attempt to preserve the past they helped to give birth to a radically new future; this has often been called the path of careers open to talent. It was no longer birth that made the gentleman, but rather the manners, and even more, the internal cultivation of the virtues that supported genuine ritual civility. Kongzi took one of the first steps when he universalized the archaic aristocratic concept of *ren* 仁 (humanity). In its elite context, *ren* probably meant something like noblesse oblige or the responsibility of the gentleman to others of his own class and to the lower classes. For instance, Louis XIV was famous for tipping his hat to any and all women who crossed his path.

For Kongzi, *ren* was transmogrified into the virtue of virtues, the veritable foundation of human culture and the proper goal of conduct for everyone. Kongzi noted that his favorite student, Yen Hui, although a commoner and a poor one at that, was able to practice *ren* for a few months, an astounding feat in the master's considered opinion. Paradoxically, in making *ren* available to everyone as a goal of ethical perfection, he made it, as Spinoza would have said, as difficult as it was rare. For example, Kongzi never claimed *ren* for himself. His only claim to fame was that he loved learning as much or more than anyone he knew and was tireless in seeking such true wisdom. Only the greatest sages, according to the scholar later counted as the "teacher of ten thousand generations," were fully men of *ren*. I should note that it was mostly men who were considered by the early Confucians masters, though there are records that women served as ministers to the great sage-kings, and hence were also considered to be persons of *ren* just as much as their male colleagues (Raphals 1998). At least from a theoretical viewpoint, all human beings could be *ren* if given the correct education and the luck to be born in the right environment. For Kongzi, and certainly for Xunzi, the only people who were able to rise above their humble origins were the sages, persons of perfect ritual action among all the other traits of true humanity.

Hidden in the thought of Kongzi and Xunzi, and perhaps obscure even to them, was the profound, revolutionary doctrine that a person was considered *ren* and *li* by conduct and insight rather than by mere birth into an elite family. If Kongzi and Xunzi made humaneness and ritual action universal ethical goals, in terms of assertive, exhibitive, and active forms of philosophical query, they also made these forms of ethical reflection the general potential property of all human beings. Human beings might be odious in some very profound sense according to Xunzi, but they were all capable of becoming sages—even if this is just an eschatological hope. It is likewise true that the early Confucians believed in a strictly hierarchical ordering of society—a view that was shared by almost every other intellectual at that time except for a few eccentric Daoists or Moists who were inclined to a strain of political egalitarianism. As we shall see in the next chapter, some Daoists even went so far as to articulate an anarchist vision of a world without rulers, something that would have shocked the Confucians.

The key to understanding Xunzi's defense of hierarchy is to understand the role of the sage within his system. The sage, for him, was the person who was able to make constructive use of active reason as wisdom or of discernment as a positive form of humane contrivance. This was why Xunzi called one crucial aspect of the sage's use of the mind-heart *wei* 偽 (contrived action), in the sense of the creation of something new or novel in civilized human social interaction (Mou Zongsan 1994; Cheng and Bunnin 2002, 327–46). Furthermore, Mou Zongsan argues that one of the key features of early Confucian moral metaphysics was the development of a concept of the mind-heart qua active reason. Reason is creative, and hence active, for all the classical Confucian thinkers, including Xunzi.[12]

The sage's positive insight as embodied in ritual action was founded on two pillars. One was the discipline of historical learning, the dedicated struggle to sift through the accumulated wisdom of the Central States that defined the civilized world for Xunzi. Here, too, Xunzi followed Kongzi who had taught about the history of the Zhou because it was only the Zhou material that he considered reliable. The implication is that Kongzi would have loved to transmit the teachings of the Shang and Xia and even farther back if he had had confidence in the historical records. As it was, Kongzi had the greatest confidence in the records of the Zhou, because the Zhou had been able to observe and refine the teachings of the Xia and Shang rulers, and the early Zhou rulers were themselves sages and could hence be counted on to transmit faithfully the full sage teachings of the early dynasties and culture heroes.

All Confucians are historians, because they believe that history can tell us something about the success and failures of the past (Nivison 1966, 1996; Graham 1986a). We can frame our responses to the problems of our days, but only if and when we pay proper attention to the teachings of the sages who have gone before. The connection of the past and present to the future was necessarily a feature of the cosmos for those Confucians who had an organic or contextualist root metaphor of reality, and especially a metaphor that was so wedded to the delight in the study of history.

The second pillar of the sage's mind-heart, the personal achievement of something beyond even a refined sense of history, was, as we have already seen, unobscured, pellucid insight into the workings of the human mind-heart, the social situation (usually defined by proper ritual action), and even the cosmos as a field of interacting forces. At least part of what Xunzi wanted us to achieve was to observe reality as it is and not as we would wish it to be. This is the genesis of his great debate with Mengzi about what traits can be predicated of human nature. Put as simply as possible, a person, in order to realize sage wisdom, must overcome the obstructions or prejudices to which the mind-heart is prone. Some writers have quite accurately suggested that one aspect of the unobstructed mind-heart is the need for the person to become a spectator of the cosmic drama without identifying all the needs of the cosmos with those of the finite person (Yearley 1980, 468–73). If we are not born into a depraved state of original sin according to Xunzi, we are certainly born to the prejudices of particular social positions and even individual talents. The problem for Xunzi is that we must overcome our subjective limitations that cause us to follow the evil and lose our grasp on the good. Moreover, Xunzi believed that human nature was such that it could end in evil just as easily as in the good. Rather like H. Richard Neibuhr's famous quip about original sin, Xunzi could have argued that if sin is not necessary, it is inevitable.

What does the historically sensitive and cultivated sage perceive at the base of a good social order? Xunzi answers that it is social order or harmony and proper hierarchy. This robust affirmation of hierarchy often offends modern readers—where is the sense of human equality that moderns prize as the mark of human flourishing? However, we must remember that Xunzi was facing a chaotic time. For him there was an obvious need for some kind of imposed social order. Moreover, he believed that any large society demanded social organization qua hierarchy. The point that differentiates Xunzi from the Legalists is that Xunzi affirmed that what was needed was to civilize hierarchy in the same fashion that we need to cultivate our unruly mind-hearts. If we can start with a bad human nature and yet end up a sage through the process of self-cultivation, it should be possible to start with social disorder of the worst kind and yet achieve a modicum of human social harmony.

Along with having a dream for cultivating the mind-heart of the sage, Xunzi also had an image of a model society as a truly prosperous country. Xunzi, unlike many other Confucians, thought commerce was a good thing for society. In fact, he encourages all kinds of specialized industry and commerce. "The circulation and transport of valuable commodities and foodstuffs is not impaired by obstructions or hindrances, causing them to be freely presented and interchanged so that 'all within the four seas will become as of one family.' Accordingly, those who are nearby will not hide their abilities and those who are distant will not hate their toilsome tasks" (Knoblock 1988–94, 2:102). The theme of being unobstructed is a major theme for Xunzi both for the cultivation of the mind-heart and for the larger world of production and trade. Following the same line of argument, Xunzi deemed that specialization of economic function is also important and to be encouraged. "Farmers need not carve or chisel, nor fire or forge; yet they have sufficient utensils and implements. Artisans and traders need not till the field; yet they have enough beans and grains" (102). He concludes with the following observation: "Thus, all that Heaven shelters and Earth supports is brought to its ultimate refinement and its fullest utility, so that the refined is used to adorn the worthy and good, and the useful employed to nourish the Hundred Clans and peace and contentment are brought to them" (102).

In contrast to Daoists such as Laozi and Zhuangzi who saw such growing complexity of the economy as one of the main problems of society and certainly not something that could ever end in promoting the good, Xunzi wanted to be realistic about what needed to be done to generate wealth and social harmony in the large, dangerous, and complicated world of late Warring States China. All forms of commerce are interconnected, whether luxury goods or utilitarian necessities. All goods must be cultivated and circulated for the common good of all. The sage-king plays his role in that "he graduates the taxes, rectifies the affairs of government, and develops the myriad things, thereby nourishing the myriads of people" (101). Xunzi might have liked markets and commerce, but like Adam Smith, he also knew that government had a major role to play in providing the context for such joyful bounty. If human nature was bad, then human beings needed a sage to help conform them to better conduct via ritual action.

THE NATURE OF THE WISDOM OF THE SAGE

Centuries later in the Southern Song, Chen Chun also recorded his reflections on how order was brought forth from the chaos that preceded the active, conscious intervention of the sages.

> From a very obscure beginning, Fuxi created the system of Change and thus opened up the universe from chaos. In their turn Shennong and the Yellow Emperor, following Heaven, established the ultimate standard. This is the origin of tradition. Emperors Yao and Shun and Kings Yu, Tang, Wen and Wu transmitted it successively, becoming the masters of the Three Bonds and the Five Constancies at the center of Heaven and Earth. They were assisted by their ministers Gaotao, Yi, Fu, Zhou, and Zhao, who carried out various measures in the empire to form the order of civilization. Confucius was unable to obtain a position to spread his doctrines. He therefore collected the standard teachings of the sages to produce the Six Classics and became the teacher of ten thousand generations. (Chen Chun 1986, 178–79)

I have chosen to quote from Chen Chun—even though he would have followed Zuh Xi in being critical of Xunzi for the theory of human nature as evil—because he narrates with precision the founding story of the sages in its standard Song dynasty form. The names might change, but this is the story of how human flourishing arose from the chaos prior to the spreading of the wisdom of the high sages of antiquity.

Chen begins the story with the great primal sage Fuxi and his creation of the system of Change. What Chen means here, and as any classically educated Chinese for the last 2,560-plus years would know, is that Fuxi was, among other things, the sage who began to assemble the *Yijing* or the *Book of Changes*. Fuxi gets Chinese high culture going by figuring out the philosophical underpinnings of the system of changes found in the *Book of Changes*. According to Chen, this system of change provides the basis for all the other insights and actions of the succession of sages who follow Fuxi. Again, this was not a problem at all for Chen Chun and other followers of Mengzi, because they concurred with the Second Sage that human nature was good. All it took was for a sage to come along and begin to codify the basic goodness found in human nature and cognized by the mind-heart.

Yet Xunzi has a problem with this Mencian-style analysis of the origin of sage ritual. It is not that he has a problem with what the sages did; he too agreed with the fundamental narrative as Chen tells it. Xunzi's major issue was disagreement about human nature. Xunzi was astounded that Mengzi would read the empirical data of Warring States China as teaching such a Confucian doctrine as "human nature is good." It seemed to Xunzi that a sage could not simply open the mind-heart and read all these good doctrines inscribed therein via the fundamental goodness of human nature *simpliciter*. The problem, again, was that the early sages, even Fuxi, were just as human as the rest of us. When they were behind the primal veil of ignorance, with a view of primordial chaos, how in the world could they be sure that they found the good and escaped human finitude, ignorance, and error? Where does goodness come from?

How we interpret the famous "Xing e" 性 惡(Nature is Evil) chapter on human perversity affects how we understand Xunzi's theory of human creativity, the very process of sage wisdom in the making. The exegesis of this thorny essay has occupied the mind-hearts of some of the best Chinese and East Asian scholars for generations. In exasperation, some have gone so far as to suggest that the whole chapter is a spurious later addition (Munro 1969, 77–78). They point out that this lone chapter is the only place in the received text of the *Xunzi* that we find the precise teaching that *xing* is evil, odious, or bad. The argument is that, if this were such a crucial point for Xunzi, he should raise this point in other essays. Be that as it may, we should follow the exegetical principle that we must not seek to amend or excise a text simply because it does not give itself over to easy interpretation. Moreover, Xunzi is certainly acerbic enough about other thinkers and their theories that this rhetorical attack on the notion of human nature as good is not out of character at all for him. Because of this, I will accept the "Xing e" as an integral part of the *Xunzi*. We shall see, as has been noted by a host of previous and contemporary scholars, that pre-Han philosophical usage is not always the same as Song or present philosophical usage. There may even be some simple way to read Xunzi's thesis without emending it out of existence; and even if there is no simple formula to interpret the "Xing e", there still might be an elegant path to follow that would lead to what Xunzi was trying to tell us.

I will illustrate the way forward on the hermeneutic path by presenting one modern interpretation based on the best of classical Chinese scholarship.[13] A. C. Graham has demonstrated conclusively that *qing* 情 (now taken to mean "the emotions" in modern Chinese), does *not* mean "the emotions" in pre-Mencian usage, but rather something more like the "essence" or the facts of the case, and we should be on our guard when we examine the term *xing* in Xunzi. It has been shown how Xunzi uses a term like *wei* (contrivance) as a highly charged positive term for the active reason and praxis of sage wisdom and conduct (Puett 2001). Xunzi, like all great philosophers, manipulates language and traditional usage to suit his advantage. Perhaps we should elevate the willingness to create new metaphors and generate neologisms or to stipulate new meanings for old terms as a transcultural trait for philosophical discourse.

The hypothesis is that we might be misreading systematically the graph *e* in the text because we are mistaking later layers of connotation for what Xunzi and his audience would have understood. Just this kind of thesis has been suggested by Liang Qixiung (1962, 52–53). The conventional English rendering of the opening sentence of the "Xing e" chapter is "Human nature is evil, [and] goodness comes from [conscious] human action." The whole of Xunzi's image as a dour thinker hangs on how we interpret *e*'s philosophical meaning. Does it really mean that *xing* per se is something completely evil or bad? The Song *daoxue* tradition took Xunzi to be saying precisely that: human nature was evil to the core. But we know that *e* may also mean "odious", "rough", "simple", or "coarse", or even "bad" in a less robust sense than a designation of ontological or cosmological evil. If we follow Liang's exegesis a bit farther, the famous sentence could mean more that "human nature is rough (odius, coarse or unrefined), and that goodness comes from [conscious] human action."[14]

If we accept Liang's suggestion that *e* means "rough" or "coarse", at last one exegetical and philosophical problem partially dissipates. This reading has the benefit of not emending the text outright, and it does make sense of the sentence within a possible philosophical world—and it would answer the criticism of the later Song *daoxue* in defending Xunzi's place of honor in the tradition of the Confucian Way. If we accept the reading of *e* as "rough" or "coarse," we can see how Xunzi was countering at least two, not one, influential viewpoints. By saying that human nature was unrefined or coarse, he was still definitely challenging Mengzi's melioristic interpretation of human nature as fundamentally good. But more than this, he could also use it to argue against a Daoist philosophical challenge as well. If Zhuangzi,—to pick a representative Daoist that Xunzi sparred with frequently—held that the essence of all things was the clod, the uncarved block, then Xunzi's thesis cleverly accepted one part of Zhuangzi's hypothesis about human nature. Xunzi could go part of the way with Zhuangzi in accepting that human nature in its primordial condition was coarse, unrefined *qi*, but he then challenges Zhuangzi by arguing that to become good, *xing* must be cultivated and not left alone to follow its own devices in being coarse or rough. Of course, Zhuangzi would have laughed and countered, "And what is wrong with being coarse? You Confucians are the fools in this little drama of self-cultivation because of your obsessive desire to improve on everything; the real path of wisdom would be, to leave things well enough alone." So Xunzi might well have had more than the obvious Mencian doctrine of *xing* as good in mind. Xunzi could still be shocking, but he might well be more shocking to Zhuangzi than to Mengzi. Xunzi could have believed that Zhuangzi's position was the more philosophically damaging one, because it goes to the real heart of the debate between Daoist and Confucian sensibilities. Mengzi's mistake is merely an empirical oversight, only indicating that the Second Sage was oblivious to the evil that human beings do right in front of our collective senses. Xunzi would still have a quarrel to pick with the shocked Second Sage, but it is not the dispute that later commentators took it to be.

What, then, was so special about Xunzi's concept of *xing* 性 (human nature)? Xu Fuguan (1975) makes the preliminary observation that Xunzi was much more empirically inclined than Kongzi and Mengzi, at least insofar as the received texts demonstrate the full range of opinions from the first two great teachers of the Confucian Way. Xu (1975, 223–62) over and over again makes the point that if actions are not concretely humane—that is, not really empirical—they count for nothing in terms of moral worth. Xunzi holds that this account of human nature contravenes the subjectivity of Mengzi's intuition concerning the mind-heart *and* human nature. Of course, a follower of Mengzi could counter, as thinkers from the Song *daoxue* school to Mou Zongsan have, that what Mengzi was really advocating was not an individualistic, solipsistic subjectivism but rather the profound deepening of an empathetic intersubjectivity. No Confucian, and Mou would include Xunzi and Zhu Xi, was interested in anything less than human flourishing as a corporate venture in intersubjective personal and social harmony. Nonetheless, the fact still stands that Xunzi affirmed that we must pay attention to the way the world is rather than just hope for the best based on moral or psychological reflection on the mind-heart of individuals. Further, Xu points out that Xunzi has some very definite views about the relationship between heaven and humanity that were different from the Confucian mainline as it came to be defined by the Song philosophical community.

The more traditional Confucian view was that *tian* 天 (heaven) was the fount of morality, and that *xing* somehow connected the two spheres of heaven and humanity (Xu Fuguan, 1975, 223–28). The truly classic exposition of this sentiment is found in the opening of the *Zhongyong*, which states, "What Heaven (*tian*, Nature) imparts to man is called human nature. To follow our nature is called the Way. Cultivating the Way is called education"

(Chan 1963, 98). The heavenly nature was then also human nature; it was what Tu Wei-ming has called the anthropocosmic vision of the Confucian Way (1989). Therefore, both Xunzi and the Daoists held a doctrine that Xu calls "natural heaven." What is important to remember is that this is a robust naturalism that has many mansions for all kinds of natural complexes (see also Lee 2005). According to Xu, Xunzi's cosmological vision owes as much to Zhuangzi's notion of a transformative and spontaneous vision of the world as to the moralizing Confucian mainline as expressed by Mengzi and the author/redactor of the *Zhongyong*. But there is at least one major difference between Xunzi and Zhuangzi in terms of worldview analysis. The Daoist notion of *tian* 天 was based on the concept of *wu* 無 (nothingness), which, of course, Xunzi totally rejects in favor of a robust Confucian realistic pluralism. The world is real, known by the senses, and brought to order by the institutions of the sage-kings. Xunzi has a very clear recognition that *tian* does not have a specific content through any easy determination of human nature as a moral norm in the sense that Mengzi wanted to argue. Therefore, human beings need the sages to establish the quality of morality for their lives and social institutions, and should not waste their time in asking questions about the arcane lore of the mysterious Dao.

Xu Fuguan then proceeds to state that we must be quite definite about what Xunzi actually meant when he wrote "Xing e" as a part of his system. For Xunzi, *xing* 性 and *qing* too are what all human beings share in being human. Xunzi gives the following examples of the way people share the same human nature: (1) All human beings desire to eat when they are hungry. (2) They all have the capacity of discriminate between white and black, good and evil, and so on. (3) They all share what makes Jie and Yu the same basic beings—namely, the undetermined desire and inclinations of *xing* (Jie and Yu are the two stock examples of ultimate human depravity as contrasted to the brilliant virtue of a true sage). Xunzi notes that both desire (*yu* 欲) and knowledge (*zhi* 知) are essential features of *xing*. Xu goes on to argue that there are two main sides of Xunzi's concept of *xing* that are often conflated but that need to be considered separately. Xunzi has an empirical bent and therefore closely relates *xing* and *qing* (emotions) as the facts or context of any given situation. What Xunzi seems to be arguing is that as human beings encounter their world, this encounter is emotional in the sense that it is an immediate feeling; moreover, these feelings take on the quality of attraction or aversion and that this quality of valuing high or low defines the capacity of the mind-heart to make all kinds of distinctions. These distinctions range from simple color recognition to much more complicated ethical judgments. In fact, Xunzi deems that *xing* and *qing* are interconnected to such an extent that they are described as the branches and roots of the same tree. Xu argues that Xunzi wants to interpret *xing* to assume *qing* for its base such that beyond the interaction of *xing* and *qing* there would be no meaningful method to describe *xing* (Xu Fuguan 1975, 228–37).[15]

As we saw earlier, Xunzi rejects any easy conflation of heaven and humanity and therefore rejects any static substance model for *xing*. David Hall and Roger Ames (2001) in their recent study of the *Zhongzong* go even farther and argue that circumstances always change and that human beings perforce must be creative and transformative in their response to the flux of the world. As for Xunzi, he can say quite clearly that "desire is the response of *qing*," which hints that *desire as response* is what *xing* actually is, or even better, what *xing* does (Xu Fuguan 1975, 237). As we have already repeatedly noted before, Confucian philosophers are often more interested in the question of what something does than what it is, isolated from other objects and events. Pushing the analogy even farther, we can say that *xing* is responsiveness, a preconscious choice between this and that. This choice does have a direction, however. *Xing* is a compound of desire and knowing, and this is why Xunzi can speak of it as a form of deliberative cognition in contradistinction to the *wuwei* 無為 (non or uncontrived action) of the Daoists like Laozi. It is ultimately contrived action and not inaction—it is a responsive human query that aims at appropriate action, or even *wuwei* if that is the path to take toward a good outcome. Xu Fuguan continues his analysis by pointing out that Xunzi actually has a functionalist definition of *xing*. For example, the nature of the eye is to see, that of the ear to hear, and so on. Therefore, the perfection of our actions is the realization of our nature as responsiveness to the world—with the caveat that our senses are functioning in as normal, healthy fashion. Furthermore, one cannot be good by going against something as primal as desire. Typical of the Confucian tradition, Xunzi holds that the trick is to civilize the desires rather than to get rid of them; moreover, why would one want to get rid of the desires when they are often pleasant in and of themselves? The desires are good insofar as they are the basis for all action; that is to say that the desires are the responses that come to be perfected in the good.

If Xu Fuguan's account is plausible so far, how do we account for the evil in human nature, which Xunzi was purportedly so keen in perceiving? Xu points out that Xunzi has a dual structure of desire mediated by the senses. Evil arises out of the capacity of desire, not the desire itself. Evil does not extend to the potential for response that is desire per se. Evil is therefore essentially a lack of control, of understanding, and of correctly responding to the way things are. Xu quotes Xunzi as saying, "The *xing* of present-day men is such that they are born having a liking for profit, and following this, the result is struggle and contention wherein courtesy and humility are lost." The crucial term here is again functional, active, and dependent on context and intelligent cognitive response. The whole force of the question of evil rests on an interpretation of *shunshi* 順是 (following this). Xu argues that the real difference between Xunzi and Mengzi is that Mengzi wanted to make the desires few, whereas Xunzi takes desire, like commerce, to be natural, something to be ordered and to follow. The two great disciples of Kongzi were not talking about the same thing when they wrote about the moral quality of *xing* (Xu Fuguen 1974, 238). Therefore, Xunzi ultimately is quite optimistic about the possibility of evoking the good, because he holds that the nature can be transformed or educated by the sage, which gives rise to conscious human action, the source of the best to be found in humankind (*hua xing er qi wei*: 化性而起偽 therefore the sage "transforms human nature and gives rise to conscious human contrivance" (238). Here again, a processive trait of transformation provides an important key to Xunzi's philosophy.

According to Xu, the real riddle of the "Xing e" chapter is why Xunzi said that human nature was *e* (evil) to prove that it ultimately had good potential? The answer revolves around the conjoined capacity to know and act, or to carry out the dictates of knowledge and yet still be linked to input of the senses. If Mengzi previously stressed the intuitive realization of the moral mind-heart, Xunzi placed great emphasis on knowledge and action guided by this knowledge. As Xunzi put it, the correct principles of humanity and justice have an order that can be known and acted upon. Xunzi was confident that even a common person could know the substance of these crucial virtues of humanity and justice and have the capacity to concretely manifest them. Xunzi equated his concept of the mind-heart with the metaphor of a *tianjun* 天君 (Heavenly Ruler who directs the person by the power of cognitive discrimination.[16]

Our intellectual capacity comes from our ability to make selective discriminations or "to know the Way," and here Xu quotes Xunzi's famous description of the mind-heart as empty, unified, and still (quiet) (241). All three qualities, when fully cultivated, allow the mind-heart to become transparent to the order of the Way so that it can apply proper standards of correct behavior to human activity. But since the mind-heart is prone to error by becoming clouded by prejudice, it must rely on the Way itself. The mind-heart does so because of its twofold nature. On the one hand, the mind-heart is an organ of desire and response; and on the other hand, it is the master of calculation and selection—the ability to make distinctions. As we have seen before, for Xunzi, having a desire requires that some kind of choice must be made, even if it is not fully conscious or rational. As the person begins to realize that the criteria of choice are objective he or she must seek the educating influence of wise sages, who in turn have relied on the pattern or order of the Way to develop their teachings. The sage provides the mind-heart of the student with something concrete, a ritual action, for the student to respond to and then extend to the conduct of the student's own life. This sagely ritual provides the mind-heart something to recognize, an object of choice. Once recognized, this choice of sage ritual loops back on itself and strengthens the will for an even more determined attempt to overcome human error. According to Xu Fuquan, such is the outline of Xunzi's complex linkage of the traits of human nature and the mind-heart. Xunzi's subtle theory was often missed by the repetition of the criticism of Mengzi that human nature is evil.

As with so many such debates in philosophy, much hinges on the definition of terms, and, as we have seen, Xunzi was prepared to use terms to suit his own purposes. I and other scholars have been tempted to say that Xunzi used terms in a novel way. Perhaps he did, or perhaps we just do not yet know the full range of debate about the meaning of human nature in the language of the Warring States era. Be this as it may, for most Chinese thinkers, whatever else it might mean, *xing* 性 does signify one of the key aspects of what it means to be human. But *xing* does not quite mean this in Xunzi's system, as he repeatedly tells us—a clear signal that he has a distinctive usage in mind. It is true, for Xunzi as for others, that we would not be human without *xing*, but *xing* is not the unique, defining trait for humanity that Xunzi wants to focus our attention on. Let us consider Xunzi's critical "ladder" passage (Lee 2005) about what makes a person a human being and not something else altogether.

> Fire and water posses vital breath but have no life. Plants and trees possess life, but lack awareness. Birds and beasts have awareness, but lack a sense of morality and justice. Humans possess vital breath, life, and awareness, and add to them a sense of morality and justice. It is for this reason that they are the noblest beings in the world. In physical power they are not as good as an ox, in swiftness they do not equal the horse; yet the ox and horse can be put to their uses. Why is that? I say it because humans alone can form societies and animals cannot. Why can man form a society? I say it is due the division of society into classes. How can social divisions be translated into behavior? I say it is because of humans' sense of morality and justice. Accordingly, from birth all men are capable of forming societies. (Knoblock 1988–94, 2:103–4)

The point that Xunzi is making is that obviously human beings belong to the natural order. But a person's distinctive feature, what we should call human nature, is a sense of duty and justice built upon an ability to form society. Hence, the real nature of human nature, if we are interested in its capacity for the good, is a result of social action rather than individual action. The good human beings do is not just from human nature but the collective deeds of human beings acting together in forming social order. This is the social order of ritual that Xunzi stresses in so many of his essays; it is a social good that is a unique manifestation of social organization (*jun* 軍). But the really crucial point to grasp is that the ability to form a social organization (a good one if informed by correct ritual) in turn depends on the ability to establish hierarchical social order.

Therefore, finally and ultimately, a person's nature rests on the ability to recognize a positive social pattern and to pick out the more useful from the less useful. This leads directly to the mind-heart's ability to recognize order by the means of difference, as we have already stressed. In "Contra Physiognomy" Xunzi writes

> What is it that makes a man human? I say that it lies in the ability to draw boundaries. To desire food when hungry, to desire warmth when cold, to desire rest when tired, and to be fond of what is beneficial and to hate what is harmful—these characteristics man is born possessing, and he does not have to wait to develop them. They are identical in the case of a Yu and a Jie. Even though wild animals have parents and offspring, there is no affection between them as between father and son, and though there are male and female of the species, there is no proper separation of the sexes. Hence, the proper way of Man lies in nothing other than his ability to draw boundaries.
>
> Of such boundaries, none is more important than that between social classes. Of the instruments for distinguishing social classes, none is more important than ritual principles. If you want to observe the footprints of the sage kings, you must look where they are most clearly preserved—that is, with the Later Kings. (Knoblock 1988–94, 1:206)

Knoblock believes that these later kings are Kings Wen, Wu, and the Duke of Zhou—again, this would also be Kongzi's favorite list. In other places the designation "Later Kings," again as in Kongzi, refers to the sage-kings of the Xia, Shang, and Zhou dynasties. As numerous scholars have noted, Xunzi places a high value on a person's cognitive and discriminative abilities. As reference to the ability to make distinctions shows, this is an ability that allows humanity, through proper ritual action, to become human. This is what Xunzi considers as human.

Xunzi was not a self-consciously ambivalent thinker. Yet the perennial tensions of Confucian discourse haunt his work. He was a realist who wanted to analyze human nature as it was and not how Mengzi thought it should be, though he shared Mengzi's vision of human flourishing when compared and contrasted to the vision of his Legalist students. In doing so he sought a secure basis for society. This basis was ritual action, manifested through true integrity, *cheng* 誠, a concept made even more famous in the *Zhongyong*. For Xunzi, ritual action was a human creation, the product of the mind-heart of the sage. Rather than trust in innate human good as Mengzi did, Xunzi preferred to rely on the socializing power of ritual. Only correct ritual action could create a viable social order. Only the greatest effort could secure humanity from the dire condition Xunzi so graphically defined as the struggle caused by the fact that "all people desire and dislike the same things, but since desires are many and the things that satisfy them relatively few, this scarcity will necessarily lead to conflict" (Knoblock 1988–94, 2:21). Ritual actions based on the distinction between a ruler and a minister provided the key for the recognition of order and hierarchy that would allow for the peaceful distribution of "things" in society.[17]

We have now returned to the social location of the aporia of sage wisdom in Xunzi's thought. How does the sage create ritual? How does the sage, attempting to generate civilizing forms, create anything at all? How did Fuxi, so long ago, discern the patterns of nature and invent writing for the benefit of humanity? We have returned to Michael Puett's (2001) question about the ambivalence of creation in Warring States China. It is at this point that Xunzi is most interesting in terms of the theme of process qua the creative advance into novelty.

THE AMBIVALENCE OF CREATION (*ZUO*) AND MORAL AGENCY IN XUNZI

As I have already suggested, Xunzi knew he needed to find a way to explain how a sage could discover the good, because human nature is, at best, odious or coarse in its original state. But before he could deal with the discovery of the good, Xunzi had to explain the notion of *zuo*作 (to create, make new). The problem was that Kongzi, as was known to all, declared that he was not a creator but rather a transmitter of traditional Zhou culture. Michael Puett renders *Lunyu* 7.1 as "The Master said: 'Transmitting but not creating [*zuo*], being faithful toward and loving the ancients, I dare to compare myself with old Peng'" (Puett 2001, 40). Moreover, the master always denied that he was a sage, and hence was barred from even contemplating creating anything whatsoever. "The Master said, 'How could I dare state that I am sagely or even humane? All that can be said is that I act unflaggingly and instruct others untiringly'" (41). We now realize that there is no one more creative than someone like Kongzi who passes down what he takes to be traditional lore, but it remained a problem for Xunzi. How could he speak of *zuo* and still claim to be a good Confucian?[18]

Mozi 墨子 and his followers presented Xunzi with an interesting challenge. Mozi and his school have been philosophically neglected based on Mengzi's charge that Mozi is one of the great heretics of early Chinese thought. However, as scholars such as Schwartz (1985), Graham (1989), Hansen (1992), and Puett (2001) have shown, Mozi played a very important role in the development of Chinese thought. For instance, Hansen (1992) argues that Mozi in many ways set the agenda for the philosophical debates in Warring States China because of his articulate challenge to all the other thinkers, and particularly to the Confucians. There is even a great deal of speculation about whether or not Mozi began life as a Confucian himself.

Further, scholars have noticed that Mozi and his school had a different reading of *zuo* from the usual Confucian position. Although we cannot be sure this is the case, the reason for Mozi's positive interpretation of *zuo* might have to do with the social location of Mozi. Although there is no conclusive evidence, it appears to be the case that Mozi could have represented the emerging artisan class as opposed to the more elite class of the Confucians as masters of ritual lore. The Moist school simply knows a great deal about the technology, crafts, and science of the day, and seeks to increase all of these domains of learning, because the Moist believes that these intellectual skills will benefit human flourishing. If compared to Daoists, Confucians were an active bunch; but the Moists were even busier doing good than the Confucians in the material world. Moreover, Mozi was passionately convinced that good arguments and explanations could change a person's mind-heart. Unlike the Confucians, who purported to dislike the arts of disputation, the Moist philosophers developed logic and the arts of disputation in the hope that this kind of intellectual technology would also promote human good.

We can see Xunzi's more positive sensibility about the question of *zuo* as a necessary trait for a sage in his praxis of moral self-cultivation. P. J. Ivanhoe (2000) has outlined Xunzi's theory of self-cultivation in terms of his debate with Mengzi. After reviewing, as I have also done, the context of Xunzi's argument with Mengzi, Ivanhoe deems Xunzi not to hold anything like the Augustianian version of original sin such that human nature is utterly depraved. For instance, Ivanhoe notes that nowhere in his writings does Xunzi incline to the opinion that someone would like to do evil things because of an evil nature. As we noted above, the real origin of evil is the situation of infinite desire competing for finite resources. "In a world of limited goods, inhabited by creatures of more or less unlimited desires, it is inevitable that the result is destructive and alienating competition. This is what Xunzi means by his claim that human nature is evil" (Ivanhoe 2000, 32).

As is well known, Mengzi's favorite metaphors for moral self-cultivation are agricultural models. Mengzi, for instance, calls the basis for human moral life the sprouts of morality—models for organic growth are always his favorites. Xunzi has a different set of moral metaphors, and interestingly enough, they are much closer to those of Mozi than to those of Mengzi. "In order to reform our bad nature, we must sign up for and successfully pursue a thorough, prolonged, and difficult course of learning. We must *re-form* our nature—as a warped board is re-formed by steam and pressure—so that it assumes a proper shape and can fit into the grand Confucian design" (Ivanhoe 2000, 32). If Mengzi has what Ivanhoe calls a developmental model based on plant metaphors, Xunzi has a re-formation model based on craft metaphors. Quoting Kant's famous dictum about human nature, Ivanhoe notes that "one cannot hope to make anything perfectly straight out of such crooked timber as man is made" (36).[19]

But if human nature is *e*, some ask, how can the sage reform it? Xunzi has an extended answer to this query.

> Someone may ask: "If man's nature is evil, how then are ritual principles and moral duty created?" The reply is that as a general rule ritual principles and moral duty are born of the acquired nature of the sage and are not the product of anything inherent in man's inborn nature. Thus, when the potter shapes the clay to create the vessel, this is the creation of the acquired nature of the potter and not the product of anything inherent in his inborn nature. When an artisan carves a vessel out of a piece of wood,

> it is the creation of his acquired nature and not the product of his inborn nature. The sage accumulates his thoughts and ideas. He masters through practice the skills of his acquired nature and the principles involved therein in order to produce ritual principles and moral duty and develop laws and standards. This being the case, ritual principles and moral duty, laws and standards, are the creation of acquired nature of the sage and not the product of anything inherent in his inborn nature.
>
> Thus, the sage by transforming his original nature develops his acquired nature. From this developed acquired nature, he creates ritual principles and moral duty. Having produced them, he institutes the regulations of laws and standards. This being so, ritual principles, moral duty, laws and standards are all products of the sage. Thus, where the sage is identical to the common mass of men and does not exceed their characteristics, it is his inborn nature. Where he differs from them and exceeds them, it is his acquired nature. (Knoblock 1988–94, 3:153–54)

Ivanhoe goes on to explain how Xunzi believed that we could find the craft to acquire sage wisdom and virtue. There is nothing supernatural about the process. It is simply a restatement of Kongzi's admonition to study and reflect on what we have studied until we get it right. "I once spent a whole day in thought, but it was not so valuable as a moment of study. I once stood on my tiptoes to look out into the distance, but it was not so effective as climbing up to a high place for a broader vista. The gentleman by birth is not different from other men; he is just good at 'borrowing' the use of external things" (136). With the borrowing comes accumulation, and with the use of reason come acquired skills and the understanding of proper ritual action.

As Puett tells the story, Xunzi did not want the sages merely to imitate nature. Xunzi's "fundamental notion was to accept the definitions of the cosmos that were becoming common but also to redefine the process of the emergence of culture" (Puett 2001, 64). But Puett makes the case that Xunzi is not here going all the way with the Moist vision of creation on a grand scale but with the patient accumulation of a set of skills. "Thus Xunzi does not claim that the sages created (*zuo*) culture like the innovators who created craft. Instead, he argues that culture is generated (*sheng* 生) from the conscious activity (*wei*) or the sages, just as implements are generated (*sheng*) from the conscious activity (*wei*) of the artisan" (67). For Puett, the next logical question is, what is conscious activity for Xunzi?

First, "The Sage's actions are described as clearing, according, and nourishing the faculties given to him by Heaven. Once the sage correctly cultivates these faculties, he will know what to do and what not to do" (68). Second, this is an orderly process rather like the work of a careful artisan. "The process of the sages training themselves to use these faculties correctly is comparable to the process of an artisan training himself to produce the implements: in both instances a highly regulated activity must be carried out in a particular way. Once this training of natural abilities was completed, the sages were then able to generate culture" (69). Although he does not want to conflate nature and culture, Xunzi, like any good Confucian, wants to keep the two within hailing distance. "Although culture was consciously made by the sages, and although such a conscious making was outside the realm of nature, culture is nonetheless, when properly instituted, the teleological (if not immediate) product of Heaven" (70).

But, once the process of balancing nature and culture has been settled, Xunzi is perfectly willing, as we have seen, for a sage to create something new. In fact, Xunzi is persistent in reminding his audience that the sage will have to create new names (and rites appropriate to new forms of social order) in order to overcome the chaotic times of Warring States China. Even if the sage were not so inclined, Xunzi recognizes that new times demand new forms of sage interventions and inventions. The mind-heart is responsive, and once cultivated can actually generate things like new names and hence rectify human behavior and culture. Hence Puett concludes that "for Xunzi, culture may be an artifice, but it is not arbitrary" (73).

Unlike the Daoist tradition that embraces transformation as the mother's milk of the Dao in wonderful speculations on cloud-riding masters, mysterious dragons, and the very permutations of the generative forces of the cosmos, Confucian are resolutely quotidian. For Xunzi, as we have already rehearsed at length, the question is, how does the sage create the good? I think that the best current discussion of this and related questions is found in the anthology edited by Kline and Ivanhoe, *Virtue, Nature, and Moral Agency in the "Xunzi"* (2000). A closely linked set of useful essays in the anthology, including most specifically the articles by Bryan W. Van Norden, David B. Wong, and T. C. Kline III, summarize the work of generations of scholars, and in doing so, the current ecumenical study of Xunzi's philosophy.

Van Norden outlines in the following way the problem of embracing the good in a world that is at best neutral and probably conducive to evil: "To summarize, for Xunzi, the process of self-cultivation begins with the performance of ritual activities which one does not yet delight in, and in the study of ritual, literary, and historical texts which one cannot yet appreciate or fully understand" (Kline and Ivanhoe 2000, 123). The difference between Mengzi and Xunzi, Van Norden argues, is significant right at inception of the process of self-cultivation. For Mengzi, we can delight in the good from the very beginning because of the growth of the sprouts of virtue found in every human person. Of course, Mengzi is completely aware of the fact that not everyone will read sprouting buds of virtue correctly or even have a clue how to cultivate these incipient virtues to the best advantage. Xunzi, however, has a different take. "Mengzi says that one does good because one desires to do good. Xunzi says that one does good because one 'approves' of doing good" (Kline and Ivanhoe 2000, 124).[20]

Other authors in the collection make the point that this kind of moral and epistemological training is not beyond a natural explanation, and in fact, we do this kind of thing all the time. We educate ourselves to ride motorcycles based on counterintuitive methods, just as classes in the arts and literature help us to appreciate forms of music and literature that we might initially not enjoy one bit. David Wong picks up this threat in his essay on moral motivation. Wong asks, "But just *how* did they [the sage-kings] use that intelligence to transform themselves?" (Kline and Ivanhoe 2000, 139). This is a critical juncture for Xunzi's ability to show how the sages "invented" ritual action. Wong agrees with Van Norden and traces this ability to Xunzi's belief that we can actually override desire via evaluative approval of alternative plans for action. "Such action would include submission to rites and dictates of righteousness, and would if practiced rigorously and consistently, result in the transformation of the desires themselves" (139).

Wong has a strong suggestion about how to solve the problem. Following David Nivison's insight that virtue in Xunzi need not be linked to any innate content, he notes that virtue is in the path of finding virtue rather than beginning with a sprout and then nurturing it. To cut to the chase, Wong believes that human beings do have a capacity to provide the motivation necessary to get the sages onto the right track. "We find such capabilities in those chapters where Xunzi describes the transforming effect of ritual and music" (147). I think that this chain of reasoning is highly convincing and resonates with Xunzi's love of ritual and music as objects of positive evaluation. As we shall see slightly later, Xunzi even has a favorite term for such a motivated will–namely, *cheng* 誠as the process of authentic self-realization of the potential for full humanity. Xunzi places so much emphasis on ritual because of "his insight that rituals are especially effective in shaping and channeling human feelings because they regulate and partially define occasions on which human beings have strong feelings of the sort that can become moral feelings" (149).[21]

There is no better way to summarize the work of scholars on Xunzi for the last century than to cite T. C. Kline's own conclusion on how the sage mind-heart was able to fashion good from the original position of human beings in a chaotic world:

> The early sages found themselves in a world in which there were already patterns that could be seen in the movements of the cosmos and the behavior of human beings and animals. Through their natural cognitive ability to perceive and understand these patterns sages were able to begin fashioning ritual and regulations that brought the human and natural orders into harmony with one another. This process built up gradually over a long period of time, each sage responding to the most pressing needs of the present situation, modifying and creating ritual as the need arose. Through participation in these rituals the natures of the participants were both expressed and transformed so that they were capable of even greater expression. The process was supported by the natural mechanisms of recognition

> and moral charisma. As the sages got closer and closer to perfecting ritual order, the moral charisma of the most virtuous individuals became greater and greater. They were able to attract and be supported by more and more people. The end result being that, with the perfection of the moral and ritual order, the sage-king was able to rule all under Heaven by virtue of his moral charisma alone (Kline and Ivanhoe 2000, 172).

Although the means are different, the final goal is analogous to Mengzi's dream of the cultivated garden of the seeds of human morality.

THE IRONY OF INTEGRITY AS SELF-REALIZATION

For Xunzi, it is the sage who creates the possibility of true human civilization, and hence the genuine creativity of the sage is the measure of all other forms of the human process as a natural complex of human transformation, both social and personal. But there is one more ironic twist I want to add before I leave Xunzi.[22] The commonplace estimation of Xunzi is that he is the grand rationalist "humanist" among the Confucian masters of the classical age. This commonplace definition, of course, is partially true and partially misleading. But Xunzi also believed in the spiritlike power of the true sage in the strong sense that he affirmed the power of the sage to transform other people and the social order. The term Xunzi chose to define this transformative power is *cheng* 誠 (integrity, true sincerity, self-realization).

Although worlds apart, Xunzi's paean to *cheng* 誠 reminds me of St. Paul's hymn to love. Paul teaches us that if we do not have love, then we are an empty, noisome vessel indeed. Xunzi teaches that if we have *cheng*, then there is hardly anything that we cannot do in promoting human flourishing. This passage from the "Bugou" (Nothing Indecorous) chapter illustrates this side of Xunzi's thought:

> As for the gentleman's cultivation of the mind-heart, there is nothing better than *cheng* 誠 (true sincerity or self-realization), for he who perfects true integrity/sincerity need do nothing else than allow humanity to be maintained and justice acted upon. With the realization of the mind-heart and the maintenance of humanity, they become manifest, and being manifest they are spirit-like, and being spirit-like they are capable of transforming; with the realization of the mind-heart and the practice of justice, there is order, and when there is order, clarity, and with clarity there is change. The transformations and changes act together and this is what is called the Virtue of Heaven. Heaven and Earth are great, but without true integrity they cannot transform the ten thousand things; although the sage has knowledge, yet lacking true integrity, he is out of touch. The exalted ruler is indeed eminent, and yet, without true integrity, he is lowly. Therefore true integrity is what the gentleman seeks to approach, and is the root of the cultivation of affairs. Only when he rests in the perfection

> of true integrity will he assemble the like-minded to himself. After having succeeded [in perfecting true integrity] the character of the person is completed and has progressed such a long way that it does not revert to its origins, and this is transforming. (Liang 1974, 29–31.[23] For an alternative, see Knoblock 1988–94, 177–78).

Xunzi believed that he was a realist who analyzed human nature as it is and not as Mengzi hoped it was. In doing so, he sought a secure basis for civilized society based on the ritual acts created by the former sages. This basis was ritual action, manifested through true integrity. For Xunzi, ritual action was a human creation, the product of sagely mind-hearts. Only the greatest effort could secure humanity from the dire condition Xunzi so graphically defined as the struggle caused by the fact that "all people desire and dislike the same things, but since desires are many and the things that satisfy them relatively few, this scarcity will necessarily lead to conflict" (Knoblock 1988–94, 2:121). Ritual action provided the key for the recognition of order and hierarchy, which would allow for the peaceful distribution of "things" in society. In this conclusion about the necessity for the sage's manifestation of *cheng*, Xunzi and the author/redactor of the *Zhongyong* would agree.

In their philosophical interpretation and translation of the *Zhongyong (Focusing on the Familiar)*, David Hall and Roger Ames make some very strong claims about how to understand *cheng*. They argue that *cheng* is best translated as "creativity". Actually, the foregrounding of the trait of creativity is not uncommon among contemporary scholars of the Confucian tradition. Mou Zongsan argues that creativity itself, which is how he translates the term *shengsheng* 生生, is the essence of the Dao itself. But no one has gone as far as Hall and Ames in making such sweeping claims for *cheng* as creativity. For instance, they translate section 21 of the *Zhongyong* as "Understanding born of creativity is a gift of our natural tendencies (*xing*); creativity born of understanding is the gift of education. Where there is creativity, there is understanding; where understanding, creativity" (Hall and Ames 2001, 105). Hall and Ames continue in section 23 with "When there is creativity there is something determinate; when there is something determinate, it is manifest; when it is manifest, there is understanding; when there is understanding, others are affected; when others are affected, they change; when they change, they are transformed. And only those of utmost creativity in the world are able to effect transformation."(105). Actually, as we have seen in our analysis of Xunzi's reflections on the creativity of the sage, there is nothing alien about the *Zongyong*'s perspective from Xunzi's standpoint.[24]

While we need not follow Hall and Ames too much farther in their exploration of the processive traits of *cheng* in the *Zhongyong*, it is pertinent to note another of their claims–namely, about the "language of field and focus." "Such language presumes a world constituted by an interactive field of processes and events in which there are no final elements, only shifting 'foci' in the phenomenal field, each of which focuses the entire field from its finite perspective" (Hall and Ames 2001, 7). Although the inspiration for Hall and Ames comes more directly from Whitehead, it is not hard to see how Buchler's notion of the metaphysics of natural complexes also applies to the the metaphor of "field and focus." According to Hall and Ames, the Dao is a natural complex with the trait of process as one of its major manifestations, if not the major one.

What is so powerful about Xunzi at this point is that he can demonstrate the integral aspect of the origins of creativity starting from a difficult place and complex nonreductive naturalism–namely, the dangerous zones of conflicting claims in late Warring States China about the proper definition of human flourishing. Creative processes can be generated from Xunzi's human domains of desire and conflict just as easily as they can be grown from Mengzi's sprouts of virtue.

I will now turn to a Daoist thinker from about five centuries later than Xunzi. Thinking about transformation and process is not only the province of the Confucians; Daoists played the game with as much, if not more, flair.

3

Coursing through the Dao

The *Liezi*

In the previous chapter on Xunzi we examined the role of the traits of process themes and prototypes (following the metaphors of cognitive science) in classical Confucian thought during the last stages of the brilliant philosophical world of the Warring States period. We now turn to the other great native school of Chinese thought, Daoism. As we shall see, the definition of Daoism is just as complicated as that for Confucianism. I will not, however, run through such an elaborate analysis of the terminological and cross-cultural comparative issues as I did when introducing the Confucians. In many respects, the Western study of Daoism replicates the engagement with Confucianism, although with one main distinction not found in the analysis of Confucianism. As W. C. Smith (1993) noticed, Confucianism almost alone among the great, self-reflective, erudite traditions of East Asia was sometimes highly praised by Western missionary scholars. If the Confucian *jing* 經 (classics) were given the gracious and respectful designation of classics, no such courtesy was extended to Daoist *jing*.[1]

Most contemporary critical scholars, as well as Daoist practitioners, argue vociferously that there is no real separation between the Zhou and Han texts and the later sectarian developments of the organized Daoist religious traditions. There were and are decisively different readings of the texts that range from theistic, polytheistic, pantheistic, panentheistic, and ritually prescriptive forms to unitive forms of mystical fusion and participation in the Dao, but each and every form of Daoism claims the classical texts as part of their patrimony. Livia Kohn (2001), representing and summarizing the work of a new generation of Daoist scholars, argues persuasively that Daoism has functioned as the main indigenous religious tradition of China in its many diverse forms over time. According to Kohn, Daoism includes what would be considered the most erudite and refined scholastic interpretations of the

Zhou and Han texts as well as divinely revealed works from the later periods of Chinese history. Along with the elite forms of recondite Daoist discourse there were also a profusion of more popular forms.

I have always found an image derived from the Buddhist tradition helpful in trying to understand the complexities of Chinese religion and spirituality. The image is that of a vast ocean and the many waves that arise and fall ceaselessly. The ocean itself is the pan-Sinitic set of cultural sensibilities that Modernity recognizes as religious or spiritual. From the generalized Sinitic culture many different organized forms, the waves, arise. Each one of the "great" or erudite or scholarly traditions of China, with their modern markers of Confucianism, Daoism, and Buddhism, can be considered iconically as huge and very tall waves that surge upon the vast sea of Chinese culture. However, there are all kinds of lower but sometimes even broader waves around the taller waves. Therefore, our ocean has the tall waves of elite religion, forms of popular religion shared by both the elite and the commoners, and a vast underlying base of folk culture shared by all the waves, tall or small or broad. Within this Chinese *imaginaire*, the *Liezi* represents a very tall, elite, philosophical Daoist wave. It shares many elite and erudite forms with its Confucian brother; moreover, both the Confucian and the Daoist share a common base of the unceasing rhythmic action of the underlying ocean of the creative matrix of pan-Sinitic culture.[2]

The reaction of the Christian missionaries to Daoism was dramatically different from the response to Confucianism. As we have seen, many of the early Jesuit missionaries had a high opinion of Confucianism. James Legge, representing the first great wave of Protestant missionary scholarship, also came to hold the highest respect for the Confucian Way.[3] In fact, Legge demonstrated, as I have shown elsewhere, that this respect was signaled by calling the Confucian texts "classics" (Berthrong 1994). By using this label for the Confucian texts, Legge made an analogy with the pre-Christian classical tradition of Greece and Rome. The early Greek and Roman classics were studied for edification by a Christian; by extension, a Christian could now also study the teachings of Kongzi and his school with confidence that there was something to be deeply appreciated in the Confucian Way. The kind of tolerance he felt for the Confucians did not extend to the Daoist religion that Legge encountered during his residence in China. But even the Confucian Zhu Xi enjoyed reading the early "philosophical" Daoist texts. Moreover, one could also make the impeccable Confucian point that if one wants to understand the historical development of Chinese thought, one must pay attention to the works of the early Daoist masters, even if only to refute them from a Confucian perspective. Frankly, I believe that most Confucians simply found them to be wondrous productions of the human mind-heart. Daoism remains a perfect counterpart to the quotidian reflections of the sober Confucian scholar, a yin counterpoint to the relentless yang of Confucianism. If we think of cosmology as embracing micro-, meso-, and macroviews of reality, Confucianism resolutely ties itself to the mesocosmic range as a species of *ars contextualis,* whereas the Daoists embrace both micro- and macrocosmic views of the ten thousand things.

Therefore, there are a number of reasons why investigating a text like the *Liezi* for traits of process is appealing. As countless generations of East Asian readers have known, the *Zhuangzi-Liezi* tradition loved to poke fun at their Confucian cousins. One of the aims of this ironic Dao is to demonstrate that the material and social world is much less solid than the Confucians would like to believe. If there is a philosophical anarchist strain in Chinese thought, it resides in the Daoist critique of Confucian social pomposity. Yet the critique is carried out with such a deft literary and philosophical touch that Confucian philosophers have cherished these Daoist texts along with their own canon. These texts, as Max Weber noted, are indeed the magic garden of the Confucian intellectual.

BACKGROUND OF THE *LIEZI* TEXT

The *Liezi*, although not nearly as well known as the *Laozi*, *Zhuangzi*, or even the *Huainanzi*, has been counted as one of the four classics of early Daoism. Furthermore, the *Liezi* happens to be one of most ironic of Daoist texts—which is no surprise, because so much of the *Liezi* is drawn from the tradition of Zhuangzi. There is an ironic wit and entertainment embodied by the author or editor of this classic of Daoist speculation that is not found in the other classical philosophical Daoist texts, with the exception of the *Zhuangzi*. Historically the text has never been nearly as popular as either the *Laozi* or the *Zhuangzi*. Notwithstanding the relative lack on interest on the part of scholars, the book was still very popular with everyone else who loved to read Daoist texts. The title was given the text because the purported author was none other than Master Lie, a character from the *Zhuangzi*.

The *Liezi* is one of those books recognized by critical traditional Chinese textual scholars as a prime representative of *weishu* 僞 書 (spurious texts). Nor is such a label surprising; there are many such texts extant. It always helped the reputation of a text to be attached to an ancient worthy, and so there was always the temptation to attribute a work to an earlier, famous author. Modern scholarship has only tended to confirm the early Chinese doubts about the authenticity of the received text of the *Liezi* (Graham 1986a). Once the seed of doubt has been planted, it is plain to see, as generations of commentators have noticed, that great chunks of the present *Liezi* text were derived in their entirety from the *Zhuangzi*. However, the problem of the provenance of the received text of the *Liezi* is not a fundamental problem for our purposes.[4]

Any reasonable elucidation of what is encompassed by these taxonomic claims about neo-Daoism and Buddhism would demand an elaborate study of the historical development of Chinese thought during the classical and postclassical periods.[5] Such a presentation, though useful, would deflect us from our search for the motifs and metaphors of process in Chinese thought and must therefore be wistfully abandoned. Suffice it to note that the received *Liezi* text probably represents quite well the eclectic intellectual currents of the Wei-Jin period. In fact, the text's combination of older Zhou and Warring States sources and newer eclectic material makes it a good place to rummage for motifs and traits of process sensibilities in one of the great transition periods of Chinese intellectual history.

THE IRONIC AND ACERBIC COSMOS OF THE LIEZI

Every time that I write in a serious fashion about Daoism I have the odd feeling that Zhuangzi and Liezi must be laughing at me in some empyrean Daoist heaven. H. G. Creel deemed Zhuangzi one of the greatest of all philosophers; moreover, as far as artistic flair is concerned, only Plato could equal Zhuangzi's astounding incantations. After forty years I am still persuaded that Professor Creel was correct. The Daoists were not only stellar philosophical raconteurs; some of them were pure magicians of words and images. Although not a literary masterpiece in the same class as the *Zhuangzi*, from which its editors borrowed so heavily, the *Liezi* is still a very stylish work. The *Liezi* is as humorous and outrageous as its classical model—understandably, because it borrows so much almost verbatim from the earlier text. But the humor is darker and the tone more ironic, sometimes almost sardonic. This style bespeaks a world in decline, the darkness of decay when Hegel's owl finally flies off into the dusk of history. The work appears to have been collected and edited by one person, or at least it seems as if there is one authorial voice to be found in the text. In the *Liezi* it is slightly safer to assume, as a pious fiction, the hand of one major author, editor, or compiler.[6]

The preface of Zhang Zhan (fl. 370CE) provides this account of the history of the text;

> I have heard my late father say, "My late father [Zhang Zhan's grandfather], Liu Zhengyu, and Fu Yinggen were all maternal nephews of the Wang family. When they were young they played together in the maternal family's house. My father's maternal uncle was Wang Zizhou and his elder first paternal cousins Wang Zhengzong and Wang Fusu (Wang Bi), all liked to collect books. They had collectively secured Wang Chongxuan's library, which totaled almost ten thousand *juan* [NB: sections or chapters of texts]. Mr. Fu's family has also been recognized scholars for generations. The three gentlemen had been friends from childhood and they competed in making copies of rare books. When they reached their maturity, having met the disorders of the Yongjia period [307–312 CE], my father, along with Fu Yinggen, escaped south in order to avoid the disaster. The carts were heavy and loaded to their capacity. Moreover, because the bandits were numerous and the road in front still long, my father said to Fu Yinggen: "Now it is unlikely

> that we will be able to preserve all that we are carrying, so let's merely select whatever items we estimate the world will want and each of us preserve and copy these works so that they will not be lost." Fu Yinggen therefore only saved his grandfather's, Xuan's, and his father, Xian's, collected works. Upon arriving south of the Yangtse there was only a part of these works left. Of the *Liezi* there was only the "Yangzhu" and "Explaining Conjunctions" chapters and the report, in three *juan*. At the time of the disorder, Liu Zhengyu became the governor of Yangzhou and came across the river to our side. Afterwards my father obtained four *juan* [sections] from Liu's home, and subsequently also sought out six *juan* from Zhao Jizi, Wang Bi's son-in-law. By collating and comparing what was and was not in the various texts, only then was he able to compile the complete edition.
>
> This book, in summary, attempts to show that total emptiness is the chief principle that governs all things, the evidence for which is that all things come to an end; divine wisdom is preserved constantly in the concentration of quietness, whereas the thoughts and reflections of desire come to grief in their own attachment to material things; but if one becomes enlightened that these thoughts and reflections of desire are like transformations and dreams, then one will not be limited, whether in matters large or small, to one realm; failure and success do not depend on mental power, and in self-governing it is best to let oneself go; if one follows his own nature then everything will be favorable wherever you go, and you will be able to tread on fire and water; and if one forgets oneself, there will be no mystery that is not illumined. This is the essence of the work. Thus what it makes manifest is often similar to the Buddhist scriptures, but its major conclusion accords with the *Laozi* and the *Zhuangzi*. Its choice of words and analogies particularly resemble the *Zhuangzi*. Zhuangzi, Shendao, Hanfei, Shizi, Huainanzi, the *Xuanshi*, and the *Zhigui* all quote its words, and therefore I have annotated it in this manner. (Yang Bojun 1965, 178–79)

This preface tells us a great deal about the nature and place of the text in the complicated intellectual milieu of Wei-Jin world. It situates the text in the difficult days at the beginning of the third century; and it does even more by telling us about the intellectual and social world of the text. Graham's best guess about the date and the composition of the text is that it was probably compiled in the early fourth century and that there is one hand at work in the final redaction of the text (Graham 1986a). There is nothing in the preface that would contradict Graham's astute estimation of the received text. As he points out, much of the text is written in the form of "parables," a common genre for the third and fourth centuries.[7]

Sadly, from the perspective of the wandering northern Chinese elite, the *Liezi* text suffered as much with its move to the south as the clan. Most of the text was lost and had to be re-created from collections of other exiled friends from north China. The preface makes it very clear that the present text is a reconstituted version of the original. The original text, however, was taken to be a genuine text from the heyday of the classical period. The proof for this was that other great classical Warring States texts quote from the *Liezi*. Even though critical scholars are dubious of the truth of these editorial assertions, the antiquity of the collected fragments was one of the reasons for preserving and publishing the new edition.

The other unmistakable note of change is the reference to the Buddha dharma.[8] The Chinese recognition of the Buddha dharma, it almost goes without saying, marks a major transformation of the social, religious, and philosophical world of China. The Chinese had never before encountered, or even imagined, that there might be a world beyond the boundaries of the Middle Kingdom that could produce anything of cultural interest for them. Of course, as we now know, the Sinitic cultural world was never completely cut off from other parts of Asia, but even compared to the minimal contact between the Greco-Roman world and India, the connections between China and the rest of Eurasia were sparse at best. What the Chinese did know, and what was crucial during the interregnum between the Han and the Sui-Tang restoration, was that the world beyond the traditional border of their empire was filled with warlike "barbarians." It would never have occurred to the Chinese that these barbarians had anything subtle to share with the educated elite. What had been shared, such as the introduction of the stirrup—which allowed for the creation of the much-feared steppe heavy cavalry—did not count for much in the Sinitic inventory of civilized behavior or ritual.

WEI-JIN PHILOSOPHICAL MOTIFS

It would be easy to have written "neo-Daoist" as a designation of the teachings of the *xuanxue* 玄學 (dark teaching), because that is the name given by many of the intellectuals during this period to their kind of work. But in terms of the *Liezi*, there is a touching Confucian note of filial piety in the preface: Zhang is doing what he can to preserve the scholarly patrimony of his clan. We also need to remember that scholars such as Wang Bi probably would have been uncomfortable with simplistic labels such as "Confucian" and "Daoist". Wang Bi, for instance, stoutly maintained that Kongzi was a more elevated sage than Laozi for the simple reason that Kongzi obviously understood *wu* 無 (nothingness)—because he did not speak of it, whereas Laozi went on about it incessantly (Berthrong 1998a, 61–70; Wagner 2000, 2003a, 2003b). Wang's point is that you do not have to explain something you clearly understand fully, but when you do talk about something, it is because you still have to explain it, at least to yourself.

Arthur Wright, in his "A Historian's Reflections on the Taoist Tradition," outlined three defining traits for the entire spectrum of elite *xuanxue* cultural forms. First, there is "an organic view of man and the universe, the notion that all phenomena (including man) are knit together in a seamless web of interacting forces, both visible and invisible. Interwoven with this is the idea of ceaseless flux: that the apogee of any of these forces engenders a reversion towards its opposite" (Wright 1970, 248).

The second theme, also cataloged by A. C. Graham in his studies of the *Zhuangzi*, is the theme of primitivism (1986a). There is a longing on the part of Daoists for the freedom to return to a simple form of organization both for individual and the society as a whole. Joseph Needham has also hypothesized that perhaps the Daoist hankering for the simplicities of rural life was the echo of a memory of life before the rise of urbanism.

The third trait defines the characteristic element of the Daoist religious quest. "A third element is the persisting belief that some men, by divers regimens—mystical, dietary, sexual, alchemical—can attain a kind of transcendence, which manifests itself in longevity, invulnerability, charisma, the ability to know and manipulate the forces around them" (Wright 1970, 248–49).[9]

Many scholars of Daoism have noticed that one of the persistent motifs of the tradition is a penchant for discussions and stories about process, flux, or transformation. The question that needs to be asked is, what kind of "process" do we discover in the ceaseless flux of the Daoist *imaginaire*? Wright did not specify process per se but rather notes that we find a cosmology of ceaseless flux as one of the defining traits of philosophical Daoism. Certainly, a ceaseless flux and Whiteheadian process share movement, change, and transformation. However, in Whitehead there is a sense that the many become one in the process of self-generativity; there is an autotelic feature to Whitehead's version of a creativity that generates actual entities without ceasing. Does a ceaseless flux define the same processive domain? Of course, Wright is trading on the ubiquitous pan-Sinitic world of yin-yang and the five forces. Given the late date of the received *Liezi* text, this is not a problem; the yin-yang and *wuxing* 五行(five phases) cosmology had stabilized long before the *Liezi* was given its final editing. In fact, it is such a commonplace feature of Chinese thought that most contemporary scholars assume that some form of the yin-yang/five phase format has been around ever since the beginning of Chinese second-order self-reflection. However, it is well to remember that although prototypes of the mature yin-yang/five phases cosmology have informed the earliest records of Chinese culture, the maturation of the stable cosmology did not fall into place in its final form until the Han dynasty (Graham 1986b). Great Confucian scholars such as Dong Zongshu and Yang Xiong seem to have played an important role in fusing all of these cosmological traits into one attempt at systematic discourse. But once in place it seemed so intuitive that it was assumed that this was about as cosmologically commonsensical as one could be.

For the sake of argument, let us ponder the ceaseless flux a bit more. As Wright notes, this emphasis on flux is not entirely random. The flux is predicated on an organic viewpoint and is defined by a set of constant alternations. The alternations are aptly called yin and yang. The organic aspect is also linked to some of the central features of the yin-yang dyad. Yin and yang are organic in a deep sense because they are connected and constantly balanced. When the yang reaches it farthest point it reverts to a yin phase, and vice versa. The whole complicated technology of *Yijing* lore is predicated on the alternation of the yin and yang in just this fashion.[10]

But is this ceaseless Daoist cosmological *hunlun* 渾淪 or *hundun* 混沌 (chaos) a process in the full-blown Whiteheadian sense of something new emerging from the flux of the various primal patterns, organic arrangements, and forces? The simple answer is, of course not. On the one hand, there is nothing in the *Liezi* that even closely resembles Whitehead's elaborate theory of concrescence that gives birth to a novel actual occasion. But on the other hand, the *Liezi*, like all of the Warring States or early Han Daoist texts, does evince a passion for the unique and singular arising from the world in flux. The *Liezi*, like the *Zhuangzi*, is a passionate attempt to get us to look closely at the multifarious qualia of the world and the wonders that reside within it, but all with an ironic tone that is distinctive.

The first step in examining the processive or transformative motifs in the *Liezi* is to examine the particular nature of the primal dyads of yin and yang. Derk Bodde provides an excellent summary when he writes in his classic article "Harmony and Conflict in Chinese Philosophy" that "in each of these dualisms the Chinese mind commonly shows a preference for one of two component elements against the other. At the same time, however, it regards both of them as complementary and necessary partners, interacting to form a higher synthesis, rather than as irreconcilable and eternally warring opposites. Thus here again there is a manifestation of the Chinese tendency to merge unequal components so as to create organic harmony" (Bodde 1953, 69). The point about the Chinese search for harmony has been repeated in many different contexts, and I will emphasize just two aspects of this dyad. First, there is a strong sense of connection between the "dualism" of yin and yang. While it is true that one pole may have more purchase in any one moment, there is the equally strong claim that one cannot have the one without the other. Even the most macho male has a yin side. Moreover, this "dualism" is eternally oscillating between the two poles, and although it seeks organic unity, there is a constant interaction between the elements that make up the event in question and the world that surrounds the emerging new organic harmony. Moreover, though Bodde does not state so in this quote, the dance never ends.[11]

Of course, the *Liezi* does not adopt the philosophical motif of process per se as its main theme. Pride of place in this regard goes to *ziran* 自然 (spontaneity). However, the connection is very strong, because without process as change and transformation, it is hard to see how the *Liezi* could make *ziran* work at all. There is nothing surprising in this textual fact, because the *Liezi*, as we have already noted, is heavily derivative of the *Zhuangzi*, and *ziran* is a key in the *Zhuangzi* text. Along with *wuwei* 無為 (uncontrived action) in the *Laozi*, *ziran* is probably as characteristic of Daoist thought as any term can be. Although spontaneity is not the same as process, such as the famous *shengsheng* 生生(generativity)—or creativity itself, according to Mou Zongsan's reading of the *Yijing*—it affords a processive and transformative thrust in the *Liezi*. These shared and even common sets of motifs certainly move around in flux and refuse to stay the same, whatever else we can say about them as markers of process.

One important aspect of spontaneity is clearly presented when we think about the moral thinking of the *Liezi*. Even as perceptive a scholar as H. G. Creel (1970) argued that there is nothing like ethical discourse in the Daoist tradition, at least when compared to the relentless focus on the ethical in the works of the Confucian masters. This is only true if we think of ethics as a deontological set of rules, and, as we all know, the Daoist are congenitally allergic to rules of any kind, especially the kind of ethical rules so near and dear to the mind-hearts of Confucian worthies. The "Explaining Conjunctions" chapter states that "in any case, nowhere is there a principle which is right in all circumstances, or an action that is wrong in all circumstances" (Graham 1960, 163). The *Liezi* goes on immediately to add a very pragmatic twist to its maxim about the nonefficacy of moral fixity. "The method we used yesterday we may discard today and use again in the future; there is no fixed right and wrong to decide whether we use it or not" (163). At least one point to draw from the *Liezi* narrative is that one does act in a moral fashion even if there is no fixed set of moral rules.

In typical ironic fashion, in the "Yang Zhu" chapter there is an elaborate story about two brothers who contravene all the conventional norms of their society in order to defend a higher (lower?) understanding of the moral condition. Yet another brother, obviously a stolid Confucian soul, works hard to bring stability and good government to the world. He still has one worry—namely, that his two brothers continue to conduct their lives in complete disregard for human sense and sensibility. One of them is addicted to drink and has a private brewery. The second brother is besotted with women and tries to seduce all the young women in his county. "Any beautiful virgin in the district he was sure to tempt with gifts and invite through go-betweens, giving up only if he could not catch her" (Graham 1960, 144). The Confucian brother sets out to reform his brothers straightaway like any prissy Confucian would, but in the end is given his comeuppance by his notorious brothers. After the elder and younger brothers have remonstrated with the Confucian brother and castigated him for butting into things he can not possibly understand, they make two characteristic proclamations. About their activities they state, "For us the only misfortune is a belly too weak to drink without restraint, potency which fails before our lust is satisfied. We have no time to worry that our reputation is ugly and our health in danger" (145). The punch line, as close as a Daoist gets to prescribing behavior for another, is: "The man who is good at ordering his own life gives scope to his nature without needing to disorder the lives of others" (145).

I have always thought this is a wonderfully ironic twist to Kongzi's well-known negative version of the golden rule—do not do unto others what you do not want them to do to you. I suspect that Kongzi would not have been at all pleased with the reproof that Zhao and Mu gave to their more orderly Confucian brother. When Zichan, the middle brother, still in a rather dazed condition, reported this encounter to Dengxi, his friend made the following comment: "You have been living with True Men without knowing it. Who says that you are a wise man? The good government of the state of Zheng is mere chance, you cannot take credit for it" (146). So much for Confucian efforts at moral reform of the self and society! The better path is that of pure spontaneity that does not deform the pure nature with which we are endowed by heaven.

Daoist spontaneity is not a fixed moral norm. This is the point that Laozi, Zhuangzi, and Liezi constantly make to anyone bothering to listen to their stories of doing the right thing in the wrong way and vice versa. There is an almost endless list of such stories in the *Liezi*. What is often amusing is that these stories are put in the mouth of Kongzi himself. Or there are times when a truly enlightened Daoist teacher confounds Kongzi as the latter blunders along in a typically constrained Confucian manner.

TRANSFORMATIONS, CHANGES, AND GENERATION

The *Liezi's* cosmology is grounded firmly in the pan-Sinitic cosmology of *qi* 氣(vital force) and the interaction of yin and yang. According to the *Liezi* persona, the sages used the notion of yin and yang to order the cosmos. What is expansive and blowing out is yang, and what is withdrawn and pulled inward is yin. As Graham noted in his introduction to the opening chapter, "Heaven's Gifts," it is almost impossible to provide a univocal translation of *qi*. Almost four decades later, Hal Roth (1999) has reconfirmed Graham's estimation of the difficulty of translating *qi* consistently in English. Roth's informed surmise is that *qi* might originally have meant vapor, but then took on the connotation of breath, and moved on to even more cosmological glory as one of the key philosophical, spiritual, and medical concepts in the whole history of Chinese thought.[12]

One of the themes found repeatedly in the *Liezi* is that things change. Nor is this an isolated insight in classical or post-Buddhist Chinese thought. The *Zhuangzi* proffered the same teaching. However, it is such a common theme in the *Liezi* that some scholars have suggested that this shows Buddhist influence. The reasoning is that one of the central tenets of Mahayana Buddhism is the lack of any essential substance all the way down. There are no eternal entities, nor does anything have a subsisting essence. All beings arise and decline. Moreover, critics also note an inordinate interest in the question of dreaming or illusion. Dreaming, of course, was a famous part of the butterfly/human dream recounted by Zhuangzi. Therefore, attention to distinguishing, where possible, between the dream and waking state was a perfectly presentable Daoist pastime. However, the linking of the world of dream to the further speculation that all the cosmos may be an illusion based on dreaming suggested Buddhist influence. The counterclaim is that here again the internal logic of the Daoist discourse moves in a parallel fashion to that of Buddhism, so it is impossible to say whether or not the *Liezi* redactor was stimulated or influenced by Buddhist texts or ideas.[13]

In order to delimit the search for themes of process and transformation, I will focus on a set of important Chinese terms (for the expanded set for both Confucian and Daoist texts, see chapter 1)—namely *sheng*, *hua*, *gai* 改, *shi* 時 and *bian*.[14] These are most commonly translated as "to give birth," "to transform," "to change," and so forth. The graph *sheng* 生, according to the New Confucian Mou Zongsan (1983, 1990, 1994), is the prime candidate for the metaphysical notion of creative process in the Chinese philosophical tradition, broadly conceived. Mou cites as the locus classicus for the notion of creativity the famous passage in the Great Appendix of the *Yijing* that says *shengsheng buxi* 生生不息 means creativity itself in a strong metaphysical sense. By this Mou means that the very nature of the cosmos is processive in nature, and that to have a cosmos means the generation of new and novel things and events. Some Chinese and Western critics argue that Mou has been reading too much process-oriented Western philosophy; while it is true that Mou was an amazingly learned scholar with a vast accumulation of knowledge of Western philosophy (he began his career as a logician) as well as of Chinese Buddhism and of every other form of Chinese thought, Mou would have demurred that his focus on *shengsheng buxi* was about as foundational and mainline to the development of all the various schools of Chinese thought as one could possibly find.[15] A literal translation of *shengsheng buxi* is "generation (or birth) without ceasing." From this Mou makes the philosophical claim that this "generation-without-ceasing" is the pan-Sinitic metaphor for creativity itself as the cosmological signifier of universal process.[16]

The opening chapter, "Heaven's Gifts," devotes a great deal of time to discerning various features of the ceaseless flux of the cosmos. The first section begins with Liezi living in the game preserve of Putian. Quoting the words of his own master, Huzi, Liezi says, "There are the born and the Unborn, the changing and the Unchanging. The Unborn can give birth to the born, the Unchanging can change the changing." (Graham 1960, 17). The Chinese for birth is *sheng* and for change is *hua* 化. These are two of the most important terms for a Daoist, or any Chinese philosophy for that matter, and through them the theory of process puts in an appearance at the very beginning of the text. A moment later the text explains, "Things for which birth and change are the norm are at all times being born and changing. They simply follow the alternations of the Yin and Yang and the four seasons" (17–18).

One could hardly expect to find a more concise definition of the processive aspects of the mature classical pan-Sinitic cosmology than what is recorded in the opening section of "Heaven's Gifts." Just after these opening sections, a section provides an example of the third of our linguistic markers for flux, change, and process: namely, *bian* 變. But before we continue reading the *Liezi*, I want to highlight one other aspect of the statement about the alternation of the yin and yang. *Bian* introduces the element of time. The four seasons are often invoked metaphorically as representing the temporal dimension of cosmic flux. For instance, the enigmatic first four graphs of the *Yijing* are explicated as referring to the four seasons or the even the four phases of the arising, success, favor, and faithfulness of anything whatsoever (Liu Dajun 1995, 3–4). Whether or not this is an accurate rendition of what these opening phrases of the text meant to the original authors is impossible to say. What is important here is that this sense of temporal development from inception to mature faithfulness is what the classical self-reflective tradition believed was being said in this most universally respected of early texts.

I am making a major point of this marker of temporality because I hold that transformative temporality is one of the key motifs of any process philosophy—and a consideration of time or temporality is probably a major topic for any reasonably complete and coherent philosophical worldview anywhere in the human world. In terms of my Sino-Whiteheadian-naturalist vocabulary, time or a strong and realistic temporal trait is crucial for the dynamic aspect of change or transformation per se. But why not just take the yin-yang model as even more primordial than the four seasons? Don't yin and yang indicate the temporality of the four seasons, from the softness of yin to the final harvest of yang? Of course this is true, but from my interpretive vantage point, one could also make the argument that the alternation of yin and yang need not be temporal in any strong sense of the passage of nature, as Dorothy Emmet would say (1992).[17]

There is another interesting turn of phrase in this early passage. This is the character Graham translates twice as "the norm." Actually, the Chinese character *chang* 常occurs a number of times as the *chang* of birth and the *chang* of change, as it were. The semantic range of *chang* includes the notion of a norm, of a rule, of something constant. In modern Chinese it also means enduring, the general, certain, lawlike, and so on. *Wuchang* 五常, for instance, are the five cardinal Confucian virtues in the sense of being the five constants of moral lives. Birth and change are indeed the norm of anything that becomes and perishes.[18]

The next cluster of passages in "Heaven's Gifts" continues this trend of thought. One of the statements I hear often about Chinese thought is that it lacks an interest in deductive explorations of topics such as the nature of being, either in its ontological or cosmological form. There may be something of a statistical grain of truth in such assertions, but the following argument from the *Liezi* should cause us to wonder if this interest in the hot topics of Western metaphysics is really completely lacking in China. Of course, one of the difficulties in making my present claim is that the passage is ironic or perhaps even nonsensical in a humorous vein. It is not that the *Liezi* or the *Zhuangzi* are uninterested in such questions, but rather that they approach them with a characteristic sense of humor that masks the serious point they are making.

Liezi says at the beginning of the passage, "Formerly the sages reduced heaven and earth to a system by means of the Yin and Yang" (Graham 1960, 18). The question then is posed, "If all that has shape was born from the Shapeless, from what were heaven and earth born?" (18). It is a sensible question indeed about how to determine the true nature of nature, and it is almost Socratic in method. If I am merely provided with examples of, let us say, virtuous action, I must still ask, what makes these virtuous actions and not just neutral behavior? It is the next set of statements that are very hard to interpret.

Liezi goes on to state that there were four "primal" traits: primal simplicity, primal commencement, primal beginnings, and primal material. I confess that I am never sure how seriously to take such lists in the *Liezi*. Is the author just making fun of more serious cosmological thinking, is it half in jest, or is the author somewhat concerned to provide a vision, metaphor, or parable of how things work? I am not alone in enjoying such a perplexing hermeneutical moment—East Asians have appreciated the ironic humor of this part of the Daoist world for more than two thousand years. But if for a moment we take the underlying nomenclature of the list somewhat seriously, it would not be without significance that the first segment of the list is the *taiyi* 太易. *Tai* is the term used in most Chinese thought when the author wants to indicate the highest, deepest, most profound manifestation of the topic at hand. For instance, within Song Confucian thought, following the *Yijing*, the ultimate is called the *taiji* 太極 "Supreme Polarity" in Joseph Adler's felicitous and apt translation of the term (in de Bary, Bloom, and Lufrano 1999–2000, 1: 672–76). The old standard translation of *taiji* was "Supreme Ultimate," but I hold Adler's new rendering to be more in line with the correlative dialectic of the Northern Song founders of a renewed Confucian philosophy such as Zhou Dunyi (de Bary, Bloom, and Lufrano 1999–2000, 1: 669–78). The play, of course, is not on the first part of the binome, but on the second graph, *yi*. This graph, of course, is used as the name of the famous *Yijing*, or the *Book of Changes*, as it is most often rendered in English. Possible meanings include "easy," "simple," "gentle," "change," "exchange," and so forth. For our point of view it would be wonderful to play on the notion that the simple or primal is actually change qua process. This is not far-fetched in terms of the history of the interpretation of the term in the history of Chinese thought. That is why the *Yijing* is translated as the *Book of Changes*, wherein "change" means transformation and process broadly conceived.

The passage in "Heaven's Gifts" goes on to state that "the Primal Simplicity preceded the appearance of the breath" (Graham 1960, 19). Given the importance of breath or *qi* 氣in all forms of Chinese self-reflexive thought, to be in some kind of state prior even to the perception of *qi* comes as a start. Yang Bojun's 1965 commentary notes that we immediately think of the Supreme Polarity of the *Yijing* when we try to interpret the cryptic remark about not even being able to sense the vital force, the breath, the vapor of the cosmos. In another passage in Yang's commentary, attention is directed to the *Zhuangzi*'s notion of *hundun* 混沌 (primeval chaos). This is the state of confusion wherein all black cows are not even yet black, much less cows. In fact, as the *Liezi* passage continues, even after breath, shape, and substance are complete, there is still no distinction between things. This is the state that Graham translates as "confusion," hence the repeated reference in the text and commentaries to the primal *hundun* or chaos.

The hermeneutical spirit that is always alive in reading classical Chinese texts tempts us to continue to limn out just what is going on in this passage. However, there is the suspicion, never far from the surface of the conscious mind-heart, that the *Liezi* text is toying with us. Of course, play is nothing to be neglected in the magic garden world of the *Liezi*. The *Liezi* glosses the enigmatic terms as "that the myriad things are confounded and not yet separated from each other" (Graham 1960, 19).

The next section of this passage keeps probing the various twists and turns of a characteristic Wei-Jin cosmology. This state of chaotic confusion, we are told, can also be likened to the simple, and the since the simple has no bounds, no shape, it too is a motif of flux. However, the "simple" has a tendency to alter, to change—the Chinese term *bian*, (to alter from one shape to another), is another one of our glosses for process. The "simple" becomes one, then becomes seven, then nine, and once ninefold. It reverts to unity. Graham translates the passage as "Then it [the final outcome of the ninefold alternation] reverted to unity" (1960, 19). The sense of the phrase is one of motion—namely, the reversion of alternation that again becomes one (with the one standing for unity in Graham's reading). Yet the "one" is merely deemed a way of trying to designate the chaos of the confusion of the myriad things. The *Liezi* then goes on to say that "unity is the beginning of the alternations of shape" (19). Even shapes, the forms of definiteness for the *Liezi* text, are implicated in the dynamics of chaotic generativity.[19]

The power of the radial metaphor resides in the fact that it causes us to ponder whether or not our more typical Western modes of analysis work well in comprehending the lesson being taught in what is called the Lao-Zhuang tradition, of which the *Liezi* is such a prominent exemplar. Lau and Ames (1998) challenge us in their study of the *Huainanzi*, to consider just for a moment, what a synchronic, radial, autotelic worldview looks like. For instance, we tend to read passages from the *Laozi* and other Lao-Zhuang texts in a linear fashion, looking for a principle that orders and causes the development of the world. But Lau and Ames articulate a different narrative structure. The Daoist might not be presenting a synchronic portrait of a world dominated by an initial, overarching principle, but rather a world in which there is an alternating pulse or rhythm to the self-order, the *ziran*, of each and every creature, thing, or event. In Buchler's terms, what is revealed is an exhibitive discourse on the generation and transformation of the things of the world. The world is displayed or exhibited to us synchronically, and we are invited to partake of as many views as the genius of the author can provide us.

The exhibitive structure, of course, can take on different personas. The Daoist can be playful, amused, and even silly. The typical Confucian persona is serious. But both the playful and serious modes pile synchronic image upon synchronic image in order to exhibit a reality to which we are invited to pay attention. A. C. Graham has argued in a number of venues that Chinese philosophers often use the device of telling the student to pay attention to the world in order to discover all the facts relevant to the case at hand, and then to choose the correct path of action. The goal, certainly for Confucians and even for many Daoists, is to find a "way" to navigate through the dangers of a hostile environment. The diagnosis of the reasons for the danger differs from school to school and from philosopher to philosopher within a lineage. One need only remember the Confucian famous debate about whether human nature is good or debased. But it is not the conclusion of the argument that is now of interest. Rather, it is what the philosophers share in common. It is the exhibitive style of exposition. It is the appeal to look synchronically at a situation from as many viewpoints as possible in order to gather as many facts as one can before acting.

Of course, this methodological point should not be pushed too far. Chinese philosophers are just as capable of developing assertive judgment as a philosophical form as are any Western sages. This is as clear as day to anyone who has read carefully the various logical treatises of the neo-Moist schools and many of the writings of Xunzi. But the point remains that it is just this rather untypical assertive sensibility that has made the neo-Moists and Xunzi somewhat odd within their own traditions, and has led to their popularity in modern times, when Chinese intellectual historians have been searching assiduously for Chinese texts that followed the assertive mode of query.[20]

Before continuing our cursory examination of the markers of transformation and process in the *Liezi*, I will take a slight detour back in time to the early days of the Han dynasty. In their translation of the first chapter of the *Huainanzi*, D. C. Lau and Roger Ames (1998) make the point that this chapter serves as a useful and careful summary of many of the main philosophical motifs of classical Daoism. As we shall see, just as in the *Liezi*, the *Huainanzi* stresses the processive traits of the Dao via its own reading of the various traditions it incorporates into its vision of the cosmos. Moreover, there is strong scholarly consensus about the date when the text was composed; Lau and Ames give it as 139 BCE. It takes its name from the Prince of Huainan, the uncle of the famous Han emperor Wudi. The story goes that the text was a gift from the princely uncle to his nephew; ultimately the gift was in vain, as the Prince of Huainan was forced to commit suicide after an abortive coup attempt against the emperor.

The title of the *Huaiananzi* chapter tells of its aim—namely, to give an account of the Dao by tracing the Dao to its source. This is obviously metaphorical language, a play on the notion of source, of the spring of meaning that flows out from the Dao. Of course, the metaphor must not be confused with the reality itself. As the *Laozi* taught all the subsequent generations of Chinese scholars, there is no literal way that we can give a name to the Dao per se. The *Zhuangzi* has a famous story about using a finger to point at the moon. Zhuangzi makes the humorous point that human beings are so benighted that they sometimes prefer looking at the finger rather than the luminous moon, but he notes that we can forget the finger once we have sighted the moon.

One more parenthetical comment. Lau and Ames agree that process is a strong motif for the *Huaiananzi*. "Since there is nothing which is not *dao*, there is no external standard against which it can be measured or corrected. This then is the meaning of the phrase, 'standing alone it is not reformed (*gai* 改).' That *dao* is unique, however, does not preclude the fact that it is processive (*shi* 時), and constantly changing" (Lau and Ames 1998, 25). The same general processive motif qua *dao* is operative in the Confucian and neo-Confucian traditions as well, but there is a difference. Especially in the neo-Confucian fascination with *li* 理 (principle, pattern, order, coherence), there is an implied source for measure and correction. The Confucians are not clueless about how to act in the mesocosmic domain of human relations and culture; nonetheless, Lau and Ames are quite correct in indicating the profound Daoist respect for the *ziran* or spontaneous traits of the Dao and all the ten thousand things.

In a typically fabulous image, the *Huaiananzi* tells of the ride of two famous charioteers of high antiquity, Ping Ya and Da Bing, as they mounted their dragon-yoked chariot: They

> Mounted the thunder chariot
> And used the cloud dragons as their six horses.
> They rambled about in the fine mists,
> Galloped around in the hazy and nebulous,
> And, ever more distant and even higher, they made the trip
> of all trips. (Lau and Ames 1988, 69)

Here again the pan-Sinitic images are layered upon each other in profuse and probably now unknown ways. We can still appreciate the richness of the language and are impressed with the ability to harness dragons to a flying chariot. Dragons, as any Chinese literatus would know, are creatures of protean qualities and wonders of the watery world of transformation. Even the means of flight, the cloud dragons, are emblematic of the flux of the cosmos.

How different this is from the stillness of Buddhism or the ontology of early Greek thought!

In the opening stanza of section 1, the Dao is described in the following terms:

Flowing from its source it becomes a gushing spring,
What was empty slowly becomes full;
First turbid and then surging forward,
What was murky becomes clear.
(61)

The images of motion and process are inscribed on the Dao from its most murky and turbid beginnings to its future clarity. What is even more evident in the Chinese text is the plethora of water radicals for the various graphs that make up the stanza. Process is even part of the formation of the graphs, and as such, would not have been lost on the educated Chinese reader. However, I do not want to make too much of the construction of Chinese graphs; this mistake was made by the early Jesuit missionary scholars and Pound and should not be repeated. The reality of the fluid undertow of the text itself is enough to make the point.

The *Huaiananzi* is an important work because it is such an exquisite rendition of Lao-Zhuang thinking. If there is stability to the Dao, it is the process of the interaction of the correlative alternations of the yin and yang. In speaking of the ability of the kings Tai Huang and Gu Wang to grasp the Dao, it is said that the kings

Move like the heavens and stay still like the earth.
Turning like a wheel without flagging,
Flowing like water without cease,
They begin and end at the same time as the myriad things.
....
Like the potter's wheel spinning, like the hub whirling,
Going full circle they start going round again.
(63)

There is process but also stability. This is an important point. Process thought need not mean aimless chaos without any stability whatsoever. Modern cognitive science often makes much the same point (Damasio 1994, 1999, 2003). While the brain is constantly reinventing and reordering itself, there are stabilities to be found both at the upper levels of cognition and at the lower levels of the brain stem. And it is always important to remember that Whitehead's magnum opus was *Process and Reality*—there really is a reality to which we must pay attention and which is stable enough for us to do so with some certainty that we will survive in the material world. From the Daoist perspective, the ultimate aim of this balancing act it is "to bring peace to the world" (Lau and Ames 1998, 63).

There is no extended set of meditations of the role of change or process in the *Liezi* like that in *Huainanzi.* There is actually a simple reason why this is the case. The various chapters of the *Liezi* are often loosely organized around a specific theme. The themes of the remaining chapters simply do not focus as specifically on the motif of transformation or process as does the first chapter. Nonetheless, there is nothing in the remaining seven chapters that would cause me to abandon my claim that the *Liezi* provides evidence for the importance of motifs of process at the twilight of the classical period of Chinese thought.

I will now turn to a montage of passages on process in the *Liezi*, beginning with one more selection from "Heaven's Gift," chapter. The Chinese term in play in this selection is *sheng* 生 (birth/generativity). "Hence there are the begotten and the Begetter of the begotten, shapes and the Shaper of shapes, sounds and the Sounder of sounds, colours and the Colourer of colours, flavours and the Flavourer of flavours. What begetting begets dies, but the Begetter of the begotten never ends. All are the offices of That Which Does Nothing. It knows nothing is capable of nothing; yet there is nothing which it does not know, nothing of which it is incapable" (Graham 1960, 20). This is another of those wonderfully challenging passages to translate from the Chinese into English. Reading Graham's rendition shows how choices must be made. For instance, Graham could have played on the lexicography of *sheng* 生to emphasize the notion of giving birth or arising. But if he had said something like "the arising," the overtones of Buddhist dharma theory would have replaced the notion of being begotten. One can only wonder if Graham's early theological training, which he abandoned before ordination, and the cadences of the King James Bible with the poetry of the Gospel of John and the creative power of the Logos influenced his translation. Could it have been otherwise? Going beyond a wooden literalism, Graham made as good a choice as possible. There is no way to ever produce a one-to-one translation playing on the Chinese *sheng* within a sophisticated text such as the *Liezi.*[21]

In the chapter entitled "Confucius" a man named Guanyin (a Daoist and not the Buddhist bodhisattva Guanyin) says:

> If nothing within you stays rigid,
> Outward things will disclose themselves.
> Move, be like water.
> Still, be like a mirror.
> Respond like an echo. (Graham 1960, 90)

The main protagonist of this chapter is Kongzi. This may seem odd, but it really is not. Daoists generally deal with the First Sage in two different ways. The first is to make fun of Kongzi or Confucians by showing, often through encounters with Daoist worthies, that they are not nearly as enlightened as they think they are. The second strategy is to make Kongzi out to be a better

Daoist than other sages—in short, to put Daoist teachings in the mouth of the greatest of the *ru* 儒 scholars.

What Guanyin reveals is the typical Daoist teaching that if we are to live successfully in the world we must learn never to stay rigid in our mind-hearts, philosophical conceptions or bodies. As the *Laozi* taught, the mark of the dead is to become rigid and unable to respond to the world, whereas the mark of the living is to be supple. The *Laozi* states that this is like becoming a baby, which is soft and without preconceived notions. Whether or not this is an accurate reading of the mind-heart of the infant according to second-generation cognitive science need not bother us much at this point. The Daoist metaphors and images are priceless, and it is one sure reason why the *Laozi* has enjoyed such cross-cultural attention wherever it has been translated from its original classical Chinese.

The last three similes in Guanyin's teachings—water, echo, and mirror—are suggestive when viewed within the larger affirmation of process and flux posited by the *Liezi* text. When we move, we must be like water. Of course, as Sarah Allen (1997) has shown, the motif or metaphor of water is one of the most powerful and pervasive traits of the pan-Chinese philosophical and literary world. Water is an important image for both Daoists and Confucians. Here we are told that to be alive we must be like flowing water. The second simile, the response to an echo, trades upon the reciprocity of ear and sound. This is yet another comparison drawing on the correlative polarity of so much classical Chinese thought.

The simile of the mirror needs some more explanation. The author would have in mind the wonderful bronze mirrors of the Han dynasty. These mirrors were more than just objects on the nightstand of an aristocratic Han lady. They were often artistic representations of Han understandings of the cosmos. The still quality of the mirror was necessary for the person to be able to respond perfectly. We must remember that the semantics of images is linked to the correlative cosmology of the *Yijing*. Whereas a modern English reader may think of the fixed quality of an image as a literal representation of the object in question, thinking of the Wei-Jin intellectual could not help but be shaped by the teaching of the *Yijing* that the images point to the ceaseless creativity and motion of the yin-yang as emblematic of the Supreme Polarity, the *taiji*. The simile, inscribed as the middle of one the three, is directed to the correlation of mirror and object more than to the idea of being still or placid. I take the *Liezi* to be teaching that we must be perfectly receptive—the action is more important than the static nature of the mirror. The implications of a mirror qua bronze object depend on the rich interconnections of the culture itself and cannot always be emblematic of the static nature of reflection without appropriation.

The next passages come from "The Questions of T'ang" chapter. This is a fascinating section because of its analysis of infinity and its brush with a philosophy of relativity. Graham, in his introductory remarks to "The Questions of T'ang," argues that the discussion of infinity ought to be taken seriously as a philosophical meditation on the status and function of the infinite. The core of this question of the infinite begins this way.

> The ending and starting of things
> Have no limit from which they began.
> The start of one is the end of another,
> The end of one is the start of another.
> Who knows which came first?
> (Graham 1960, 94)

This is a fascinating passage for a number of reasons. While the topic of infinity, as we shall see, draws the author farther and farther into the murky depths of something and nothing, for our purposes it is crucial to note that process is understood as endless. There is no fixed doctrine of substance to help things out in terms of ultimate beginnings or endings. It is just process all the way down.

The passage continues with one of the most convoluted answers in the whole of the *Liezi* to the question of the infinite.

> It is nothing which is limitless, Something which is inexhaustible. How do I know this? [NB: Graham notes that there is a lacuna in the text here by noting that the commentator Zhang Zan writes, "Since it is called Nothing, how can there be an outside? Since it is called Void, how can there be anything within it? [Graham then goes on to reconstruct what must have been the gist of the undamaged argument.] But also there is nothing limitless; there is no exhausting, but neither is there any inexhaustible. That is why I know that they are limitless and inexhaustible, yet I do not know whether they may be limited and exhaustible. (95).

This does make some sense when one places the passage in the context of classical Daoist thought, which is loath of make something of the origin of the process of the Dao. The limits, as Graham argues in the notes to this passage, are neither the something that is simply larger than anything else nor the smallest thing, which is simply smaller than anything else. The problem with the above solution is that it is no solution at all, because the infinite is without bounds of any kind. However, it is perhaps unwise to press the assertive point too far. As Graham states, "Chinese arguments of this kind present great difficulties of interpretation. In this section I have made a point of translating very literally, and confining my interpretations (which are disputable) as far as possible to the notes" (96).

The last passage of my montage of processive motifs in the *Liezi* is found in the last chapter of the book, "Explaining Conjunctions." According to Graham, this is the most heterogeneous chapter in what is a very eclectic work. If there is an overall theme to the collected material, it is that we should be very skeptical about placing any trust in a fixed standard of judgment. The line in question here says, “Therefore the sage trusts the transforming process of the Way [聖人恃道化], and puts no trust in cunning or skill” (161). In all respects this is a typical Daoist admonition against using some kind of fixed convention, as would Confucians, to judge a situation. From the Daoist viewpoint of the *Liezi* we know that there is neither any rule that is always right nor any action that is always wrong. Any interpretation tending toward action, depends on the context.

The passage also seems to cast a shadow of a doubt over the more commonly proffered Daoist understanding of “knowledge”—namely, a knack or spontaneous action without the willful, pernicious torque of self-interest to cause us to go astray. No, here even skill is rejected. But there is still an element of trust on the part of the sage in play. The Chinese term *shi* 恃, which Graham translates as “trust”, has the connotation of relying on, depending on, feeling secure with, and so forth. It is not trust as one of the cardinal virtues of Confucianism, but certainly would be the state of someone with *xin* 信 (trustworthiness). The image is apt. The sage relies or leans on the very process of the Dao rather than on any human cunning. In the end, it really is process all the way down.

Texts such as the *Liezi* were critical of Confucian politics. Sometimes later religious Daoist sectarians were much less adverse about entering into active political life, even to the point of openly rebelling against the empire. We will now take a short look at another interesting byway of the Daoist version of process as transformation and as the freedom of spontaneity. Some “Daoist” thinkers made the jump from affirmations of cosmological spontaneity and freedom to discussion of the potential freedom of persons. Alone among early Chinese intellectuals, some followers of the spontaneous Dao in the tradition of the *Zhuangzi* and the *Liezi* manifested anarchist sensibilities, especially during the very creative Wei-Jin period.

TORCHES OF CHAOS AND DOUBT: ON THE POLITICAL EDGES OF EARLY ELITE DAOIST TRANSFORMATION

One of the best definitions of the word “classics” for any cumulative philosophical or religious tradition is that they are works with what hermeneutic scholars call a surplus of meaning. In this case, one of the surplus areas has to do with notions of generativity, transformation, growth, and process. Zhuangzi wrote, “The torch of chaos and doubt—that is what the sage steers by. So he does not use things but relegates all to the constant. That is what it means to use clarity” (Watson 1968, 42). The irony here is that the constant is change itself; this is hardly the kind of constant norms or laws so dear to the mind-hearts of Confucians or Legalists.[22]

The question that intrigues me is whether or not process thought can have an elective affinity with radical social theory, if not action, and if so, what form such an affinity would take. Does reflection on process as change and transformation bleed over from questions of cosmology and ontology into the practice of human social ethics and ultimately to the question of the governance of the human social order? Does a recognition that the cosmos is in the grip of change hint that human governments can change as well? Is there, in short, a radical political cast of process thought? Can process cosmologists easily transform themselves into anarchists or antiauthoritarian theorists? Classical elite Daoist texts are useful to interrogate about views of governmental authority, because they often seem to be the least political of Warring States philosophy.

Historically there is no necessary link between radical political thought and Daoist religious communities. While the Daoists might have sought to establish alternative utopian states, Daoists, like their Confucian cousins, had difficulty thinking outside the box of the imperial Chinese state theory. The very success of the Han made it a model for all future Chinese political theory. One might replace the emperor with another emperor, but it was not till the arrival of the Western powers in the nineteenth century that Chinese intellectuals began to consider something beyond the imperial state as possible for the Chinese political world.

But, there have been many antiauthoritarian Chinese thinkers, including even conservative Confucians; many Confucians supposedly gave their lives in protest against the draconian policies of the first Qin emperor. A great Ming-Qing Confucian intellectual historian, Huang Zongxi (1610–95), detested the illegitimate tyrannical power of the late Chinese imperial state, even though he continued to accept the idea of the state and even the imperial institution. Huang called for a drastic reform—reform that you seek to preserve (de Bary 1993). But even this most radical of Confucian critics of tyrany still believed that the best way to deal with the crisis of political authority was to reform the governmental authority profoundly but without recourse to eliminating imperial authority as the source of social order (Tan 2003).

Laozi reminds us in his eightieth chapter of a time when there were no large state structures, and he clearly commends this form of nonstatist solution to social problems (Ivanhoe and Liu 2002, 83). One could hear the chickens and dogs from another village and not even bother to wander over to see how things were going over there. However, other scholars do not take Laozi's wistful memories of late Neolithic village life so seriously and always remind us that Laozi has his eye on giving advice to late Warring States rulers. Nonetheless, as A. C. Graham has defined it, there is an element of primitivist thought in some Zhou philosophical texts (1981, 1989). We can define "primitivist" as something akin to the libertarian sensibility that the less government the better. One question any exegete of the *Laozi* needs to ask is, does the primitivist strain identified by Graham in the *Zhuangzi* actually equate to a libertarian love of uncontrived action or spontaneous action that should be applied to the political realm, or is it just nostalgia for a dearly remembered past? Scholars such as Graham and Needham et al. (1954–) have argued that memories or even contact with Neolithic life would have been entirely possible when the *Laozi* was composed. On the edges of the Warring States cities there had to be many small villages that preserved older–and from Laozi's viewpoint, gentler–forms of social organization than those of the ever more militaristic world of the contesting major powers of the time.

And finally, there are some anarchistic thinkers, such as Zhuangzi in some of his moods and the later Bao Jingyan (ca. third and fourth centuries), who actually questioned the authority of any state system. In the writings of the great alchemist Ge Hong (283–343) (Ware 1966; Saley 1978), Bao is remembered as having written an account of the golden age of the great sages suggesting that it was a time of *wujun* 無君 (no rulers) (*juan* 48. 1a, in Ge Hong, 1966). Given that the early sage-kings mentioned by Bao were taken as the paradigmatic example of great rulers by the rest of Chinese social theorists, this was a bold claim for Bao to make. Although Chinese thinkers from Mengzi on were audacious in providing theories about how a minister should remonstrate with—or even, in extremis, remove—an unworthy ruler, it never seemed to have occurred to them, save for Bao Jingyan, to devise a theory that would do away altogether with rulers.[23]

PROCESS AS RADICAL SOCIAL ACTION

That we even remember this early Chinese anarchist is because Ge Hong in *juan* 48. 1a of the *Baopuzi* preserves a discussion of Bao's theory about government without a ruler (Ge Hong, 1966). Ge happened to preserve this tidbit of strange political theory along with recipes for immortality and other topics of interest to the Wei-Jin intellectual world. As a theory about society without rulers or a lord, *wujun* provided as concrete a definition of anarchism as one could want.[24] That such anarchist ideas would be lurking in the neighborhood of certain forms of Daoist thought would hardly have surprised the functionaries of the Chinese state. Egged on by Confucians, Chinese politicians were always worried, that thinkers such as Yang Zhu and Bao Jingyan were potential subversives, because they lacked any respect for the majesty of political authority. It was only a short step from advanced egoism to the debauched notion of anarchy. Somehow the flux of the cosmos was analogized by Daoist intellectuals to the practice of government. There is yet another reason for this foray into early Chinese social theory. All too often the world of East Asian thought has been taken to be the home of hopelessly conservative political theory—the political opposite of any kind of social transformative praxis. Hegel is famous for his condemnation of all forms of Asian philosophy as static and with no progressive content or form (Clarke 1997, 2000). In its of political theory, only the emperor is free, and hence there is no real freedom whatsoever to be found in society. But there are some interesting radical political ideas in the early Sinitic world that cluster in the same intellectual space, to use the terminology of Randall Collins (1998), as intense Daoist speculation on the trait of process. In an era of debates about Eastern and Western social ethics, with a particular focus on human rights, I will hold that a fairly radical defense of the dignity of the person free from authoritarian government should not be seen as a merely fortuitous and idiosyncratic development of the West but rather as part of the common heritage of all humankind. We can thank Hegel, as noted before, for giving a psuedophilosophical defense of some of these antiquated claims about Chinese political culture. I counter that the Chinese have been just as interested in personal dignity—and, by extension, the freedom of the person—as any other people (Tan 2003; Angle 2002). Of course, the Legalists actually tried to perfect a totalitarian state and were roundly condemned by Chinese intellectuals for more than two thousand years as providing a perfect example of bad government. Many later Confucians defended human dignity against the claims of tyranny, even by sacrificing their lives and the lives of their whole families (Elman 2000).

Some have argued that the true nature of Confucian philosophy does not run completely counter to the goals of creative freedom for the person and society. Even modern defenders of Confucian liberal thought such as Wm. Theodore de Bary, however, would be the first to admit that the imperial Chinese state was adept in using Confucians and Confucian rhetoric for its own purposes (1991a, 1998). The struggle between what can be called imperial Confucianism and elite philosophical Confucianism was and is epic. The imperial state wanted to use Confucianism as a support for an absolute state, especially in the Ming and Qing periods. But, if such modern Confucian philosophers as Mou Zongsan are correct, then we can make the strong case for human freedom, creativity, and dignity as the basis for classical, early modern, and contemporary Confucian thought (Cheng and Bunnin 2002; Bresciani 2001).

Mou Zongsan's defense of the Confucian concept of human freedom runs like this: First, Mou never defends nor forgets the use to which the Confucian Way was put by the imperial state. Mou, in fact, is a harsh critic of imperial Confucian rhetoric as a form of authoritarian discourse. It is all too clear to Mou that imperial or state Confucianism was an attempt to foster a paternalistic authoritarian theory on the population. Second, and more importantly, Mou acknowledges that this imperial or statist theory does not mesh with the real philosophical basis of the pre-Han Confucian masters, at least down to Mengzi. True, Mou notes, Xunzi, the last great pre-Han Confucian master, did defend the role of the state more vigorously than did Mengzi, but Mou does not deem Xunzi to be in the mainstream of Confucian political or philosophical discourse. The reason that Mou advances this rather surprising thesis about early Confucian antiauthoritarian discourse is his belief that the main emphasis in Confucian political theory ought to be found in the creative powers of the person to respond to her or his environment in an autonomous fashion. Mou suggests that we can call Confucian moral thought a philosophy of moral metaphysics in which the final test of true humanity is the development of a strong moral will that acts in a creative manner within society while ordering society for the good of all. This is, according to Mou, the classical teaching of the sage within and the king without (Mou Zongsan 1983).

PROCESS AND PROTEST IN THE *LIEZI*

Doubtless, thinkers such as the Wei-Jin redactors of the *Liezi* thought of themselves as working within a tradition that had its origins in the thought of Laozi and Zhuangzi. If we now perceive that this elite "Daoism" was not quite the kind of unified movement that it once seemed to be for Han academicians, this does not mean that those who followed their perception of antiauthoritarian qua primitivist thought to the font of the two revered masters did so in good faith and with a very plausible reading of the texts. If a scholar wanted to criticize the state as an illicit and inhuman form of social organization, he or she could certainly turn to the "tradition" of Laozi and Zhuangzi for the basic form of antistate discourse. Even such a great antiauthoritarian Confucian as Huang Zongxi in the late Ming and early Qing could not really conceive of a state without a ruler as Bao Jingyan had done in the Wei-Jin period (de Bary 1993).

But if there is no state to enforce social norms and laws, or to generate cultural authority and respect, how does Zhuangzi's or Liezi's society operate? Clearly, there is a pattern of deference to those who really know or have a perfected skill or knack. And what do these people know? Put in a typically paradoxical fashion, they know nothing at all, or they can be said to "know" the Dao itself. This is actually a very complex statement, and it is one of the reasons for the great charm of Zhuangzi's writings. Zhuangzi's point was that we mistake true authority, the command of an excellent skill or craft, for the illegitimate and systematic aggression of the state and petty rulers. Zhuangzi was antiauthoritarian for both theoretical and practical reasons.

Some might object to a claim for authority in any sense within Zhuangzi's vision of the cosmos. On the surface, Zhuangzi does seem to reject any claims to knowledge, and by analogy, the authority that knowledge would bring. The argument goes like this: If there is no praiseworthy state for Zhuangzi, and there clearly is not, then the traditional (political) mode of authority is denied out of hand. One could then fall back on the idea that real authority is that of intellectual, moral, or technical craft excellence. But Zhuangzi is especially adept at poking fun at those who would profess to be moral or wise or know much of anything at all. In all cases he undercuts any appeal to knowledge of morality as it was found among his contemporaries such as Kongzi or Hui Shi. Both Kongzi and Hui Shi (the paragon of sophistic disputation) are made either to look foolish when they debate with Zhuangzi or, even more effectively, they themselves are often presented as preaching Zhuangzi's own theories, quite to the consternation of their followers and friends.

Zhuangzi discovered that wit and humor, including a keen and biting irony, was often more effective in dealing with philosophical antagonists than long dialectical arguments. One might object that wit is not a substitute for a carefully crafted argument about truth, but no one argues that Zhuangzi was not a master of his deflating craft. But when the job of radical deconstruction of reputations for theories or wisdom or goodness was done, there is still in Zhuangzi a respect for a special kind of wisdom of the sort that in the West would be called knowledge in a robust sense of embodied and cognitive discernment.

If there is some kind of knack or wisdom appropriate for human flourishing, it is also definitely not part of conventional political wisdom according to the *Liezi*. If we were to construct some kind of political vision from the *Liezi's* philosophy, it would be antiauthoritarian and antistate, though it would not necessarily reject all claims to "authority" as illegitimate. As Whitehead, relying on his interpretation of Plato, once observed, the victory of civilization is the victory of persuasion over force. Although Liezi would never have phrased it this way, I suspect that he would very much have appreciated Whitehead's insight into the proper role of authority in interhuman relationships. I have noticed that although Zhuangzi's and Liezi's fabulous collections of idiosyncratic characters engage in the most outré acts based on the most spontaneous decisions, these actions are rarely vicious. Neither Zhuangzi nor Liezi resort to torture, murder, rape, or robbery—though they know people who do these awful things. In short, I would rather fall into the bemused hands of Liezi than into the clutches of Li Si, a minister of a Legalist state.

Almost by definition, to be a Daoist in the *daojia* 道家mold of Laozi, Zhuangzi, and Liezi was to harbor suspicions about the role of authority in governance and distaste for Confucian social theory. However, it also strikes me that the connection is historically tight but not conceptually established. There is no reason why the Daoists should take this role based on their particular interpretation of process. Process is such a strong feature of so much of the Chinese tradition that we might well ask, if change and transformation are so central to the pan-Sinitic cultural worldview, then why don't we find more antiauthoritarian or anarchist thinkers in the tradition? This is an interesting point, but we must abandon it, for it is now time to revisit the Confucian masters of the Song dynasty and see what they make of the trait of process, for these Song Confucians read the Daoist texts with as much relish and with as much appreciation as any other members of the Chinese elite.

4

Daoxue

Zhu Xi and Chen Chun

Ever since Joseph Needham suggested in the mid-1950s that there was a strong affinity between Whitehead's organic philosophy and Zhu Xi's grand neo-Confucian synthesis, many scholars have pondered the scope and nature of this cross-cultural comparison between the thought of the Anglo-American philosopher and the Southern Song literatus.[1] Making things even more complicated than Needham's analogy, estimates about the value, even the viability, of cross-cultural comparative studies have fluctuated widely over the last three decades. While most scholars allow begrudgingly that we navigate our worlds by means of various forms of comparisons others hold that if we are not almost fanatically careful about the process of comparison, we will end in hegemonic disregard for the identity of the topics.[2] As we shall see, Lakoff and Johnson (1999), among others, make the strongest possible case for the role of comparison as the foundation of all second-order reflections such as philosophy and theology.

This chapter will pick up our conversation about Confucianism begun with the discussion of Xunzi. We will move over a thousand years and across great transformations in Chinese society from the late Warring States period (sixth to third centuries BCE) to the Northern Song and Southern Song dynasties (960–1279). Even to those who disagree with his interpretation of the teaching of the *ru* 儒 masters, Xunzi represents the intellectual culmination of the first great epoch of the Confucian Way. The works of Zhu Xi and his disciples such as Chen Chun come to represent the second great turning of the Confucian wheel as exemplars of the *daoxue* (learning of the Way). . Zhu invented the notion of the *daotong* 道統 (the transmission of the Way) as a method to differentiate his philosophy and exegesis of the classics from the teachings of other Song masters such as Wang Anshi, Hu Hong, and Su Shi, and even of Shao Yong, for that matter (Bol 1992; Berthrong 1998a).

This commitment to a theory about the revival of the Confucian Way is certainly part of the grand narrative Zhu and other *daoxue* masters tell about the *daotong*. The simple version of the story is that the Confucian Way is the articulation of the insights of the sage-kings of antiquity and hence is the foundation of any and all civilized personal and social order. Obviously, Xunzi agreed with this assessment. But according to Zhu, after the death of Mengzi (289 BCE) things began to go wrong. Xunzi, though a Confucian scholar, was definitely not a sage in the same sense as Kongzi or Mengzi—at least according to Zhu Xi and, in fact, most post-Song Confucian literati. According to Zhu, it was not until the rise of the four Northern Song masters—Zhou Tunyi, Zhang Zai, and the two Cheng brothers—that the true intent of the ancient and classical sages was revivified. Modern historians of Confucianism either smile or frown at the hubris of the authors of this new Song ideology. Nonetheless, it has become an important part, though always contested, of the *daoxue* version of the grand historical narrative of the Confucian Way. Moreover, because Zhu's version of the Song Confucian revival of *daoxue* became the basis for the civil services examinations after 1313, no Chinese scholar could avoid having to learn Zhu's narrative history in all its historical and philosophical details.

The very name that Zhu Xi chose to accept for his school—namely *daoxue*, is instructive. Zhu Xi is implying strongly that the Confucian Way was occluded during much of its previous history—in fact, ever since the death of Mengzi. He is claiming that, if properly understood, the Northern Song masters were the only Confucians to have revived the ancient and classical Confucian Way since Mengzi. He is asserting that this particular study of the Way based on the teachings of four Northern Song masters is really "the" Way when compared and contrasted to other versions of Confucian discourse. Some of his colleagues used the term *daoxue* as a joke, and others called Zhu's pretentious narrative *weixue* 偽學 (a false, contrived learning).[3]

What is fascinating in studying the Song Confucians is to see how the terms of debate about process and transformation retain the marks of their classical Confucian heritage and how the trait was both transformed and refined—how it ramified within the *daoxue* of Zhu and his disciples. I will adopt here what might seem a somewhat unorthodox procedure: I will first analyze the work of Chen Chun 陳淳 (1159–1223), the disciple, and then proceed to an analysis of Zhu Xi 朱熹, the master.

Why study the student's work before the teacher's? From the time of the Southern Song to the modern period, Chen Chun, an influential philosopher of the Southern Song dynasty, has been recognized as one of Zhu Xi's most important students and interpreters (J. Zhang 2004). His fame rests on a short philosophical glossary he composed for students of the emerging Teaching of the Way tradition based on his close study of the teachings of Zhu Xi. This philosophical dictionary served as an important introduction to the longer works of the Southern Song tradition of Zhu Xi. For eight hundred years

Chinese, Korean, and Japanese students have employed Chen's philosophical glossary as an aid to understanding the complexities of Zhu's great synthesis. Although not a systematic philosophical treatise in the Western sense of linear exposition of a complete system of speculative thought, the *Beixi ziyi* 北溪字義 (hereafter referred to as the *Glossary*) was an ordered account of twenty-six key terms drawn from Zhu Xi's corpus and personal teachings. Moreover, as Wing-tsit Chan (Chen Chun 1986, 1–32) has argued in his introduction to the English translation, Chen was always and everywhere a careful and faithful expositor of Zhu Xi's thought. Chan believes that the *Glossary* was a faithful and accurate presentation of Zhu Xi's mature thought. Secondary classics often bring a precision to the primary texts that are useful in interpreting the words of the classics. They make what was suggestively vague in original texts more explicit. An expository secondary classic is a blessing in that it can make the teachings of a philosophical or religious school more explicit and clear, but it can also close off the fruitful ambiguity of the primary classic. Chen believed that he was providing faithful documentation of his teacher's own close reading of the classical Confucian texts as revived by the Northern Song masters. Chan, with great appreciation of Chen's achievement, writes, "The *Pei-hsi tzu'i* [*Beixi ziyi*] is much more than a study aid; it is the ultimate message from Neo-Confucianism" (Chen Chun 1986, 32).[4]

Because of its importance in the foundation of the pan-Asian *daoxue* discourse, there is certainly warrant for a close reading of Chen's *Glossary.*[5] However, there are two other substantial reasons for choosing this text rather than others from the same period in the Southern Song and early Ming. For one thing, the *Glossary* is a coherent text. It passed under the eye of Chen on its way to publication. Such was not always the case with other major works of the emerging Teaching of the Way school. Many of their most interesting writings came from their conversations with their students or from their correspondence with friends. But this is not really the main reason for choosing the *Glossary.*[6]

In *Science and the Modern World,* Alfred North Whitehead made an astute point about secondary classics as useful guides for philosophical research:

> When you are criticizing the philosophy of an epoch, do not chiefly direct your attention to those intellectual positions which its exponents feel it necessary explicitly to defend. There will be some fundamental assumptions which adherents of all the variant systems within the epoch unconsciously presuppose. Such assumptions appear so obvious that people do not know what they are assuming because no other way of putting things has ever occurred to them. With these assumptions a certain limited number of types of philosophical systems are possible, and this group of systems constitutes the philosophy of the epoch. (Whitehead 1925, 48)

It is the background that supports the foreground. This holds as true for second-order systemic reflection as it does, according to the accomplished neurologist Antonio Damasio (1994, 1999), for the neurology of cognition itself. Chen is eager to show where Zhu is doing something novel within the world of the growing Song tradition. Sometimes what is unsaid, as we shall see, can be more interesting than what is explained. As an exegete of the master, the follower does have to take the time to explain more simply what is going on and is helpful in gauging the major sensibilities and quirks of an emerging system.

Chen was traditionally a controversial thinker because of the precision of his exposition of *lixue* 理學 (Teaching of Coherent Principle). He was always considered one of Zhu Xi's favorite and most astute students. Zhu thought highly of Chen; and the feeling was reciprocated. Chen sought to explain to other students the complexities of Zhu Xi's *daoxue*, and he was well known in his local region as a fine teacher of Confucian thought and practice. The *Glossary* is certainly not an exhaustive treatment of the *daoxue* philosophical vocabulary, and it is a shame that it is not more comprehensive, because Chen really did have a knack for explaining very clearly what Zhu's position was. Wing-tsit Chan makes the claim in his translation of Chen's *Glossary* that we cannot find any instance where Chen deviates from Zhu's philosophy. This is the main reason that the text has been so well received over the centuries in East Asia.[7]

The Glossary focuses our attention on those aspects of Zhu's philosophical vision that are different from those of other Song thinkers. Chen's task is to show how Zhu understood these contested or reinterpreted terms; the implicit subtext is that Zhu departs from other readings in order to recover the true teachings of the Dao. There is a whiff of stubborn pride in being able to access true wisdom, and other Confucians found it irritating in its claims for a privileged insight into the Confucian Way. Of course, Chen tried to make the case that in every instance Zhu has solid classical warrants for departing from other interpretations of Confucian cultural history and classical texts. It was the novelty of Zhu's philosophy, though expressed as ancient wisdom, that Chen wanted to present to the scholars of future ages.

Much of Zhu's thought is scattered in typical Confucian fashion among his various commentaries, short treatises, ritual texts, poetry, and voluminous correspondence. Chen sifted through Master Zhu's thought and organized *daoxue* thematically. Qian Mu (1971), another brilliant contemporary Confucian scholar, has provided an even more extensive organization of Zhu's thought in his multivolume *Zhuzi xin xuean*. Qian's massive study almost serves as a sophisticated, interpretive index to Zhu's thought, topically organized. One can only wish that Chen had written as much as Qian about Zhu's thought.

THE PLACE OF *LIXUE* IN THE DEVELOPMENT OF NEO-CONFUCIANISM

Let me first offer a sketch of the history of Confucian discourse as Zhu Xi understood it. Then I will show whether or not we can interpret this Chinese philosophical system as a form of process thought and as a form of robust naturalism. Further, if Zhu's and Chen's thought can be judged as a Southern Song version of process thought, how will that modify our understanding of process thought as an ecumenical movement? And if there is sufficient warrant for the label "naturalism," then Zhu's *lixue* can become an active partner in dialogue with the various streams of the North American naturalist philosophical world.

It is important to remember that the *daoxue* movement created by Zhu Xi was controversial from its beginnings. Zhu himself, later to become the master of the entire "orthodox" tradition, died while under condemnation for proposing a strange and heterodox new understanding of the Confucian classics. Zhu Xi has often been likened to Aquinas in terms both of the scope of his synthesis and the impact of his thought. It is somewhat curious that Zhu and Aquinas were both under bans of various sorts at their deaths. It was only later that the sheer power and massive weight of their collected works forced other intellectuals and the official keepers of orthodoxy and the imperial examination system in China to acknowledge and socially legitimate the fact that they were truly the masters of their traditions. It is now clear, as it was not in their times, that Zhu and Aquinas were uniquely able to synthesize the work of their predecessors and to add their own unique marks of philosophical genius to these creations.

In short, Zhu Xi believed that he was reviving the proper interpretation of the Confucian classics based upon the insights of his Northern Song masters (Bruce 1973; Bol 1992). In order to understand what Zhu meant and achieved by his synthesis, we will review the development of Confucian thought as it relates to Zhu's hermeneutical and philosophical project.[8]

Zhu's theory about the development of the Confucian Way is a famous part of his philosophical synthesis. Not only did he elevate his favorite Northern Song teachers to semicanonical status, but also he tried to show how the mainstream of Confucian thought flowed from the classical sages and masters of the Zhou dynasty to his beloved Northern Song masters. The most pertinent feature of his theory of *daotong* was that the truth of the tradition was passed down from sage to sage as a form of intellectual and/or spiritual communication, a transmission not only of the letter but also of the spirit of the teachings of the classical sages and early masters of the Ruist Dao. This in itself was not a shocking theory, for the simple reason that many Confucians before Zhu had given a great deal of thought to how to describe the historical contours of their growing tradition. However, Zhu gave the whole debate about how to define the true Confucian Way a twist by noting that mere preservation of Confucian documents was not what he meant by the real transmission of the Way. Rather, Zhu argued that the crucial issue was to get the spirit, ideas, and meanings of the sage rather than merely memorizing vast numbers of canonical texts (though many scholars did just this). This was certainly not an innocent reading of the tradition; scholars such as Michael

Nylan (2001), Peter Bol (1992), and Hoyt Tillman (1992a) take grave exception to this being the only possible way to understand the historical transmission of the Way. For instance, Nylan argues that Zhu does not really do justice to the intent of the great commentarial traditions that flourished from the Han to the Tang dynasties.

Zhu Xi pressed his interpretation based on the premise that if you did not understand the real meaning of the sages as embodied in their texts, then you were simply not part of the transmission of the Way. This did not mean that you were not a Confucian. Zhu would acknowledge that a commitment to the Confucian Way made you a Confucian. The problem was that mere commitment to the textual tradition was not enough, even if it was a necessary station on the road to the Dao. Zhu believed that a study of scholars such as Xunzi, Dong Zongshu, Tang commentators, or a fine Song scholar such as Hu Hong would make his point (Levey 1991). All of these men were Confucian scholars; where they went wrong is that they did not truly comprehend the essential meaning of the sages. According to Zhu, if the meaning of the sages was lost, the transmission, *sensu strictu*, was lost.

Zhu argued that Mengzi was the last classical Confucian to understand the Confucian Dao. After Mengzi, scholars lost this true Ruist Dao until the famous Northern Song masters actively retrieved it. As mentioned, Zhu identified these masters as Zhou Dunyi, Zhang Zai, and the two Cheng brothers. It was only with these four scholars that the Mencian mainline of Confucian wisdom reemerged into the light of day. Needless to say, many Song scholars disagreed with Zhu's reading of philosophical history. The great debate was joined about who was really in or out of the orthodox transmission of the Way.

The Confucian community agreed that Kongzi was the most important of the early classical authors, though in no way the sole founder of the tradition. According to Confucian lore, the actual founders of the Ruist Way were the sage-emperors of the mythic and historical past. Kongzi himself focused much of his attention on the trio of King Wen, King Wu, and the Duke of Zhou—for the simple fact that Kongzi averred that he had proper documentation for the teachings of the Zhou founders, and that he lacked such evidence or records for the more ancient sages.

Based on his historical understanding of the teachings of the sage-emperors and kings, Kongzi proposed a fundamental return to the Way of the sages. According to Zhu Xi, this revival demanded a reform of the person through self-cultivation and of society through the formation of governance based on correct ritual practice. Out of these two beginnings the whole of Confucian thought unfolded. In order to provide a guidepost for students of the Way, the tradition affirmed that Kongzi edited or wrote the various works known collectively as the Confucian classics. Later scholars came to doubt that Kongzi himself actually wrote or edited all the works attributed to him, but they never questioned that Kongzi's spirit hovered over all the classics as repositories of sagely wisdom, history, and plans for social and personal renovation.

According to Zhu, the Way was transmitted and expanded by later disciples of Kongzi and then definitively by Mengzi. For instance, Xunzi, although the most philosophically astute of the early masters, was not considered part of the orthodox transmission of the Way because of his arguments with Mengzi. Even sincere Confucians could go wrong if they did not understand the essentials of the Confucian Way.

The Confucian Way now entered its long medieval doldrums. Zhu was convinced that the Han and Tang scholars simply lost their way amid the huge and verbose commentaries they appended to the canonical texts. This decline in the Confucian Way opened the door for the revival of Daoism and the arrival of Buddhism in China. Zhu understood that these two traditions were the most dangerous rivals to the Confucian Way. And the most dangerous for Zhu was Buddhism. Zhu, and Chen after him, would often remark that some forms of Buddhism seemed to be very close in form to his Confucian Way. Later critics find this an ironic statement, and the less charitable among the critics agree with Zhu to the extent that they also see the similarity between Zhu's *daoxue* and certain forms of Buddhism, but they say that is because so much of the *daoxue* teachings of Zhu is borrowed, however unconsciously, from Buddhist and Daoist teachings.[9]

Mou Zongsan defends and documents a reading of neo-Confucianism history that is responsive to the Buddhist challenge but does not depend on Buddhist materials to build its new syntheses, at least in its emergence in the teachings of the Northern Song masters.[10] Mou's main defense of a "stimulation theory" derives from his analysis of the fundamental sensibilities of the Confucian tradition. Mou holds that Confucianism is a form of inclusive naturalism and humanism that is realistic, relational, and pluralistic—and more than capable of being creative when confronted by new philosophical alternatives such as the arrival of Buddhism in the postclassical medieval period and with the importation of modern Western philosophy after the nineteenth century. At one point—a point to which we will return—Mou argues, quoting a famous phrase in Chinese philosophy, that the very nature of reality is *shengsheng buxi* 生生不息, which Mou Zongsan (1994, 31–32) glosses into English as "creativity itself." A more literal translation would be something like "generation without cease." Critics of Mou have countered that this translation of an early Chinese insight should not be immediately identified with any one Western school of thought; the theme of creativity—indeed, the very term itself—has become identified with the work and school of A. N. Whitehead. Nonetheless, Mou did believe that there was a strong, even essential, process theme to be found in the Confucian tradition. According to Mou, this processive, pluralistic, and realistic sensibility was present from the beginning of the tradition and was only sharpened and made clearer in the Song revival of Confucian thought.[11]

The question that we will now pursue is, did Zhu and Chen have strong roles for the trait of process in *daoxue* thought? And if so, what was it? My argument follows Mou's argument that for Zhu and Chen process and transformation play important roles in *daoxue* philosophy. But process for Zhu and Chen was a complicated question; in fact, careful attention to Zhu's philosophy is one of those places that will help to globalize or expand our notion of the process movement.

CHEN CHUN'S *GLOSSARY*

The *Glossary*, as masterfully translated into English, annotated, and supplemented by Wing-tsit Chan, runs to 164 pages. The text is broken down into two chapters and is organized around twenty-six sections. The first section begins with an analysis of *ming* 命, which Wing glosses as "mandate," "destiny," "order" and "fate." While *ming* is undoubtedly a very important Confucian term, this is still a rather odd way to begin a glossary, because *ming* did not have this kind of pride of place in other presentations of Zhu's philosophy. Philosophical beginnings are never innocent.

From the perspective of modern Confucian philosophy, *ming* is not a very promising starting point. Thomas Metzger (1977, 127–34) has pointed out that *ming* gives the impression of being an unwanted guest in the New Confucian revival banquet. Metzger hypothesizes that this is because the New Confucians are extremely sensitive to the contemporary criticism that all Confucian thought is authoritarian and oppressive from root to branch. For instance, the great critics of the May Fourth generation could think of nothing better for Confucianism than to throw it on the scrap heap of history. The Marxist revolutionaries followed the lead of the May Fourth intellectuals. Mao, who did love certain aspects of traditional Chinese culture such as classical poetry, showed only scorn for the Confucian Way.

Although the New Confucians did not share Mao's hatred of neo-Confucianism, they were sensitive to the drastic need to reform the tradition. The old patterns of authority and control that were so useful to generations of emperors would never do in the world of democratic ideals and universal declarations of human rights. In any case, the New Confucians shied away from an exposition of *ming*, with its overtones of command, as the place to begin the reformation of the Confucian Way. Both the critics of Confucianism and the New Confucians agree on the need to break the bond between what has been called imperial Confucianism and the reformed or philosophical Confucianism advocated by the New Confucians. Mou Zongsan was as convinced that the old order, as represented by the conflation of Confucian philosophy and governmental structure, needed to be broken if Confucianism were ever to enter into the modern world as something other than historical anachronism.

What interested Chen about the role of *ming* is the fundamental *daoxue* question about the cosmological formation of things or events. If there is no creator God, then how are the ten thousand things generated so often and so successfully? Chen reasons that when anything at all emerges as some definite object or event—that is to say, when it emerges out of what he calls the "great transformation"—there must be some a point when it becomes the specific thing and not something else. "This is similar to giving an order," he says (Chen Chun 1986, 37, J. Zhang 2004, 236).[12]

Hall and Ames in their multivolume study of Confucianism make an intriguing point about the concept of order without someone or something to bring about this order (such as God in Western Christian theology). Not only do they reject any overt theistic import to Confucian thought, but they also argue that the *ru* tradition does not even have anything like the Greek concept of principle or *arche* lurking in its formulation by Kongzi or any other early Ruist master. On the contrary, Hall and Ames deem that what we have in the Ruist accounts of the origins—or even better, the continuity of the cosmos is ceaseless creation without a creator—an insight also shared by Joseph Needham. This order with no one to order it is like the Daoist notion of spontaneous action among things, and may be the root vision of the entire classical Chinese world, the Confucians included. This is a highly contested point. Zhu Xi himself was more agnostic when asked about the role of *tian* 天. Zhu thought that in ancient times there might have been a theistic interpretation of *tian*, but this is not a direction that he persues. Rather, Zhu is much more concerned to develop, based on the philosophy of Cheng Yi, an interpretation of *tian* as an expression of the creative principle of the cosmos as manifested in all objects and events rather than to posit a special role for a creator deity.[13]

The issue posed by Hall and Ames traffics with two issues: creativity and action. There is nothing strange about the role of action in the Confucian tradition as I have argued elsewhere (Berthrong 1994, 1998a). Ruist philosophy and social theory have always been an activist movement. Even scholars such as Brooks and Brooks (1998), who posit a very austere view of the genuine writings of Confucius, note that the First Sage was what we would now call a public intellectual interested in the politics of his day. Even the more sedentary or speculative Song literati were activists in the sense that they were concerned with good government and efficient social policy. Of course, some were actual political activists, such as Wang Anshi and his critics in the Northern Song. For these Song revivalists, the basic worldview was realistic, pluralistic, and activist even if they did not bother to fully articulate such a vision; the formulation of the worldview was left to thinkers like Zhu and his followers. There was a great deal of disputation about details of the worldview, yet it was realistic, pluralistic, and actively transformative and generative for all the *daoxue* masters.

It does turn out that this is indeed the case for the action theory of the Song-Ming-Yuan-Qing Ruist philosophers; ceaseless action is predicated of all aspects of the new Song revivalist worldview. For instance, the notion of *qi* 氣 as vital force, matter-energy, or any of the other clumsy ways that the

Chinese term has been expressed in English shows that the translators are seeking a way to talk about *qi* as suspended between the more categorically independent Western notions of action, force, and matter. The early Jesuits were not entirely wrong when they called Zhu's system a form of materialism. It was. But *qi* manifested formal and spiritual traits as well. The problem was that, based on *qi*, it was also an active, realistic, and pluralistic system as well one of vital force creating the things and events of the cosmos. Any worldview with *qi* as a major component is going to be a tricky one for Western philosophers and theologians to handle, at least until we reach the wonderfully protean world of modern physics. In modern quantum physics we discover a language that would have delighted Zhu and his disciples.

In the opening section on *ming*, Chen provides clues about the direction in which he wants to move the discussion of order and the destiny of things. He notes that *ming* has two meanings (Chen Chun 1986, 37–39; J. Zhang 2004, 237). It can be articulated in terms of principle (*li*) and vital force (*qi*). Even a casual student of Zhu's philosophy immediately sees what Chen is trying to accomplish. Zhu was famous for his theory of principle and vital force; or more properly put, he was famous for exploring the relationship between principle and vital force. The question of how principle and vital force combine in order to generate all the things of the world is a key metasystemic or second-order question for Zhu. It is such an important topic in Zhu's thought that his version of *daoxue* was often called *lixue* (the teaching of principle).

Another common label for Zhu's philosophy was to call it Cheng-Zhu 程—朱 *lixue* 理學 (the "principled" teaching of Cheng and Zhu). Although both of the Cheng brothers are included in the label, later intellectual historians note that it is really Cheng Yi who is most like Zhu in his interpretation of principle, a fact that Zhu readily admitted. In the later tradition, this proclivity for principle is contrasted to the great alternative, *xinxue* (the teaching of mind). The great paladin of the teaching of the mind-heart was, of course, Wang Yangming. Wang, with typical Confucian modesty, argued that he did not invent this philosophy, but merely was following the lead of Mengzi and Song worthies such as Liu Jiuyuan (see Tillman 1992a).

The two great labels are not without irony. While there is good reason to call Zhu's metasystem a teaching of principle, this does not mean that Zhu was not as much transfixed by *xin* 心 (the mind-heart) as any other philosopher of a Lu-Wang inclination. Qian Mu (Qian 1971, 2:1–38) has conclusively shown that Zhu wrote enough about *xin* to warrant being called a philosopher of the mind-heart. In fact, as Qian and Mou have proved, it was Zhu's struggle to understand *xin* that began the great philosophical turn in his late thirties and early forties. There are now a number of accounts, including my own, of this final phase in the development of Zhu's mature thought.[14]

The presenting question for Zhu, during his philosophical awakening in his late thirties, was what the proper analysis was of the human mind-heart. How should we understand it, and how should we cultivate it in order to enter the path of true learning? As we noted before, Zhu's mature philosophy is often linked to the work of the Cheng brothers. They provided him with the key material for his theory of principle. But it was Zhang Zai who provided the key for understanding the mind-heart. Moreover, it was with this new reading of the mind-heart that Zhu was firmly launched onto the path of his mature philosophy. What Zhu took from Zhang was that the mind-heart was the union of vital force and principle—or more specifically, as Zhang Zai thematized the connection, that the mind-heart united the formal human nature with the emotions. Commenting on Zhang Zai's famous epitome, "The mind-heart commands and unites man's nature and feelings." Chen Chun said, "This is especially simple in language but complete in meaning" (Chen Chun, 1986, 60; J. Zhang 2004, 252; I have modified the translation with *xin* 心 as mind-heart).

Zhang's pithy formulation of the mind-heart illustrated how the Song revivalists gave a new level of hermeneutic understanding to the traditional lore of the Confucian Way. Zhang's solution to the definition of the mind-heart played on two levels of meaning. The first was that of the formal nature of reality, for which Zhang appropriated the old concept of *xing* 性 (human nature). There has been considerable debate as to whether we can call *xing* human nature in the classical literature; however, by the time of the Song revival, there is little doubt that this is what the term came to mean. "Human nature" defined the formal pattern, order, or principle that was given by heaven to human beings. It was that mandate, or *ming*, that caused the thing or event to be what it was in a formal, patterned sense.

Qing 情 (emotions) was an equally ancient term. Here too there is a great deal of contemporary debate, best summarized by Graham (1986a), about what *qing* meant to the classical authorities. It is more and more clear that it probably meant a number of different things. As we discover new classic texts in archaeological excavations, we are beginning to see the outlines of the debate about human nature, the emotions, and the essence of what it means to be human. Whatever *qing* meant in the Zhou and early Han, it came to be inextricably linked to the emotional side of human life by Song times. Moreover, it became identified with vital force perceived as the pristine locus of the emotional components of human life according to *daoxue*.

In short, according to Zhang Zai as interpreted by Zhu Xi, the mind-heart unified or linked the two traits of human nature: the formal side of reality and the emotions, or dynamic side of reality (as defined by *qi*, or the vital force of all that is). Furthermore, both Zhang and Zhu held that the mind-heart itself was the most refined form of vital force. Its particular essence was its ability to comprehend form or human nature as part of the human cognitive process. It is the perceptive and cognizing element of humanity. *Xin* can sense and react to the formal side of being; it can interpret the principle of humanity as endowed by heaven to the emotions, and vice versa. This was just the key to interpreting human nature that Zhu was searching for.

By using Zhang's formula about the mind-heart, Zhu was able to fuse a great deal of Northern Song theory about vital energy and principle into the characteristic architectonic of meaning that was his philosophical trademark. This was the *fons* of the theory of the unity of *li* and *qi* that became the hallmark of his version of Song philosophy. Along with becoming the benchmark for all future philosophies derived from the Song revival, it also bequeathed a particular philosophical problem to neo-Confucian discourse. It is one thing to state that the mind-heart unified human nature and principle, it is another to give reasons why this is the case.

Zhu Zi was not only known for defining and cataloging the essential traits of the world; he was perhaps even more famous for giving reasons why this was so. This is the origin of his purported "rationalism." It is certainly not much like the rationalism of the Age of the Enlightenment in Europe, but it was nonetheless different from a great deal of Confucian discourse. One of the things that many modern Western philosophers have noted about Chinese thought is that it lacks a concern for rationally analytic discourse. What this complaint boils down to is that Confucian thinkers declaim without explaining or offering dialectical defenses of their positions. In this regard, the Confucians are more like dogmatic theologians who are out to teach a form of religious life and less like philosophers interested only in giving a rational justification of the nature of things as they think they really are. Of course, in an age grown weary and skeptical about the claims of technical rationalism, it seems less odd to fuse pragmatic concerns for life and interpretation into a more unified whole. This was, of course, the classic purpose for the systematic metaphysics in Western thought throughout most of its history.

What makes Zhu and Chen uncharacteristically "rational" is their attempt to give reasons for some of their statements about how the world works. Zhu and Chen work on two levels. The first, as we shall see, concerns the analysis of the mind-heart as the bridge between *qi* and *li*. Second, they give a meta-account of how this works for the entire structure of the world. It was this account or speculative *ars contextualis* that made Zhu's philosophy famous or infamous, depending on one's level of agreement or disagreement with the fundamental ideas operative both in the concrete cultivation of the mind-heart and in the broader reflections on the constant conjunction of vital force and principle.[15]

It was obvious that Zhu's teaching about the relationship of vital force and principle was complicated. Zhu's students questioned him repeatedly about how they should understand the doctrine. But by the Southern Song, Zhu's disciples believed that they understood what he was talking about in his various discussions of the relationship between principle and vital force. In fact, vital force was as close to a metaphysical concept as one could find in the period. It was such a ubiquitous player in the *ars contextualis* of the Song that no one, it seems, felt the need to define it with great precision or care. Master Zhang Zai had already explored the world of vital force; Zhu, though the Evidential Research scholars disagreed, thought that all he was doing was correctly weaving Zhang's reflections on vital force in to its proper place in the tapestry of the Northern Song masters.[16] For instance, according to Qing philosophers such as Wang Fuzhi, Zhu committed a category mistake when he taught that principle was in any way prior to or superior to vital force (Black 1989).

Although I can understand how Wang Fuzhi came to his conclusions, I also believe that there is another line of defense for Zhu. I have called this defense the observational priority of recognition and the theory of actuality. What I take Zhu to be claiming is that, in terms of our normal epistemological reactions to the world, we learn about new objects and events by recognizing something different, some novel pattern that attracts our attention—namely, *li* 理 as a coherent, ordered principle or pattern that makes the thing or event stand out from the rest of the ten thousand things and events. Of course, such recognition of difference is predicated upon the coherent recognition of a pattern or principle. But this does not mean that this principle is ever separate from vital force. This reading makes sense when we remember that the great power of the mind-heart is that it is the subtlest aspect of vital force and has the ability to recognize principle. It is this recognition of principle that happens first, that is all. It is not an ontological division. It would be fair to claim that Zhu's epistemology is wrong and that this is not the way the mind-heart encounters and interprets the world. But this is a different point from the argument so dear to the Qing critics that Zhu was a dualist who separated vital force from principle, which is not the case. All Zhu was trying to do was to describe phenomenologically how we learn about the world. Zhu was a firm believer in the fact that vital force and principle are always found together in the world itself. To borrow from Justus Buchler, Zhu has a theory of ontological parity and not of ontological priority. Zhu over and over again taught that principle is not ontologically prior to vital force or vice versa. In this sense, Zhu was not a cosmological or ontological dualist.

Zhu actually had a theory that is quite distant from any Western form of dualism. It is a vision of reality that revolves around three modal traits and one ultimate goal. In previous studies I have called these the domains of form, dynamics, and unification. To this list I will add the idea of actualization or perfection in order to explain not only what Zhu thought but where he thought it would lead. The schema is this:

- *Formal*: Supreme Ultimate *taiji* 太極 qua coherent principle or *li*, order and pattern; human nature
- *Dynamic*: *Qi* as vital force or impulse; the energy of emotion
- *Unification*: *Xin* as mind-heart; the unity of human nature and emotion
- *The Goal of Actualization*: *Cheng* 誠 as reflection of humaneness (and the other virtues)

Zhu instructs anyone who cares to listen that this schema (in my terms, not his) can never be read as distinct ontological levels of reality. All of these elements are found together, beginning with the primordial unity of vital force and principle. Nonetheless, Zhu also presents this analysis as a species of processive *ars contextualis* because he wants to present reasons for saying that the world works this way.[17]

It is important to remember that Zhu and Chen ultimately defer to the judgment of the *Zhongyong* that "*cheng* is the beginning and end of things" as a way to point to the final goal of human flourishing. The *Doctrine of the Mean* is chiefly concerned with showing how sincerity leads to ultimate self-actualization; and while I appreciate Hall and Ames's definition of *cheng* as creativity, one need not go along with their Whiteheadian translation to appreciate the point of the processive and transformative nature of *cheng*. In fact, only when a person can embody true *cheng* can the person form a trinity with heaven and earth in their unceasing nourishing powers. Therefore, Zhu will often use a common bamboo fan as a teaching tool in order to describe the relationship of principle and vital force, but perhaps not in terms of self-actualization, because it is something simply materially made and not something that partakes of the creative process of heaven and earth in intentional, intersubjective, living terms.

The distinction between a living person and a nonliving fan cannot be pushed too far. There is a religious strain in the thought of Zhang Zai that was embraced by Zhu and Chen; it sees life and process everywhere. Zhu and Chen are sensitive to this almost mystical, world-affirming Confucian vision about the living unity of the cosmos. But they are not Daoists and do not dwell too much on nonhuman goals or the outcomes of objects and events. They prefer to focus on the ethical life and follow the Confucian tradition that holds that human beings are the most refined ethical agents in the world. Xunzi held that although other living creatures have ethical potentials, only human beings have the possibility of cultivating all the major virtues. It was only a human person who could embody all the virtues and hence become a humane person. For instance, my poodle Fafner can be loyal but cannot create a complete civilized society, because the poodle lacks a method of efficient communication (a language that forms a culture over time) common to all. Fafner is often ethical, but sometimes very unethical when he makes off with freshly washed socks as toys. I am convinced, following Xunzi and Leibniz, but not Descartes, that dogs do have a sense of right and wrong, or perhaps it is merely the awareness of not wanting to get caught with the sock. In any case, Xunzi's point is that marking levels of cultural complexity is a way of recognizing significant divisions in the animate world. Human beings have the potential for all the virtues and, via a common language, for the creation of culture. Perhaps this is just a complicated way of saying that humans have goals for their lives, always mediated by culture and language.

PROCESS AND TRANSFORMATION WITHIN *DAOXUE* 道學 PHILOSOPHY

After a long detour, we return to Chen's exposition of *ming*. Immediately after he has explained the basic meanings of *ming* as mandate, he goes on to stress that principle is to be found within the vital force as the two primal material forces of yin and yang. "In actuality . . . the process of production and reproduction (*shengsheng*) 生生 [不息 *buxi* or 不已 *buyi*] as without ceasing or without stopping; going on and on has gone on without ceasing from time immemorial" (Chen Chun 1986, 38; J. Zhang 2004, 237). The term *shengsheng* is key to Chen's argument about the creative nature of *ming* 命. As mentioned, Mou Zongsan often argues that *shengsheng* and the phrase *shengsheng buxi* cosmologically represent creativity itself; Chinese dictionaries define it as "production and reproduction and so forth." As the *Book of Changes* says in the Great Commentary, "The great virtue of Heaven and Earth is called 'generation'" (Lynn 1994, 77).

Chen Chun argues that vital force needs something to direct it, and this, of course, is the role of principle. The basic principle itself is that of immemorial production and reproduction. It is a principle of cosmic generativity without a beginning or end. "Principle is in material force and acts as its pivot. This is why as the great transformation functions and prevails, production and reproduction have never stopped" (Chen Chun 1986, 38; J. Zhang 2004, 237). Chan is here translating *qi* as "material force." As we have already seen, there is no single and elegant translation of *qi*: "vital force," "material force," and "matter-energy" are all shots at capturing in English some of the protean semantic meanings of the Chinese original. In the very next section, Chen states, "The production of man and things does not go beyond the material forces of yin and yang (passive and active cosmic forces)" (Chen Chun 1986, 39). Wing-tsit Chan himself added the paraphrase of "passive and active cosmic forces" in his translation to characterize yin and yang.

We will now jump forward to the opening concept in the second chapter of the *Glossary*. This is *dao* 道. To those familiar with Zhu's great *Reflections*, it may seem somewhat strange that Chen did not begin the *Glossary* with *dao*. In the introduction to the translation of the *Glossary* Wing-tsit Chan makes the point that if Chen Chun is anywhere originative, it is his choice of *ming* as the opening motif for the explication of *daoxue*. As we know, Zhu himself always preferred, whenever possible, to delay speaking of ultimate matters or abstract concepts until the student was grounded in the more mundane elements of the Confucian path. Actually, Chen commences the section on the Dao by stating that it is indeed a path. Of course, this is the ur-meaning of *dao* as a way that can be walked consistently.

Chen then proceeds to give a short historical review of various meanings that have been attached to the Dao. He takes particular pains to differentiate the Confucian view of the Dao from the Daoist view. Chen thinks that

Laozi and Zhuangzi go wrong because they interpret the Dao as something completely transcendent. According to Chen, "In the learning of the School of the Sage, there is nothing that is not concrete" (Chen Chun 1986, 107; J. Zhang 2004, 285–86). What Chen means here is that for anything "to be" in the sense of existing as a thing or event means that it must be a union of vital force and principle. "Tao is not external to things and affairs as something empty" (Chen 1986, 107). This is the root quarrel that Song Confucians believe they have with Daoists and Buddhists. The world, according to the Confucians, is neither vacuous nor empty.

MASTER ZHU'S CONVERSATIONS

It is now time to cross-check our search for the processive motifs in Chen's *Glossary* against the works of Master Zhu. If Wing-tsit Chan is correct about Chen's faithfulness to the spirit and letter of his teacher's philosophical vision, then we should find similar expressions of the importance of traits of process in Zhu's own writings, letters, and conversations. This indeed turns out to be the case, as we shall discover.[18]

It is clear that there are parts of Zhu's works that deal more particularly with the philosophical motif of process. For instance, the first six sections of the *Zhuzi yulei* (hereafter referred to as the *Conversations*) are fruitful locations for discovering Zhu's ideas about process within the context of his meta narrative of principle, vital force, human nature, and the mind-heart. I will therefore check my assessment of Chen's processive motifs against material found in the first six sections of the *Conversations*. Another extremely useful anthology of Zhu's thought is the *Zhuzi quanshu* or *Complete Works of Master Zhu*. The title is a misnomer, at least in English, because the *Complete Works* is really another anthology of selected writings by Zhu compiled in the Qing dynasty.[19] However, it is considered the best of the genre of Zhu anthologies and can also be employed for my purposes, in this case specifically *zhuan* 49 and 50. These two chapters are concerned with Zhu's theory of principle and vital force. The *Complete Works* is especially useful because it also adds material from Zhu's letters and other writings to his conversations as recorded in the *Zhuzi yulei*. When cross-referenced against each other, these texts provide the learned consensus of what the *lixue* school thought Master Zhu was teaching. The other obvious choice for referencing motifs of process is *Reflections on Things at Hand* (Chu Hsi and Lü Tsu-ch'ien 1967), the famous anthology of Northern Song masters compiled and edited by Zhu Xi and his good friend Lu Zuqian (1137–81).[20]

The first section of the first chapter of the *Conversations* (Q. Li 1973, 1:139ff.) begins with an exchange about the Supreme Polarity or *taiji* (I have accepted Joseph Adler's suggested translation [de Bary, Bloom, and Lutrano 1999–2000, 1: 669–76] of *taiji* 太極in his rendering of Zhou Tunyi's *Explanation of the Diagram of the Supreme Polarity*). As any older account of the revival of Confucian learning in the Northern Song dynasty attests, Zhou's short study *Diagram of the Supreme Polarity* was hailed as the opening manifesto of neo-Confucian philosophy. The critical phrase is *wuji er taiji* 無極而太極 (The Nonpolar and yet Supreme Polarity) (de Bary, Bloom, and Lutrano 1999–2000, 1: 673) Adler also provides an excellent summary of the philosophical issues involved in interpreting the role of the Supreme Polarity in Zhou's foundational secondary classic.[21]

Chen Chun is able to trace the Confucian lineage of *wuji* back only to the mid-Tang period. Clearly Chen was eager to show that *wuji* did have a reputable Confucian pedigree. "'With whom did the theory of the Ultimate of Non-Being (*wuchi/wuji*) originate?' Master Liu (Liu Zongyuan, 773–819) spoke in his *T'ien-tui* [*tiandui*] (*Questions and Answers on Heaven*) of 'The ultimate of the *wu-chi*'" (Chen Chun 1986, 120; J. Zhang 2004, 293–94).[22] The next relevant source is Shao Yong, but this would hardly have been comforting to the emerging *lixue* school, because Zhu Xi had intentionally excluded Shao from his list of authorized Northern Song masters. Later Confucian textual critics were not slow to point out that *wuji* was probably adopted from Daoist, if not Buddhist, sources and hence should not be employed for secondary classic status by serious Confucian scholarship.[23]

In fact, the Supreme Polarity is the perfected formal trait for Zhu Xi. The very term "Supreme Polarity" is a name for principle as the informing pattern of any object or event—and yet the most formal element is also the most active, the veritable pivot of creation. If my hypothesis about the formal nature of principle is right, then process is an essential aspect of the Supreme Ultimate/Polarity and we can confirm that process really is a foundational trait of Zhu's thought. Like James's turtles all the way down, we do indeed find process consistently throughout. There is simply no way to avoid process in Zhu's mature *daoxue*. In order to test—albeit gingerly—this hypothesis we will review the opening two sections from the *Conversations*, but first we will examine the section of Chen's *Glossary* on the Supreme Polarity.

Chen Chun's query begins by noting that the Supreme Polarity is not some thing; that is, it is not one thing among the other things among the ten thousand things found among heaven and earth. Chen queries as to whether or not it is the most encompassing name for principle. Zhu Xi responds, "The Supreme Polarity is the principle of the ten thousand things of heaven and earth" (Q. Li 1973, *Yulei* 1.1). There is nothing surprising about this opening. It has been repeated endlessly by any exposition of Zhu's thought and is considered a hallmark of the *lixue* style. There is a quality almost reminiscent of modern Anglo-American analytic philosophy in this most Confucian of philosophical treatises. Chinese philosophers are often chided, if noticed at all, by analytic colleagues for not paying attention to a careful examination of terms. Yet a scrupulous study of philosophical language is precisely where Chen and Zhu begin. Perhaps attention to the "meaning of meaning" is not always characteristic of Confucian thinkers, but when they need or want to, as witnessed in this exchange between Zhu and Chen, they can be as analytical as they need to be. Perhaps they are merely letting the magic of philosophical language enchant them—but then, language is one powerful medium for inducing bewitchment from and to the world.

The emphasis in Zhu's response falls on the motif of polarity, which, no doubt, is one reason that *taiji* became such a potent icon and symbol for the Song *daoxue* revival. Along with the stress on the complementarity of the polar oscillations of the yang-yin forces, Zhu reinforces the notion that any discussion of the Supreme Polarity is perforce an exposition of principle per se. For instance, he says that "when we speak about the ten thousand things, each of the ten thousand things has a Supreme Polarity" (Q. Li 1973, *Yulei* 1.1). The second query by Chen reinforces the theme of polarity in the first response. It begins again with the yin-yang forces and then moves on to a discussion of other important polar terms, such as "substance" and "function," within the common Confucian dictionary of philosophical terminology. The *Glossary* section ends by noting that even in human breathing we find the alternation of taking in and letting go. Life is in the motion of air moving in and out of the lungs.

The second set of query-and-response dialogue segues neatly into Chen's summary of Zhu's teachings on the Supreme Polarity in the *Glossary*. In this section, the focus moves from the polarities of yin and yang, substance and form, and the rhythm of breath toward a consideration of the relationship of principle and vital force. The correct understanding of the complex interaction of vital force and principle became one of the dominant themes for all later *lixue* scholars. A great deal depends, according to this debate, on the correct interpretation of Zhu's explanation of the relationship of these two key motifs. If, as some scholars argue, principle is considered ontologically prior, then vital force is secondary in precedence and we have a dualistic system. The terms of the debate were codified as a "one origin" or "two origin" theory. The dual origins would be principle and vital force in some balance or combination of prior and later. A one-origin theory could privilege either principle or vital force as the font of the ten thousand things. In many ways this is a more fruitful way to frame the debate among Song and post-Song thinkers than the more prevalent dichotomy between the school of coherent principle (the Cheng-Zhu school) and the school of heart-mind (the Lu-Wang school). The problem with the classification into principle and heart-mind is that both schools embrace these concepts vigorously. The better point of entry, as some classical Chinese scholars have noted, is to ferret out the balance or priority assigned to principle and vital force in a philosopher's system.

Of course, Zhu Xi's hypothesis has been identified as a prime example of a "dual origin" *eryuan* 二元 (theory). Note well, however, that whatever else the "dual origin" theory might be, it is not a replica of the stereotyped form of Western dualism condemned in contemporary philosophical movements such as deconstructionism and theologies of liberation. But the point is a fascinating one, because it also has implications for process thought. The question then is, if process is central to Confucian thought, then where is the main source of process to be found? Is process found in principle or in vital force? Or in some combination of the two? And if in combination, what is the balance, ratio, and so forth? This was obviously a difficult point to articulate for Zhu, or at least his students had a hard time understanding what the master was trying to teach them. My sense is that Zhu was trying to balance at least two different modes of interpretation or pedagogical strategies. I have called these the "priority of actuality" and the "priority of recognition."

When we recognize some object or event, we have to ask ourselves, how do we recognize the object of our attention, of our concern? Rather like Whitehead, Zhu Xi argued that the act of human recognition, or the basic human epistemological stance, is to identify the pattern of the object or event in the first instance. I believe that it is crucial to remember that Zhu is talking not just about material objects but also about events. In both cases Zhu argues that we become aware of a pattern of difference. Whitehead's way to express a parallel insight was to note that human beings learn by the method of difference. We notice an elephant in an empty room but do not think about it in its absence.[24] Hence, for Zhu the basic point of differentiation is recognition of the pattern of the object or event being observed.

As for the actual encounter with things and events, there can never be an allotment of vital force that is not completely fused with the appropriate principle. Moreover, Zhu notes that the processive quality for any thing or event is a gift of the specific allotment of vital force. It is *qi* 氣 that is prevalent or prevails. The semantic range of *liuxing* 流行 (to prevail) ranges from the notion of being something in vogue to something new that becomes a fad, to the transmission of a disease (in modern usage); and to the sense of movement, of flowing, of transmission. It also has the sense of something that pervades whatever it encounters. The nature of actuality, according to Zhu, is the flowing quality of principle linked to vital force.

Other scholars disagree. Some, such as Wang Yangming, Wang Fuzhi, and Dai Zhen, deem that Zhu gives both ontological and cosmological priority to principle.[25] While there is a case to be made for this interpretation of the principle–vital force connection, Zhu himself took pains to explain that any simplistic notion of valuing principle higher than vital force is a mistake. The two, though playing different roles, simply can never be separated in the actual world of things and events. Chen Chun made the same point in the *Glossary*, and we now turn to the section on the Supreme Polarity in that work.

Chen Chun begins his explanation with the statement, "The Supreme Polarity is simply the undifferentiated and maximum principle. It cannot be described in terms of material force [vital force] of physical form" (Chen Chun 1986, 115; J. Zhang 2004, 290). One of the philosophical charms of Chen, at least for those who like analytic, propositional forms of thought, is that this is the kind of query he attempts at the beginning of his explanation of Zhu's theory of the Supreme Polarity. Chen next, as one expects from him, cites the appropriate locus classicus for the Supreme Polarity in the Confucian primary canon. This is the *Appended Remarks*, a commentary on the *Yijing*. Of course, this is not just any commentary and was associated with Confucius almost from time immemorial, and the passage in question states that "the *Change* [or *yi* as change or the title of the *Yijing* as the "Book of Change" or "Changes"] has the Supreme Polarity" (Chen Chun 1986, 115; translation paraphrased; J. Zhang 2004, 290–91). Arthur Waley, the great translator of Chinese texts, once remarked that the true ability of a scripture is to have a surplus of meaning, and this short phrase fulfills Waley's test of being a scripture. The *Yijing* is a book about change and transformation. Chen comments on the *daoxue* position and writes, "Change is nothing but the change and transformation of yin and yang" (Chen Chun 1986, 115). This proposition includes two of the most important semantic markers for the process motif—namely *bian* 變 and *hua* 化, which are translated by Wing-tsit Chan as "change" and "transformation," respectively.[26]

Chen Chun reads the famous opening sentence of the *Diagram of the Supreme Polarity* in the same way as François Jullien does: as the characteristic Chinese method of exposition by indirection. The term *er* 而 is explained in the following fashion: "The word *er* (also) is merely a slight conjunction and does not mean to break the sentence into two sections" (Chen Chun 1986, 116; J. Zhang 2004, 291). Jullien, commenting on the *Analects* 7.37 passage that contains three repetitions of *er*, takes it to be an empty word "implying both opposition and simultaneity" (Jullien 2000, 239). There is a dialectic here governed by *er*, but not the agonistic dialectic of the Greeks. The term "empty word" is a standard Chinese term for a class of common grammatical particles in Classical Chinese. The distinction is made between empty words (that is, words that are merely grammatical in form) and full words (that is, words that express content).

Jullien has an interesting argument about what is going on with this kind of polar thinking. It is, he believes, oppositional, but it is not a contrast between two different levels of the real, as it would be for someone like Plotinus. There is no separation between what is and what becomes, between appearance and the truth of ultimate reality. It is rather an opposition "between the unending flaunting of things, which, as such, is distinct, and the 'eminently subtle internal coherence' that makes this process possible" (245). The passage Jullien is studying is also from the *Yijing* and reads, "Words are twisted but reach the center / Things are both flaunted and hidden" (Jullien 2000, 245). What is important in the manifestation of things is not some eternal or surpassing form but rather the variations that obtain between what is flaunted and what is hidden. In slightly more sober terms, Hall and Ames have argued that one of the chief features of early Confucian thought is its use of a "field and focus" model for reality. Things come into focus or are flaunted in front of our eyes and then are hidden again in the vast, obscure, wonderfully pregnant field of the Dao.[27]

In these philosophical venues Jullien finds that the Confucian seeks a process rather than an essence or substance. There is no world of pure forms or any other world beyond the one we inhabit. We have the shifting dance of signifiers and signified, always looking askance from this perspective and that; the aim, if there is one, is a global vision of the whole and not the substance of the one pure truth, whatever that would mean in the allusive world of Chinese poetics. "The Chinese point of view—of a reality in process—can illuminate things on this score, for if there is to be an effect, there must be a development; and for there to be a development, it must occur at a stage prior to the situation" (2000, 300). According to Jullien, this conception of "an effect *unfolding through immanence* brings us to the heart of the question of the indirect and can illuminate it from within" (300). Later we will return to the question of causation and effect in process thought as interpreted by Dorothy Emmet.

Jullien argues that for the Chinese literati the quest is not a search for meaning in the text or painting. Rather, the literatus "makes himself available" or waits in an uncontrived (*wuwei*) mode to mature, to develop. The literatus "waits for it to *mature* within him" (355). This, of course, does make "sense" in a tradition that seeks self-cultivation and the maturity to know how to act without action. "Like any event, meaning is not about action . . . but about *process* . . ." (355). Process itself is an end in itself and not something on the way to a more secure essence. The path is in the walking, the poetry in the indirection, the emotional encounter in the moment. Perfection is a process, a habit always changing, and not some final end.

Chen Chun is very clear that the Supreme Ultimate is coherent principle in one of principle's many manifestations. Towards the end of the discussion of the *taiji*, Chen writes, "The reason why the Supreme Polarity is described as 'ultimate' is because principle is most central, most correct, most exquisite, most refined, most spiritual, and most wonderful. It is perfect and reaches the highest degree and nothing can be added to it. Perforce, it is called ultimate" (Chen Chun 1986, 120; J. Zhang 2004, 293–94). There is never a possibility of getting away from the question of principle in Zhu's thought. We must now turn to principle to continue the hunt for process.

DEAD PRINCIPLES AND LIVING HORSES

Chen Chun's discussion of coherent principle 理 in the *Glossary* is actually much shorter than one would expect for such a major and controversial concept. It is this compression and suggestive ambiguity that has made the debate on the nature of *taiji* so extended and passionate throughout East Asian and now the wider world of the cultural Chinese diaspora. Chen Chun commences by noting that in general terms, principle and Dao denote the same thing. The Dao, which he has discussed in the previous section, is based on the metaphor of a road that people travel. The notion of motion is clear, but principle is that which provides a form of definiteness to any thing or event, including the trait of living action. Again, there is no more exhaustive study of the living nature of principle than Levey's study (1991) of the emergence of Zhu's mature *daoxue*. Be this as it may, there are immediate problems with talking about principle in this fashion, both for the East Asian *lixue* traditions and for the modern comparative study of these traditions. If so many modern interpreters, ranging from Lau, Allan, Hall and Ames, and Jullien are correct, then a search for a pure definition of principle goes against the grain of the very different communication strategy so familiar to any student of East Asian thought.

However, Chen Chun does appear to be so much closer to the Western forms of propositional or assertive discourse in his discussion that he provides a perfect place to begin pondering the place of principle in Zhu's thought. Of course, the place of principle has been identified as a key issue ever since Zhu began to teach his students what he had learned from the Cheng brothers about principle. Although there are many ways to approach the question of how to interpret Zhu's understanding of principle, here I will choose the issue of whether or not principle can be described in process terms. Baldly put, if there is no place for the trait of process in principle, then how can *daoxue* be discussed as a species of process philosophy? It would then be a case of a dead principle riding the live horse of *qi*, as many East Asian critics beginning with Wu Cheng (1249–1333) have asserted (Gedalecia 1999).

Many other East Asian philosophers have argued that, to the contrary, Zhu's reliance on principle is precisely a nonprocessive trait in his metanarrative. Of course, this depends on how the question of "process" is asked. My favorite query is one that gained a great deal of currency in the East Asian philosophical world and was first made by Wu Cheng in the Yuan dynasty. Wu asked, can a dead rider (principle) ride a living horse (vital energy)? Zhu has used other illustrations such as the trigger mechanism of a crossbow as a representation of principle. Wu, however, put his finger on the problem: Zhu's metaphor really does not help us, because it is mechanical. A trigger assembly is a non living device, and there is still the prior quest of human, living agency. How does principle make its way among the living?[28]

In the terms I have developed—namely, the systematic traits of form, dynamics, unification, and the final goal of harmony—the query now has to do with whether or not "form" qua principle as its prototype can carry a process trait or whether it is hopelessly static, dead, and ungenerative—dare one say essentialist and foundationalist? I have come to believe that Zhu would have affirmed the process-trait of principle even if the methods and metaphors he used to explain and defend his view were not entirely persuasive. Later Confucians have, with real merit, gone in both directions on the issue of the living or dead nature of principle. Perhaps one problem comes also from my use of the term "formal" for principle. It is crucial to remember that the formal trait here is that of a pattern for an emerging thing or event and not a perfected essence implanted like a pit in the middle of a peach. It pervades the emerging object or event but is not "something definite" prior to the emergence of the object or event per se. The pit, solid though it certainly is, grows from the principle qua pattern as surely as does the flesh of the fruit.

I take Zhu Xi's constant responses to his students about the inseparability of principle and vital force to refute the appearance-and-reality gambit so common in post-Platonic Western philosophy. Richard Rorty admonishes modern Western philosophers to abjure the dubious pleasures of seeking presence and essence, because this search for essence and true reality is a mistaken linguistic application of the appearance/reality dualism. We surely need dualities or conceptual dyads, Rorty agrees, but only as a way to better describe the world. Rorty calls this a panrelational pragmatism. Rorty's apt characterization of this processive turn runs thus: "They [that is, pragmatic, antiessentialist thinkers] are trying to replace the world of pictures constructed with the aid of these Greek oppositions [NB—such as the appearance-reality opposition] with a picture of the flux of continually changing relations" (Rorty 1999, 47). Actually, a "flux of continually changing relations" is not that bad a summary of Zhu's general interpretation of the unification and harmony of principle and vital force.

Chen Chun commences the discussion of the unity of a generative *li* with a dynamic *qi* by making a distinction between principle and the Dao. Although Chen believes that generally the two terms represent the same thing, they are designated by two different words. Chen concludes that this means that there must be some difference between the meaning of principle and the Dao/Way. The Dao is a way, and Chen believes that it is a metaphor for a road on which people travel. This makes a great deal of sense from the perspective of Lakoff and Johnson, who believe that metaphors of roads, of travel, and of moving from one point to another, are common in many kinds of philosophy.

Chen then goes on to explain a second difference—namely, that Dao is a broad term whereas principle is "more concrete" (Chen Chun 1986, 112; J. Zhang 2004, 288–89). Moreover, Chen immediately adds that principle "has the idea of being definitely unchanging" (Chen Chun 1986, 112). Of course, this is precisely the kind of statement that has led generations of Chinese, Korean, and Japanese critics to posit a static formalism at the heart of Zhu's philosophy. Chen continues by stating that what he means by the unchanging trait of principle is that it is a "specific principle (*tse/ze* 則) of what a thing should be (*tang-jan/dangran* 當然)" (112).[29]

The next section of the *Glossary* explains how principle is linked to *xing* 性 (human nature or dispositions). Here Chen also shows how principle is correlated to *yi* 義 (justice, moral principles), the second of the five major Confucian virtues. Chen quotes one of the Cheng brothers, who said, "That which is inherent in things is principle. That by which things are managed is moral principle [NB: *yi*]" (Chen Chun 1986, 113; J. Zhang 2004, 289). There might be some confusion for the English reader, but principle or *li* 理 is quite distinct from Chan's moral principle or *yi* 義. *Yi* means "the right," "righteousness," "morality," and "justice," to list only a few of its Western analogues. A more literal interpretation that brings out the parallelism of the two phrases is: "In things principle acts; in situating things [principle] acts justly." The point that I am trying to tease out is that the active quality of principle or justice is not static but rather speaks of actions—"principling" and "justicing," if we must, even if this is hard to verbalize in standard English. Principle means to be in proper relationship with the nature of the thing and in proper relationship to other things and events.

In order to understand what Chen means by pattern or form, we need to move back to a section in the *Glossary* that contains his study of the notion of the Dao. Actually, Chen's section on the Dao is about six times longer than the section on *li*. Remember that the preferred self-designation of the movement begun by Zhu Xi was *daoxue* or "the teaching of the Way." The other common term, *lixue* 理學 or "teaching of principle," was applied to differentiate Zhu's philosophy from that of other Song-Ming Confucians, and especially from that of Wang Yangming and his followers at a later time. Of course, many of Zhu's contemporaries thought that it was the height of arrogance to arrogate the name of the Way for the opinions, and controversial opinions at that, of only one branch of the Northern and Southern Song Confucian revival. The argument revolved around how broadly the notion of the Dao should be interpreted. Remember also that "Dao" was actually a more important term than "principle." "Dao" was the most general term for the proper path of Confucian assertion, exhibition, and action. Dao was the royal road for Confucian self-cultivation. Therefore, it made sense to defend Zhu's specific interpretation of the pan-East Asian philosophical mainstay.

Chen starts the *Glossary*'s Dao section by playing on the metaphor of Dao as a road. He notes that a road is only a road if more than one person walks on it. "The general principle of Dao is the principle people should follow in their daily affairs and human relations" (Chen Chun 1986, 105; J. Zhang 2004, 284). Moreover, the source of the Dao is none other than *tian* 天itself. Here Chen quotes Zhang Zai's statement, "From the Great Vacuity, there is Heaven. From the transformation of material force (*qi*, 氣 vital force) there is the Way" (Chen Chun 1986, 105; Zhang 2004, 284). Chen interprets *tian* not in theistic terms but as what is naturally so of itself (*ziran* 自然). Although *ziran* is most commonly linked to Daoism in general and Zhuangzi in particular, it was also part of the general Chinese philosophical vocabulary and could be used for perfectly legitimate Confucian purposes. Some later critics of *daoxue*, such as Wang Fuzhi, would have liked to see principle as well as vital force encompassed by creative spontaneity, according to Alison Black (1989).

The argument that then follows is enough to make one embrace Hall and Ames's hypothesis that a field-focus metaphor for Chinese metasystems is better than the whole-part metaphor more common to much Western philosophy. It is one possible answer to the question of a dead principle (rider) riding a living horse. Chen deems Zhang Zai to be arguing that principle is *tian* 天. Moreover, "Obviously principle is not something dead just lying there. As the material force [vital force] of the One Origin spreads out, it produces man and things" (Chen Chun 1986, 106; J. Zhang 2004, 285–286). And if this were not enough, Chen directly says: "This is what it is when one traces the source of creative process" (Chen Chun 1986, 106). The term that Wing-tsit Chan translates as "creative process" does indeed carry the semantic load of transformation as "creative response" to the living situation. Principle is then the various patterns, the lines and veins, such as found in a piece of jade or bamboo—that give us direction for our task of self-cultivation. While it can be called a formal trait, as I have done in the past, it is really a pattern, a focus; it is what emerges when a person seeks to follow the Dao or Way of *tian*. In the end, Chen puts his active spin on the Dao by noting that it is "the principle according to which daily human affairs should be conducted and the road on which people past and present all travel" (Chen Chun 1986, 106). Here again motion as the process of travel in a moral direction is crucial to Chen's understanding of the Dao.

Slightly later in Chen Chun's explanation of Dao, he comes back to the question of the relationship of principle and vital force. If it is true that principle penetrates or pervades everywhere, it is equally true that vital force is everywhere and at all times as well. The processive trait is highlighted: "Prominent principles are seen in the process of the creation, the development, and the nourishment of things" (Chen Chun 1986, 109; Zhang 2004, 286–87). In terms of Hall and Ames's metaphor of the field and focus, vital force is the field and principle provides the focus. Both are equally in the grip of the process of creation.

In section 12 of the chapter "On the Substance of the Way," which begins the *Reflections on Things at Hand*, Zhu Xi and Lu Zuqian selected a passage that is of interest in our quest for the processive traits of Song Confucian thought. Section 12 begins by stating, "Wherever there is influence, there is necessarily response. All actions are influences" (Chu 1967, 13). In Zhu's own commentary on the *Conversations*, he says "Everything in the universe is governed by the principle of influence and response, whether universal creation or human affairs" (13). There is a ceaseless creativity afoot in the cosmos, but it does have an order. The reciprocal balance of influence and response governs the order of the universe, both in terms of cosmic process and in terms of its outcome in human affairs. In the thirty-fourth section of the same chapter, quoting Cheng Hao, the point about reciprocity is made yet again. "Within heaven and earth there is only the process of action and response. What else is there?" (Chen Chun 1986, 27). In short, what is there beyond the process of action or influence and response? Beyond the process there is nothing more real, more substantial, or more true to the nature of the cosmos.

One could go on with the bricolage of quotations from Chen and Zhu—but is it necessary at this point? I believe that process, as part of the *daoxue* cosmology, is without a doubt one of the main traits or motifs of Song thought as exemplified by Zhu Xi and Chen Chun, even though it was not their main concern. Above all else, Zhu and Chen sought to revive a passion for the Confucian Dao as a way of getting the Way for oneself in service to others. Ethics is never far from the heart-mind of any Confucian. When students and colleagues ask about how to characterize Chinese thought, I always hesitate before answering. For instance, when asked if there is anything like Western metaphysics, ontology, or cosmology in Confucian thought I will aver that, if pressed to allow for at least one analogue, cosmology comes closest to what Chinese thinkers occasionally indulge in as philosophers. But even here the analogy should never be pressed too far. I go on to say that my favorite broad Western grand designation is "axiology." I say axiology because it includes ethical and aesthetic sensibilities, and does approach what someone like Zhu Xi was trying to accomplish.

From Zhu's perspective, when we ask the question of *what* the essential nature of some thing, person, or event is, we must modify the way we think about answering such a question about origins and goals. Zhu prefers to talk about *how* a person comes to make choices about the world and the resulting action in it. A New Confucian of the last generation, Mou Zongsan, has argued passionately and repeatedly that what we find here is a moral metaphysics. The key motifs of the moral metaphysics of the Song-Ming world rest on axiological premises. To be real, to actualize the person, is to become a harmony of the patterns of principle, the dynamic activity of vital force through the moral decisions and actions of the cultivated heart-mind.

The structure of the arguments that Zhu Xi and Chen Chun propose always follows a typical Song-Yuan-Ming pattern of exposition. Chen and Zhu are fond of providing us with a series of analogies about how principle is active in the sense of "causing" people to act in certain ways. Now, Chen realizes that this seems somewhat odd, because at the same time he is writing about the active trait of principle, he is maintaining that principle is not some thing or event that can act on other things and events. Principle is the norm, the pattern of an event or thing, and not the actual thing or event. Principle only becomes definite when it is found, as it always is, as the pattern within vital force chosen by the heart-mind for action. Principle subsists within any person or event; however, it is equally true that we can also recognize principle as pattern in the world beyond our person. This is one reason to emphasize study so strongly: we study, among other things, the writings of sages to see the principles they actualized in their conduct. We try to discern how we, too, can appropriate principle in order to act with moral integrity in life.

The key here is the axiology of the norm, the action of principle. Principle as a norm functions in two ways. The first is to coordinate the unification of principle and vital force into the specific form of definiteness for the emerging person. The second is to afford the sense of appropriateness for the particular quality of the principle as it comes to order the person in the specific situation. For Zhu and Chen, to become is to make choices and to accept some form or norm for our conduct. Merely to become something is not enough. We always stand in relation to something definite to other persons and are hence acted upon by them and act on them in turn. The world really is defined by influence and response.

As I have remarked before, Confucians do not always follow the assertive road of query. They are also committed to exhibitive and active modes of query. When you are tempted to ask, what is the essence or defining characteristic of the Confucian Dao qua principle, they tell you a story. Plato, who could tell a good story, still required dialectical argument or formal definitions. Yet if Lakoff and Johnson are correct, the world of metaphors found in stories is probably as good a way as any other to point toward a valid argument about the nature of things. A story indicates a direction. My favorite story about the normative nature of the Confucian Dao is found the *Analects*. It is a story told by Kongzi's most favored disciple, Yan Hui. Yan Hui, for whom the master so deeply grieved when Yan Hui died young, was one of the patron saints of the Song Confucians. He was the model student and even, according to Kongzi, resided in *humanity* for three months.

This is what Yan Hui said about the normative quality of the master's teaching:

> The more I look up at it, the higher it soars; the more I penetrate into it, the harder it becomes. I am looking at it in front of me, and suddenly it is behind me. The Master is good at drawing me forward a step at a time; he broadens me with culture [*wen* 文] and disciplines my behavior through the observance of ritual propriety [*li* 禮]. Even if I wanted to quit, I could not. And when I have exhausted my abilities, it as though something rises up right in front of me, and even though I want to follow it, there is no road to take. (Ames & Rosemont 1998, 128–129)

Anyone who has recognized how hard it is to be good at anything at all can understand what Yan Hui is bemoaning here. All of us have had that brilliant teacher, or that friend who could pick up spoken languages (even Chinese) within two months, or play music well enough to make your spirit ache. It is there before us, and sometimes along with Yan Hui, it feels like there is no more road for us to follow. Yet the master refuses let us stop at any one place; the master demands that we move forward, exhausted or not.

And yet, and yet. It is always there, the nagging doubt that we have got it just right. The trick is to learn how to respond to the "it." From the viewpoint of Confucian self-cultivation, the ability to discern the "it" of our common moral tendencies is the beginning of wisdom. The shock—the emotional dynamics, if you like—comes from the ability to compare and contrast what "is" with what "is not;" to compare and contrast what "is" and what "should be." I do not want to excessively rationalize this moment. It is more emotional than purely cognitive, and this is what the Yan Hui story expresses so well. There is recognition, discernment of the moral Way of the master, and yet there are moments when one simply cannot rationally discern the way forward. Even more, there are moments when the fleshly heart-mind is tired; and yet there is still the insistent nagging of the spirit to compare and contrast what "is" with what "is not," what "is" with what "has never been on land or sea."

The stock Confucian answer to the question of why Yan Hui feels the way he does is that his master has nurtured his seeds of virtue into life. Because his moral consciousness has awakened, even though he is fatigued in the extreme, he cannot forget that he has seen a vision rising up around him everywhere; and like the peaks of a mountain before the traveler, there is both challenge and promise. The challenge is to surmount the mountains; the promise is to find the wonderful valley on the other side. However, the problem becomes even deeper when the master then points out more mountains and holds out the promise of even more valleys.

Dorothy Emmet has a wonderful way of describing the symbolic nature of stories such as Yan Hui's. She says, "I shall call this their *promissory* character" (Emmet 1998, 198; italics in original). This is a fine characterization of the drive toward the future found in Yan Hui's lament. The road is forward in both space and time. The reward is a promise; but a promise is never an ending in and of itself within the Confucian Way. Emmet continues her discussion of the role and power of symbols in human life by noting, "Some of the great recurrent symbols . . . have a power of pointing forward to meaning beyond that which is consciously seen and given to them in any one time" (198). Moreover, "It is perhaps a quality of a good religious symbol that the person who produces it builds better than he knows" (Emmet 1958, 196).

Emmet provides the reader with a perfect illustration of the power of symbols. She has reproduced a picture of the common Near Eastern Winged Sun disc. She cites authorities in the field to the effect that this was a image in common usage from Egypt to Persia; moreover, it was clearly known to the Jews and was even used in Malachi 4:2 for the purposes of Jewish religious life. She then goes on to quote from two hymns of Charles Wesley that use the Winged Sun as a symbol for the illuminating tendencies of the Christ. "We have here an illustration of a symbol traveling into other cultures, and acquiring fresh associations as it gets established in liturgical usage" (Emmet 1958, 196). Many of the diverse terms of the Confucian vocabulary, I believe, function as symbols or metaphors that accumulate new meanings over time. However, this Enlightenment project in favor of verbal newness obscures, for those who take neologisms to be a index of creative thought, the enduring ability of Confucian discourse to add new meanings to old terms. We have seen how the Song philosophers did this as they reinterpreted their classical heritage.

As a powerful Confucian symbol, the term *xing* 性is most commonly translated as "human nature" or "dispositions." There has recently been a lively debate about whether or not it is proper to use the fairly common English expression "human nature" to fit what the Confucians called *xing*. The main counter argument goes something like this: True, the Confucians are talking about being human, but this does not mean that they, like so many Western philosophers, are seeking to depict an assertive, perfect definition of the ultimate essence or substance of the human person. Rather, the Confucians are talking about a set of tendencies that all human beings seem to share to one degree or another.[30] One of these human dispositions is to be creative in transforming self and cosmos, what Xunzi would praise as contrivance and Mengzi would laud as nurturing the seeds of humanity.

This is an "open" social sentiment that provides, if there ever was one, a way to improve both individuals and society. According to Dorothy Emmet, Bergson understood as much in his argument about the social nature of morality in *The Two Sources of Morality and Religion*. Dorothy Emmet describes this creative moment in the following terms: "Such feeling is a deep kind of stirring out of which ideas and images may be produced; it is not just the kind of emotion which has become a habitual stock response to a ready-made stimulus" (1958, 150). Bergson tends to go on about this creative moment in such a romantic fashion that many people tend to forget the insight itself and dismiss it as a merely rhetorical flourish. Yet Emmet's tribute to Bergson could be equally applied to Xunzi's vision of the work of the sage in providing metaphors to live by and to cultivate the wisdom needed to realize the ethically informed life. "To Bergson this intuitive feeling is a manifestation of creative energy; the person charged with it is living as a spear head of the *élan vital*, the creative impulse of life, pressing forward against the resistance of mechanized routines of habit and custom to a new stage of development" (150). Perhaps Xunzi would not have liked these thoughts about the passage of nature and its creative advance into novelty as much as I do, because he loved custom and habit as the teachers of virtue. But Xunzi favors only good customs and habits and not the strict legal system advocated by the Legalists who helped to found the first empire. These habits and customs are good because they are useful in creating a better world.

The Song Confucians sought to offer comfort to those who hold that all pragmatic, relational, perspectival (or ordinal, in Buchler's sense of location), and process thinkers tend to undermine serious commitments to a robust ethical system and strong social order. In fact, one of the main criticisms leveled against the Confucian tradition in East Asia was that it was too conservative and too authoritarian in its ethics of ritual action. The critics of the Chinese May Fourth Movement argued that Confucianism was not even a small part of the solution to the modernization of China but rather one of the main problems. Modern Confucian revivalists counter that there is nothing at all in the basic insights of the tradition that is inimical to the modernization of East Asia. What is usually under debate is the relationship of a revived Confucian sensibility with modern ecumenical science, the market economy, modern human rights discourse, and democratic institutions. The rise of industrial East Asia has demonstrated in the most empirical of terms that a culture with Confucian cultural DNA can take to science and the global business market like a duck to water. The real question now remaining is whether or not a revived Confucianism can make peace with democratic institutions and human rights.[31]

Confucians have never lacked the ability to believe and practice their tradition, even if they have never been sure that they can fathom the ultimate truth of the Dao or codify it in a perfected philosophical vision. The consensus of the learned and a desire to keep on learning and applying what has been learned have served Confucians well enough to create the longest-running civilization in human history. One need not be in search of absolute truth, a perfect method, and essences in order to have moral backbone, great art, and a sophisticated and cohesive social order.

It is now time, after three visits to Chinese philosophical sites, to return to the modern global city and see if we have glimpsed a way to expand process as a philosophical movement.

5

Modern Permutations

North American Naturalism and Global Philosophy

NORTH AMERICAN NATURALISM: CREATIVE PASSAGE

We have now come full circle in our search for themes, motifs, and traits of process; we have traveled in space and time from the end of the Warring States period in China with Xunzi, into the third- and fourth-century Wei-Jin dynasty with the author/redactor of the *Liezi*, and into the Southern Song dynasty with Zhu Xi and Chen Chun. We now return to contemporary North America. In the North American philosophical and theological world, Whitehead is universally acknowledged as the modern progenitor of process thought, although various pragmatists and assorted naturalists also share this honor. William James, for instance, is as much a philosopher of process and pluralism as is Whitehead, a fact that Whitehead would have been the first to acknowledge. However, as many critics have argued, if process is such an important self-reflective philosophical trait, it must find representation in a wider world of discourse. This is the burden of Nicholas Rescher's short study of the Western history of process philosophy (1996), wherein he identifies the theme of process articulated by many philosophers long before Whitehead began writing about it.

I trust—perhaps "hope" would be better—that I have made a case for a global exploration of the theme of process in previous chapters. That the notion of process can be found everywhere from the early pre-Socratics to the Daoists and Confucians in classical, medieval, and Song China demonstrates that Rescher was correct in his assumption about the scope of the philosophical theme of process. Process does turn out to be very much part of the global philosophical scene, both diachronically and synchronically in terms of its articulation by philosophers as distinct as the author of the *Liezi* and A. N. Whitehead. Yet I have become more and more convinced that in order to understand the nature of what philosophers and theologians have encompassed by the trait of process, we must broaden our speculative vision. As I will explain below, it makes sense to see Whitehead as part and parcel of the larger American naturalist movement, within which, of course, the pragmatists are the most famous group of thinkers.

To make the case about the trait of process in a global comparative perspective, we need what Robert C. Neville calls vague philosophical categories, as articulated in a set of studies on the methodology of comparative philosophy and theology (2001a, 2001b, 2001c). Neville's theory is easy to explain but hard to carry out according to critics of the comparative studies in religion and philosophy.[1] All Neville really means is that when making comparisons among philosophies and theologies we need to find general comparative categories that will focus on questions of similarity and difference demonstrated by comparing various philosophies and theologies. In this regard Neville is responding, at least in part, to Jonathan Z. Smith's call for a clear methodology for comparative study. According to Neville, vagueness of categories does not mean a lack of clarity as to the methods, aims, techniques, and goals of the comparative enterprise. For instance, a suitable candidate for framing theological comparison could be the category of religion considered diachronically or synchronically. However, as are so many other areas of human life, appearance can be deceptive. For example, finding a suitable definition for what a modern Western intellectual takes to be religion (or takes to be philosophy) is a devilishly difficult task. For those who like tidy definitions, to be told that the pleasure of the study of "religion" is found in the path and exploration of the concept but not in any assertive precision about initial stipulations, is scant solace.

Whitehead suggested, that a cosmology implies a religious viewpoint and that many modern Westerners now have adopted a new and decidedly naturalistic and processive cosmology; if so, the Confucian tradition will certainly have a lot to say to modern Western religious and philosophical thinkers about the nature of religion in the modern world. The Confucians and Daoists not only have held views about the trait of process that share strong affinities with the views of many modern Western pragmatists, naturalists, and process thinkers, but they have also struggled to find ways to relate the transcendent/ultimate to the particular/immanent world of mundane human life. For Confucians, the mesocosmic domain of quotidian human life is as much a site of the holy as anywhere else it could possibly inhabit. Modern New Confucians such as Mou Zongsan, Tu Weiming, and Liu Shuxian (1998, 2003) call this respect for the human lifeworld a form of immanent transcendence.[2]

For many citizens of North America who have embraced late Modernity as a form of nonreductive naturalism, such a Confucian-like cosmology of immanent transcendence or dual transcendence has become an exemplar of their operative vision of the way the world works. The rhetoric of the holism of the ecology movement is a perfect example of this cosmological paradigm shift. The ecology movement is not merely descriptive; it seeks to make normative judgments about what is good for humanity and indeed the whole of the cosmos (Tucker and Berthrong 1998). This is a discourse of transcendence, at the least, beyond the mere selfish needs and goals of humankind. It seeks to find a harmony between human beings as one species with all the other natural complexes of the world in order to maximize the potential for life, and life abundant. Zhang Zai, another of the great Northern Song Confucian masters (Chan 1963, 495–517), has become one of the patron saints of the ecology movement because of his short essay, "The Western Inscription." To many modern ecologists, Zhang's short statement speaks to how human beings ought to treat each other amid the ceaseless processes of nature as the manifestations of *qi* 氣. This is an implied respect for the passage of nature such that human beings need to be properly attuned to the order of the natural world. At no time in the previous history of humankind have Western intellectuals been better prepared for a dialogue with Confucians in terms of emerging cosmologies.

Theories about worldviews can die or be abandoned just like various scientific paradigms can be revised or simply given up in the light of a better paradigm. Many modern and liberal Western Christians have a new paradigm, and they are desperately looking for a new religious vision that will connect their faith with their reason. Whitehead's process philosophy and the theology it inspired is one form of a modern cosmology that leaves a place for the religious dimension of life within a worldview that allows contact with other dimensions of late Modernity's diverse cultural manifestations. I will argue that Confucianism (and Daoism as well) also provides such a model for connecting reason and faith in a world without supernaturalism or the total transcendence of God.

The philosophical trait of "process" is another broad term that defies any simplistic definition. I have become more and more convinced that we must, following Neville's insight about the usefulness of vague categories and Smith's caution about comparative research, seek a wider vision of what constitutes the trait of process in different cultural worlds. Process as a philosophical trait resides in many different cultural matrices, and we need to have a larger scope for our exploration of its constituting traits than merely trying to find various examples of process to compare and contrast around the world and through history.

As I worked through the Chinese and Western texts on the theme of process, and most especially treatises about the contemporary American philosophical scene, I was struck that most scholars consider philosophies of process to be a subgroup of a broader category. This broader category is that of naturalism as a specific form of American philosophical discourse (Kuklick 2001). Without putting too fine a point on it, there seems to be an elective affinity between the special class of philosophies of process and the broader world of American naturalism. [26]

In order to provide the context for comparison with Western accounts of the theme of process, a number of previous chapters have been devoted to Chinese Confucian and Daoist thinkers such as Xunzi, Liezi (assuming that there was someone of this name), Zhu Xi, and Chen Chun. These Chinese intellectuals demonstrate that an interest, even fascination, with themes of process did not arise from Whitehead's brow alone—or for that matter merely from the impressive lineage of Western philosophers and theologians outlined by Rescher. What has become clear is that process (as it is understood in Whitehead's mature philosophy) can be found in other philosophical traditions. Illustrations have been drawn from the two great streams of indigenous Chinese thought—namely, Confucianism and Daoism. However, nothing valuable is ever easy, as Spinoza so rightly observed. I am convinced that by paying attention to the Chinese case studies, we can expand our collective understanding of process as an important theme for contemporary global philosophy.

In order to extend the discussion both diachronically and synchronically, I am redirecting our focus to various interrelated strains of modern North Atlantic philosophy. Specifically, I will focus on a range of diverse thinkers who collectively share, in the technical and restrictive sense that I will define below, a nonreductionistic naturalist sensibility. I have become convinced that Whitehead's version of process/organic/relational philosophy is, in fact, part of a larger North American philosophical adventure—namely, the exploration of naturalism. The first question, therefore, is one of historical definition. What is North American naturalism?

If there is a consensus about the (North) American default position in philosophy, pride of place usually goes, and rightly so, to pragmatism. My hypothesis is that pragmatism, while certainly the most famous, expansive, and important of American philosophical traditions, is actually part of a larger family of three interrelated philosophical types and traditions that can all be called forms of naturalism. First, more attention has been paid to the great pragmatist lineage beginning with Peirce, James, Dewey, and Mead than to any other group of American philosophers, and again with good reason. Second in line as a paradigmatic school of the naturalist connection comes A. N. Whitehead and the disciples of process/relational philosophy and theology. As its name implies, the Whiteheadian tradition is taken to be the radial prototype of all process-based modern philosophies. The third family type is naturalism per se as a distinct movement in American philosophical history, and this includes thinkers most often associated with Columbia University, but also other philosophers and theologians.[26] For the purpose of exploring the theme of process, I will deem the work of Justus Buchler as representative of the type of "naturalism" made most famous at Columbia University. In complete candor I should note that although Buchler did not reject entirely the title naturalism for his mature philosophy, he did demand that he be allowed to define naturalism in his own fashion.[26] This third group of broadly defined American naturalists also includes scholars such as Richard McKeon,[26] Stephen Pepper, Robert Corrington,[26] and the teams of David Hall and Roger Ames and George Lakoff and Mark Johnson. What ties this eclectic group of philosophers and theologians together is their agreement that human beings are integrally part and parcel of nature; Lakoff and Johnson have most emphatically called this a "philosophy in the flesh."[26]

These are the three current major divisions of what I define as American philosophical naturalism, and I assert that all three major types have paid a great deal of attention to the theme of process. Of course, each individual philosopher and all four ideal types of American naturalism have widely divergent ways of depicting process as a philosophical theme.[26]

The accompanying chart of the major traditions and players will help illustrate the range of thinkers I include in this ideal typology of "American philosophical naturalism."[26] Of course, Whitehead and Emmet are English, but are included because both lived in North America and have influenced process thought.

AMERICAN PHILOSOPHICAL NATURALISM

Pragmatism	Peirce, Kaufman James, Rorty Dewey, Mead
Process/Relational	Whitehead, Cobb Hartshorne, Neville[a] Loomer, Ford Meland, Griffin Emmet, Frisina Grange, Suchoocki Keller
Naturalism & Hermeneutics	Randal, Wieman[b] Buchler, Langer Hall and Ames, Corrington McKeon, Pepper Lakoff and Johnson, Toulmin[c]

[a]Neville might object to being placed in the process-relational camp.
[b]Wieman could also be assigned to the process tradition equally well in some respects.
[c]Toulmin (and one could include his colleague Jonson) is added because of stellar work on reviving casuistry as a form of naturalistic ethical reasoning as well as providing a naturalistic account and defense of reason itself.

Robert Corrington,[11] who makes extensive use of Justus Buchler's formulation of a metaphysical ordinal naturalism, argues that naturalism initially seems a fairly harmless and even vague philosophical viewpoint: "There is a sense in which philosophical naturalism is a fairly harmless perspective. All that it initially claims is that the human process is but one process among innumerable others, even if it shares many features, via analogy or proportion, with the rest of nature" (Corrington 1994, 9).

Corrington moves on quickly to state a distinction that many American naturalists feel compelled to make. Historically, both professional and lay audiences have often identified naturalism as a form of materialism. Although some naturalists are materialists, there is no reason why all naturalists need be materialists, and Corrington rejects this easy identification. He believes that naturalism cannot be reduced to a species of materialism for the following reason: "Nature cannot be characterized by any single metaphor or conceptual scheme. Its vastness and sheer multiplicity belie our attempt to frame a compelling and adequate metaphysics that would somehow open out the ultimate essence of trait contour of nature" (16).

Like Buchler before him, Corrington affirms the fact that nature is more than some kind of material container in which the human drama is acted out: "Naturalism is not a distinct perspective within philosophy so much as a necessary starting and ending point for all reflection that wishes to honor the locatedness of the human process within vast orders of relevance that are not themselves human products. Naturalism is the formalization of our natural piety before the world" (16). Corrington's project of elaborating his ecstatic naturalism is useful because he very clearly recognizes the religious element of naturalism present whenever we realize that the human process, to use Buchler's language, has a transcending moment situated within the vast web of natural complexes. As Corrington writes, "Initially, ecstatic naturalism can be defined as that moment within naturalism when it recognized its self-transcending character. Naturalism is self-transcending when it understands the eternal power of the transition from preformal potencies to the realms of signification within the world" (18).

But, even if we preliminarily accept Corrington's contention that process theology is really a form of robust naturalism, why not simply call all of these three groupings "process" philosophy or theology? It has been reported that Bernard Loomer, who himself is credited with inventing the name "process philosophy," later decided that this was something of a mistake in nomenclature. Loomer preferred to call Whitehead's achievement "process-relational" philosophy and theology. Moreover, Loomer's opinion is that this process-relational philosophy is rational-empirical in method and that "the emphasis is naturalistic" (Dean and Axel 1987, 20). Bernard Meland, a member of the movement known as the Chicago school of empirical theology, also strongly defended the naturalism of a philosophy and theology committed to an explication of process as a primary trait of the present cosmic epoch (1962, 1988).

In short, a strong argument can be made that process-relational philosophy cum theology is a robust naturalism, and that naturalism is the more inclusive "vague category."

I call this version of naturalism "robust" because it does not reject a religious interpretation of reality. In fact, Whitehead, Loomer, Hartshorne, Meland, Wieman, Griffin, Corrington, and Neville all affirm an active and persistent role for God in the constitution of the world. These thinkers, unlike more traditional Christian theists, deny that God violates the normal operating procedures of the natural world. God works within the world such that God is a cocreator of the world along with all the creatures of the world. For these theologians, God really does exist and really interacts with the world. In fact, they argue that God interacts with all the other creatures in a most natural way as the supremely relative qua supremely related creature. Because of this supreme relationality, God does not need any supernatural interventions in order to be God. While not the normal Western theistic definition of God, it is a novel contribution, offering a different voice about divine reality in the modern world. Even Lakoff and Johnson, hardly theologians per se, still have a place for spirituality and religion in their philosophy in the flesh as a metaphoric enterprise. I suspect that many of the Song Confucians would recognize this Western idea as compatible with their broad understanding of the Dao.

Bernard Meland, although influenced by Whitehead, defends his version of the naturalist vision as a form of empirical realism. He argues that many Whiteheadian philosophers were seduced by the wonderful precision of *Process and Reality* into abandoning the appeal of the radical and persistent empiricism of Whitehead, an empiricism that Whitehead himself adopted from James. In his later writings, Bernard Loomer (Dean and Axel 1987) came to agree with his longtime colleague at the University of Chicago, Meland, in reaffirming the empirical and naturalist sensibilities of process-relational philosophy and theology. Meland repeatedly defended the continued use of Christian theistic language within the emerging sensibility of religion as a form of radical empirical realism. "Being *saved*, yes, being *saved through grace*, implies being released to participate with fuller sensory powers in wide, wide planetary life, not being rescued from this earthly pilgrimage" (Meland 1988, 154). Meland himself called the trait of process the Creative Passage.[26] Moreover, Meland hoped that this new empirical realism qua process-relational theology could allow the Christians among modern people to sing an old song again in a new world.

Another instance of contemporary philosophy in a naturalistic mode is what I will call metaphoric philosophy. Since 1980 the linguist George Lakoff and the philosopher Mark Johnson have collaborated on a remarkable interdisciplinary venture leading to a bold revision of the Western philosophical tradition. Central to their collective vision is the pivotal role of metaphor in the construction of human thought. This interest in metaphor, especially with a focus on what Stephen Pepper (1942) called root metaphors in philosophical systems, is not surprising, given their extended joint philosophical enterprise based on contemporary studies in cognitive psychology and philosophy.

It has often struck me that the Confucians, including philosophers like Xunzi in the classical period, Zhu Xi in the Song, and Mou Zongsan in the modern period, have undertaken the task of naturalizing the spiritual dimensions of the Confucian Way for over two thousand years. As more North Americans come to share a nonreductive naturalist mood or sensibility, the Confucians might indeed have something to share with modern Americans in search of a form of philosophical worldview or spirituality that is naturalist in temper and yet has a profound religious dimension to it. In fact, I believe it is the case that Confucians, like the Buddhists and some Daoists, demonstrate how to be spiritual without any robust theism. God moves from being a transcendent person to being the Dao to being thought of as a wonderfully potent natural complex. Or as the New Confucians such as Mou are wont to say, we really have in religion an expression of immanent transcendence.

ONTOLOGICAL PARITY

Clearly not all American philosophy can be collected under the banner of a focused interest in the trait of process; yet many American philosophers have shown a fascination with the themes and traits of process. Nonetheless, many forms of historical and contemporary analytic and language philosophy are against any mention of such metaphysical speculations as are found in Whiteheadian process thought. True, some analytic or language philosophers might evince an interest in what the term "process" means, but they would not share Whitehead's mature conviction that process is a key to understanding reality. Therefore, I will narrow my focus to only those three parts of the American philosophical public I listed above.

We need a robust, open interpretation of what the world includes according to the American naturalist tradition. Justus Buchler has provided us with just such a conceptual tool by coining the phrase "ontological parity". Buchler's theory of ontological parity was developed, at least in part, through a dialogue with Whitehead (Buchler, 1974; 1990). In passing, I note that it is also clear that for Buchler the theory of ontological parity is likewise a defense of pluralism as both ontology and cosmology. Like Emmett, Buchler harbored great appreciation for Whitehead's philosophy and paid it the supreme compliment of informed criticism. What bothered Buchler about Whitehead's vision was that he thought he detected a flaw in the way Whitehead went about trying to find and define the "really real" elements of the cosmos.

Buchler's point is actually both astute as a criticism of Whitehead and fairly simple to grasp. That it is simple does not detract from the power of Buchler's caveat concerning Whitehead's attempt to discover the "really real" elements of this or any world whatsoever. Buchler began by noting that Whitehead was critical of incoherent philosophical systems. However, Buchler detected what he called "a strain of arbitrariness in Whitehead's system." Buchler argues that Whitehead has two trends in his philosophy that work toward contrary ends. The first trend, according to Buchler, is Whitehead's drive to understand the basic components of this or any cosmos and to boil down these components into a finite list of types of existents or entities. According to Buchler, this is Whitehead's search for a definition of actual entities or occasions. The second trend, Buchler asserts, is found when Whitehead then tries to decide which of his basic types is the prototype for the "really real." According to Buchler this is a mistake.

In order to move the conversation forward, Buchler compares and contrasts two principles he finds in constant play in the history of philosophy. While Buchler draws his examples from the history of Western philosophy, I believe Buchler's point is also illuminating for the Chinese Confucian tradition. Buchler's two principles are ontological priority and ontological parity.

> Let us contrast a principle of ontological priority—which has flourished from Parmenides to Whitehead and Heidegger, and which continues to flourish in unsuspected ways—with a principle of parity. In terms of the latter, whatever is discriminated in any way (whether it is "encountered" or produced or otherwise related to) is a natural complex, and no complex is more "real," more "natural," more "genuine," or more "ultimate" than any other. There is no ground, except perhaps a short-range rhetorical one, for a distinction between the real and the "really real," between being and "true being." (Buchler 1990, 30–31)

A bit later, Buchler offers a slightly different rephrasing of the principle of ontological parity: "The principle of ontological parity could be stated in positive terms, and without dependence upon the conceptual associates of 'reality,' to the effect that all discriminanda are obtenances, regardless of what else they are in comparison with one another. For certain purposes of emphasis and controversy, the principle commends itself in this [weaker] form. To say that every complex obtains underscores the idea that anything identified, whether as framed or as found, has an inviolability merely as such" (53).

Before we continue, let me explain Buchler's notion of a natural complex. Buchler calls his philosophical enterprise a metaphysics of natural complexes. Moreover, he is clear that he prefers the richness of the principle of ontological parity to the constraints of ontological priority in terms of defining what a natural complex entails. Buchler begins the *Metaphysics of Natural Complexes* with "Whatever is, in whatever way, is a natural complex" (1). In his later study of poetry, Buchler offers the following observation: "The expression 'natural complex' (which we have been abbreviating as 'complex') applies to whatever is, and therefore to whatever can be dealt with; to what is produced by men as well as to what is not. . . . The term 'natural' is important, not as a qualification used in order to concede that some complexes can be 'non-natural'; but on the contrary as a reminder that *all* complexes are aspects of nature; that there is no complex that can be dismissed or exorcised." (Buchler 1974, 103)

Later in the same paragraph Buchler goes on to argue that the notion of a natural complex allows us to talk about whatever poetry or art or fantasy would like to index. The use of natural complex allows us: "to talk of whatever it is that poetry may be concerned with and to include in the 'whatever' not only public space-time particulars but any kind of actualities—actual parts of animals, actual traits of an illusion, actual revolutionary ideas, actual components of a dream; and any kind of possibility . . ." (103).

Buchler coined the phrase "natural complex" because, like Whitehead, he believed that philosophers often incline toward a principle of priority in which concrete objects are considered more real than other things as possible discriminanda. But according to Buchler, the world is so much richer than just "thingness." We live in a world of poetic imagery and fantasy, of revolutionary dreams of liberation, of standard poodles, of possibilities of love and hatred. This concept would make sense to someone like Zhu Xi, who would argue that a ritual gesture or an embodied ethical action is just as real as anything else.

Moreover, Buchler held that these real things were individuals: "Most philosophers assume that individuals are the prototype of being. They are the 'real existences' which as it were underlie or carry all other aspects of being. They alone are visible, and all else is inferred, or found lurking here and there, around, between, and behind them" (55). This kind of reified ontological sense of the priority of one level of natural complexes over another is definitely not the case for Buchler; it is the poet who honors all the variety of complexes "may be said to be the chief exemplar of the principle of ontological parity" (56).[26]

There is something appealing in the way Buchler goes about talking about orders and natural complexes when we reflect back on Zhu Xi's and Chen Chun's *daoxue* philosophy. For instance, one of the key terms in Zhu's philosophy is *li* 理 (coherent principle, form, pattern).[26] Such principles as forms and patterns are exemplars of the kind of natural complexes or orders that so fascinated Buchler. Zhu uses *li* as a way to indicate the order of a thing or event such that it obtains its distinctive ontological integrity when compared and contrasted to other things and events. Even more, Zhu is always hesitant to indulge in a metaphysical principle of ontological priority. Zhu is always at pains—if not completely successfully, according to his critics—to argue for parity between form as principle and vital force, for instance.[15] The question, however, remains: How are we to understand the relationship of form and dynamics if we press Zhu Xi for something more than a cosmological account? Is there an ontological dimension, even perhaps implicit and unexpressed, lurking in *daoxue* discourse?

A NATURALIST ONTOLOGY FOR THE TRAIT(S) OF PROCESS

One of the most common criticisms of Whiteheadian-style process thought made by other philosophers and theologians is that the mature system lacks a proper ontology. Whitehead is not without a defense of his method, nor is he apologetic about defending a cosmology rather than using the other related twins of Western philosophy—namely, ontology and metaphysics.

Whitehead warned repeatedly that we should not be seduced into thinking that we have everything figured out. He admonishes philosophers not to fall prey to the search for the Holy Grail of dogmatic Enlightenment and analytic philosophy, the perfect dictionary. He forever counsels us to be cautious, to seek clarity and perfection and rigor, and then to doubt our results immediately. According to Whitehead, the best we can hope for is an asymptotic approach to truth: "Philosophers can never hope finally to formulate these metaphysical first principles. Weakness of insight and deficiencies of language stand in the way inexorably. Words and phrases must be stretched towards a generality foreign to their ordinary usage; however such elements of language be stabilized as technicalities, they remain metaphors mutely appealing to an imaginative leap" (1978, 4). Of course, we have a dream of a scheme of principles, but this is only an ideal that we can never reach. Postmodern philosophers go even farther: we should abjure any such search for a perfect dictionary and a set of clear and distinct principles. However, I think that Whitehead would have liked Lakoff and Johnson's appeal to metaphors as a way to express whatever insight we have into the structure and meaning of the cosmos; metaphors honor the strong empirical side of Whitehead's process thought.

Actually, there are places in *Process and Reality* (and in *Adventures of Ideas*) where Whitehead takes a shot at defining what metaphysical first principles might be. The first principle is, "That the actual world, in so far as it is a community of entities which are settled, actual, and already become, conditions and limits the potentiality for creativeness beyond itself" (Whitehead 1978, 65). As previously indicated, Buchler, just to mention one serious student of Whitehead who shares a fascination with speculative philosophy, criticized the way Whitehead privileges the discussion of what constitutes a community of "real" entities. For Buchler, Whitehead's understanding of these actual entities is too restrictive in scope. Buchler offered his metaphysics of natural complexes as a way forward for someone like Whitehead sans the mistake of granting an ontological privilege to only one aspect of the cosmos, namely, actual entities. But what Buchler would like is the naturalism and pluralism of natural complexes assumed by Whitehead in this first principle. Attentive readers will immediately sense the hovering spirit of Plato and his receptacle transformed into the extensive continuum. Nor would the reader be wrong, for one of Whitehead's most famous dictums is that all Western philosophy is but a set of footnotes to the divine Plato.

Whitehead then writes, "The second metaphysical assumption is that the real potentialities relative to all standpoints are coordinated as diverse determinations of one extensive continuum" (1978, 66). Whitehead's extensive continuum is a very austere statement of a first principle. "An extensive continuum is a complex of entities united by the various allied relationships of whole to part, and of overlapping so as to possess common parts, and of contact, and of other relationships derived from these primary relationships" (66). Although Whitehead does not himself talk very much about other universes, he thinks that any universe, as far as he can tell, would have to be an extensive continuum with these kinds of allied relationships. These alternative universes might even have their own metrical geometries that would be very different from our own, so different that we could not even recognize them if we encountered them. If we know by the method of difference, and the differences are the specifics of the relationships in this cosmic epoch, we might be completely blind to alternatives to our own embodied world. Lakoff and Johnson, for instance, never tire of reminding us that we know the world through being embodied and that our cognition depends on and is derived from the very specificity of this particular human interaction of brain, body, and world.

In part 4 of *Process and Reality* Whitehead explains his theory of relationship in terms of the mutual implication of extensive whole and part in terms of the actual entities. Hall and Ames again pick up this part of Whitehead's philosophy, though they prefer the metaphor of field and focus to Whitehead's talk of wholes and parts. "Some general character of coordinate divisibility is probably an ultimate metaphysical character, persistent in every cosmic epoch of physical occasions. Thus some of the simpler characteristics of extensive connection, as here stated, are probably such ultimate metaphysical necessities" (Whitehead 1978, 288). Mutual implication or relationship is what is crucial here. "If you abolish the whole, you abolish its parts; and if you abolish any part, then *that* whole is abolished" (288). The extensive continuum is the means by which entities or natural complexes are connected with one another in any specific cosmic epoch. "Thus the continuum is present in each actual entity, and each actual entity pervades the continuum" (67).

Extension, which is the various relations of whole to part—overlap and contact, for instance—expresses or serves as a background for the field and focus of the natural complexes of the world. "Extension, apart from its spatialization and temporalization, is the general scheme of relationships providing the capacity that many objects can be welded into the real unity of one experience" (67). As Whitehead notes just slightly later, extension "is the most general scheme of real potentiality, providing the background for all other organic relations" (67). But Whitehead is very cautious here. He only wants to talk about the actual entities of this cosmic epoch. It is for this reason that he sticks with cosmology rather than a general metaphysics that would also include a robust ontology.[16]

The Confucians were, like Emmet and Buchler, fully capable of sustaining a cosmology that was pluralistic, naturalistic, and processive without recourse to any notion of divine intervention or creation. Building on the work of the late Qing Evidential Research scholars, Zhang Dainian (2002) has confirmed the pervasive role of themes of process, change, and transformation throughout the history of Chinese thought. According to thinkers as diverse as Xunzi, Liezi, Zhu Xi, and Chen Chun, there was and is an order to nature without a transcendent God as creator of the created order, although there is still a very strong religious dimension to all three forms of Chinese discourse. Whatever order there is to be found in the cosmos comes from the complex interactions of the objects and events of the world, to use the *daoxue* language instead of Whitehead's language of actual entities. The Confucians, for instance, would agree that what order we find is the outcome of the action of actual entities, but they felt no need to define God as some special type of actual entity. Nor did they spend a great deal of time looking for the really real objects of cognition. Along with Emmet they would agree that there is a passage to nature that embodies a strong commitment to the trait of process in the analysis of the world; with Buchler they would probably like the notion of a natural complex as far as it could be equated with the concept of the Dao both in its plural manifestations and its role as *taiji* 太極, the Supreme Polarity.[17]

Therefore, I will argue that Buchler's metaphysics of natural complexes might be just the kind of vague general category that allows for a comparison and articulation of the naturalist project found among the American naturalists and various Chinese Daoist and Confucian thinkers if we are interested in defending a robust trait of process within some modern forms of pluralistic process naturalism.

OLD AND NEW CONFUCIANS

It has been a constant temptation to focus even more on the New Confucian Mou Zongsan, because of his reaffirmation of the centrality of process and creativity at the core of Confucian discourse.[18] Of course, I have made use of Mou from time to time, but now I will focus directly on Mou's theory of process. One reason that I have hesitated to make more immediate use of Mou to buttress my claims about the role of the trait of process in Confucian thought is that some might make the following counterclaim. Critics are quick to point out that Mou, along with almost every other Chinese philosopher from the beginning of the twentieth century, was heavily influenced by contact with and appropriation of Western thought. Many of the great modern Chinese philosophers spent significant time studying in Japan, North America, or Europe and often took advanced degrees from universities in these areas. Therefore, it is hard to say just how much of their thought is derived from traditional Chinese sources or is drawn from their teachers in the West.

The case of Feng Youlan (1895–1990) demonstrates the (supposed) problem of intercultural philosophical conceptual contamination. Feng studied at Columbia University during the height of the neorealist movement. When Feng returned to China he became famous for his critical studies of the history of Chinese philosophy. His most renowned study of the history of Chinese philosophy, translated into English by Derk Bodde and still a basic English text for the study of Chinese philosophy, set the tone for all his later research projects. In fact, he continued to work on revisions of his history of Chinese thought until his death. Sometimes it is hard, even for students of his thought, to figure out if the revisions of the history were caused by changes in his own thinking or were merely the outcomes of the demands of the Communist Party for him to revise his history in light of the latest changes in party doctrine.

Along with Feng's influential historical studies, he wrote a series of books that expressed his own constructive speculative philosophy in the 1930s and 1940s. Feng called these a new philosophy of principle in homage to the work of Zhu Xi. Feng chose this designation because he saw himself as reviving the kind of neo-Confucian thought adumbrated by Zhu Xi's *lixue* 理學. However, other scholars, while acknowledging Feng's skill in renovating Zhu's vision for a modern age, also saw the long hand of Feng's Columbia teachers in his reexpression of the unity of principle with a diversity of manifestations. In short, the criticism runs that although Feng thought that he was being faithful to Zhu Xi and other classical and neo-Confucian philosophers, he really was reading them almost exclusively in the light of the neorealism of his Columbia teachers. The criticism seems to assume that there is a correct, perfect, or pristine kind of reinterpretation of a tradition open to later scholars.[19]

Mou Zongsan's situation was somewhat different. Although he mastered much Western philosophy, he never studied in the West or Japan. Mou himself is extremely clear about his claim that the trait of process is an essential, indeed, foundational—feature of the Confucian Way. This claim is supported by one of his characteristic, if contested, philosophical positions. Mou vehemently defends the notion of the *daotong* 道統 (transmission of the Way). Zhu Xi did the same, and is, in fact, one of the founders of the Song theory of the *daotong*. However, Mou disagrees with Zhu not about whether there is a transmission of the Way but about how to define the various schools involved in transmission. What is even more important for Mou is to define what he calls the mainline of the transmission. Mou often uses the metaphor of the taproot of a tree to describe what he is proposing; he takes a large tree as a metaphor for the Confucian tradition as a historical or cultural artifact. Just as a tree has many roots and branches, it usually has one main root. This root Mou defines as the Mencian mainstream of the Confucian Way. In Umberto Bresciani's translations from one of Mou's last major works, this is how the master defines the true transmission of the Dao:

> The line of the Confucians, starting from Confucius speaking of *ren* (to practice *ren* in order to know Heaven), passing through Mencius' speaking of the mind-heart being nature (to develop one's mind and heart in order to know nature and so then to reach knowledge of Heaven), already contained the tendency of aiming at ethical metaphysics under this perfect doctrine (of the Confucian *summum bonum*). Then it advanced further through the *Zhongyong*, which spoke of the Heavenly Destiny (*ming*) granting to humans their natures and of the perfection of sincerity (*cheng*) as well as of the full realization of one's nature, then reached down to the *Book of Changes* speaking of penetrating into the innermost spirit and knowing the flow of cosmic change: at that point the ethical metaphysics under this perfect doctrine was already basically complete. The Confucians of the Song and Ming dynasties inherited these pre-Qin doctrines, and brought them to perfection. (Bresciani 2001, 378)

This is just the kind of elegant restatement of the *daotong* that irritates other Chinese intellectual historians. The philosopher Fang Dongmei (1899–1977) was also perplexed with Mou's rather strict adherence to the orthodoxy of the *daotong* (Besciani 2001, 271–299; Cheng and Bunnin 2002, 263–80). Fang simply did not believe that we could limit the exuberance of the Confucian philosophical tradition to one line of orthodox transmission. This would, Fang points out, actually privilege the Song philosophers much more than is defensible, and this move would be even more constraining if we were to pick one line of the Song achievement and exclude all the others from notice or consideration. Fang—and among the early generations of the New Confucians, Xu Fuguan—also shared this sentiment, and wanted to honor the pre-Qin philosophers as much as the Song and Ming masters. Furthermore, Fang simply points out that the Song masters owed heavy philosophical debts to the Wei-Jin Daoists or *xuanxue* (obscure learning) thinkers as well as to Buddhists. The history of Chinese philosophy, Fang believed, is the story of the fruitful interaction of many schools of thought. Modern Confucians ought to be able to appreciate Xunzi, Wang Bi, and the great Tiantai master Zhiyi as much as Mengzi, Hu Hong, Cheng Hao, Zhu Xi, Wang Yangming, and Dai Zhen. To borrow a Christian metaphor, the habitats of the sages and Kongzi have many mansions. Both Bresciani (2001) and Cheng and Bunnin (2002) chronicle the opinions of those who demur at a too restricted list of Confucian masters and materials.

Here I completely agree with Qian Mu's chronological typology of Confucian history, which is broken down into six distinct but interconnected phases (Bresciani 2001, 263). Using a different descriptive terminology, I use the same six divisions in *The Transformations of the Confucian Way* (Berthrong 1998a). My version merely names the epochs of the transformations of the Confucian Way after their historical periods without trying to find philosophical tags for each of them.

Notwithstanding my agreement with Qian Mu and others in their objections to Mou's historical typology, I do agree with Mou's philosophical archaeology of the early Confucian texts. Mou is not simply reading Kant, Leibniz, or Whitehead back into the early canonical Confucian texts.[20] In Mou's later constructive speculative philosophy, he claims that Confucianism is the taproot of the Chinese intellectual tradition. While he does not deny the role of other pre-Qin philosophies such as Daoism, Moism, or Legalism, he strongly affirms Confucianism as the essence of the Chinese cultural tradition, even when stimulated by the great Wei-Jin master of the *xuanxue* 玄學 and the profound achievements of the high Tang Buddhist philosophers. And at the heart of this Confucian tradition is a deep appreciation of the trait of process. As a modern philosopher, Mou feels it is entirely appropriate for him to make use of Daoist and Buddhist sources for the reconstruction of Chinese philosophy, even if pride of place still resides with the lineage of Kongzi.

The first stage of the argument about creativity and process is taken from the third section of the twelfth chapter of *Special Traits* (Mou Zongsan 1994, 130–33). One of Mou's favorite passages expressing the processive nature of the Confucian vision is a line from one of the poems of the *Book of Odes*: "Ah! The will of heaven, profound and unceasing" (130–33). This unceasing quality is, Mou believes, the content of the virtue of heaven. Moreover, it is this virtue of heaven, according to the *Zhongyong*, that is given to each human being in order to realize full humanity. Rather like the Holy Spirit, the virtue of heaven moves everywhere, and in fact there would be no here or there at all if the virtue of heaven were not unceasing in its creative actions. And Mou concludes that finite human intellect cannot penetrate into an understanding of the unceasing nature of the virtue of heaven; this simply indicates to us the depth dimension of the Dao. Mou is not afraid to recognize the religious dimension of this teaching. He quotes Mengzi, who is in turn quoting Kongzi, to the effect that except for the text of the *Book of Odes*, how can a scholar know the Way? The poems reflect a primordial aesthetic insight into the nature of the Way and the proper sentiments and reactions of the sages and the people to the unceasing creativity of the Dao.

Next, Mou argues that philosophically there is a root meaning for the notion of *ren* 仁 (humaneness) in the *Analects*. He believes that the nature of humaneness in the *Analects* is "best expressed in penetrating the meaning of 'the fundamental root of the nature of creativity itself'" (Mou Zong shen 1994, 130–33). According to Mou, it is exceedingly difficult to express in an assertive or propositional form this fundamental insight into the root of nature being creativity itself. Mou believes that in the Western Christian tradition, it is only God who expresses, reveals, or manifests creativity itself. But Kongzi saw *ren* rather than *shangdi* 上帝 (God) as the ultimate foundational trait of all the things of the cosmos. Moreover—and here Mou separates himself and the Confucian tradition from Christian theology—this trait of creativity itself as process "is not something superadded to the motive force of the life of each thing. This 'foundational root of the nature of creativity itself' is also later called the 'real potential of the decree of life.'" (130–33)

In the sixth chapter, Mou outlines how he believes the canonical records of the classical sages conduce to the understanding of the Dao as the root of creativity itself (45–56). The search for such an understanding of creativity allows Mou to set the general context for such a philosophical claim, and it arose in the humble beginnings of the Confucian notion of study as the means to understand the Way of Heaven. What Mou is looking for, and he notes that he is using modern language to describe the function of *xue* 學 (study) in the Confucian project, is the function needed to transform epistemological knowledge into life-values, and to transform these life-values in such a way that the person can manifest a virtuous nature. When study becomes transformative such that we comprehend life-values as expressions of the moral mind-heart, we find that study, Mou asserts, becomes a form of awareness in the most meaningful manner of being in the world. According to Mou, Kongzi understood how we could proceed from the lowly studies of simple empirical matters to a higher penetration of the virtuous nature, which in turn will allow the person to become unified with the Way of Heaven. Mou believes that the mutual comprehension of the person and heaven is part of the spiritual life of the Confucian quest for sage wisdom. But of course, as Kongzi noted, the comprehension of true and transformative life-values is not easy. It was not until he was fifty years old that Kongzi deemed that he knew the Will of Heaven. The later Song scholars took this idea of the flowing forth of the Will of Heaven as the principle of all the things and affairs of the world. Here too Mou finds the constant trait of process at the heart of the Confucian Dao.

Mou continues to track the flowing forth of the Will of Heaven into one of his favorite texts, the *Zhongyong*. The realization of the immanent and transcendent finds its full manifestation only in the extending of *cheng* 誠 as the perfecting self-actualization of the flow of creativity itself. Human beings, according to the *Zhongyong*, have an essential role to play as mediators between heaven and earth. In fact, when human beings do play their proper role, they form a trinity with heaven such that all three phases of the creative process find a proper order or pattern of actualization. The *Zhongyong* teaches that it is the sage who can extend the realization of creativity itself. The entire process takes transformation of the moral mind of humanity as its goal. Hence the *Zhongyong* concludes that *cheng* is the true realization of the Way of Heaven. As we shall see, David Hall and Roger Ames, based on an analogous interpretation of the *Zhongyong*, translate *cheng* as "creativity" *simpliciter*. Mou makes the claim that the reality of *cheng* in the *Zhongyong* and Kongzi's teaching about *ren* are identical.

Here Mou claims that *cheng* as creative realization is identified with the Way of Heaven, whereas the humaneness of Kongzi has the special traits of purity, vastness, and depth, so that its effects in terms of human culture are limitless, and hence humaneness can also be identified as the Way of Heaven. Mou writes: "We cannot do any harm by writing it out in a string together with the following form. . . . The decree of heaven, the way of heaven (in the *Book of Odes*, the *Book of History* and other ancient writings) = to humanity (of the *Analects)* = of realization/*cheng* (the *Zhongyong)* = creativity itself [an English gloss by Mou] = a principle of creativity [Principle of Creativity again by Mou in English gloss] = a fundamental principle of life transformation (this is an old name for the principle of creativity, which is the principle of life transformation) (Mou Zongsan 1994, 53)."

And just to make sure that we have not missed the main point of this string of intentional meanings, as Mou would say, he writes immediately hereafter that the theory of realization found in the *Zhongyong* expresses the real metaphysical viewpoint of the Confucian tradition. This viewpoint is what Mou calls a moral metaphysics, and he deems this Confucian formulation to be the perfected expression of the summum bonum. All of Mou's work in the late 1960s, 1970s, and 1980s hammers home this point, ending with another book of nineteen lectures on Chinese philosophy and a book on the summum bonum as the discernment of transforming life-values for the sage within and, hopefully, the king as an ideal ruler without.

Along with his constant concern for explaining the continuing relevance of the Confucian *daotong*, Mou is a stout defender of the moral mind-heart theory he traces to the teachings of the *Zhongyong* and Mengzi. As Bresciani (2001), Cheng and Bunnin (2002) and Liu (2003) chronicle, Mou is merely one of many New Confucians who sustain a robust commitment to the moral mind-heart in the tradition of Mengzi in the classical world and scholars such as Hu Hong, Cheng Hao, Wang Yangming, and Liu Zongzhou in the Song and Ming dynasties, just to mention a short list of Mou's favorite paladins of genuine Confucian moral metaphysics.[21] However, Mou makes an important distinction in regard to two modes of expressing the philosophical vision of the Mencian mainline—namely, a moral formulation and a cosmological formulation found in the early canonical texts. According to Mou's philosophical typology, the root of moral sensibility, and the root metaphor for the Confucian tradition, is best expressed by Mengzi, whereas the cosmological approach is found in the *Zhongyong* and the *Yijing*. Without recourse to a proper explication of both the moral and cosmological modes, Mou does not think that we can understand the full richness of the Confucian doctrine of human nature founded on creativity itself as the taproot of cosmic process.

In the eighth chapter of *Special Traits* Mou outlines his theory of the moral and cosmological interpretations of *xing* 性 (human tendencies, human nature) (Mou Zonshan 1994, 73–82). In the cosmological mode, nature is taken to be the *tianming* 天命 or "the Mandate/Will of Heaven" as it is commonly rendered in English. Mou plays with the metaphor of *tianming* as a function of the official duty of heaven to provide creativity itself to human beings as their true nature. This definition plays nicely on the ancient notion of *tianming* as the Mandate of Heaven within all the classical schools of Confucianism. Mou argues that cosmology, following the insights of the *Book of Changes* and the *Zhongyong*, is not just the story of the formal, material, or mechanical relations of things and events. Rather, the real Confucian cosmology is the ability of human beings to transform the given circumstances of life by means of the perfection of their moral mind-hearts. Hence, the quintessence of creativity becomes the true nature of human nature when it is fully realized as *cheng* 誠 (genuine self-actualization). This self-actualization always has the potential to overcome the inherited structures of the past in the free exercise of the moral mind-heart. Mou ends lecture 8 by giving a set of interconnected short quotes from the pre-Han canon to the effect that creativity itself as the endless process of the interaction of the Dao is what nature really means for human beings. There is hardly a more robust affirmation of the role of process in any modern philosophical system, East or West. Mou is certainly a philosopher of process in Rescher's sense of process philosophy as philosophy with a strong motif of process and transformation.

FROM OLD TO NEW

If Heraclitus is revered as the first philosopher of process in the Western tradition, the *Yijing* 易經 (*Book of Changes*) holds a special place of honor in the Chinese tradition as the foundational text for systematic reflection, with a special place for theories of change or transformation. The *Yijing* is often seen at the beginning of the Confucian canonical texts, and its interpretation is certainly difficult in the extreme. The problem rests in its cryptic nature, its antiquity, and its complex, layered construction. Modern scholars believe that the earliest layers of the text, along with some of the poems of the *Book of Odes* and a few sections of the *Book of History*, are the oldest classical Chinese texts preserved from the Zhou dynasty and perhaps even the Shang dynasty.

It is the famous long section or "wing" of the *Yijing* known throughout history as the Great Commentary that speculates on the place of process and transformation in the cosmos. As the Great Commentary tells us, "It is by means of the *Changes* that the sages plumb the utmost profundity and dig into the very incipience [*ji* 幾] of things. It is profundity alone that thus allows one to penetrate the aspirations of all the people of the world; it is a grasp of incipience alone that thus allows one to accomplish the great affairs of the world" (Lynn 1994, 63). It is because of statements like this that some modern New Confucian philosophers such as Chung-ying Cheng (1991) argue that the trait of process has been at the forefront of Chinese philosophical speculation since its very beginnings in the Zhou dynasty. To know how things begin and interact with other things one must, according to this reading of the *Yijing*, know something about the process of change and transformation. "The Master said: 'As for the *Changes*, what does it do? The *Changes* deals with the way things start up and how matters reach completion and represents the Dao that envelops the entire world. If one puts it like this, nothing more can be said about it.'" (Lynn 1994, 63).

It is the *Changes*, for instance, that introduces Confucians to a concept that became so important to the Song masters—namely, the Great Ultimate or Supreme Polarity as the *taiji* 太極. "Therefore, in change there is the great ultimate. This is what generates the two modes [the yin and yang]" (Lynn 1994, 65). Northern Song dynasty philosophers such as Zhou Dunyi and Shao Yong regarded this as the warrant for regarding the whole cosmos as the vast set of interlocking processes that we human beings call things and events. It is the Dao as a vast cornucopia of natural complexes of infinite variety and ever-changing patterns of stillness and movement ending in harmonies of completed action. "The great virtue of Heaven and Earth is called 'generation' (Lynn 1994, 77). The key term that Lynn translates as "generation" is *sheng* 生. Most commonly, *sheng* means "to give birth," "to produce something." The *Changes* tells us that the very virtue of the cosmos is to produce and produce without ceasing (*shengsheng buxi* 生生不息). This also becomes Mou Zongsan's favorite Chinese expression for "creativity itself."

Kongzi (or whoever actually edited the Great Commentary) has tales to tell about how all of this came about in the first place—namely, the ur-act of composing the trigrams and hexagrams that became the veritable images of the world itself.

> When in ancient times Lord Bao Xi ruled the world as sovereign, he looked upward and observed the images in heaven and looked downward and observed the models that the earth provided. He observed the patterns on birds and beasts and what things were suitable for the land. Nearby, adopting them from his own person, and afar, adopting them form other things, he thereupon made the eight trigrams in order to become thoroughly conversant with the virtues inherent in the numinous and the bright and to classify the myriad things in terms of their true, innate natures. (Lynn 1994, 77).

I have always found it fascinating that one of the common views about classical China is that it lacks cosmogonic myths about the origin of the world, notwithstanding the work of contemporary scholars such as Anne Birrell on Chinese mythology (1993) to the contrary. There is nothing quite like the opening of Genesis or the prologue of the Gospel of John, which announce the beginning of a wonderful drama with God as the author and human beings as the audience. However, the story of Lord Bao Xi, one of the early sages according to Confucian cumulative tradition, strikes me as a perfectly fine foundational myth for a naturalist tradition. It is just sages and their fellow human beings exercising a natural processive creativity all the way down.

The Great Commentary continues the story about the death of Lord Bao Xi with a chronicle of the cultural achievements of other sage-sovereigns such as Lord Shen Nong, the Yellow Emperor, and the sages Yao and Shun. In short, it is the usual cast of sage-heroes who helped to classify the world and bring order to all the people under heaven: "With their numinous powers they transformed things and had the common fold adapt to them. As for [the Dao of] change, when one process of it reaches its limit, a change from one state to another occurs. As such, change achieves free flow, and with this free flow, it lasts forever" (Lynn 1994, 78). As the great Wei-Jin commentator Wang Bi notes, "If change is allowed to flow freely, it will never be exhausted. This is why it can last forever" (78).

Considering the role of the *Yijing* in Chinese intellectual and religious history, it is as if Heraclitus wrote a whole foundation myth and commentary on his cryptic remark that all things flow, and this remark then became a classic statement of the whole philosophical tradition. Or, just as Whitehead said that all of the history of Western philosophy is a series of extended footnotes to Plato, (Whitehead 1978, 39) one might say the whole history of Confucian speculative philosophy is the history of the elaboration of the trait of process. But this is far too rhetorical, because it would constrain the flow of change itself. That is the problem of interpreting and living with change; the sage needs to understand the flow of change and transformation and to adjust to whatever new circumstances emerge out of the ceaseless generativity or *shengsheng buxi* of the Dao. Even if we do not go all the way with Cheng Zongying's claim that the *Yijing*'s philosophy of process stands at the root of all future Chinese (and even East Asian) speculative philosophy, there is still the historical fact that the trait of process was embedded in the earliest and most influential sedimentations of Chinese folk and elite culture.

We will now catapult from the world of early classical China to the twenty-first century. One question remains: how can reflection on the philosophies of change and transformation of the *Yijing*, Xunzi, the *Liezi*, Zhu Xi, and Chen Chun throw any illumination on current problems in philosophy in general and in process thought in particular? Here is one example. If Kuklick (2001) is correct in his history of philosophy in America, there has been a long trend toward the naturalization of philosophy since Jonathan Edward's founding of American philosophy. Edwards is remembered as a great philosopher and a theologian. But it was the theology that drove the philosophy; moreover, Kuklick argues that this is a motif of religious elements giving rise to philosophical discourse that runs right down and through the rise of pragmatism and other characteristic forms of American naturalism.

LIYI FENSHU—PRINCIPLE IS ONE, ITS MANIFESTATIONS MANY

Confucian philosophers have a predilection for describing their cosmological thought-worlds in pithy axioms that seek to encapsulate their vision. One of the most famous of these is the axiom *liyi fenshu* 理一分殊, which the

Northern Song Confucian philosophers understood to mean that principle is one, while its manifestations are numerous (Yao 2003, 1:367–68). Of course, a great deal of contested philosophical debate is encoded in this simple phrase. It became one of the most famous teachings of Zhu Xi and his *daoxue* school. I believe that it can now contribute to the conversation about creativity with the American naturalist tradition. *Liyi fenshu* played a pivotal role (which is something of pun, as we shall see), in Zhu's Song school, and it can possibly play a similar role in the debates I have described about the trait of process in contemporary philosophical circles. It is a crucial step if Whiteheadian process philosophy is to expand from its American origins into the ecumenical world of global comparative philosophy—and philosophical theology as well.

My contention is that Zhu Xi's favorite axiom of *liyi fenshu* provides an alternative version for a process explanation of how things hang together. If Neville (1992, 1995a) wants to defend a theory of God as the undetermined creator of all finite determinations, a philosopher such as Justus Buchler declines to hold theo-volitional theism as a necessary element for a robust metaphysics that can account for the determinations of things and events, even divine events and spiritual realities. For Buchler, God is another natural complex—no more and certainly no less than any other natural complex. In one sense this is rather like Whitehead in that everything that is must be deemed a natural complex and not something that can be ontologically discriminated from other natural complexes in terms of priority. However, every natural complex prevails in unique ways, and God might indeed prevail in unique and powerful ways from the perspective of Buchler's ordinal metaphysics of natural complexes.

American philosophers, including Buchler, have struggled to leave the supernatural world of the teachings of the Western revealed religions behind them as the foundation of their worldviews. But there is the persistent query from philosophical theologians such as Neville as to whether or not it is possible to save the religious elements of life when the supernatural foundations of so much Western religion are gradually abandoned. Can the sense of the transcendent survive after the acids of Modernity have done their corrosive work? Or are we all doomed to live forever in Weber's iron cage of instrumental reason? And if not wanting to cohabitate with the ferrous touch of instrumental reason, are we left with a simplistic bhakti religion of faith in some divine creator ex-nihilo? Are we suspended between just getting clear about ordinary language games *or* becoming enthusiastic evangelicals?

My hypothesis is that Confucian discourse (and Daoist thought found in the *Liezi* as well) can throw a different light on the problem of the loss of the supernatural foundations of religion and yet sustain and nourish the yearning for some naturalized form of transcendence as an explanation of how finite things find harmony, the harmony of what Neville calls essential and conditional features of things and events. This, the Song Confucians like Zhu Xi thought, was what was expressed so perfectly with *liyi fenshu*.

From a modern Confucian viewpoint, what is needed is a balanced view that allows for a theory of immanent transcendence (see Berthrong 1994 for an account of immanent transcendence). New Confucians such as Mou Zongsan and Tu Weiming have argued that the classical Warring States Confucianism and the revived Confucianism of the Song and Ming periods can provide just such a balanced view of the demands of immanence and transcendence. The modern New Confucian reasoning runs thus: Neville, as a Christian theologian with strong Platonic root metaphors, is passionately concerned to protect a notion of transcendence, albeit a special kind of qualified transcendence, although he is just as uninterested in a defense of classical supernaturalism as are naturalists such as Buchler and process thinkers such as Bernard Loomer, Lewis Ford, and David Ray Griffin. What Neville yearns for is to find a place for what Mou called the vertical dimension of Confucian thought. This vertical dimension is the aspect of creativity that allows for the harmonies of the essential and conditional traits of each and every object and event.

Mou sounds a note of balanced appreciation for a naturalist like Buchler who wants to parcel out creativity to each and every creature, object, or event and not just assert that to God alone goes all the glory of determinate creativity. This is the horizontal dimension of cosmology wherein creatures are mutually related one to another and impact each other in diverse and sometimes profound ways. Nor is Mou's vision a form of panexperientialism or panpsychism as defended by David Ray Griffin (2001) or Charles Hartshorne (1967). Mou's *daotong* is a robust doctrine of immanent connection or relationship between the creatures, objects, and events of the world. Actually, Mou would also probably reproach all of these philosophers for excessive rationalism, the besetting sin of the entire Western philosophical tradition, according to his view. What one really needs, Mou repeats, is true intellectual intuition into the fundamental nature of the moral mind-heart of heaven, earth, and humanity. Anything less than such a synthetic vision of the Dao as the Supreme Ultimate or Ultimate Polarity is a flawed version of an epistemology seduced by technical rationalism, ending in a needlessly truncated vision of the endless harmonies of the world of ceaseless creativity.

Mou argues that a proper Confucian understanding of *liyi fenshu* is a theory that does justice to both the transcendent and immanent dimensions of the ever changing, processive, and pluralistic creative world of our present cosmic epoch. According to Mou, who claims the massive supporting weight of a host of witnesses ranging from the classical period to the variety of Song, Yuan, Ming and Qing periods, one can have both transcendence and immanence within the ambit of the Confucian Dao. One can find a place for the determinate creativity of each creature and also reverence for the transcendent unity of each creature as a manifestation of the ceaseless transformative power of the Dao. In fact, one can only understand the Dao in terms of the harmony of the creature as it finds the expression of its proper principle. One can have glimpses of ultimate values, even of the Supreme Ultimate or *taiji* 太極 in its glory as the principle of reality and ceaseless creativity itself manifesting itself as the sacred in all the divers objects and events of the secular order. From Mou's vantage point, one does not need to sacrifice the immanent for the transcendent or vice versa.

Within modern Western philosophy, a perfect example of the desire to save transcendence without supernaturalism is Whitehead's complex doctrine of God's primordial and consequent natures. One may also cite the work of process philosophers such as John Cobb (1965), Lewis Ford (2000) and David Ray Griffin (2001). However, it sometimes really helps to invite other philosophical voices to join the conversation. I also hazard the observation that such intercultural philosophical conversation is now inevitable in the new global city.

One of the cardinal insights that the Song Confucians sought to encapsulate under their rubric of *liyi fenshu* is, in Western terms, a fundamental axiology. Whatever else Confucian philosophy is, and it is indeed many things, it is always axiology. This is the reason that so many Western students of Chinese thought have argued that the core of Confucian thought is its social ethics. Or, from a slightly different point of view, David Hall and Roger Ames have argued at great length for an interpretation of the aesthetic *and* ethical dimensions of the classical Confucian Dao. Mou Zongsan, as we have already seen, calls this fundamental sensibility "concern consciousness." Ultimately Mou's "concern consciousness" and Hall and Ames's defense of the aesthetic dimension of the Confucian legacy are both manifestations of the axiological unity of the Confucian Dao; they are different manifestations of the same basic point.

Hall and Ames have argued at great length that one of the key metaphors of Confucian thought is that of a field-focus orientation toward the analysis of the objects and events of the world. The field-focus model has been part of their extended analysis of the classical origins of Confucian (and Daoist) philosophy. They argue, for instance, that a field-focus model is a much better way to interpret Confucian cosmology than Whitehead's part-whole model. The definition is this: "A particular is a focus that is both defined by and defines a context—a field. The field is hologrammatic; that is, it is so constituted that each discriminated 'part' contains the adumbrated whole" (Hall and Ames 1987, 238). For Daoists, the field defined by the various particulars is the Dao itself. Confucians arrange matters slightly differently. "In the early Confucian tradition, a similar implicit cosmology is captured in the relationship between *tian* as field and the determinate world as focus" (239).[26]

Hall and Ames keep coming back to the field-focus model, especially when they want to stress the aesthetic nature of Confucian and Daoist philosophy: "The Chinese conception of aesthetic order, in contrast to the rational understanding of order, is characterized by the multi-perspectival organization of particular details. Such order is not a function of 'locus' (the placement of items in such a manner as to realize a formal pattern) but of 'focus' (the construal of the particular elements in a field from the perspectives of focal centers." (239).

Although they do not engage in a dialogue with Justus Buchler's naturalism, Hall and Ames's description of the alternation of field and focus meshes neatly with Buchler's theory of natural complexes that endlessly entail each other from the "beginngless beginning" (as the Daoists would say) to the Christian apocalyptic end of time. In the last volume of their trilogy on early Confucian thought, *Thinking from the Han*, Hall and Ames carry out an extended discussion of how the field-focus model is the best way to understand the nature of the formation of the self according to Confucian and Daoist lights.

In defending their field-focus model, Hall and Ames even invent a neologism to suggest the particular and persistent flavor of Confucian and Daoist discourse when compared and contrasted to Western models. They call this *ars contextualis* (the art of the contextual). "Among the majority of classical Chinese thinkers, there is resort neither to *ontologia generalis*, a 'general ontology,' nor to *scientia universalis*, a 'science of universal principles.' It is the 'art of the contextualization' that is most characteristic of Chinese intellectual endeavors" (Hall and Ames 1998, 40). They go on to state, "Since there is no overarching context determining the shape of other contexts, the world is an open-ended affair comprised by 'thises' and 'thats' construable from any number of distinct perspectives" (40). Here again I am struck by the affinity to Buchler's natural complexes and Zhu Xi's *daoxue* notion of *liyi fenshu*. Moreover, this art of the contextual is relentlessly driven by values, both aesthetic and also moral in the case of the Confucians. If you are not happy with the idea of an *ars contextualis*, fundamental axiology is not far from the range of meanings that Hall and Ames attribute to their neologism. Mou's concern consciousness is also close in the sense that it also revolves around the axis of the vertical and the horizontal elements of the Confucian Dao.

Following this line of argument, Mou Zongsan accused Zhu Xi of departing from a true understanding of the Dao as concern consciousness in line with Mengzi and later Song scholars such as Hu Hong and Cheng Hao. Zhu's deviation was toward a *scientia universalis* as a cosmology indebted to a profound reflection on the nature of *li* as order, coherent pattern, or principle. There is little doubt that Zhu and Mou disagree in their interpretation of *liyi fenshu*. For Zhu the fundamental principle of order has its own name, that of *taiji* as Supreme Ultimate or even better, in Joseph Adler's felicitous translation, Supreme Polarity (de Bary, Bloom, and Lufrano 1999–2000, 1:669–76). Actually, as Zhu Xi interprets Zhou Dunyi's "Explanation of the Diagram of the Supreme Polarity," it does make a great deal of sense to talk about the *taiji* as the Supreme Polarity, and not just because of the eternal balancing act of the alternating forces of the yin-yang powers, although that is also part of the picture. *Ars contextualis* is always about relationship, about the dance between natural complexes. This is what makes it a unique philosophical sensibility. The metaphor of a supreme polarity spins gracefully at the center of concerned attention. The Confucian sage is balanced, harmonious, and timely. The sage brings focus to a complex field of interacting and ever-changing forces.

The movements of *taiji* as a mesocosmic cultivation of the person can become, in the harmonious flow of a master, a symbol of the interaction of the transcendent and the immanent, the vertical and the horizontal. The one order, the Supreme Polarity of the interaction of yin and yang, becomes the veritable pivot of creation as ceaseless creativity. The focus becomes particular, and the sage can follow the dictates of the mind-heart without violating any of the rituals of heaven, earth, or humanity. Focus becomes one; and the one adds particularity to the field, and the field is increased by one, as Whitehead would say about the category of the ultimate. "The many become one, and are increased by one" (Whitehead 1978, 21). Principle (or creativity) is one, and its manifestations are many. Both the Song *daoxue* master and the Anglo-American philosopher sought to explain, in their different worlds, immanent transcendence.[23]

From a Confucian and Daoist vantage point, Whitehead is obviously trying heroically to correct a bias toward bad interpretation of transcendence and supernaturalism in the mainstream Western philosophical and theological tradition. What thinkers as diverse as Xunzi, the author of the *Liezi*, and Zhu Xi offer is hope that such a project will bear its own fruit in a comparative mode in the future as the world becomes ever more intellectually and spiritually interconnected. Furthermore, if hermeneuts such as Hall and Ames are correct, there is a future for the language of process in Western philosophy as it engages in a more profound dialogue with various strains of the Chinese tradition. Mou Zongsan and the contemporary theologian Gordon Kaufman (1993, 2004) would agree. Creativity itself is a foundational trait of the Confucian tradition beginning with the earliest layers of the *Book of Changes*. Even Zhu Xi holds to such an insight about the importance of "ceaseless production," though according to Mou, Zhu went wrong in all kinds of other ways. Mou thought it would be hard to abandon faith in the creativity itself and unceasing process and still remain within the Confucian camp.

This is not an easy teaching about the trait of process or transformation. If we accept Mou's argument about Zhu Xi for the sake of argument, even one of the greats of Confucian philosophy got many of the details wrong. Nonetheless, the emphasis on the processive (and relational) nature of the world remains plainly in view in the extensive writings that constitute Zhu's corpus. Furthermore, according to Mou, the Confucian tradition has a religious dimension that is almost impossible to miss.[24] The only way to avoid the religious dimension of the Confucian tradition is to demand that any and all religion be perfectly in sync with the contours of the Christian theological deposition. Mou and countless other students of global culture argue that such a restrictive definition of "religion" simply does not work and causes needless misunderstanding of the traditional thought of China and the rest of Asia. The Confucian tradition begins with a piety toward the Mandate of Heaven; here Zhu Xi and Chen Chun would agree completely. One simply does not need to be overtly theistic in a supernaturalistic sense in order to be profoundly committed to the vertical dimension of the Dao.[25]

The growth of interest in various forms of the American naturalist tradition indicates that Confucian philosophy with its commitments to immanent transcendence, a naturalist religious sensibility, and a processive philosophical outlook might just find a warm reception at the beginning of a new millennium on both sides of the Pacific (see Metzger 2005 for a discussion of the political aspects of this dialogue). For instance, the Confucian penchant for, and love of, metaphor resonates with the philosophical insights of second-generation cognitive scientists and philosophers as expressed by the kinds of research projects on metaphor led by George Lakoff, Mark Johnson and Antonio Damasio. One of the enduring Confucian and Song *daoxue* metaphors for reality is the Supreme Polarity, and here again there is strong affinity between modern American metaphoric philosophy and classical and Song-Ming Confucianism. Of course, the differences are just as fascinating as the similarities. Moreover, Justus Buchler, representing one of the classic schools of American naturalism, would have appreciated why the Confucians defended the role of metaphor so strongly.

The appreciation goes thus: The Confucians, as fellow naturalists, have their own interpretation of the religious dimension and how it is expressed via the contours of various natural complexes, such as images of *tian* 天 as heaven, *tianming* 天命 as the Mandate of Heaven, and *taiji* as the Supreme Polarity. One would expect two entailments from the Confucian perspective. First, metaphor is always important, because the art of knowing, of becoming wise, is always involved in moving between different cognitive domains. One must constantly balance (to use the language of Mou Zongsan), the vertical and horizontal dimensions of the Dao.

Second, metaphor serves the religious dimension as a natural complex in terms of exhibitive query so central to Confucian self-cultivation. Confucianism is not just about careful exposition or assertive discourse, though obviously in the hands of Xunzi, Zhu Xi, and Chen Chun it can seek clarity about terminology as a crucial aspect of the complex path of *daoxue* self-cultivation. Following Buchler's typology, Confucians are just as concerned to articulate exhibitive and active forms of judgment as they are to proclaim assertive propositions about the nature of reality. In the Confucian case, from Kongzi to Mou Zongsan, if one does not embody the Dao and act out of this embodiment, then one cannot claim to really know the Dao. One might be a good scholar, but one is not a sage or a worthy. The religious dimension comes with knowing the Dao as the principle or order of the values appropriate to human beings in community. This knowing makes the person one with the Dao such that the principle or pattern of order tends toward a harmony of achieved or perfected value, but any such value only has meaning within the larger community. Being Confucians, the values most often discussed are mesocosmic moral values. But as Zhang Zai wrote in the *Western Inscription*, these values spread throughout the whole cosmos. Ultimately, the whole cosmos must be treated as one's own body, one's own family (de Bary, Bloom, and Lufrano 1999–2000 1:682–84).

By now I hope that I have convinced the reader that the history of process thought can be expanded beyond the confines of the Western tradition. As Nicholas Rescher pointed out in his introduction to process metaphysics (1996), if process as a philosophical trait is as important as modern process philosophers claim it is, then it should have an extended history in the Western tradition. Rescher proceeds to outline the history of the trait of process. I have attempted nothing as grand. Rather, I have sought to explore this subject in the Chinese tradition to see if it can expand the notion of process so dear to Whitehead and his disciples. My answer is, yes, process is an important feature of many Chinese philosophers in general and in the specifics embodied in the teachings of Xunzi, the *Liezi*, and Zhu Xi and Chen Chun. In order to bring the account of Chinese thought up to the present, I have also made extensive use of the modern Chinese New Confucian Mou Zongsan.

The case of the Daoist text of the *Liezi* is the least surprising in terms of process and transformation. Scholars of the Daoist literary tradition, of which the *Liezi* is such an important example, have long noted the Daoist proclivity toward notions of change and transformation—in short, traits of process. The Confucian examples might be a bit more surprising, at least to those who have not kept up with the contemporary revival of the study of the Confucian Dao since the 1970s in East Asian and the Euro-American academic settings. One dominant image of Confucianism has been that of an entrenched ritual orthodoxy, given over to the preservation of the past cultural glories of the ancient sages. But one can be seduced by Confucian rhetoric about the love of the past. On one level, it is absolutely true. Confucians love and venerate the past; and Confucians have been consistently the most assiduous of historians. However—and I hope that I have made the case—Confucians share processive sensibilities that are just as strong as their Daoist confreres, though harnessed for different purposes. Daoists seek to become immortals, or at least many of them claim to want to do so. Confucians want to promote human flourishing. As Herbert Fingarette explained so well (1972), Confucians seek the sacred in the secular.

More and more modern North Americans also seek the sacred in the secular. The problem is that their inherited religious traditions have not been very adept at such naturalist religious quests. And if Whitehead is correct, even the mainstream of the Western speculative philosophical world has likewise not been very good at understanding the role of process as a religious motif. Religion has sought the unchanging, the eternal. The problem with substance metaphysics is, what do you do with process? The problem becomes even more pressing when there is a paradigm shift that includes a renewed appreciation of the trait of process in Western speculative philosophy and theology.

Here the Confucian tradition should give some hope to people who think that acquiescing to the claims of process means the loss of any certitude or commitment to ideals. This need not be the final answer. Confucians have been process philosophers and profound religious thinkers, even nonreductive naturalists, who have maintained an unbroken record of personal and social ethical reflection about what ought to be done to promote human flourishing. That process is an important philosophical trait does not mean that all human relationships are to be discounted. Confucians can also begin to speak to modern Western religious thinkers who seek to balance the claims of immanence and transcendence.

Process, transformation, or change is everywhere, but at its heart, according to the Confucians, is humaneness as the ceaseless creativity of the Dao. As each person seeks the harmony of the Dao, he or she shares in a larger field of relationship that begins with the family and extends to the whole world. This is the only world that we have, and it is natural. But it is also luminously divine. It is complex, but also harmonious. Human beings seek harmony and sometimes find it. These markers of ethical perfection, these natural complexes of the sages, these metaphors of the Way, become the Mandate of Heaven for each person as the Supreme Polarity of the interaction of heaven, earth, and humanity.

Appendix

The Alchemy of Process

FROM THE CHRISTIAN CABALA OF RAMON LLULL TO THE NEW AGE

As I explored some of the historical background of the varied flora and fauna of the trait of process, one particular pathway seemed a natural site for wonderful tales of change and transformation. This was the Daoist tradition of China and East Asia. I then asked the question, if it is the case that Chinese philosophers have often described their field as a combination of Confucian, Daoist, and Buddhist sensibilities, what then of the various combinations of traditions that have comprised the Western tradition? Of course, in terms of philosophy there is the perennial contrast between those who embrace the divine Plato and those who follow the analytic and comprehensive Aristotle. Along with Whitehead's observation that all of Western philosophy is a series of footnotes to Plato (Whitehead 1978, 39) could be added the observation that Western philosophers and theologians have cultivated either a Platonic or Aristotelian sensibility.

As noted before, Max Weber once remarked, Daoism is the magic garden of the Confucian literati elite. The esoteric or occult path of the West never shared this ambiguously positive cachet with its Daoist cousins. The occult side of the Western tradition has always been suspect by both philosophers and theologians for all kinds of reasons, some good and some bad. Western intellectuals were always suspicious that Western occult esotericism was in league with, if not the devil, the most naive kinds of secular and religious superstitions.

My encounters with the vast expanse of the Western esoteric landscape began with some background explorations on the notion of change or process found in various New Age movements. Hence, rather than beginning with the beginning of the Western esoteric tradition—whenever the beginning of Western esotericism could possibly be—I began my explorations at the present moment of the modern esoteric revival. I read carefully Wouter J. Hanegraaff's *The New Age Religion and Western Culture* (1998) in search of the traits of process. As it turns out, New Age religion does have a place for the trait of process in many of its divergent formulations. Themes of change, transformation, and other forms of process are important aspects of the New Age. The very theme of the New Age is one of the progression of old religion into a new religion, the New Age, which places its focus, in varying degrees of emphasis, on the role of personal and social change and transformation. As we have seen, these were also favorite themes in the Daoist tradition at the other end of the Eurasian landmass. As Hanegraaff and other academic students of the New Age and other offshoots of the Western esoteric traditions have documented, the New Age's fascination with the trait of process was shared by many of its antecedents in the history of the Western esoteric landscape.

I framed a research question: How far back and in what form does the trait of process reside in the Western esoteric tradition? Or does the New Age fascination with process simply reflect the fact that the New Age is representative of the rise of process-style thinking in later Western Modernity? It was a fascinating search, but I quickly came to realize that to test any kind of meaningful hypothesis about the place of process in the Western esoteric tradition demanded historical skills beyond anything I could muster at this time. Hence, I decided that I would simply frame a hypothesis for future research. The hypothesis to be tested was this: Does the Western esoteric tradition, broadly conceived, have a more prominent place for the trait of process when compared and contrasted to the more established mainline of Western philosophical and religious history?

If Whitehead was right that the mainline Western intellectual tradition sided with substance worldviews, might not the shadow world of the esoteric arts and magic reveal a more exalted place for process? If the Daoist tradition expresses the yin side of Chinese thought, does the same hold for the Western esoteric tradition? And if the Daoists have found a fecund place for process in their cosmologies, does the same hold for the Western esoteric traditions?

As I quickly discovered, this esotericism is very much like the mainline Confucian metanarrative: the origins of Western esotericism can be tracked back in time about as far as one wants to go. In fact, one can even trace its beginning back to the founding actions of God, which is the historical limit for a theistic cosmology. Kongzi believed that he was teaching the ancient wisdom of the sage-kings, and many Western esoteric masters held a theory that they teach or preserve the ancient wisdom of the very first divine philosophers about the nature and destiny of the cosmos. One version of the Western theory holds that the god Hermes himself imparted celestial wisdom to the earliest teachers of humanity.

There is, of course, a problem in exploring such terrain, because the world of esoteric speculation and praxis is not exactly the elysian fields of Western or Chinese thought. Plato had his cave and a dividing line between real knowledge and mere opinion, and any Confucian gentleman would feel a similar repugnance at delving too deeply into the murky, magical side of Chinese popular religion, wherein all manner of things go bump in the night. Both sober sets of elite scholars call this superstition. In the Western scenario the problem is even more complicated because of the long-standing penchant to label all such countercultures as heretical, if not diabolical.[1]

DEREGULATING RELIGION IN THE MODERN WORLD

Reality and religion have been deregulated in the modern world.[2] Some scholars and theologians have noticed the emergence, or reemergence, of underground traditions identified with the Gnostic, magical, and theosophical strains of Western thought. Wiccan witches have joined the interfaith council of Salem, Massachusetts, in order to promote a better understanding of their neopagan faith. There is a delicious modern irony in the thought of a witch sitting with the descendents of the Puritan divines in Salem discussing interfaith projects. Acceptance of new movements such as Wicca is not found everywhere, and sometimes for good reasons.[3]

The whole field of occult studies is arcane in the extreme. Even the terms used to describe the various commonly identified aspects of the esoteric as part of the occult world are confused. Moreover, although there is a constant appeal to antiquity for many of these traditions, even the term "occult" itself is a nineteenth-century neologism coined by one of the leading French ritual magic revivalists in Paris. Of course, to the outsider gazing into this world of shadows, all the various manifestations of the occult world look like black cows on a very dark night. Nonetheless, there are differences between this quixotic band of roving witches, cunning women and men, magicians, druids, and followers of the New Age, much less postmodern philosophers abjuring the search for static foundationalism. And this just looks at the esoteric side of the Western world, and not the various Chinese manifestations of the mysterious and wonderful.

Alchemy, on the other hand, has been around for some time in European, West Asian, South Asian, and East Asian cultures; it has existed since the classical and medieval periods of all of these foundational forms of Eurasian high culture. Its existence in Europe is a good example of the persistence of esoteric knowledge and tradition in the Western world. Historians of Middle Eastern, Islamic, and Chinese cultures (such as Joseph Needham and Mircea Eliade) have demonstrated that human beings in diverse cultural settings have been fascinated by the lure of the transformations promised by the alchemical crafts.

The field of occult studies, of which alchemy is a part, is contested ground both within and outside its ever-changing boundaries. Let us dwell for a moment on three modern movements: high ritual magic, Wicca, and the New Age. While all three are likely to be lumped together in popular media and communal perception, this "continuity" of form and function is hotly denied by at least two of the three groups. At least in its modern forms, high ritual magic is a relatively recent phenomenon, having its major points of origin in France and England in the nineteenth century. Of course, practitioners of the craft of ritual magic, such as the famous (or infamous) Aleister Crowley (Sutin 2000), argue that they are participating in a much older movement. In fact, many magicians would claim that they are practicing one of the most ancient forms of religion ever devised by human beings—and that the spiritual elementals and spiritual powers have always been humankind's familiars.

The movement that preserves the name "Wicca" is of even more recent origin, at least according to sound academic scholarship (Hutton 1999). But in this case, too, the claim is made that its adherents are reviving the ancient ancestral religion of nature found throughout Europe until its suppression by the Christian church. At least the claim for the struggle between witches and the followers of Judaism and Christianity has solid support in the most ancient of Western religious texts—namely, the Bible. We are instructed to suffer not a witch to live and are enjoined to never practice necromancy. However, modern Wicca's foundational texts are probably mostly of twentieth-century origins.[4]

Could there be some link between those who think that things change and those who hold to their own patch of the Western esoteric tradition? In pondering this question, I read Hanegraaff's *New Age Religion and Western Culture* (1998) with a growing fascination. I had begun with the desire to check whether or not I had misinterpreted the role of New Age Religion in the pluralism of North American spiritual life in another study (Berthrong 1999), and in doing so I recognized a number of persistent themes that run across and through much of the complex phenomena of New Age religion. Not the least of the themes was a proclivity for expressions of process, or at least a willingness to embrace personal and social change and a concomitant fascination with the workings of such change.[5]

Unlike exoteric religious movements, such as Confucianism has always been, esoteric traditions swirl about in a world of magic and secret formulas, incantations, and, according to the orthodox guardians of Western religious sensibilities, even worse kinds of traffic with the forces of darkness and the prince of evil. A case in point is the great Renaissance translator Marsilio Ficino. Ficino was patronized and protected by the Medici family, but even this made the renowned translator/scholar a nervous man. He constantly reaffirmed his devotion to the Catholic Church and argued that the work he was investigating—namely, the newly received Hermetic Corpus—was orthodox. Ficino was well aware of the medieval traditions of esoteric ritual magic and desired to escape the imputation that his work was in any way like the black arts of the Middle Ages. Not even Ficino, with his impressive Medici patron, wanted to be known as a magician; being a magician was dangerous business during much of the history of the Western world.[6]

The Renaissance was a time when origins (and magic) were taken seriously. With all newly recovered Greek texts flooding in from the East, Western scholars lived in a heady time. The Hermetic Corpus offered to take the Western Renaissance scholars back to a period even before Plato and Aristotle. The same spirit lived in these scholars as it would in the leaders of the northern Protestant Reformation. The new texts offered to give scholars access to the most ancient and pristine forms of wisdom. If the Protestant theologians of the next generation would seek to return to the text of the Bible, scholars such as Ficino sought a return to "first philosophy."

Yet as I read more about these matters, I was struck by one strong strain of evidence against my hypothesis of the linkage of esotericism and the trait of process. It became clear to me that most practitioners of the esoteric paths in the West shared the same basic philosophical heritage as their more orthodox colleagues—namely, some form of Neoplatonism. It appears that the default philosophical position of the Western world is Neoplatonism as inherited from and interpreted by Augustine at the end of the classical Greco-Roman world and then modified again and again until challenged by the recovery of some of the texts of Aristotle in the High Middle Ages. Of course, Neoplatonism comes in all flavors, ranging from Plotinus, Proclus, Iamblichus, Damascius, and Augustine to John Scotus Erigena and the theologians of the late medieval world. Until St. Thomas Aquinas began to challenge some aspects of the received wisdom of the West by incorporating the new philosophy of Aristotle and the Arab commentators on "the Philosopher" (Aristotle), a rather essentialist Augustinian Neoplatonism was dominant. Nor did Aquinas ever break completely from Augustine; such a schism would have been unthinkable till much later in Western intellectual history.

With its verities of eternal forms, most Neoplatonic philosophers were not prophets of process, though forms of change were part of their philosophy as the soul moved from the mundane world to more refined steps on the great chain or ladder of being. However, this kind of static essentialism is more a mark of Augustine (see Gunton 1997) than of the late Greco-Roman Neoplatonists such as Iamblichus, Plotinus, Proclus, and Damascius. Although it is almost impossible to reconstruct, all the late Neoplatonists shared a concern for the ritual magic of theurgy, and it is in this world of theurgy that motifs of process and transformation abound (Shaw 1995; Rappe 2000).[7] But theurgy was not something that was passed on to the victorious Christian theologians of late antiquity and the medieval Scholastic masters in the common practice of the faith.

In fact, nervous orthodox religious and secular authorities have suppressed many forms of Western esoterism wherever and whenever they pop up, regardless of the kind of philosophy they expressed. And rise up they do again and again. As with Chinese popular yin-yang theory, every good orthodox teaching demands some heterodoxy in order to give it meaning as part of the dyad of orthodox self and heterodox other. As many scholars of the Western esoteric tradition argue, the New Age, just to mention the most notorious of current esoteric revivals, is simply another in a long list of subterranean religious manifestations latent in Western philosophical and religious culture.

The connection between the esoteric or occult traditions and philosophical traits of process has turned out to be conceptual rather than historical—at least as far as one can tell at this point, based on the best critical historical scholarship. The rhetoric of both the Western occult or esoteric traditions and Western process thought is that of an outsider. Why would this be the case? Take two examples: alchemy and ritual magic. Both alchemy and ritual magic, among countless other dimensions of the esoteric bricolage, are concerned with change and transformation. Things that seem stable are transmogrified from one thing into another. The magus seeks the power to take what is below and turn it into a simulacrum of what is above. The alchemist has learned the secrets of nature and can transform the base into the noble and perhaps even find the secret of eternal life.

Isn't the world of witches, magicians, alchemists, and a stray magus or two far removed from sober philosophical (much less theological) thought? Yes and no. As the Sufis remind us, experience is both sober and drunk. We must also heed Whitehead's salutary injunction that it is the role of philosophy to explain experience rather than indulging in clever feats of explaining away various features of the world that the particular philosopher may not approve of. In short, if there is a Western esoteric tradition that erupts and flourishes from time to time, there ought to be a place for the examination of its claims within the general purview of process thought.

In the main body of this book, I have explored the notion of process thought as part of the naturalist tradition of the last two centuries in North America.[8] Parallel to the world of temperate philosophical study is the world of Western esoteric, occult, theosophical, or magical religion. As I have already noted, there was and is always something suspicious about looking into the history of the occult, esoteric, magical, and theosophical. Nonetheless, there are certain features of the history of occult philosophy, especially beginning with Ramon Llull in the thirteenth century, which merit our attention. First, Llull, who lived and was inspired by the religious and philosophical pluralism of the Spain of his day, helped to introduce Cabala (the Christian version of the Jewish Kabbalah) into Christian theology. His style of thinking had a great impact, as we shall see, on various Renaissance thinkers and, through that tree of learning, down to the world of contemporary New Age religion. While these connections with the Western esoteric tradition may not endear process thought to orthodox Christian theologians, it is an interesting and perhaps not so minor footnote to the expansion of our understanding of the fascination with process themes in Europe and beyond.

One intriguing feature of the occult and esoteric philosophers of early modern Europe is their (relative to the orthodox) ecumenical openness to other philosophical and religious traditions. Although many of these thinkers remained, at least according to their own lights, Christians, they demonstrated a marked willingness to consider dialogue from the Jewish and Islamic worlds as important parts of their intellectual and spiritual agenda. For instance, one of the main features of the early modern occult movement was the creation of a Christian Cabala. Furthermore, there was always an element of spiritual practice in these movements. The more orthodox Christian authorities were always worried that these occult philosophers were too much interested in magic—especially evil ritual magic. However, this element of praxis would have been perfectly comprehensible to various strains of the Chinese tradition—even if the occult worldview would have seemed somewhat odd. But then, Confucians were used to dealing with their Daoist cousins, the occult masters of the Chinese world.

Yet another feature of this story is the link, as demonstrated by Margaret Jacob (1981), between the radical religious esoteric movements of the Renaissance and what she calls the "radical" Enlightenment. The whole Enlightenment project is seen as one that rejects the more fanciful elements of the European Christian traditions, yet, as Jacob shows in quite a bit of detail, there was another side of the early English and Dutch Enlightenment that was tightly connected to the history of the occult via such early modern movements as the Masons and other radical religious movements. The English and Dutch radical religious thinkers had no hesitation in drawing connections between their sense of political transformation and a more dynamic, vital view of nature and the cosmos. Nonetheless, these historical connections are hard to trace because of the nature of many of the secret societies. Because of potentially dangerous conflict with both the political and ecclesial powers of their day, the English, Dutch, and French partisans of the radical Enlightenment were ever so cautious about their public personas, even if they were prolific in their publications denouncing the old order. It is always salutary to remember that Newton was an alchemist as well as the founder of Newtonian science.

The story becomes even more convoluted when we include contemporary fusions of science and religion. Here, as in so many other respects, the figure of Darwin and evolutionary theory cannot be avoided. Just as evolutionary theory caused havoc with orthodox Christian theology, so too did it awaken the trait of process from the long slumbers induced by an Augustinian Neoplatonic fixation on the formless and timeless perfection of the eternal great chain of being, including the unchanging precision of ideas. Many scholars have commented on the impact of evolutionary theory on religion and philosophy. Once evolutionary theory made its impact, related movements such as historicism emerged as well. One common theme of all of these nineteenth-century intellectual movements in North America was, as Bruce Kuklick has written (2001, 160), "The whole of the nineteenth century's emphasis on change and development. . . ." Change and process were back, and Whitehead would give them a final touch in the next generation of Harvard's philosophy department.[9]

One of the themes of the older esotericism was that all of nature is alive. I remember talking with a friend who was a practicing alchemist in San Diego; he told me that plants and even rocks have an emotional life, albeit on a slower time scale than human beings. One of the marks of being alive, as the *Laozi* noted so long ago, is the art of being supple, of changing with circumstances, and of following the spontaneous flow of the Dao. The tide has turned so radically that, for many of these contemporary cosmologists, the Neoplatonic reverie for eternal images of the divine is the truly strange doctrine. Change, transformation, and the effects of history and circumstance now reign where the older unchanging ideas once reigned. Process is supreme.

Why should there be such a close connection between the new cosmology of process and new religious thought in the West? The title of David Noble's *The Religion of Technology: The Divinity of Man and the Spirit of Invention* (1999) shows the new link between religion and the spirit of invention, itself a manifestation of a philosophy and theology of change.

PARADIGM SHIFTS

The realization that we are living in a time of redefinition of many aspects of human culture is not new; process cosmology and a new religious cosmology are emerging. My concern is perhaps even more foundational: the amazing but often unnoticed shift in God-world relations that characterizes the rise of the late modern world. Such a shift, I argue, goes on unabated in late Modernity and into postmodernism regardless of whether we assume that there is something in postmodernism that merits its separation from late modern sensibilities. Robert Neville (1992) has ironically called this historical period "paleo-Galactic," because no one wants to be at the end of anything when it is much more enjoyable to be at the beginning of something new.

As evidence of this particular philosophical and religious paradigm shift, recall the famous article by Robert Bellah (1970), reprinted in *Beyond Belief*, on global religious evolution. Bellah is asking us not to look at changes in specific doctrines or teachings from various religions, in his case most specifically from early modern and modern East Asia and Europe, but at the profound transformation of religious sensibility per se. For an even more provocative example, call to mind David Lodge's fantastical description of the loss of hell by a group of English Roman Catholic graduate students in *The British Museum Is Falling Down*. The characters in Lodge's novel wake up one morning to find that they have lost hell, literally. The very idea of such a place as hell, which the students recognize as part of the religious life-view of their parents and grandparents, has become so alien that they cannot imagine that they have lost hell, because hell no longer makes sense to them.

Bellah argues that one of the chief characteristics of global religion, at least since the axial age (5th Century BCE–6th Century CE), has been the pervasive sense that God or the religious ultimate becomes ever more distant from the world of human beings, leading to doctrines of God as the wholly other. A doctrinal version of this sensibility is the notion of strict transcendence as defined in early modern Christian theology by both Protestants and Catholics (though this pertains to Catholics less so at least in terms of formal academic theology). Strict transcendence means that God is God and does not depend on the world for anything at all, though the world is believed to depend for its very existence on the gracious creation and support of God. Joseph Bracken, in a discussion of Thomas Aquinas's unwillingness to apply Trinitarian theology to God-world relations, writes, "Rather, in line with the philosophy of antiquity as carried forward by Origen and Augustine, he conceived God as the transcendent Creator of the world to be utterly simple and thus lacking in any intrinsic relationship to creation" (Bracken 2001, 182). There are all kinds of philosophical problems, no doubt, with such a monodirectional view of God-world relations, but these will not detain us here.

The real problem is that, along with the ontocosmology of such a rigid view of transcendence, all kinds of other visions of reality trail along in its wake. If God is spirit, for instance, and the world material, and if God is good and the world at best highly suspect, things of material nature are ethically problematical. The rest of the list of problems with the logocentric philosophies and theologies of the West is well known; feminist theologians have been in the forefront in showing how this radical separation of God and the world has induced a denigration of women in general and sexuality in particular. There is a world of pure ideas, the world of men, and then there is the world of women, the world of matter, of dirt, of impurity, and so forth. Study after study has attempted to demonstrate how such a set of views of God-world relations has implacable implications for real women, because women are depicted as more earthly (and therefore, ungodly) in their essential beings. It clearly also has implications for the sexual relations of human beings as well.[10]

Bellah then goes on to note that something is happening to perceptions of God-world relations in late Modernity. Late modern or postmodern people conceive of god-world relations based on a dramatically different model than that of Bellah's Tokugawa neo-Confucian scholars and Puritan New England divines. It is as if, Bellah writes, strict transcendence collapsed sometime after the Enlightenment. Somehow it does not make sense in the twenty-first century that God is absent from the world in the way formulated by the logic of a radical doctrine of divine transcendence. There are flurries of theories that try to explain what has happened. Bellah, for instance, notes that the late modern view of God-world relations now resembles the early religious sensibilities of human beings when the gods and the world were coimplicated in one organic connection. Early modern Western missionaries called this primitive thought, but their great-great-great grandchildren embrace such a view of God-world relations as New Age spirituality. As above, so below, and the two are now intimately *interconnected* once again.

Nonetheless, I need to stress an important caveat here about the trait of transcendence. Whitehead once wisely wrote that an adequate philosophy is one that explains objects and events and does not seek to explain away things that are not initially convivial to the contour of its own categorical system. Just because modernist and postmodernist theologies reject one notion of transcendence does not mean that such new imaginative reconstructions of traditional theology do not need to be able to explain what transcendence meant for Augustine, Aquinas, Duns Scotus, and Calvin—much less Barth and Tillich. However, even in respecting the theological sedimentations of the revered past, we must continue to be bold to explore the alternative logics that lead inevitably to a different bricolage of spiritual discernment. The description and the articulation of present religious experience are just as foundational as historical hindsight into the various trajectories of theological ethics. It is especially important when modern sensibilities appear to be dramatically divergent from the second-order normative prescriptions of classical systematic theology and the ethical injunctions that flow from those classical teachings.

Let us consider another example about paradigmatic worldview shifts. I have found that many of my theological students now deeply appreciate the various teachings of Native American Elders or other representatives of the primal religious traditions of the world. There are obviously a number of reasons why this is the case, but I believe that worldview transformation is very much part of the picture. The reason for this is that many Native America Elders enunciate, in highly diverse forms, a worldview wherein the divine reality and the mundane world are part of a continuum of interaction and intersubjective self-formation that fuses the immanent and transcendent inextricably. This sense of the absolute connection of the divine and the quotidian is immensely appealing to my students, because it is the way the world functions as they now see it. A completely transcendent deity simply no longer makes sense to them. When they read Calvin or Barth, the early and late modern Christian acceptance and worship of a totally transcendent deity expressed in their writings does not fit the student's sense of God-world relations. The Native Elders better express their understanding of God-world relations than many early modern Christian theological giants. In short, my students have felt a need to readjust their notions of what constitutes transcendence in a fashion that appreciates rather than disregards the spiritual teachings of the primal religions of North America (and of other parts of the world as well).

This kind of interfaith encounter, of course, is problematic for the more conservative and orthodox Christian students when they realize that they actually rather appreciate what the Native traditions have to teach on some topics, especially in ecological theology and ethics. They express a sense of considerable cognitive dissonance when they realize that the Elders make more sense than Christian theologians when the conversation moves to respect for the natural world. One of the components of being bathed in the acids of modernity is to encounter alternative worldviews; but more than mere encounter, there is a willingness nowadays to take the worldview of the radical "other" seriously. What is going on here? I would say that this probably has something to do with the relationship of their worldview to what they believe the Christian churches have everywhere and always taught. The easiest way out of the predicament for my perplexed students comes when I try to show that their relationships to a religion and to a specific cosmological worldview are not always the same thing; I explain that worldviews qua philosophical doctrines come and go, whereas the great axial age religions have demonstrated a tremendous staying power. Christians, for instance, have made use of Stoic, Neoplatonic, Aristotelian, and various early modern philosophies in their theologies and can certainly make effective use of different or new philosophical traditions when the need arises.

At least one thing that links all these variegated forms of discourse for my students is that these diverse worldviews, as alternative cosmologies, have a place of honor for the philosophical trait of process.[11] In this embrace of process my students sense a connection between ancient Daoist texts, the teaching of Native Elders, and contemporary process thought. Can the world of alchemy, of esoteric transformations of the person, be far behind? The age of process may indeed usher in a new age even more profoundly different in terms of worldviews than most New Age religionists can even imagine.

NOTES

1. INTRODUCTION

1. The *Analects* is the most authoritative text for the early thought of Kongzi.

2. In Mahayana Buddhism in China, debates about the trait of process abound, perhaps because of the Chinese transformation of Buddhism via dialogue with Confucians and Daoists. The Buddha would probably have thought any extended discussion of the notion of process was another metaphysical question not conducive to liberation. The Buddha might even be correct in his rejection of such metaphysical speculation for the religious path. The intense debates about the question of change, of illusion, or of judgment itself suffuse the writings of the grand philosophical schools of Tang dynasty Chinese Buddhism such as Tiantai and Huayan. As Brook Ziporyn (2000) has shown in his study of Tang and Northern Song Tiantai masters, this question of the basis of axiology was the focus of a great deal of intense theoretical speculation and praxis. It was these kinds of debates within the world of Tang and Song Buddhist circles that have led scholars to argue that we cannot even conceive of Song *daoxue* apart from the stimulation of Buddhist elite philosophy. In fact, the Buddha had little time for metaphysical debates per se. He argued that there were two classes of arguments that could never be answered. The first set were questions that in principle cannot ever be answered, such as the question of whether or not the world has a beginning or end in time. The second was something like how many grains of sand are there to be found along the banks of Ganges River—an empirical question that is simply very hard to give an accurate answer to. This second kind of profitless question could be updated to ask, how many fundamental (and not so fundamental) particles make up the universe? There might be a discrete answer, but we can never be sure that we will have the technology needed to give the correct or proper answer at any given moment. Moreover, the Buddha went much further. These kinds of questions that are so dear to the mind-heart of a philosopher simply are not conducive in the search for the proper means of liberation from samsara. The Buddha was a preacher or enlightened teacher and not a philosopher. His aim was liberation from suffering and not the discussion of metaphysical and other kinds of philosophical issues, although his followers in both South Asia and East Asia became some of the most sophisticated and astute metaphysicians the world has ever known.

3. Kaufman (1993) makes the interesting point that we already live in a complex world that gives the lie to the notion of strong relativity among different religions. Kaufman notes that all the various historical religions of humankind are engaged in intense dialogue with each other as mediated by the globalizing forces of Modernity. Hence the theologian can no longer affirm either a stance of strict separation of the religions or a complete relativism.

4. Patton and Ray (2000) have reprinted Smith's essay on the magic of comparison and assembled a set of responses to the questions raised by Smith's work as well as Smith's own further reflections on the uses and abuses of the comparative method in philosophy and religious studies.

5. Having cast stones at the opaque house of philosophy, I think modern Western (and hence most Christian) theology hardly fares any better. For instance, Radical Orthodoxy, a new player on the block, is a perfect example of historical bricolage built up around rummaging within one tradition in order to become postmodern. In the name of restoring the historical truths of the Christian faith, Radical Orthodox theologians (such as John Milbank) root around in the history of the Christian movement, flying from century to century in search of the timeless truth of revealed religion. There is even a subtext within Radical Orthodoxy of unmasking those dupes who helped the pristine Christian faith go astray by whoring after other gods—in this case, certain late medieval theologians and various early Enlightenment philosophers; good Radical Orthodox theologians are set on getting the train back on the right track. But what if the new track is designed by and built with Buddhist and Shinto sensibilities by Japanese engineers in a Shanghai factory? Theology is always so selective. No one wants to bring everything back; I doubt that even the Radical Orthodox want to return to religious murders, burnings at the stake, the water test for witches, the theological defense of slavery, and other charming and creative forms of ecclesial mayhem. Sometimes statements issued by the Vatican also play this game of cut-and-paste. Bits of scripture and snippets of older papal documents are presented as the always-present and never-changing breath of the Holy Spirit. The whole enterprise of Radical Orthodoxy in both its Protestant and Catholic forms seems like whistling past the graveyard. What is sad is the lack of faith in human reason, creativity, and the movement of history. Of course, the Radical Orthodox will retort by saying that all of these appeals are to outmoded forms of Modernity that must be rejected out of hand. But the real question remains, what are your methods and principles of selection in philosophy and theology, especially when the vision is cross-cultural in scope?

6. In the modern West, Alfred North Whitehead taught that the trait of process qua creativity thematized the idea of change. Moreover, Whitehead then went on to assert that the idea of process, which should have been a vital trait in any adequate philosophical system, has been shortchanged or elided in much of the history of Western philosophy in favor of metaphysics that privileged substance over process. Late in his life Whitehead wrote book after book to rectify this oversight and return the trait of process to its rightful place of honor in the standard lexicon of philosophy. Furthermore, a number of scholars, beginning with Joseph Needham in the second volume of the vast *Science and Civilisation in China* project (1954–), have noted that the Daoist and Confucian traditions in China (and by extension, in Korea and Japan) always have acknowledged the key role of process in the works of

many different philosophers over twenty-five hundred years. Studies of the classical Confucian Xunzi, of Daoist intellectual history with a special focus on the late *Liezi* text, and of the Southern Song Confucian *daoxue* of Zhu Xi and Chen Chun have convinced me that Needham was correct in his estimation of the importance and centrality of themes of process in various segments of the Chinese philosophical and religious traditions.

7. Buchler was the last in the line of the classical American naturalist tradition as I shall define this broad set of American philosophical traditions (1974, 1990). The concept of a natural complex was the capstone of Buchler's philosophical corpus. As we shall see, however, Buchler's notion of the trait of process as a natural complex does not resemble Whitehead's theory of process very much save for the fact that Buchler sees human culture as the achievement of human processes within a vastly larger domain of other natural processes or complexes. Rather like Whitehead's early student, Dorothy Emmet (1992), Buchler saw the need to speak cogently about the role of process in the natural world but was not moved to adopt Whitehead's elaborate cosmology in order to buttress the trait of process as part of what Emmet called the passage of nature.

8. The most famous example of such an exploration of process and creativity is the collective work of the team of David Hall and Roger Ames. They published a series of important works (see the reference section) in order to defend the processive nature of many famous Chinese texts and traditions.

9. A major lacuna in my presentation is my unwillingness to expand my exploration of Chinese sources to include texts from the vast world of Chinese Buddhism. This is an especially egregious flaw in anyone studying the rise and flourishing of neo-Confucianism. I confess that so much has already been done in the study of Chinese Buddhist thought that I do not believe that I could, as a nonspecialist, add much of interest. Therefore, I would refer readers to publications by experts in Buddhist studies for reflections on this issue. However, and this has been noted by many scholars of Chinese Buddhism (including those in Korea and Japan), I do agree that the Chinese proclivity for finding a prominent role for the trait of process is manifested in various schools of Buddhism as much as in Confucian and Daoist texts.

10. I have decided to call the contemporary period of modern Western philosophy "Modernity". Although I am not fond of capitalizing too many terms, Modernity probably deserves special treatment. Other students of the phenomenon of "Modernity" have noticed that there is no one term that defines what authors mean when they try to talk about the "modern" Western world. Of course, the main reason for such problems in nomenclature is that we are still living in the modern world, even if we embrace the concept of the postmodern. It is always hard to know what to make of one's own time in relation to the past and the future.

11. I need to add immediately that Rescher has a high opinion of Whitehead's philosophical contributions. The point Rescher wants to reinforce is that no one philosopher stands alone, even if he or she does become famous for pinpointing some new feature of our self-reflective world.

12. As any student of Chinese thought knows, the terms "Daoism", "Buddhism" and "Confucianism" are themselves products of Modernity. They are Western terms for diverse Chinese intellectual realities. Of course, Chinese intellectuals have a

robust history of philosophical and religious typology themselves. However, in the ecumenical scholarly world of the twenty-first century, the terms "Daoist", "Buddhist" and "Confucian" make as much sense to colleagues in Beijing, Hong Kong, and Taipei as they do in London, Paris, Boston, and Berkeley.

13. The choice of the *Liezi* is not as odd as it might at first seem. Of course, the obvious choices would be the *Laozi*, the *Zhuangzi*, or the *Huainanzi*—texts much better known both in China and in the West. However, the *Liezi* has been accepted as one of the principal early Daoist texts, though the text as we now have it has always been somewhat suspect. The general scholarly consensus is that our present received text is a later forgery. Clearly, much of the material of the text has been lifted from the *Zhuangzi*. Most scholars now believe the text was finally assembled after the fall of the Han dynasty, and perhaps even as late as the fourth century CE. But this very textual problem is also a blessing. The *Liezi*, hence, represents a work nicely situated between the early writings of Xunzi and those of Zhu Xi, not only temporally but also because of its obvious Daoist leanings. It helps that there is also a brilliant English translation of the text by A. C. Graham (1986a), arguably the finest sinologist of his generation and also an astute philosopher. And finally, like the *Zhuangzi*, the *Liezi* is a thoroughly entertaining read.

14. It is always dangerous to assert that some newly noticed trait in philosophical discourse is really anything new at all. Jacques Barzun (2000), hardly a proponent of politically correct multiculturalism, has written that most of the seeds of twentieth-century thought and sensibilities derive from the last decade of the nineteenth century and the first decade of the twentieth century. The stuff of life, according to Barzun, has been transformed into the stream of life, of movement, of process, if you will. To make his point, Barzun, quotes William James as saying, "The most notable and influential chapter was James's redefinition of the mind. It is 'first of all a stream. Chain or train does not express it; it flows'" (Barzun 2000, 660). This Jamesian stream that flows comes to define the nature of the mind-heart, literature, and common speech. The rush to embrace change, transformation, or process as an essential philosophical motif was first codified in the *Principles of Psychology*; moreover, Whitehead was a great fan of James; and one suspects he would have appreciated the work of scholars such as Buchler, Lakoff , Johnson, and Damasio (1994, 1999, 2003) in second-generation cognitive science and philosophy, and modern cosmologists such as Swimme and Berry (1992, 1996).

15. A scholar make a choice in calling the tradition(s) in question "Cabala" or "Kabbalah". I will use "Cabala" to indicate the Christian appropriation of a major medieval Jewish religious movement.

16. I also focus on the Confucian tradition because of my desire to respond to the work of Hall and Ames over the last two decades (1987, 1995, 1998, 2001). Hall and Ames have completed a series of jointly authored books focusing on early Chinese thought; the range of their work includes both Western and Chinese philosophy, but the "one thread" that holds it all together is the Confucian tradition. My citation of Kongzi's enigmatic comment that his thought is held together by one thread—which he does not actually define—is apropos of the work of Hall and Ames. They make a number of important and controversial points in the context of developing a sophisticated intercultural history and hermeneutic of philosophy. In his earlier writings, Hall (1973) was known as a skilled exegete of Whitehead's philosophy. However,

Hall moved beyond a scholarly exposition of various features of Whitehead's thought, specifically a philosophy of human culture, and toward his own philosophical vision. Hall's early work, which influences his later contributions to his joint cooperation with Ames, is definitely part of the world of process thought (Hall 1982a, 1982b).

I will revisit these points later in my arguments about the role of process in Chinese thought. However, I want to applaud one aspect of the Hall and Ames collaboration immediately. Hall and Ames strive to make us all aware that classical Chinese Confucianism is not just some truncated version of Western social ethics or simplified pragmatism. They defend the strong thesis that Chinese thought, for a number of reasons, is structured and articulated in ways different from the mainstream of Western European thought. There are the obvious historical and geographical reasons I have already noted; but Hall and Ames press farther by arguing that we miss a great deal about the unique character of Chinese thought when we do not attend carefully to its different way of viewing the world. For instance, Ames and Hall contend that rather than being a philosophical tradition focused on static substances, there is a process sensibility in Chinese thought that must be understood; otherwise we simply miss the point that thinkers such as Kongzi, Mengzi, and Xunzi want to make in terms of presenting their Confucian worldview.

17. Edward Slingerland (2003) has recently been using Lakoff and Johnson's theories of metaphor in his studies of classical Chinese texts both in a major study of the notion of *wuwei* 無為 (uncontrived action) and in the analysis of a number of other major Chinese philosophical figures.

18. The case of Vietnam is much less clear. Many scholars have assumed that Vietnam, because of its close connections with the Chinese empire for over two thousand years, must have been strongly influenced by Confucian thought. Some contemporary scholars urge a contrary view. They claim that the Confucian influence on Vietnam was not nearly as strong as that felt in Korea or Japan. However, serious research on the development of Vietnamese Confucianism is only now beginning in earnest.

19. Thomé H. Fang (1981, 109) strongly agrees with Mou's interpretation, and in fact makes extensive uses of Whitehead's process philosophy in his explanation of the development of what he calls the primordial Confucian tradition. "Metaphysically, the philosophy of change is a system of dynamic ontology based upon the process of creative creativity as exhibited in the incessant change of time as well as a system of general axiology wherein the origin and development of the idea of the Supreme Good is shown in the light of comprehensive harmony." Fang could hardly have made the point more strongly.

20. Among American theologians with a strong interest in pragmatism and naturalism, Gordon Kaufman (1993, 2004) has been a strong voice in promoting a more naturalistic philosophical and theological vision. He has come to champion the notion of creativity in three broad senses as responsible ways for modern theologians to deploy God-language in the modern world. First, we are all children of the great first act of creation, the big bang of the cosmologists that in itself remains a grand mystery and yet iconic as an act of pure creativity. Second, human beings are resolutely biocultural creatures who are part and parcel of the created order. Third, human beings also follow what Kaufman calls cultural or social trajectories; religion and morality are such trajectories and are prime exemplars of

the human contribution to the mystery of creativity. While creativity is not to be identified with the trait of process per se, Kaufman represents, along with fellow theologian Robert Corrington, a religious sensibility that connects and articulates a naturalist perspective.

21. For one of best discussions of the nature of Chinese religion in general and Confucianism in particular, see Yu (2005). While Yu notes that his work will not put an end to what has been an endless debate, his small book does go a long way in clarifying many of the issues involved in the complex debate over the centuries.

22. Kongzi, according to Lewis, was one of these teachers beyond the immediate control of the state who became famous teachers of various versions of the Dao—although his own tradition notes that the master did occasionally serve his domain as a minister with various portfolios. The *Analects* represents the beginnings of the tradition of one Warring States intellectual lineage. However, what distinguishes the Ruist followers of Kongzi from the other schools qua extended discourse lineages is that they did arise from the larger pool of *ru* as ritual masters and teachers. This gave the proto-Confucians a pool of possible recruits to their version of literate *ru* culture. Furthermore, because of their mastery of ritual and the ritual texts, there was always a local market for these *ru*. The other famous lineages of the Warring States period cut their intellectual teeth in distancing themselves from the *ru* scholars qua proto-Confucians.

23. I have always found it somewhat curious and instructive that many of the most famous *ru* scholars seemed to have had a sharp sense of identity when confronted with the indigenous and foreign schools. For instance, the great Tang thinker Han Yu (768–824) became famous for denouncing Buddhism and arguing for a return to the classical culture of the Warring States (de Bary, Bloom, and Lufrano 1999–2000, I: 568–86). Moreover, Han Yu's curriculum for this proposed reform made use of the traditional Han Confucian classics as well as the works of selected later Confucian thinkers (Bol 1992). At least Han Yu knew that he was not a Buddhist. In the Southern Song dynasty, Chen Chun, the disciple of Zhu Xi, was equally aware that he was not a Buddhist—or a Daoist, for that matter. As we have seen, he included sections in his philosophical glossary that sought to refute the philosophies of the Buddhists and Daoists. Chen certainly had a very robust *ru* identity.

24. Ben-Ami Scharfstein (1989), among others, has noted that once the theme of relativism, even in the mild form of ordinal naturalism (Ross 1980), has been entertained, then it becomes an outrider for a more radical form of philosophical skepticism and relativism. This, at least, is a contested teaching Confucians took from their readings of Daoist texts such as the *Zhuangzi* and the *Liezi*. I would go one step further and add the traits of pluralism and of process to Scharfstein's list of thematic camp followers of relativism and skepticism.

The implications and entailments that weave process, pluralism, relativism, and (sometimes) skepticism together in Chinese and Western philosophies of process are virtually impossible to untangle. For instance, one argument is that we are talking across philosophical domains—we are committing all manner of category mistakes. Second-order reflections on the traits of process, relativism, skepticism, and pluralism belong to the disciplines of speculative philosophy. In short, to decide that the world is pluralistic and processive, much less realistic, is to utter classical ontological or cosmological statements, which in turn are grounded in doctrines or insights into what is taken to be the ultimately real "something" of the cosmos. The other extreme would be to declare the universe a static block of just one infinite and eternal substance understood as completely and splendidly sui generis.

25. Many students of comparative philosophy and the history of religion are dubious about synchronic claims for ideas jumping, like a forest fire, from one cultural epoch or culture to another (Christian 1987). There is a much stronger concern for the cultivation of careful diachronic historical studies that focus on one school, person, tradition, or cultural area even while acknowledging that comparison is an inevitable part of the intellectual enterprise. But Scharfstein still does have a point that when one begins innocently with a realistic pluralism, both weak and strong forms of relativism and skepticism often follow. Moreover, in the case of the Chinese examples I have chosen, there is also a concomitant concern for exploring a range of possibilities for the trait of process.

26. One of the first descriptions of Mou's thought can be found in Thomas Metzger's (1977) study of Chinese intellectual history, in my 1979 dissertation, and, in even more careful and rich detail, in Matthew A. Levey's 1991 study of the complex structure of Zhu Xi's philosophy.

2. XUNZI

1. There is a great deal of debate over the question of how to parcel out the periods of Chinese thought. In other publications (Berthrong 1998a, 2000), I have argued that what is universally considered the golden age of Chinese thought comes to an end with the unification of the Qin empire. While many other scholars, and for good reasons, will argue that one also needs to include the Han dynasty (206 BCE–221 CE) as part of the golden age, I have always been persuaded that the Han period is not a part of the classical age, even if there is a great deal of continuity between the end of the Zhou and the rise of the Han. Since Xunzi probably died just at the transition point between the old world of the Zhou and the new imperial world of the Qin and Han, I locate him as one of the last of the great classical thinkers.

To begin with Xunzi 荀子 (ca. 310–210 BCE) as a paragon of process might seem somewhat strange, based on the standard interpretation of his place at the end of the first great classical age of Chinese philosophy. He has always been something of an enigma within the Confucian tradition, and most pointedly since the Song revaluation (or better, devaluation) of his status in the Confucian Way almost a millennium after his death.

2. Legalist philosophers such as Hanfeizi and politicians such as Li Si, who ended life as a minister for the Qin empire, denounced their Confucian teacher on both pragmatic and ideological grounds. First, Li Si and Hanfeizi argued that Confucianism was a failure because rulers could not bring peace to the feuding Chinese multistate world by endlessly repeating Confucian moral bromides. If a Warring States ruler wanted to rule the entire Chinese world, then he would have to forgo the pleasures of Confucian ethical self-cultivation in favor of Legalist rigor in social policy. Second, Li and Han disputed their teacher's basic conviction that only morality and correct ritual action could provide the basis for restoring order to the chaos of late Warring States China. Rather than babble on endlessly about the wonders of ethical rule, a ruler needed to remember one basic fact: People like pleasure and fear

pain, and political control meant ruthlessly applying this psychological insight to the empire based on strict laws based on this sober assessment of human character.

3. Mou Zongsan, as the most systematic philosopher of his generation of New Confucian public intellectuals, adds another interpretive note to the concept of concern consciousness as one distinctive root metaphor for Confucian culture. He does so in a series of publications in the 1960s and 1970s. Mou argues that the distinctive root metaphor qua categorical articulation is moral metaphysics (Mou Zongsan, 1983, 1990, 1994), a relational cosmology governed by creativity itself as manifested in the active reason of the mind-heart of the sage. Mou contends that this typical Confucian philosophical sensibility of a moral metaphysics emerges most clearly in the thought of Mengzi. Although Mou places Xunzi outside of the Mencian mainline or taproot of the cumulative Confucian tradition, he concedes that Xunzi still represents, albeit in an idiosyncratic way, characteristic Confucian claims about concern for self and others and the creative relationship of intersubjectivity as the basis for the human person. Mou actually allows for the fact that Xunzi follows a distinctive line of thought that can be traced through the text of the *Great Learning* and into the work of Cheng Yi and Zhu Xi in the Song period. On Mou's reading, Zhu Xi's grand Song synthesis, although always taken to be a pure representation of Mengzi, is really much more in sync with Xunzi's worldview. And finally, Mou is explicit in defending the thesis that there is a strong religious dimension to be found in all forms of classical Confucian thought, a dimension of what Mou calls "vertical transcendence."

4. While it would be enjoyable to review Xunzi's place in the development of early Chinese thought, there are sufficient fine intellectual and philosophical histories of this period that can be consulted—such as those by Wing-tsit Chan (1963), A. C. Graham (1989), Benjamin Schwartz (1985), Chad Hansen (1992), Paul Rakita Goldin (1999), T. C. Kline III and Philip J. Ivanhoe (2000), and Janghee Lee (2005)—for an overview of Xunzi's place in early Chinese thought. These works will explain how Xunzi interacted with Legalists, Daoists, Moists, other Confucians, and what the Chinese call the "hundred schools" of the Warring States world. Although somewhat overlooked in the early Western study of classical Chinese thought, more and more competent students of Chinese thought are looking again at Xunzi's philosophical achievement.

5. Lee (2005) has an excellent discussion of how to understand the naturalism of Xunzi's complex philosophical vision.

6. The Chinese text for the first part of the discussion of and quotes from Xunzi is found in Jiyu Ren's (1979) edited four-volume history of Chinese philosophy. Like many mainland scholars of his generation, Ren has the highest regard for Xunzi. It is always interesting to see how a Chinese Marxist reads a Confucian master. Many of the things that made Xunzi a black sheep of the classical Confucian world made him much more acceptable to Marxist historians. The broad outlines of Ren's exegesis comport well with the solid Chinese scholarship for the last few decades—if we discount the obligatory Marxist tags inserted into the narrative during from the Maoist era. However, Professor Ren remained a committed Marxist—and Marxists, in their own fashion, are also philosophically concerned to show how process and transformation are important aspects of the ideology of any important mode of production.

There is also now a magisterial complete translation and study of Xunzi in English. Between 1988 and 1994 John Knoblock published his translations of Xunzi with extensive commentary and exegetical notes. All scholars of classical Chinese thought are in Knoblock's debt. More recently we also have the work of A. S. Cua (1985) on Xunzi's epistemology; Edward J. Machle (1993) on Xunzi's theories about nature and heaven; Paul Rakita Goldin (1999) on Xunzi's philosophical achievement; and a fine set of interpretive essays on various aspects of his thought edited by T. C. Kline III and Philip J. Ivanhoe (2000).

7. Much later, Hu Shi, one of the great modernizers of the study of Chinese philosophy, wrote, "In short, this naturalistic conception of the universe and life is not necessarily devoid of beauty, of poetry, or moral responsibility, and of the fullest opportunity for the exercise of the creative intelligence of man" (Cheng and Bunnin 2002, 87). Although a stringent critic of traditional Confucianism, Hu, along with Xunzi, Zhu Xi, and Mou, agrees on the vertical power of the Sinitic worldview.

8. The whole question of borrowing and influence in Warring States texts is perplexing both in terms of theory and in terms of the facts on the ground—or in the ground, as the case may be (Puett 2001, 2002). We are rarely clear when we use terms such as "borrowing" or "influence" when we talk about how ideas or terms wander from one thinker to another. The only way we can be clear about such migrations would be if the author told us directly that he or she was borrowing an idea from another thinker and in what fashion. Of course, this does happen all the time. But even when we find such transparent confession of intellectual borrowing, postmodernists muddy the water again and question our ability to know what the first author really meant, and even if we knew what the first author intended, would it really matter to later readers? What is important, they say, is how the reader makes use of what is read and appropriated in his or her own lifeworld.

9. One of the more interesting features of the study of classical China these days is that more and more archaeological finds are enriching our corpus of early Chinese texts. When new highways are built or shopping malls constructed, new texts have, from time to time, turned up—literally. These texts are showing us all kinds of new links between different thinkers in the classical period. Without these new texts we formerly had to guess about who was writing what and when. For instance, we now know that the early Daoist texts such as the *Laozi* have a textual history that is much more ancient that we had previously believed. Similar kinds of new perspectives have also emerged for Confucian studies. Formerly it was assumed that the attribution of a text like the *Zhongyong* to the immediate family and disciples of Kongzi was a pious legend. We are no longer sure. Newly discovered texts indicate that the *Zhongyong* might just have had it origins very early in the history of the development of the Warring States *rujia* 儒家 (The School of Ru).

Old exegetical tests for the dating of documents have to be reexamined with all the new texts being found almost daily in China. One of the rules I was taught when I began my study of Chinese philosophy in the 1960s was that, if a text is philosophically sophisticated, it must be late. If we find a complicated cosmology embedded in a text, for instance, I was taught to consider seriously whether this was not later added by the hand of a redactor. This addition of later materials need not have been carried out, I was assured, with any malice of forethought on the part of the redactor. The later editor might sincerely have believed, being part of the later lineage of the text, the he (and it probably was "he" in classical China) was adding useful material or an explanation of something that was obscure in the ur-text. What is wondrous to behold is the ever-expanding map of the intellectual history of China that is now available to the international scholarly world. So, although I still assume that the trait of stillness has a Daoist pedigree for Xunzi, even the idea of stillness might indeed turn out to have been a part of the Confucian tradition for longer than anyone previously anticipated (Yearley 1980, 465–480). If complexity of philosophical discourse has now been proved to be much older than previously suspected, why not a Confucian appreciation of the stillness of the mind-heart as Xunzi explained it in "Dispelling Blindness"? From the systematic side, it really does not always matter where the idea first came from; it is what the philosopher does with the concept that is critical.

10. What we now know, based on the most extensive study of the topic by Christoph Harbsmeier's 1998 contribution to *Science and Civilisation*, is that Chinese scholars periodically evinced interest in rhetoric and informal and formal logic (see also Lloyd and Sivin 2002). The most important of these in terms of formal logic would be what is called the neo-Moist texts and later Buddhist studies of logical texts imported from India. Chinese scholars were perfectly capable of formulating sophisticated logics, as witness the recent studies by scholars such as Harbsmeier and Graham on the Moist logical texts. It is still an interesting comparative question as to why the study of logic did not become as pronounced in China as it did in the Western world. Of course, for a Confucian such Xunzi, it would have been difficult to admit that he was borrowing directly and positively the material of countertradition such the logical texts of the Moist school.

11. Xunzi had a complex and controversial theory of human tendencies or nature. He had, according to his own lights and in contrast to the other deluded Confucians of his day (and much less thinkers such as Mozi, Zhuangzi, and Laozi), a very clear understanding of the difference between nature as the natural order or environment of human life and the conscious role of *wei* 偽 as human contrivance. Even the term Xunzi chose to explain the special role of sage wisdom in founding humane conduct and civilized society was rhetorically loaded. The term *wei* often means something which is false, such as in *weishu* 偽書 (falsely compiled books). Laozi had his *wuwei* 無為 (uncontrived action), but Xunzi wanted to contrast this with his ideal of contrived action in the positive sense of the sage actually understanding the Great Ordering Principle and then doing something about it. This was contrived or human action done in conformity to moral dictates and would eventuate in rites conducive to human flourishing. For a brilliant study of Xunzi's notion of human nature, see Stalnaker (2006).

12. Mou is aware that the flowering of speculation on the trait of active reason only comes much later in the Song and Ming dynasties, but he is adamant that its roots were to be found in the soil of classical China—albeit in an imperfect form in Xunzi's texts. The mind-heart of the sage, having overcome the delusions and obstructions of the natural world, which is the common fate of all humankind, as Xunzi taught, is able to become the constructive molder of correct social conduct. The sage reacts to and sees the proper order of the world because the sage is no longer blinded by the power of false passions or even partial truths. Not that the sage has some kind of paranatural ocular powers or sense of smell or touch or any other form of sensory perception; the sage is merely dealing realistically with the world of Dao as a set of natural complexes.

13. In this regard I have found Xu Fuguan (Xu 1975) and Liang Qixiung (Liang 1962, 1974) especially useful because of the fact that they epitomize the best early modern critical Chinese scholarship on Xunzi's work. Parenthetically, Xu notes that Xunzi is not directly concerned with what Mencius said about human nature, even though Xunzi is critical of the Second Sage. Xu believes that Xunzi did not have the received text of the *Mengzi* although he would have been familiar with the Mencian oral tradition from his residence at the famed—and perhaps fabled (Lloyd and Sivin, 2002)—Jixia Academy.

14. Liang is suggesting, among other things, that there is a parallelism between how Xunzi is reshaping the meaning of *e* and *wei* in directions that are designed to make his philosophical point rhetorically. As I noted above, the term *wei* was not a graph with purely positive connotations; any student of Chinese thought has run into the common bibliographical category of *weishu* (forged books). But as Liang observes, following the earlier commentary of Yang Liang (ca. 818), *wei* in Xunzi's thought means conscious and reflective human activity. Its balance shifts from the negative to the positive. But does this work for *e*? Does simply moving to the meaning "simple" or "coarse" really parallel the other semantic shift? This would be harder to defend, because, as we have also already seen, Xunzi is not a particular fan of the simple or rustic state. It is the role of the sage via contrived action to reform and polish the dull jewel of the human-mind heart.

15. The complexity of semantic differentiation is an important point (Puett 2001; Kline and Ivanhoe 2000). It might well have been the case that Xunzi was not using the emerging Confucian philosophical lexicon in the same way Mengzi had. For instance, A. C. Graham (1986a, 7–66), in a classic article on the Mencian theory of human nature, has shown that there was a great deal of semantic shape-shifting going on with both *xing* and *qing*. Later Song *daoxue* Confucian scholars were prone to interpret *qing* as "emotion," "passions," and "desire," whereas it really has the meaning of something like "the way things really are" in the classical period of Confucian philosophical discourse. This is one reason that the Song *daoxue* scholars had problems in reading Xunzi; it did not occur to them that their common term for the passions or emotions was not used in the same fashion in the Warring States period.

16. Although it arrived to late for me to incorporate its numerous insights into this chapter, I would urge that anyone interested in Xunzi (and comparative philosophy and theology) consult Aaron Stalnaker *Overcoming Our Evil: Human Nature and Spiritual Exercises in Xunzi and Augustine* (2006).

17. When we think about the "later kings" as he calls them, we must ask, "And how do we know them?" We have the records of the sage-kings and are able to check their sense of discrimination against our own. The rites as shared patterns of human interaction, such as a majestically complex court ceremony, like everything else unique to human society, become the gift of language, both spoken and written. It is language, as the supreme form of making distinctions, that separates us from the other animals. We are human because we are social, and we are social because of language. It is language and the culture of remembered language that gives us the social memory to transmit ritual distinctions from one generation to another.

Of course, there was one other problem. There was also a hallowed tradition among Confucian intellectuals that recognized the expressive limitations of language.

In the Great Commentary of the *Yijing*, it says (I paraphrase), that writing or written records do not completely match the spoken word, and even the spoken word does not perfectly express the ideas of the speaker. Nonetheless, one of the things that we do have is the written record of the sage-kings. Although they would not have put it this way, I think that the early Confucians would have approved of Justus Buchler's division of the modes of discourse into the assertive, exhibitive, and active modes of query. The sages did not only leave their written records but were equally memorialized for the quality of their lives as examples of how to speak and exhibit the graceful qualities of civilized conduct and ritually appropriate actions.

18. In what follows I rely on the work of Michael Puett in his *The Ambivalence of Creation: Debates Concerning Innovation and Artifice in Early China* (2001). Puett has carefully outlined the problems that early Chinese philosophers encountered when they tried to think of what creation meant as a technical philosophical term. Simplifying Puett's account, Xunzi had to address at least three other philosophers in framing his own account of creating. First, he had to find a way to work around Kongzi's strictures against a too robust version of creating new things just for the sake of novel creation. Second, he had to respond the challenge of the Moist philosophers. And third, he had to address Mengzi's views about the nature of the sage's creativity.

19. Ivanhoe argues that Mengzi and Xunzi actually share the inventory of Confucian virtues, ritual actions, and social obligations necessary for human flourishing. The argument is how we steam and shape the crooked timber of humanity. "Thus, a warped piece of wood must first await application of the press-frame, steam to soften it, and force to bend its shape before it can be made straight. A dull piece of metal must first be whetted on the grindstone before it can be made sharp" (Knoblock 1988–94, 3:151). Ivanhoe defines the real debate about human nature between the two Confucian masters in these terms: "Whereas Mengzi saw these practices and obligations as the refined manifestations of our nascent moral nature, Xunzi viewed them as wholly *artificial*, the accumulated wisdom of past sages" (Ivanhoe 2000, 33). As scholars have noticed before, the task of gathering together the conventions of sage wisdom into an accumulation of virtue is essential for the moral task of reforming human nature.

20. Van Norden provides a subtle reading of Xunzi's argument by positing that Xunzi actually builds on Mengzi's argument about desire and approval. Earlier, Van Norden states that if Aristotle defines humanity in terms of reason, Mencius defines humanity in terms of evaluation. For Mengzi, we are evaluative animals, and the process of evaluation is based on the dialectic of desire and approval. But from Xunzi's point of view, at least when seeking moral judgment, "no amount of desire can override approval. Approval simply trumps desire" (Kline and Ivanhoe 2000, 124). But because desire is such a strong force in human life, "one must be *trained* to delight in ritual and morality" (123).

21. Wong likes Van Norden's hypothesis, but he does not think that it will work to answer the question of the sage-kings' creation of good rituals and proper names. The key is rather that "Xunzi is attempting to show how human beings could transform themselves into moral beings when their original nature is to seek the immoral. The basis for the transitions is precisely this seeking after what they lack" (Kline and Ivanhoe 2000, 144). The sage, therefore, can use the evaluative sense of the lack of the

good to seek after the good. Wong offers an alternative interpretation: "For Xunzi the desire to do good and the sense of duty are not original to human nature but derived from calculation on what is in our self-interest" (145). But this just extends the chain a bit farther, because Wong notes that we then have to ask "how self-interest turns into love of and delight in morality" (146).

Kline's article is a concise summary of the problem, and serves to conclude our examination of Xunzi's understanding of the process of creativity as defined in the artifice of the sage-kings. Using the analogy of piling up for the ability of the sage to create good names and ritual, Kline writes, "If we gradually pile up water into a deep pool, dragons will come of their own accord to dwell in its depths. Likewise, for human beings, 'if we pile up good deeds to complete our moral charisma, then godlike undertaking will come of its own and the mind of the sage will be complete in it'" (Kline and Ivanhoe 2000, 170). For Xunzi, the power of the creative process is a profound ability to *hua* 化 (transform) human beings. "Xunzi describes the power of the gentleman or sage to order society as the power to transform (*hua* 化) those around him. In order to explain this transformation, Xunzi often uses the metaphor of resonance in sound" (Kline and Ivanhoe 2000, 170). Van Norden, Wong, and Kline all point to the fact that human beings can be moved to approval by ritual action and music because these kinds of experiences are so closely linked to our ability to have desire and evaluate these desires. There is a clear sense of aesthetic delight and motivation at play here.

22. The irony that I refer to is that *cheng* is a major concept of another Confucian text of this period, the *Zhongyong*. *Zhongyong* has always been considered to express the mainline Mencian position and to be, therefore, on the other end of the Confucian spectrum of thought from Xunzi.

23. For an alternative translation, see Knoblock 1988–94, 1:177–78.

24. In their introduction to the translation of the *Zhongyong* Hall and Ames (2001) provide a philosophical defense of their translation of *cheng* as "creativity." They note, as did Chen Chun in the Southern Song, that the conventional early meaning of *cheng* was either integrity or sincerity. Hall and Ames derive the notion of creativity from an interpretation of integrity. "In a world of changing events, 'integrity' suggests an active process of bringing circumstances together in a meaningful way to achieve the coherence that meaningfulness implies. As such, 'integrity' suggests a creative process" (61).

In fact, Hall and Ames defend the radical thesis that if "the Chinese world is better characterized in terms of process understandings than in substantive concepts, then one must reckon that in such a world, 'things' (*wu* 物) are to be understood as processes (happenings) and events (happenings that have achieved some relative consummation)" (32). They quote section 24 of the *Zhongyong* to the effect that "Creativity is self-consummating (*zicheng* 自誠), and its way (*dao*) is self-directing (*zidao* 自道). Creativity is a process (*wu*) taken from its beginning to its end, and without this creativity, there are no events" (32). According to Hall and Ames, building on their previous three books on the early Confucian tradition, all of this process takes place within a field-and-focus model of the world. In the case of the sage, "Creativity involves both the realization of the focal self and of the field of events, the realization of both particular and context. Self-actualization is a focal process that draws upon an aggregate field of human experience. And field and focus are reciprocally realized" (32).

3. COURSING THROUGH THE DAO

1. However, there is the second kind of distinction made most cogently by H. G. Creel (1970) between "philosophical" and "religious" Daoism. Although the sharp distinction between these two strains of Daoism has come under sustained and warranted attack in contemporary scholarship, it is still important as a hermeneutic device to help distinguish between different kinds of texts in the ever-expanding world of living Daoist traditions, schools, lineages, and transmissions. Philosophical Daoism was construed to be a pure form of brilliant, witty, and sometimes ironic cognition as defined most cogently in the *Laozi* and *Zhuangzi*. Religious Daoism was then taken to be every other kind of material generated over the long history of Daoism in East Asia. In this chapter we will examine a later "philosophical" text, the *Liezi* 列子. The *Liezi* ranks right after the *Laozi* and the *Zhuangzi* as one of the most important early Daoist texts drawn from the elite ranks of Chinese society.

Notwithstanding the close connections among all forms of Daoist thought, for a long time the later organized forms of religious Daoism that arose at the end of the Han dynasty in the second century were deemed by many early Western scholars of Daoism to be at best a misreading of the classical texts and at worst a farrago of common superstitions. In this regard, both the early scholarly Western missionaries and the Confucian literati shared a common assessment of Daoism. The classical texts, including the *Laozi*, *Zhuangzi*, *Huainanzi*, and *Liezi*, were appreciated as works of philosophical and cultural worth, whereas the lineages of the post-Han Daoist sectarian religious movements were considered a falling away from the primal purity of the best Daoist thought. Only within the last three decades has this old dichotomy between the various trends in Daoist thought been effectively challenged (Kohn 2001; Kohn and Roth 2002; Miller 2003). We are now aware of the spiritual or religious bent of the entire Daoist tradition, and that all the texts we conjure and catalog as Daoist are connected to China's great indigenous elite and popular religious cultures.

2. The main difference between the current definitions of Confucianism and Daoism is that scholars now argue that it was the later scholarly Protestant missionary James Legge who "invented" Daoism in its modern full glory by giving it a name in English. It was the earlier Jesuits who forged early Modernity's understanding of Confucianism. Of course, all Legge actually did was to give new labels to various sections of works that had long been identified with Daoism in the Chinese tradition. As we shall see in the next chapter, Chen Chun (1159–1223) was perfectly happy to speak of Daoists as contrasts to the teachings of Kongzi and his school. However, the crucial distinction is that in the Chinese case the designations derived from bibliographical needs rather than from early Modernity's desire to catalog separate "religions." The underlying passion in both cases was to classify a set of texts. In the Chinese case the organizational principle was often based on a sense of lineage rather than religious typologies. But of course, the Western drive to catalog the diverse Chinese cultural sensibilities makes sense once early Modernity's definition of "religion" was applied to the Chinese material; many scholars have noticed, as noted above, that there has always been an intimate connection between all the indigenous Chinese "religions" and the family. Nonetheless, the Han scholastics who composed the early Chinese bibliographies that organized pre-Han texts were not primarily interested in discovering "religions" in the same sense that a Jesuit who wanted to discover what the religion of the Chinese literati really was. Religions

as conceptual radial prototypes, to use the language of Lakoff and Johnson, are the inventions of early Modernity and the later Enlightenment project. Tomoko Masuzawa (2005) has a fascinating study of the Western "invention of world religions." While primarily interested in the later aspects of this endeavor, much of what she writes has a bearing on the question about how Western missionaries and scholars have struggled to understand and catalog the rich religious diversity of the world beyond the early modern Western purview.

3. For a magisterial study of Legge's life and thought, see Girardot (2002). Over and over again Girardot demonstrates how Legge's opinion of Confucianism improved over a long and productive scholarly life, often causing friction with other missionaries who wished that the master of Chinese translation had a less positive view of the Confucian Way.

4. The basic facts about the history of the text are these. In the *Zhuangzi*, there are a number of stories about a Daoist worthy by the name of Liezi or "Master Lie." Because books often take the name of their purported authors in the classical period in the Zhou and Han dynasties, someone came up with the idea of writing a book claiming to be the words and deeds of the legendary Liezi. However, the text as we have it today is now thought to be the creation or edition of a fourth-century editor or redactor. We shall explore some of the detective work that went into this conclusion, because it helps to situate the Liezi as a product of the late classical period and the beginning of the long middle period of Chinese intellectual history.

In fact, the question of the provenance and dating of the text are one of the reasons for my interest in the text in terms of themes of process. The early Fourth century is a period that marks the end of classical period of Chinese thought in a decisive way and is known traditionally as the Wei-Jin period after two of the dynasties from the era. Of course, scholars argue that the real end of the classical period comes somewhere in the Han period. What they are trying to describe is the clear differentiation in cultural sensibility found in the works of the last decades of the Zhou and the early days of the Han and the kinds of writing preserved after the fall of the Han and before the rise of Buddhism. The third and fourth centuries are typically categorized as the age of the flourishing of neo-Daoism and the arrival and "conquest" of China by the Buddhist *dharma* (Wagner 2000, 2003; Zücher 1959; Ziporyn 2003).

5. There are many fine studies of the thought of the period that can be pursued by anyone interested in the twists and turns of late Han and Wei-Jin intellectual life, such as Xiao Gongzhuang's history of Chinese political thought (Xiao 1979).

6. Besides, it is a very good read; and this is not only the case in original classical Chinese but also in the accurate and felicitous English translation of A. C. Graham.

7. Even in the preface to one of the Daoist classics family and family relations are critical. Quite clearly this is not just any elite family. The lineage of the text is connected to the most famous of the third-century intellectuals, the justly famous Wang Bi. Wang, who died in his early twenties, wrote two of the most famous commentaries in the history of Chinese thought. One was on the *Laozi* and the other on the *Yijing*. The commentaries were so good that the received texts of both books, in Wang's edition, became secondary classics in their own right. Generations upon generations of Chinese literati have read the two classics through the lens of Wang Bi's precocious genius. Moreover, Wang is also recognized as a major philosopher in the neo-Daoist style, though titles such as "Daoist" or "Confucian" are too constraining for someone

like Wang Bi. He was an original. I can think of no philospher who died so early and has yet left such a major legacy (Wagner 2000, 2003). Even Jesus survived to his thirties and Kongzi and the Buddha had long lives.

The preface paints a picture of the difficulties of life in the Wei-Jin period even for the rich elite. Civil wars abounded, and if the civil war battles were not enough, bandits and foreign raiders compounded the difficulties. Many of the great Han clans did just what Zhang's family did: they moved south. The south at this time is not as we think of it today, or even as it was in the Song period. It was a world of mystery and water; it was dramatically different from the dry north China plain that had been the cradle of Chinese culture and the seat of all the Chinese states and imperial dynasties. As the elite families moved south, they tried to take as much of their treasured classical culture with them as they could. As Zhang tells the story, one of the things the family took was the text of the Liezi.

8. Along with the political decay of the Han state, there were also other indicators of a profound social change at the end of the Han period. In a recent study of the commentarial art of Wang Bi, it has been demonstrated that a whole new mind-set appeared in the post-Han courts. Someone like Wang Bi could flaunt convention, both social and intellectual, and win praise and scholarly immortality by doing so (Wagner 2000, 2003). It is this kind of bold attack on social convention that has given rise to the term "neo-Daoism." The neo-Daoists were certainly not simply commentators on the early classical Daoist texts in the same way that such scholastic commentary was a proud activity of the Han erudite elite. Much to the contrary, the "neo-Daoist" revivalists sought to thumb their noses at the scholarship of the Han; if stuffy Confucian convention was mocked, then so much the worse for Han Confucian thought.

9. Wright was not part of the group of scholars who divided Daoism neatly between the philosophical and religious poles. This is the form of dialectic described by Chung-ying Cheng, albeit for Confucians, as integrative rather than the typical Western agonistic clash of differing forces (C. Cheng 1991). What Cheng defines as Daoist (and Confucian) is a proclivity to comprehend seemingly contrary forces as balanced along a continuum and not as diametrically contrasting or contesting entities, processes, fluxes, or substances. In the Confucian case this manifests itself in the love of harmony and the desire to design ritual behavior such that conflict is abated if not eliminated altogether.

10. It is the basis for what Graham (1986b) and others have identified as the correlative structure of Chinese cosmology. It is not an agonistic battle between good or evil, light or heavy, male or female. Rather, it is the oscillation between the two inseparable poles of reality in the making. Men and women, for instance, are an intricate balance of yin and yang, the five phases, and the social conditioning of the larger cultural world. In the 1950s Joseph Needham (Needham et. al. 1954–), so often a pioneer in Chinese intellectual history, in his second volume followed Zhong Dongsun and named this typical Chinese cosmological approach "correlative" or "dialectical thinking." He argued that the classical Chinese intellectuals did not typically employ a subject-predicate proposition to frame their discourse and hence did not rely on the Aristotelian identity-difference logical framework. Rather, Needham said, "Relation (*lian* 連) was probably more fundamental in all Chinese thought than substance" (2:199). Needham elaborates the relational and organic sensibilities of the classical

Chinese tradition in the following fashion: "Where Western minds ask '*What* essentially is it?,' Chinese minds asked '*how* is it related in its beginnings, function, and endings with everything else, and *how* ought we to react to it?" (2:200).

Actually, according to Bret Hinsch, Dong Zongshu defined yin-yang as complementary but also added a highly stratified twist to the definitions. Without doubt, yang was superior in position and authority to yin, according to Dong. See Hinsch 2002, 143–157. According to Hinsch this marked a decline in the status of the feminine in western Han thought, a tendency that sadly continued throughout much of Chinese social history.

11. In terms of both the Confucian and Daoist theories, the highest manifestation of organic unity is the sage or immortal as the mediator between heaven and earth. Although the details are different, and sometimes even the nomenclature, the sage (or immortal, as the Daoists would say), is taken to represent the best synthesis possible for a human being. For instance, the sage will follow a pattern of involvement and withdrawal from the intercourse of life and society as the need arises. While the Confucians are much more focused on the social nature of life, they too did think that there were times when opting out of society was the proper course for the sage-in-training. Of course, the Daoists were famous not only for their withdrawal from society but sometimes for their disdain for society on any terms. All students of Chinese thought know the saying that Chinese literati are Confucian in office and Daoist in retirement. Or, as Max Weber so aptly observed, Daoism is the magic garden of the Chinese elite. Moreover, the whole world could count as the garden in a metaphorical sense. It was also a garden that would change during the seasons of the year and with the passage of the years themselves.

12. Along with the notion of polarity and reciprocity, mention of yin-yang in the *Liezi* also assumes various forms of change, transformation, birth and flux. The *Liezi* is not a metaphysical text by any stretch of the imagination. If he were challenged by such a notion, I can only imagine Liezi mocking the whole idea of metaphysics as a science. What physics? What science? And what things could he possibly be talking about would be the retort. Moreover, the aim of the work is not philosophical in a propositional/assertive sense; we will return to this question in the last chapter when we review the American naturalism of Justus Buchler. Rather, the Liezi text focuses its attention on questions of life and death and living in perilous situations. If it teaches anything, it is a perspective on the cosmos that allows us to be detached from the more common concerns generated by living toward death. It asks us to look at the big picture and to take it with a pinch of salt and a willingness to laugh at our all too human pretensions of control and wisdom.

13. Whatever the outcome of such questions of intellectual influence is, it would not detract from the point that in either scenario, the flux, birth, and transformation—in short, common metaphors for process—are very much in conceptual play. In fact, anyone consulting either Graham's English translation (Graham 1960) or the critical Chinese edition of Yang Bojun (1965) will discover that themes of process and flux abound.

14. Hall and Rosemont (1998, 281) in their translation of the *Analects* have another list of key Chinese terms for change or process, as we noted in chaper 1. They list five important terms: (1) *bian* or to gradually change over time; (2) *yi* the change of one thing or pattern into another; (3) *hua* or the complete transformation one thing

or event into another; (4) *qian* as the change from one place to another; and (5) *gai* or the correction or transformation of one thing into something else based on another principle or model. For someone like the redactor of the *Liezi*, *ziran* qua spontaneity also needs to be added.

15. This is in fact just what Professor Mou told me in a personal interview in the early summer of 1974 in Hong Kong. Professor Mou graciously agreed to meet with me based on a letter of introduction provided by one of my professors. After about twenty minutes of drinking tea, Professor Mou walked me over to one of the small classrooms in New Asia College and asked me to explain to him my understanding of Zhu Xi. He knew from our short conversation and the letter of introduction that Zhu Xi was the focus of my dissertation. I threw caution to the winds and explained as much as I could about Zhu Xi, knowing all too well that I was speaking to probably the most important interpreter of Zhu Xi in the known universe. After I had talked about fifteen minutes, Professor Mou went on to discuss the issues at hand with me for about two hours. At one point he paused to ask me why I was using Whitehead to interpret Zhu Xi. I was beyond being amazed by his erudition at this point, but still went on to mutter that I thought that process philosophy was a good way to interpret Zhu's style of Song moral metaphysics in Western philosophic terms. Professor Mou agreed graciously, but then went on to say that while he has toyed with this idea for a while, he was presently more inclined to use Leibniz or Kant for this task. Mou's own favorite Western philosopher, of course, was Kant. I was properly impressed; awe would better describe my mental condition at that point.

16. Before I review material from the opening sections of the *Liezi*, let me quote some of my favorite lines about the ubiquity of change qua process from the chapter "Confucius." "Anything at all that we see, we always see changing. You are amused that other things never remain the same, but do not know that you yourself never remain the same" (Graham 1960, 82). The dialogue in this parable is between Liezi and his teacher, Huzi. Liezi loves to travel. The tradition introduces Liezi as someone who wanders through the world by riding on the clouds. But of course, Huzi chides his student because he misses the real point of the flux of the cosmos. True, Liezi observes the *bian* 變 (change) of the cosmos, but fails to understand that his own personhood is as much in control of the *bian* of the cosmos as anything else whatsoever.

17. Again, following my Sino-Whiteheadian categories of form, dynamics, unification, and harmony as a final goal (Berthrong 1994, 1998b), the yin-yang forces could as well stand for the formal aspect of the emerging things or events. I will provide a much longer explanation of this set of categories in the next chapter. The yin and yang are, among other things, forms of definiteness in the sense that they stand over against each other in terms of patterned contrast. They are, it is true, complementary, but this reciprocal relationship is still one of difference. The sunny side of the mountain can be distinguished from the mountain in shadow. Of course, I do not also want to deny that yin-yang can also have a temporal dimension, although yin-yang need not always be temporal. But by adding a distinctive temporal element, the strong point would be made that "time" as temporal transition is an important aspect of the cosmology of the *Liezi*. It takes time for things to develop; one of the abilities of the sage is that he or she can sense in imperceptible beginnings the very first stirrings of something that will grow in greatness over time. Time is very much a crucial trait of process, although it is not the only element in the emergence of any thing or event.

18. One of the reasons that scholars have guessed at the late (fourth century) dating of the text is this kind of philosophical discussion. It comes about as close to classical Western cosmology as early Chinese thought is likely to approach. Some critics have even wondered if this shows a distinct Buddhist influence, because this kind of speculation through cosmological parables on the nature of what is can certainly found in mature Mahayana thought that was then making its way into China. However, John Makeham (1995) has made a strong case for just this kind of discourse about names and actuality being highly characteristic of the circles in which the Zhang family moved in the Wei-Jin period. Here again we do not need to immediately posit some external influence or even stimulation to find Wei-Jin intellectuals debating about the nature of being qua being. Of course, as Graham himself has shown, just how the Warring States, Han, and Wei-Jin disputers about the Dao went about thinking about the nature of being or existence was dramatically different from the way their Western counterparts at the other end of Eurasia did (Graham 1989).

19. As I cautioned above, it is exasperating to make the *Liezi* fit the assertive (and mostly propositional) mode of exposition so popular in Western thought. As Justus Buchler taught, however, not all love of wisdom need be expressed in assertive judgments. Along with the assertive mode of judgment are the active and the exhibitive. For instance, when we do something, when something changes or is transformed, attention, query, and judgment are directed such that "'bringing about' is the central trait attributable to our product; we produce in the mode of active judgment, we judge actively" (Buchler 1974, 97). Or when the actual "process of shaping and the product as shaped is central, we produce in the mode of exhibitive judgment, we judge exhibitively" (97). There is a suggestive parallel between Buchler's exhibitive judgment and some of the points in the last set of passages in the *Liezi*.

Another way to understand the exposition found in the *Liezi* text has been offered by D. C. Lau and Roger T. Ames (1998) in their commentary on their translation of the first chapter of the *Huainanzi*, another of the famous early Daoist classics. Lau and Ames argue that the author of the treatise called the *Yuandao* [Tracing Dao to Its Source] uses a "radial" form of exposition. This is a genre that has "an emanating and centripetal 'radial' order" (Lau and Ames 1998, 10). As we shall see, the notion of a radial prototype is also an important element in the metaphoric philosophy of Lakoff and Johnson. Radial exposition is a relentlessly synchronic rather than diachronic way of developing a theme. While there might be a radial hub for the motif being developed—say, the source of the Dao in this case—there is no search for an overarching principle or logocentric founding presence. The world is ordered, but the order is something that arises from the process of self-generation. The favorite Daoist way to name this is *ziran*, or the autogenerative process of the cosmos. The point made by Lau and Ames is very much in line with the much more extended argument developed by Hall and Ames in their trilogy on Confucian thought. There is order but no master principle and certainly no appeal to the creation of the cosmos out of nothing through the act of a transcendent God. As Joseph Needham observed, there is creation without a creator.

20. Moreover, a great public intellectual and youthful genius such as Wang Bi, mentioned in Zhang's preface as being a friend of the family, as it were, can be referenced as a philosopher fully capable of taking the Lao-Zhuang metaphoric and exhibitive style as an invitation to serious second-order reflection on the nature of being

and nonbeing (Wagner 2000, 2003a, 2003b). The fascination with what the Western mainline speculative traditions would call metaphysical, ontological, or cosmological questions need not always be attributed to the influence of Buddhism. Wang Bi, for example, lived before there could have been any major impact of Buddhism on his thought. By the time of the preface to the *Liezi* the situation changed, and reference was made to the Buddha dharma as something analogous to the kinds of speculations about illusion and reality that became more and more popular during the gentle Buddhist conquest of China. It would be intriguing to know whether or not these questions of the relationship of illusion to being and nonbeing in the received *Liezi* text do show the emergence of Buddhist themes in what is a superlative Lao-Zhuang compilation. Unless new texts are uncovered archaeologically as new shopping malls arise in modern China, we will probably never be certain whether this is the case of not.

It is fascinating to imagine what Wang Bi would have made of the opening sections of "Heaven's Gifts." From my perspective, it is an exhibitive tour of many of the ways cosmology was expressed in classical China. It is almost beside the point as to whether or not it was meant in jest, or how much play is mixed with serious intent. The upshot of any reading is that we are forced to pay attention to the question of ultimate or not-so-ultimate beginnings. Furthermore, many of the process themes that have been identified as core elements of a Lao-Zhuang Daoist sensibility are front and center for anyone reading the text, whether it is read as an elaborate joke or as an ironic commentary on the more serious side of Chinese philosophical history.

21. I am inclined to take the whole passage as a perfect example of the *Liezi* playing with *sheng* as yet another sedimented marker of process. The specific things are begotten, made, become definite, and then die. This is a motif that the *Liezi* and classical Daoism share with Buddhism. As the Buddhists teach, it is the dharma of compound things to fall apart. Nothing ever stays the same, but all is subject to the cycle of birth and death. From the *Liezi*'s perspective, this is the nature of That Which Does Nothing—it is the *wuwei* 無為 that engenders all but what is it in and of itself. If we could give an accurate definition of *wuwei*, it would not be true *wuwei*, because it would simply then have become some one thing correlated to all the other myriad things. This is not the office, the *Liezi* teaches, of That Which Does Nothing.

22. The *Zhuangzi* has always been recognized as a text of transformation and change. The case of the *Laozi* is somewhat more complicated because of the favorite motif of the *Laozi* is *wuwei* 無為, which has often been glossed as "inaction" or "nonaction"; or perhaps "uncontrived action" is a way to describe what is at stake in *wuwei*. For an elaborate discussion of the role of *wuwei* in classical Chinese thought, see Slingerland (2003).

23. The term "Daoist," as we have noted before, began life as a bibliographic classification originally devised by the Han historian Sima Tan and perfected by his son Sima Qian. Because it is a bibliographic category, it can cover a multitude of sins. Someone like Bao Jingyan becomes a Daoist because someone else preserves an account of his thought in a text that is considered Daoist.

More recently, scholars such as the late Michel Strickman, have pointed out that we would be better off if we used the term "Daoist" for the great religious traditions that arose at the end of the Han dynasty and claimed the name for themselves forevermore. Strickman puts his case succinctly when he writes: *Taoist (Daoist)* is potentially a clear, unambiguous technical term denoting China's indigenous higher religion, and should not be debased by being made to serve as a denomination for everything Chinese that does not fit our own notion of what is Buddhist or (still worse) 'Confucian.' Finally, what is to become of 'philosophical Taoist?' I earnestly hope that this term will be allowed to revert to the original restricted usage of its Chinese model, *tao-chia* (*daojia*), as a bibliographic classification" (*History of Religions*, 17: 3 & 4, 166).

Strickman believes that the great early texts such as the *Laozi* and the *Zhuangzi* belong to what he calls the prehistory of Daoism as he defines it—namely, the great high religion of China in the post-Han dynasties. Most contemporary scholarly students of Chinese philosophical and religious history share much the same sentiment about the problem of defining Daoist and Daoism (Kohn and Roth 2002; Kohn 2001). Perhaps yet another way to look at early texts such as the *Zhuangzi*, *Laozi*, *Huainanzi*, and *Liezi* is to view them as part of the collective patrimony of classical Chinese culture. A perfect example is the *Yijing*, a text claimed and used by every imaginable school of Chinese thought. Although Zhu Xi would never have taken the *Zhuangzi* as a Confucian text, he knew the thought of Zhuangzi as well as he knew the canonical Confucian classics. These texts are simply part of the classics in the same sense that Western scholars take Plato and the Stoics are representative of the elite culture of the Greco-Roman world.

24. Moreover, the great modern historian of Chinese political thought, Xiao Gongzhuan, has written more extensively about the various anarchist tendencies in early Chinese thought in his magisterial study of early Chinese political theory (see Xiao 1979). Over and over again Xiao demonstrates various protoanarchist elements in Chinese political thought. However, Xiao does not attempt to show that there is a unified philosophical position that lies at the base of all of this radical social theorizing, including Bao's theory of a world without rulers.

4. DAOXUE

1. I had the pleasure of discussing this point with Joseph Needham in the early 1980s while conducting research in Cambridge. It was fascinating to listen to his account, because he actually knew Whitehead personally. Although he thought it was an interesting analogy, he wanted to make sure that I understood that it should not be pressed too far. The differences between the thinkers was as important to Dr. Needham as were the similarities between what he took as two prime examples of the philosophical style he labeled organicism (Needham et al. 1954–, 2:458, 474).

Alison Black (1989) provides one of the most sagacious and suggestive interpretations of Needham's organic metaphor in her study of the philosophy of Wang Fu-chih. Black basically agrees with Needham that some kind of organicism is part and parcel of most neo-Confucian philosophy. However, she calls Wang Fu-chih's particular version of post-Song Confucian philosophy a form of expressivism. Black's intent is to sharpen the definition of what we mean when we call a philosophy organic. In her reading of Wang Fu-chih, she takes Wang to be critical of Zhu Xi for not recognizing the truly dynamic aspects of all categories, even including *li* as the principle or pattern of order.

2. Jonathan Z. Smith's classic article on the "magic" of comparison warns the unwary comparativist about the potential solipsism of comparisons between different religious traditions (Patton and Ray 2000, 23–44). Yet Smith and the authors in

Patton and Ray's anthology all agree that we inevitably indulge in comparison; the trick is to find ways to mount fruitful comparisons rather than merely fanciful ones. I still wonder whether or not this attempt to discern the difference between good and bad magic represents a kind of lingering proclivity in the Western scholarly student of religion to root out heretical or unorthodox teachings in order to protect the pious faithful from the wiles of skilled magi. Is comparison some kind of illicit magic, an intellectual sleight of hand we all must be wary of? Lakoff and Johnson (1980, 1999) chime in with their insight that we live by metaphors and, in fact, all our elite forms of second-order cognition are compounded out of the act of comparison via conceptual metaphors.

The critique of any comparative project is that we will become, on the suspicious reading of comparison as wayward wandering in vineyards that are not ours, intellectual neocolonialists hijacking other people's ideas and cultural artifacts for pleasure and profit—raiders of living ideals and lost treasures. The thesis is that to compare is to control, and ideas can be controlled just as much as territory and conquered populations. Of course, this hermeneutic of suspicion is correct in at least one major sense. We do seek to control our discourse, to make whatever sense we can of our data and the theories we bring to them, both as articulate methodologies and as much vaguer general cultural perspectives and sensibilities. Be this as it may, modern metaphor philosophers such as Lakoff and Johnson, appealing more to modern cognitive science than to the humanistic history of the interpretation of metaphor, again argue that at the end of the day all our philosophies, ideologies, or hegemonic discourses arise from our comparative engagement with the world—we live by and through our metaphors. It is comparison all the way down. Of course, comparisons, as cultural artifacts or natural complexes nested within other natural complexes, can be judged better or worse, informative or disruptive, enlightening or dreary. If one shares Confucian cultural roots, then the real question then is not whether one can do without comparison (and its train of metaphors) but whether one can civilize the comparative process in the service of human flourishing—which is often Xunzi's point about the role of ritual in complicated social settings. Like social and educational hierarchies, metaphors and comparison are the very stuff of complex social orders.

3. In terms of comparative philosophy, the term *dao* 道 ought to qualify as a first-rate vague general category. For instance, the notion of *daoxue* is just as broad a suggestion for a metaphysical category as is Justus Buchler's theory of natural complexes, which will be discussed in much more comparative detail in the next chapter. In chapter 5 on modern permutations of the trait of process, I will defend the thesis that *dao* might well be as good a general term for the explication of processive naturalism as Buchler's more recent theory of a natural complex. There has never been a grander and more expansive and culturally ramifying notion of a natural complex qua the matrix of all reality than the Dao. At least within East Asian philosophical cultures, when intellectuals were pressed to provide a grandly expansive name for their category of the ultimate, or even nonultimate (or "nonpolar," as Joseph Adler urges us to translate *wuji* 無極 in *daoxue* discourse) as we shall see, they turned to the ubiquitous Dao. When Zhu Xi taught about the widest range of anything whatsoever, he used the term *dao* as his vague general category of choice. As we shall see, the trait of process is a critical manifestation, to use his language, of the Dao in the concrete world of objects and events.

4. One more terminological digression is in order. There are a number of terms that were used by Zhu Xi and later Confucian scholars to name the various schools that developed from the Northern Song Confucian revival. *Daoxue* was one favored by Zhu, but his teaching was also often called *lixue* 理學 (the study of principle) as well. It was also sometimes know as *xingli xue* 性理學 (the study of nature and principle). Because Zhu Xi followed most closely the teachings of the Cheng brothers, especially the younger brother Cheng Yi, and because both were famous for this emphasis on the trait of pattern or order as principle, it was natural that *lixue* was later sometimes called "Cheng-Zhu *daoxue*." As we shall see, Zhu and Chen had a complicated theory about how Dao as pattern or order as principle is linked as an explanation of how the world works. Even later, the Cheng-Zhu lineage was contrasted to its great rival, namely the *xinxue* 心學 (teaching of the mind-heart) of Lu Jiuyuan (1139–1193) and Wang Yangming (1472–1529). And last, but not least, there was the Qing reaction to both Zhu and Wang; and it became the school of Evidential Research or *hanxue* 漢學 Han Study (the study of Han dynasty philosophy). Whether these are really good labels is a matter of great debate within the history of Confucian philosophy. Nonetheless, and probably with fairly good reason, scholars will often use the term *lixue* to designate Zhu's version of *daoxue*. From Zhu's perspective, *daoxue* is clearly the more inclusive term.

5. Actually, there are two levels of defense of this claim that should be mounted even before I make claims for the *Glossary*. First, there are those who now wonder why we continue to bother with *daoxue* texts at all. They say we now know that the history of Chinese, even Confucian, thought is so much wider and richer than that given by Zhu Xi and his students. And that is true. Scholars such as Bol (1992a) and Tillman (1992) have demonstrated the diversity and intellectual range of Song philosophical discourse. But none of this increasing range of vision of the historical development of the Confucian tradition obviates the fact that Zhu and his school remain one of the main branches of the Confucian Way. One can love Zhu and others equally well; and one can realize that the more we know about the colleagues and critics of Zhu, the more we will know about him and his school. The great modern New Confucian Mou Zongsan is one of the most relentless critics of Zhu's philosophy, and yet few would argue that scholarship on Zhu would be impoverished without Mou's trenchant critiques of Zhu's *daoxue*.

Second, there are scholars now who would expand the critical point made above and argue that we need to expand our study of Chinese thought beyond even an inclusive interpretation of the Confucian Way so that it also comprises all the other traditions and movements that dominate the Chinese religious and intellectual landscape. For instance, we must now be careful students of all forms of Daoist and Buddhist thought, practice and institutions. Moreover, we need to pay careful attention to all the various movements that have been lumped together as folk religion and social praxis. Here again, I agree. But I would make the simple point that Zhu Xi and his school are important as a part of the complete landscape of Chinese intellectual, social, and political history. What is really needed, when we are working as Chinese intellectual historians, is reciprocity of interest rather than condemnation of individual fields of study. In short, the more the merrier.

6. Textbooks as paradigmatic examples of secondary classics offer an intriguing entrance into the interpretation of a tradition. They represent, when they become secondary classics, a synchronic overview of the views the particular school wants to

defend. In the case of the *lixue*, the other obvious choice for a famous secondary classic is *Reflections on Things at Hand*, the anthology published by Zhu and his good friend Lu Zuqian (1137–81) as an introduction to the thought of the Northern Song masters. Both secondary classics provide a portrait of how Zhu's *daoxue* wanted to present itself to its scholarly audience. The *Reflections* selects the texts from the Northern Song philosophers deemed essential to an informed understanding of the teaching of the Way. Most editions of the *Reflections* automatically include Zhu Xi's commentary on the Northern Song texts. Moreover, both the *Reflections* and the *Glossary* were designed to be texts for students and other scholars seeking entrance into a new way of looking at the world. In fact, both Zhu and Chen wrote in a comparatively simple style of classical Chinese; Zhu even often wrote in what we now understand to be a form of Song vernacular Chinese. The reason for this was that Zhu (and Chen) very much wanted to communicate as clearly and as widely as possible with the aspiring literati students of their day. As textbooks, the *Reflections* and *Glossary* have been access points for generations of Chinese, Korean, and Japanese scholars seeking an understanding of the complex world of Zhu Xi's grand philosophy. Chen himself discovered *daoxue* when one of his teachers gave him a copy of the *Reflections*. As a text, the *Glossary* is especially useful for the analysis of key philosophical motifs for Zhu's *lixue*.

7. For an even more extended scholarly discussion of the text, see J. Zhang (2004). While Zhang essentially agrees with Chan's assessment of Chen's fidelity to Zhu's thought, he does point out that Chen could be creative in his elaboration in the thought of Zhu Xi.

However, the text also drew criticism because of its very precision. We must remember that many critics of Zhu Xi argued that his form of *daoxue* was overly intellectualistic and missed the spirit of the Northern Song masters as true Confucian masters and not just pedantic scholars of archaic texts. Depending on one's point of view, Chen Chun might be considered the prime disciple who was even more pedantic than the master and therefore encouraged a false style of scholastic methodology for *lixue*. Furthermore, Chen has the reputation of being contentious in defending Master Zhu Xi, whereas Song literati culture favored a search for harmony than the encouragement of sharp disputation.

8. I have written extensively about this matter in *The Transformations of the Confucian Way* (Berthrong 1998a), as have many other Western and Asian scholars over the last fifty years, and these studies can be consulted for a more detailed telling of the story. The basic history of Confucian thought is now fairly clear in outline, even though there are areas of considerable debate still to be resolved pertaining to how to periodize the history of the cumulative Confucian tradition(s).

9. In fact, the arrival of Buddhism was completely transformative of the Chinese world. It was the first time that the Chinese had ever encountered another sophisticated civilization replete with a complex and compelling alternative vision of the cosmos and the role of human beings caught between samsara and nirvana. The Chinese were entranced with Buddhism. It was also significant that Buddhism arrived during the Han dynasty, which in many respects signals the end of China's classical age; like the fall of imperial Rome, it marked the end of a golden age. The classical world of the Shang, Zhou, and Warring States and then the Han imperium was definitively over. This caused a great deal of anguish on the part of Chinese

intellectuals, but Buddhism offered an interpretation and a way out of the pain of mundane life. Buddhism was an alternative philosophical and religious worldview to Confucianism and Daoism, and the Chinese eagerly explored in earnest the various permutations of the Buddhist dharma over the next eight centuries. Buddhists offered both theory and liberation via the praxis of wisdom and compassion.

Even many Confucian scholars have pointed out repeatedly that many distinctive neo-Confucian themes come directly from the experience with Buddhism. For instance, it would be impossible to think of Zhu's theory and practice of "quiet sitting" without various forms of Buddhist meditation. The real debate is between those who see this as a mild stimulation of the Confucian imagination or a wholesale borrowing, if not plundering, of Buddhist ideas, practices, and worldviews.

Even the most ardent proponents of the stimulation theory of the relationship of Buddhism and Song Confucianism, such as Mou Zongsan in the modern period, admit the massive impact that Buddhism had on Confucianism. Zhu Xi once even pointed out that when you went out into nature looking for a scenic spot, almost inevitably there was a Buddhist compound there, and if not a Buddhist monastery, then a Daoist temple. Mou Zongsan has made the case for a stimulation theory in his multivolume history of the rise of the Song-Ming Confucian movement (Mou Zongsan 1968–69). Mou tries to prove that the Song Confucians did not consciously borrow material directly from the Buddhists. Rather, the Northern Song masters made use of previously unnoticed or underutilized themes, motifs, vocabulary, and practices within their own Confucian heritage in order to respond to the challenge of the Buddhist dharma. In this sense the Buddhists stimulated a Confucian response. For instance, the Song Confucians provided the Confucian tradition with a much more sophisticated set of philosophical positions than had ever been the case before.

10. In his own explanatory works, Mou Zongsan does make use of Buddhist and Daoist materials in his reconstruction of the Confucian Way. For instance, he believes that the Buddhist insight to the two-tiered nature of the mind-heart is a vital contribution to the formulation of an adequate New Confucian philosophy of life.

11. The question of borrowing or stimulation continues to be hotly debated today. Although I see the point of the borrowing thesis, I still tend to give more weight to the stimulation theorists for what I take to be good reasons internal to the development of Confucian philosophy. First, the various forms of Mahayana Buddhism that the Song Confucians knew well, such as Tiantai, Huayan, and Chan/Zen, had already been Sinizied rather thoroughly. That is to say, these schools of Chinese Buddhism themselves were examples of successful intellectual philosophical and religious hybridization with native Confucian and Daoist sensibilities and patterns of thought and action. However, I do not want to suggest that Buddhism in China had stopped being Buddhist. The point that I am making is that by the Northern Song, Buddhism had become a very Chinese kind of Buddhism. It often asked very Chinese kinds of philosophical questions and gave answers that would have surprised their South Asian confreres.

Second, I have been persuaded by Mou Zongsan's careful textual and historical exposition of the Song revival that stimulation is a better way to put the issue than the charge of outright borrowing. Of course, a great deal will depend on what we define as borrowing and stimulation. What Mou means is that much of what the Song masters did was to make explicit what had only been implicit in the earlier Confucian tradition, albeit with a clear recognition that they never would have gone in these directions until and unless they had been pushed to do so because of dialogue with Daoist and Buddhist thinkers. For instance, Mou claims that Confucianism had always been realistic, pluralist, and processive in orientation. These themes had never been linked in a coherent, systematic manner, but this did not mean, according to Mou, that they were not there from the beginning of the Confucian tradition. They were some of the foundational roots or basic metaphors of the whole edifice. They could be found quite easily in some of the early texts such as the *Analects*, the *Mencius*, the *Zhongyong*, *Yijing*, and the *Daxue*, just to mention some of the more important classical texts used by the Song revivalists. It is interesting to note that Mou agrees with the Song usage of texts rather than a more traditional affirmation of the five classics per se. The Buddhist challenge forced or invited the Song masters to refocus their intellectual floodlights on these tacit or underutilized aspects of sedimentation of Confucian discourse.

12. Actually, in her study of Wang Fuzhi's alternative interpretation of principle and vital force, Alison Black (1989) has a very suggestive account of why Chen might have begun the *Glossary* with a section on *ming*. Black notes that "the general import of his [Wang's] argument was to remove from *t'ai-chi/taiji* the concept of generative source and define it as a principle of harmony characterizing yin and yang" (65). In short, Black argues that Wang is critical of Zhu for giving the Supreme Ultimate/Polarity pride of place and also for mistakenly giving the Supreme Ultimate the sense of something with generative command power over the emergence of the ten thousand things. As Wang himself wrote, "What the Supreme Ultimate is in fact is simply the blended harmony of yin and yang" (Black 1989, 66). Black interprets Wang to mean that "according to this passage, *t'ai-chi* [*taiji*] is not a physical or metaphysical *entity*, but a *state* of perfect harmony characterizing the dually constituted *ch'i* [*qi*]; or it is to be treated as an entity it is merely *ch'i*-in-harmony" ([Page?]). This goes to the heart of the argument between one reading of Zhu and the alternative interpretation of someone like Wang, who believes he is much more faithfully following the teachings of the Northern Song master Zhang Zai. This would also be the reason why Zhang and Wang were seen as champions of a "one source" cosmological theory as opposed to the "dual source" theory of Zhu and his followers. For Wang, it really was just *qi* all the way down.

In terms of comparative philosophy, Black urges a reading of Zhu Xi that makes *taiji* something abstract as well as the locus of the generative power of pattern within the emergence of the various things and events of the cosmos. The crucial point Black makes is this: "The element of transcendence that *li* 理 contained in Chu Hsi's philosophy and that was certainly expressed in his concept of *t'ai-chi* (which was still for him a generative source) distinguishes Chu Hsi's view from Wang Fu-chih's" (Black 1989, 67). This is a very useful exegetical insight. Zhu and Chen probably do want to make a case for the generative impact of a form of definiteness coterminous with the emergence into concrete reality of anything that can be conceived of as some object, thing, or event. On the other side of the great neo-Confucian debate, "Wang traces the essential diversity of things to the yin and yang modes of *ch'i*. He takes pains to show that the unity existing between them is not something that can be reified as logically antecedent. This was the mistake, he thinks, made by some Sung philosophers with regard to *t'ai-chi*, the Supreme Ultimate" (63). But again, we must be very careful to define just what we mean by terms such as 'antecedent' and 'transcendence.' I will argue in this and later chapters that there can be a very robust version of naturalism that has a place for something like Zhu and Chen's notion of *ming*, *li*, and *taiji* as symbols of the forms of definiteness that are the very nature of anything that becomes in any sense whatsoever. Zhu and Chen could counter that there is nothing wrong in beginning with the analysis of things as distinct one from each other based on their observable patterns—even if they are not ontologically disparate.

Black's point about Zhu's use of pattern or principle and Chen's presentation of *ming* to introduce this aspect of *daoxue* becomes even more fascinating in light of the extended three-volume study of the emergence of the classical Confucian tradition published over the last decade by David Hall and Roger Ames. A cornerstone of the argument of Hall and Ames about the Confucian tradition (and Chinese philosophy as a whole) is that it manifests a world without a creator—and here they agree with Needham's and Black's interpretation of Wang and, to a more limited extent, Zhu and Chen. Hall and Ames mean this to be a strong argument. Few would dispute the first part of their claim that the Confucians never had a theory of an omnipotent creator God such as we find in Judaism, Christianity, or Islam. Confucianism can never, from an emic viewpoint, be construed as a form of radical theo-volitional monotheism. The only persistent counterargument to this claim was the proposal put forward by the early Jesuits that Confucianism really was based on a belief in the Lord on High as documented in some of the earliest strata of the five classics. According to the Jesuits, this primal, pristine form of natural theology was gradually lost over the succeeding generations. By the time of the Song revival, this pure or original theism had been replaced by an atheistic account of the origin of the cosmos. Moreover, the Jesuits believed that Song neo-Confucians were also confirmed materialists.

This is an intriguing hypothesis, and some educated literati, as well some modern Confucian theorists, were persuaded by the Jesuit claim about the role of heaven as a creator that was found in the early canonical texts and became converts to the new Christian religion. However, there was and is a difference between accepting that there was a Lord on High to be found in the earliest layers of the classics and making the second step to accept the whole Genesis account as it would have been preached by early modern Jesuit missionaries. Many Ruist scholars baulked at swallowing the whole Catholic tradition, even if they were intrigued by the Jesuit exegesis of the Confucian classics. For instance, the Ruist scholars reasoned that the notion of creation ex nihilo simply does not follow from the recognition of the reality of the Lord on High as an important element of the early Confucian worldview; nor did the whole theory of the Trinity, the role of church, and Christian claims to the keys of the kingdom that seemed to follow seamlessly to many Ming or early Qing literati.

13. What is intriguing about Ruist cosmology, from the perspective of the early Jesuits down to Hall and Ames, is the question, if there are no principles of action and even no creator, what is the source of action? Prior even to the question of the creativity of a sage is the "problem" of the source of action. But is the question of the source of action a problem for the Song revivalists? No doubt it was a problem for the Jesuits, but this does not mean that it was a problem for the Song-Ming Confucians or an early Qing philosopher such as Wang Fuzhi. Why should it be a problem, given the realistic, pluralistic, and active orientations of the tradition? If the world, as we shall see, is one of ceaseless transformation, the coming to be and the passing out of existence of myriad things, and of their mutual influences and interactions, action would definitely have to be one of the prototype metaphors of the whole worldview.

14. I have found, along with most of the works of Qian Mu, Tang Junyi, and Mou Zongsan, the contemporary studies of Zhang Liwen (L. Zhang 1981), Liu Xiuxian (1982), and Chen Lai (L. Chen 1990) of particular use in interpreting the thought of Zhu Xi. In terms of Zhu's religious thought, Julia Ching (2000) is extremely informative.

15. A perfect example of the gravitational force of Zhu's mature thought is illustrated in the work of the Qing Evidential Research school. This school, the last great flowering of Confucian philosophy before the disruption of the imperial Confucian world by the Western powers, did not agree with Zhu's vision of reality. In their terms, Zhu came too close to creating a Confucian form of dualism. This is not the common Western dualism of matter and mind, of the physical and the spiritual; yet from the perspective of someone like Wang Fuzhi, Zhu did fall into the trap of misunderstanding the proper relationship of vital force and principle. The criticism was that Zhu made principle the hegemon of vital force. The Qing critique was that Zhu tended in the direction of falsely privileging principle at the expense of vital force. With other scholars I have previously acknowledged the difficulty that Wang Fuzhi and others have noticed: I believe that Zhu left himself open to such a legitimate criticism of his *li-qi* theory. I do not believe that this was Zhu's intent, but mere intent is not enough. Sometimes there are reasonable inferences that can be drawn from the work of a philosopher that do not follow the inclinations of the master.

16. For a fascinating discussion of vital force and sixty-three other key terms, see Dainain Zhang's own philosophical glossary (D. Zhang 2002).

17. Although I have explained in detail the tripartite metasystem of Zhu and Chen in previous publications (Berthrong 1994, 1998a), a very short outline here of what is meant by the three modalities and one goal will provide a background for the further discussion of process.

The first modal trait is form. This is the element of principle that Zhu and Chen found so prominent in the works of the two Cheng brothers. The term *li* 理, as mentioned elsewhere, means "pattern," "order," or "form." One of its most archaic definitions was that of the boundaries of a field or the striations in a piece of jade. It is the pattern that a thing takes on when it becomes definite. The most important principle or pattern for Zhu and Chen for the person is the distinct principle of human nature. This is the pattern or form that a person receives from heaven. I have defined it as the formal element of anything that is. It is also what allows us to recognize and discriminate one thing from another. It is also the first thing that we often recognize when we perceive something, even if we are not certain about our perceptions. Just because principle is formal in terms of a specific pattern, this does not preclude an active role for principle per se (Levey 1991). Such an "active" reading of *li* 理 is a highly contested point, and I will return to it. To repeat: to be formal is not to be ontologically or cosmologically static per se—a pattern can be a lure for action.

The second modal trait is the dynamic trait or modality. The most obvious candidate for the dynamic trait of vital force is *qi* 氣. Just as the Cheng brothers supplied Zhu and Chen with the theory of principle, Zhang Zai was the patron of vital force theory in its neo-Confucian application. On the mesocosmic level of human life, it was always identified with the emotional side of human activity. The emotions, though they certainly had their own principles, were thought to represent something else, something more protean. The emotions are what give impetus to human life; vital force is alive, active, but somewhat directionless. It moves but not always prudently.

According to Zhu, vital force needs principle in order to discipline its raw and unpredictable activities.

The third modal trait is the unification of the first and second traits of form and dynamics. The traits of principle and vital force need to be unified in some manner for there to be anything at all. For a human being, the mind-heart brings unity to the passionate, active vital force and principle. Ideally, the mind-heart should bring unity to the principles appropriate to human life. However, unity can be better or worse. The search for unity must be balanced so that vital force and principle are correctly conjoined. Nothing can exist until and unless there is this unity of vital force and principle. As Alison Black (1989) has noticed in the thought of Wang Fuzhi, there is always a triadic pattern to a great deal of neo-Confucian discourse. The most famous triad is that of heaven, earth, and humanity.

Although Zhu prefers to discuss the unity of vital force and coherent principle in terms of the mind-heart, he also notes that even more mundane items such as fans have their own unity of vital force and principle. For a fan to merit the name of a good fan it has to fulfill its function of providing cooling air for the person. The quality of the fan's construction out of paper and bamboo strips can be high or low. A fan that falls apart because it was not carefully crafted would be an example of failed unity—it did not live up to its name as a good fan. But if the fan or a rice cooker works the way it is supposed to work, then there is a successful unity of vital force and principle.

The fourth element is what I call the hope or goal of actualization, thematized by the notion of *cheng* 誠. Without wanting to sound too much like Aristotle, I believe that Zhu desired to answer the question of ultimate reasons and causes, albeit in a very different mode from that of Aristotle. This is where Song *daoxue* moves toward the world of religious discourse, or at least toward examination of comprehensive reasons. There are ultimate reasons for us to act as we should, and Zhu and Chen want us to understand these ultimate goals. They are ultimate in the sense that you can only fully understand them if you embody them. Zhu is forever teaching his students, as would Wang Yangming, that the proof of knowledge is in action and the virtuous life. To simply say that you understand something and prove to be unable to carry out that understanding in praxis means that you do not really understand the unity of the mind-heart with vital force and pattern/order. The Confucians have a resolutely axiological and pragmatic turn to their version of process thought.

The favorite term that Zhu and Chen used to pinpoint the goal-like nature of the unity of vital force and principle is *cheng*. There is nothing surprising about this choice, and as we have seen, Xunzi also wrote about the importance of *cheng*. Various translations of *cheng* have been suggested, the most common being "sincerity" or "integrity." Moreover, *cheng* has an impeccable Confucian pedigree because it is such an important concept in the *Doctrine of the Mean*, the most "metaphysical" of the Four Books according to Zhu and Chen. By the time of the Song revival, *cheng*'s semantic range had expanded considerably. Chen begins the section on *cheng* by noting that it indeed does mean both loyalty and faithfulness, and hence continues to bear the early signification of sincerity. Chen goes on to note that *cheng* represents "a description of natural principle, whereas loyalty and faithfulness have to do with human effort" (Chen Chun 1986, 97; J. Zhang 2004, 278). Here again we see Chen's method of presenting both the formal and dynamic side of any trait.

Chen wants to show that in the Song revival, *cheng* has become a key term for the goal, the principle or formal order, of human self-cultivation. It comes to represent the real and true; it illustrates the lack of error and the actualization of virtue that is the ultimate goal of human life. After presenting a series of metaphors drawn from the classical and Song literature, Chen proffers another definition of *cheng*: "In the case of man, it is simply that in the operation of this real principle, what has been endowed in him naturally manifests itself" (Chen Chun 1986, 98; J. Zhang 2004, 279). Just before giving that definition, Chen quotes Hu Hong (1106–61) to the effect that "*cheng* is the way of destiny" (98). Chen shows how *cheng* as the manifestation of principle in the cultivated life is linked to the mandate itself.

I have hesitated to place the modality of goal with the other three traits, because I am not convinced that it works the same way as the other three. If one reads enough of Zhu and Chen, it is clear that the formal, dynamic, and unifying traits are used over and over to show how things and events come into being. When the specific focus is on human beings, then Zhu and Chen resort to the classical language of virtue and self-cultivation. This is completely consonant with the mesocosmic focus of Confucian inclusive humanism and naturalism. Moreover, Confucian discourse never strays far from its axiological moorings in social ethics. After the analysis of how something functions, Zhu and Chen will almost inevitably show how this functioning is connected to ethical concerns. The path is ethical and should be defined in terms of the classical vocabulary of the Confucian Way.

For human beings there is always a complicated goal to be sought, especially for the ethically motivated *daoxue* philosophers. Of course, Zhu and Chen are careful to respect the processive, spontaneous nature of the ethical quest. They remember the various students of Kongzi who report how the master constantly challenged them to keep moving along the path of virtue. The path is long, and the burden of walking the path is heavy. One not only carries the responsibility for personal self-cultivation, but also struggles with the burden of what the Confucians call "this culture of ours." Would Zhu and Chen want to argue that there is a similar goal for the bamboo and paper fan mentioned before? On one level, they would maintain that the fan illustrates the unceasing combination of formal and dynamic traits. But it would be pushing the language of human self-cultivation a bit too far to use the language of *cheng* without significant hedges.

18. There is always a question about how to find thematic material in Zhu's extensive corpus. Unlike Xunzi in the classical period, very few of Zhu's works are sustained essays on a particular philosophical motif; however, the lack of a prolonged philosophical genre does not signal a lack of interest on Zhu's part in exploring the key motifs of the tradition as he understood it. For instance, Zhu is famous (or infamous, depending on one's point of view) for his elaborate and repeated discussions with friends and students about topics such as principle, vital force, the Supreme Polarity/Ultimate, human nature, the cultivation of the mind-heart, social policy, and so forth.

For anyone interested in reviewing the range of Zhu's thought about these philosophical issues, Qian Mu's five volume *Zhuzi xin xuean* (Qian Mu 1971) is a carefully arranged and exhaustive anthology of Zhu's works. Qian has thoroughly collected the relevant material from all of Zhu's own works and has interspersed the selections with his own commentaries. Qian's work is, among other fine characteristics, literally an annotated index of Zhu's thought. A student of Zhu's work can be fairly sure that Qian has assembled most of the relevant sections of Zhu's thought; moreover, a student is always free to consult the original texts in Zhu's own words.

19. There is now another modern Chinese collection by this name recently published in Shanghai that is indeed (in twenty-seven volumes) a truly complete edition of all of Zhu Xi's works.

20. This work was designed to be a ladder to the understanding of the classics. Zhu Xi had already drastically altered the Confucian genre of the classics by creating the Four Books from texts selected from the much larger canon that he argued epitomized the teachings of the sages. Of course, Zhu never intended the Four Books to replace the study of the rest of the canonical thirteen classics, but he did strongly believe that his commentaries on the Four Books were a necessary pedagogy for any student trying to appropriate the classics for the sake of the cultivation of the self in service to others. Because Zhu held that the true meaning of the classics had been obscured since the Warring States, and had indeed only been reclarified again in Northern Song, he and Lu believed that an anthology of some 622 items from the four "orthodox" Northern Song masters would be an aid to young men as they began their study of the classics. The *Reflections* did become just what Zhu and Lu hoped for, a secondary classic that was read in conjunction with the study of the *daoxue* program of moral, intellectual, and social reform.

Zhu Xi (1967), inveterate commentator that he was, revisited the various items in the *Reflections* in other writings, and Wing-tsit Chan has also included many of Zhu's comments on the selections in his annotated translation, thereby providing us with a detailed exposition of what Zhu thought his Northern Song masters were trying to teach. Furthermore, Allen Wittenborn (1991) has translated another collection of Zhu's comments on the *Reflections*, giving us an even richer set of texts to contemplate. One who can read only English, therefore, can actually experience some of the same style of reading Song texts (that is, the genre of extended commentary) that a student of *daoxue* would have undertaken. The Song tradition was committed to a commentarial style, and although this is not a common form for modern Western philosophers, if one is patient enough to work through the various levels of commentary the general ideas of Zhu Xi become clear. Of course, there is one tradition—namely, Judaism—that also carries out much of its second-order intellectual reflection by way of commentary. And we would do well to remember that commentaries played a much more prominent and elevated role in the Western Christian world prior to the victory of the Enlightenment project and the full vigor of Modernity.

I once gave a lecture on the religious dimension of the New Confucian Mou Zongsan at the University of Toronto. At the end of the lecture, several members of the audience were still perplexed about the religious dimension of the Confucian tradition. However, an orthodox Jewish colleague said that he had no problem recognizing a tradition as religious when scholars wrote commentaries and placed such a strong emphasis on the reading of its classics.

21. I particularly like the translation, because it captures so well the relational nature of so much Song speculative philosophy. The semantic issues are of some interest here and directly pertain to the processive motifs of Song Confucian philosophy. The opening line of Zhou's text is very short, but concision has never harmed the status of a classic line within a classic text. It reads simply *Wuji er taiji* 無極 而 太極. Although there are not as many commentaries on Zhou's *Explanation* as there are on the equally enigmatic *Laozi*, there has been almost as much ink spilled in trying to explain the meaning of this five-graph sentence as there has been on interpreting what Laozi meant by "the Dao that cannot be named."

The analogy to the Daoist sage Laozi is not accidental, either. The main "classical" problem for Zhu, though perhaps not for Zhou, was that the two phrases *wuji* and *taiji* exuded the fragrance of Daoism to refined Confucian noses. Adler translates the line as "Nonpolar (*wuji*) and yet Supreme Polarity (*taiji*)" (Adler, in de Bary, Bloom, and Zufrano 1999–2000, 1:673). The connective *er* is often overlooked, and as Adler notes, can mean "and also," "and yet," "under these circumstances," or just "and." *Er* does not help in deciding on any one obvious philosophical reading of the line. The problem is that *wuji* had a Daoist provenance rather than a Confucian heritage. It appears in early Daoist texts such as the *Laozi*, the *Zhuangzi*, and the *Liezi*. Not a very propitious beginning for a Confucian manifesto. Needless to say, Zhu Xi and Chen Chun exert considerable exegetical ingenuity in trying to provide the Nonpolar with a respectable Confucian reading and pedigree.

Julia Ching, in an appendix to her 2000 study of the religious dimensions of Zhu Xi's thought, has an extended discussion of the exegesis of this critical sentence.

22. However, such concerns about the terminological purity of Zhu Xi's and Zhou's reflections on *wuji* are only tangentially related to my concern for understanding the role of process in Zhu's thought. The more interesting issue is the role of the Supreme Polarity qua conceptual modality in the larger structure of Zhu's and Chen's philosophy. Among all of the various elements of the emerging Zhu system, principle and the Supreme Polarity have been interpreted as the most abstract, stable elements of the whole edifice. In three previous studies, for instance, I have argued that principle plays what I call a "formal" role in Zhu's thought. My basic argument, which I have already outlined above, is that any event or thing for Zhu can be analyzed in terms of its formal, dynamic, and unifying traits—with an appropriate goal for the process thrown in for good measure. For instance, the human person has a formal nature, a dynamic allotment of vital force, and the emerging unity of the heart-mind. The aim for Zhu is not merely a formal and actual unity, because that would only make sense as a harmonization of the three traits. In human terms, this results in the various practices of self-cultivation central to the educational program of the *daoxue* movement. If there is a goal for the actualization of form and dynamics via unification, it is the special harmony of ethical cultivation and habituation that ultimately produces the worthy person. Although there are many arguments about how this harmony is to be achieved, there is no Confucian project as theory and praxis without attention to self-cultivation in some form or another. For a model exposition of the range of Confucian debates over these questions of cultivation, one need only consult Ivanhoe 2000.

23. It is interesting that the *Complete Works* section specifically devoted to the Supreme Polarity, after beginning by noting that the Supreme Polarity is another name for principle, immediately starts with a quote from the *Conversations* as recorded by Chen Chun. This makes a great deal of sense, because Chen, as noted before, was Zhu's student best known for a fascination with the systematic and rational elements of *lixue*. See K. Li 1977, 2:1065.

24. Zhu Xi often liked to use the example of a common fan to make his point. The fan has vital force surely, but we recognize that it is a fan because it has a certain shape, function, and form. Zhu always goes on to say that there would be nothing to recognize at all without vital force. Vital force provides the physical allotment of any emerging thing or event. While recognition begins with noting difference and

marking presence, actuality is a combination of both principle qua pattern and the vital force that is being principled or patterned qua vital force.

25. Dainian Zhang's excellent study of the history of important philosophical terms in Chinese thought (D. Zhang 2002) provides an excellent discussion of these issues, including great Qing Evidential Research scholars such as Dai Chen.

26. Chen then goes on to say that the principle of the why or how of change and transformation is nothing else than the Supreme Polarity. Chen's next move is typical of his hermeneutic style. After having provided us with a succinct definition of the true meaning of the Supreme Polarity and its appropriate Confucian bona fides, he then explains how the term has been persistently misunderstood from the Han period on, and also includes the mistaken interpretations attributed to Laozi and Zhuangz. It is only with Zhou Dunyi that we again have a positive exposition of the Supreme Polarity.

27. Jullien continues his account by noting, "The logic of this process can thus be conceived of not by using fixed—and therefore isolable—formula but only by taking into account its sequence" (2000, 245). Although Jullien is not interested in defending Chinese thought as one specification of a global family of traditions, he does argue that motifs of process play a major role in pan-Chinese rhetorical strategies. Jullien goes about his task by focusing on the strategies of absence and indirection in Chinese poetry, prose, literary theory, philosophy, and painting.

28. Other philosophers—Wang Yangming being the most famous, but also equally astute Qing thinkers such as Wang Fuzhi and Dai Zhen—were also worried about the dead principle riding the living, dynamic horse of vital force. Among modern New Confucians this has remained an important philosophical topic. For instance, Mou Zongsan wrote a great deal about Zhu Xi's philosophy and decided to declare it, along with Cheng Yi's thought, not to be the mainline of Mencian Confucianism. This is a doubly startling announcement. First, for centuries Zhu's version of Song Confucian philosophy had been considered by most literati to be about as mainline as possible. In fact, it was so mainline that it was adopted as the official basis for the all-important civil service examinations from 1313 until 1905. Second, Mou argued that Zhu's thought, though Confucian, was merely a branch on the tree of Confucian learning; and moreover, it was a branch that had more in common with Xunzi than with Mencius. One suspects that Zhu Xi and Chen Chun would be shocked if they could still follow the development of Confucian thought. Zhu and Chen believed that whatever else they were doing they were very much in the orthodox mainline that ran directly from Confucius to Mencius and then to Northern Song masters.

Mou Zongsan's point is that Zhu's focus on principle was entirely too cognitively retrospective an engagement with the world to be a proper process or dynamic encounter with the cosmos. Mou traced some of this problem to Zhu's interpretation of the *Great Learning*'s call for the examination of things (*gewu* 格物). According to Mou, Zhu was asking us to look backward at the fixed history of things and events rather than to focus on the path ahead or the truly proper habits of the heart. It was entirely too historically bound and almost legalistic in the sense of being dominated by past precedent rather than future ethical projection. Of course, Mou recognized that such careful attention to past achievements was part of the Confucian Way, and most specifically to be identified with the *Great Learning* and Xunzi. Mou, most dramatically in his *Nineteen Lectures on Chinese Philosophy* (1983, 401), noted that this is not surprising from his viewpoint, because he believed that the *Great Learning* was a representative text of the Xunzi style. In fact, Mou mused that we could say that Zhu Xi was, unwittingly, Xunzi's revenge on Mengzi. What Zhu did was to valorize a most Xunzi-like philosophical position while all the time proclaiming that it was the purest form of Mencian orthodoxy.

29. At this point in the unfolding of Chen's explanation it is so tempting to believe that we have found a Song version of Platonic forms. Although I am not a particular adherent of Wittgenstein's philosophy, his warning about the bewitchment of language floats ever so gently into the interpretation of the emerging principle as a standard or pattern of the conscious mind. We run the risk of becoming seduced and enchanted by such a long history with forms, essences, and monadic substances that we are tempted to attribute these interpretations to the Chinese *daoxue* words. However, it is a lure that needs to be resisted for a number of reasons.

Mou Zongsan has said that real Confucian thought is always moral metaphysics. While some modern or postmodern scholars might demur about metaphysics, few will gainsay the fact that Confucians do tend to think, if not always act, in moral terms. Though principle does not change, it is subject to deliberations about what is excessive or deficient. It is the proper correlation—the relationship, as it were—between too much and too little. Moreover, if these images are spatial, it is important to remember that they can also be put in temporal terms as well. In any event, what does not "change" in seeking the end of virtue does need process between the excessive and deficient in becoming a standard or pattern for conduct. Chen concludes this section by giving illustrations about the proper standards of ethical virtue and conduct by noting the various actions of rulers, ministers, fathers, and sons. He then also gives an example about the human foot poised for ritual action as a manifestation of ritual action as a formal trait of principle.

30. The opposing view is that a set definition, an assertion about the final essence or common nature of what makes us human, was not what the Confucians were really talking about. Rather, the better way to describe what was going on is to describe *xing* 性 as natural human tendencies. In fact, this is precisely how Hall and Ames (2001) translate *xing* in their philosophical translation of the *Zhongyong*. This is a familiar debate, as we saw in the chapter on Xunzi. Both Mengzi and Xunzi agreed that human beings must cultivate their *xing*, but Xunzi disagreed vehemently with Mengzi about whether or not you could specify the *xing* as purely good without a heavy dose of social, moral, and spiritual self-cultivation. If we do not embrace the notion, based on an essentialist desire for a perfected assertion about the invariant nature of human nature, we can see that Xunzi was both agreeing and disagreeing with Mengzi, because neither of them subscribed to an understanding of *xing* in terms of a fixed, essentialist assertion about a perfect definition. Rather, Xunzi and Mengzi were arguing about just how many human tendencies needed to be recognized and nurtured.

If we look at their argument in this fashion, we can see it as a variation of both the classical and the revived contemporary American pragmatist notion of warranted description and argument. What Xunzi argued was that along with the ability to cultivate sagely virtue there is also a tendency in human beings to be self-interested, and this distorts our ability to nurture other natural tendencies unless we are aware of this more negative side of our inclinations. What makes Xunzi a Confucian is that he passionately does believe that we can cultivate the virtues he identifies with Kongzi. The problem is that Mencius only gives us part of the picture needed for successful self-cultivation. Xunzi never tires of telling us what other philosophers got right and what they got wrong. What they get wrong comes, often, from their limited viewpoint. In this regard, Xunzi would agree with Zhuangzi that we are all like the frog at the bottom of the well looking up at the sky. The frog thinks, on impeccable subjective and empirical grounds, that the sky is a rather small blue patch above its head. Xunzi would counter that if the frog would only climb out of the well, he would immediately have to redefine his notion of sky. He would also need to discuss his definition with other frogs outside the cavern of the well. And so it goes.

Xunzi, as we saw, then takes the argument about natural tendencies one step further in his theory of *li* as ritual action. The discussion there is about the proper methods to cultivate the self so that it can overcome the power of inordinate self-interest. Xunzi believed most strongly in the power of education directed toward the inculcation of Confucian virtue. Another point that distinguished him from Mengzi was his belief that virtue was a human artifact. For Xunzi this did not mean that virtue and ritual were any less real for being social conventions. In terms of Justus Buchler's metaphysics of natural complexes, Xunzi held to the ontological parity of virtue along with other artifacts. That would be the burden of Xunzi's suggestion that virtue was *wei* 僞, something constructed by human skill and understanding—a human artifice. If Mengzi liked to talk about nurturing our common tendencies to do the good, Xunzi talked about the steaming of wood in order to fashion it into a powerful bow. Human inclinations were like the crooked wood that needed the steaming process of the sage in order to transform them into something useful.

Where do we then, according to Xunzi, find a pattern for the bow? "From the sages" was his stock reply. It was by studying carefully the teachings of the ancient kings and worthies that we could find direction for our intersubjective social construction of reality. Because of his commitment to ontological parity, Xunzi held that these intersubjective social constructions were just as noble as any natural seed we might nurture in Mengzi's sense of immediate ethical recognition. Xunzi proposes that even the most ordinary human beings need to follow the advice of the sages. The sages, of course, are those who are able primordially to entertain the symbols that will stimulate others to follow the path of Confucian virtue. The ability of the sage to articulate what needs to be done in a creative moment is a mark for transformation if there ever was one for Xunzi's narrative of the Confucian Way. This is an "open" social sentiment that provides a way to improve both individuals and society. According to Dorothy Emmet, Bergson understood as much in his argument about the social nature of morality in *The Two Sources of Morality and Religion*.

31. The debate rages around the so-called set of Asian values articulated and defended in the first place by the leaders of the government of Singapore. Whatever we make of the credentials of Singapore as a Confucian society—skeptical scholars point out that Singapore is really the nineteenth-century creation of the British imperial system—and its Confucianism follows the carefully crafted authoritarian blueprints of its leaders, other countries in East Asia are adapting themselves quite well to both democratic systems of government and social commitment to basic human rights. South Korea, Japan, Taiwan, and even Hong Kong (as a special case within China) demonstrate these commitments to democracy and human rights. Taiwan is probably the best example, because it is becoming a vibrant democracy and a crucible

for human rights discourse. Taiwan is also the society that most diligently tried to preserve its Confucian heritage. Of course, the more cynical among us could counter by saying that, yes, Taiwan did have a Confucian heritage, and like any modernizing East Asian society, once the people had even a modicum of freedom they abandoned the restrictive bonds of Confucian social teachings. The jury is still out on whether New Confucianism can become a partner in democratic and human rights sensibilities and social institutions.

5. MODERN PERMUTATIONS

1. For a stimulating discussion of the history of the notion of comparison in religious studies, see Patton and Ray (2000). This set of essays includes Jonathan Z. Smith's 1982 original essay "In Comparison a Magic Dwells" plus some further reflections on the use of comparison in religious studies. Buchler would be pleased with the positive reclamation of the magic in the sense that magic, as the authors use it, is a good example of what Buchler calls human judgment in the exhibitive mode. The editors say that they reclaim a positive reading of magic in order to make the case that comparative religious studies are often more like art than a strict demonstrative science. Buchler would see this as recognition of the difference between the assertive and exhibitive modes of judgment when applied to the comparative study of religion. And of course, as Smith notes, no one can really do without comparison in the study of religion or in other dimensions of human thought, action, or passion.

2. I could make a case for also using Charles Hartshorne's language of dual transcendence here to name the cosmological sensibility that always sees the ultimate as linked to the ceaseless generativity of the world, to borrow from Song dynasty neo-Confucian cosmological language (Berthrong 1994). As the neo-Confucians (Yao 2003, I: 367–68) were willing to tell anyone who wanted to listen, principle is one, but its manifestations are multifarious (*liyifenshu* 理一分殊). The harmonies of the past enrich and stimulate the present. The yin-yang forces endlessly dance together to throw up something creatively new at every movement. One of the favorite terms for the Confucian sage was "timeliness." This simply means that the Confucian sage expects newness and has the capacity to transform the new into creative patterns for human flourishing while honoring the precepts and principles of the past.

3. I might be able to enlist the support of the late Dorothy Emmet in support of this interpretive strategy. Emmet was an early student of Whitehead, and in fact traveled from England to Harvard in order to study with Whitehead in the 1920s. She was the author of the first, and still one of the best, comprehensive studies of Whitehead's late philosophy. Although always respectful of the achievements of her revered teacher, Emmet paid Whitehead the supreme philosophical compliment of taking his work seriously enough to be critical of it when she thought such criticism was warranted. One point of which Emmet remained convinced was Whitehead's insight that philosophers must find a way to speak intelligibly about the trait of process.

Emmet's last book, *The Passage of Nature*, returned to her reflections on Whitehead's grand theme of process, albeit on her own terms. In fact, Emmet's book is a fine example of the modern English analytic sensibility. Being clear about all things is probably not a final resting place for philosophical query, but it is never completely wrong to ask for as much linguistic clarity as possible when contemplating vague philosophical themes. Emmet archly notes that philosophers talk about process a great deal but are seldom clear about what they actually mean. She justifies her interest by stating, "It seems to me that we live in a world of processes—goings on—not just of facts and events; and this is important theoretically" (Emmet 1992, 1). Emmet then proceeds to lay out what she thinks we profitably say about the nature of process and processes.

In her caustic English way, Emmet writes "There is a contemporary movement calling itself 'Process Philosophy' which runs a journal *Process Studies*; this is concerned largely with exegesis and development of Whitehead's philosophy, and I am not aware that it carries discussion of Process as such" (ix). Emmet wants to set her elucidation of the traits of process within a larger metaphysical enterprise, a form of what she calls a revisionary rather than descriptive metaphysics, following Strawson's distinction of these two types of metaphysical discourse. "I set all this [the topics of the book] within a metaphysics of what, adopting a phrase of Whitehead's, I call 'the passage of nature'" (ix). She would agree, as we shall see, with Buchler in his depiction of nature. Emmet believes that passage means that something is going on in the world. Moreover, nature is taken to be a vague category for "the world in the widest sense, along with its contents, properties and ways of working." (1) One of the ways the world works is via processes.

Emmet breaks rank with Whitehead and later Whiteheadians insofar as she does not replicate Whitehead's journey into his later metaphysics—she thinks that his later vision is so complex that we lose our philosophical way in the endless thickets of multiplied categorical specifications. I think she would have preferred it if Whitehead had developed a more restrained naturalism based on his fundamental philosophical intuitions rather than the baroque splendor of *Process and Reality*. She draws the title and inspiration for her form of chaste naturalism from *The Concept of Nature*—"The past and the future meet and mingle in the ill-defined present. The passage of nature is only another name for the creative force of existence" (Emmet 1992, 1). Perhaps we need to reconsider the dominant place of Whitehead's process philosophy as a species of naturalism in order to have a better grasp of the global reach of the trait of process as an important comparative philosophical and theological theme. This does not mean that we should neglect Whitehead's achievement but that we should try to place it in the context of the emergence of the broad river delta of American naturalist traditions.

4. I was initially tempted to call this category "Columbia and Beyond." Although the label "naturalism" was often applied to the work of many philosophers working at Columbia from Dewey through Randall to Buchler, naturalism describes an American philosophical sensibility that finds expression far beyond Morningside Heights. Another label could be "eclectic," and this is the kind of label the Chinese bibliographers would use when they had to fit a number of different neatly into a single category.

5. John Ryder (1994) sustains the same position concerning Buchler's role in the development of the American naturalist tradition in his collection of representative essays by American naturalists in the twentieth century.

6. One also needs to take note of the work of Walter Watson and David Dilworth when mentioning Richard McKeon. These two philosophers, based on the initial work of Watson, have attempted to extend the work in the "architectonics of

meaning" made so famous in McKeon's seminars at the University of Chicago. Watson began the project with *The Architectonics of Meaning: Foundations of the New Pluralism* (first edition 1985; new edition 1993). Watson's articulation of a new comparative philosophy was soon joined by the publication of Dilworth's *Philosophy in a World Perspective: A Comparative Hermeneutics of the Major Theories* (1989). There are two salient and appealing points about this project from the perspective of naturalism. The first is that Watson and Dilworth are resolutely multicultural in their choice of philosophers, writers, scientists, and theologians analyzed. They make the point that philosophy is now, or ought to be, much more than the study of the history of Euro-American traditions scattered around the modern world. With their commitment to a pluralistic vision of the history, problems, and courses of world philosophy, Watson and Dilworth are also concerned with the notion and role of metaphor in philosophical discourse. This interest in metaphor is not surprising, given the basis of their philosophy in Aristotle as interpreted by Richard McKeon.

7. Corrington (1994) names his specific formulation of the American naturalism movement "ecstatic naturalism." John Deely, in his forword to the book, describes how Corrington is placed in the historical development of American naturalism. Moreover, Deely also provides an alternative chart, based on Corrington's work, of the players in American and Continental naturalism. The first category is descriptive naturalism, and this includes Dewey, Santayana, and Buchler. There are two forms of honorific natualism. The first group focuses on spirit and includes Schelling, Emerson, and Heidegger. The second group is focused on creativity and includes Whitehead, Teilhard, Hartshorne, and Neville. The third category is ecstatic naturalism and includes Peirce, Tillich, Bloch, Jung, Kristeva, and Corrington. Although a very different chart, and including a number of Continentals, it does at least recognize a major movement that we can (vaguely in Neville's sense of vague categories) label "(American) naturalism."

8. In terms of moral philosophy, a second addition to "philosophy in the flesh" as an analysis of metaphoric philosophy is a plea for the revival of a medieval and early modern discipline: casuistry as a form of ethical reasoning attentive to case studies (Jonsen and Toulmin 1988; Miller 1996). Although Pascal dealt a devastating blow to the casuists in the seventeenth century, a number of contemporary ethicists and intellectual historians are making the case for the relevance of a revised casuistry for the modern world. The point that I will argue, however briefly, in this book is that such a modernized casuistry is a form of ethical reasoning that fits superbly with global process thought, given casuistry's commitment to the pluralism of ethical theory, the centrality of relationship, and the contextual nature of its unique form of ethical reasoning. A key statement of the need for a renewed casuistry is found in Jonsen and Toulmin 1988. I believe that casuistry, at least as Jonsen and Toulmin define it, is naturalistic to the core and also incorporates a willingness to include themes of process as part of rational ethical deliberations.

9. Bruce Kuklick (2001) organizes the history of American philosophy quite differently, yet he too recognizes a naturalist movement in American philosophy beginning with the pragmatists, though he believes that the pragmatists remain idealists to the end. However, with Dewey's commitment to instrumentalism, the way forward to a recognizable naturalism was underway in New York and in other sites around the country. Here again the hand of Darwin and evolutionary theory is easy

to discern, according to Kuklick. "Naturalism derived from Dewey's view that Darwin had allowed him to 'naturalize' Hegel: the growth of culture, previously associated with the march of an infinite thought, could now be socially located" (190). Nonetheless, Kuklick goes on to explain, "Naturalism was indeed more of a mood than a reasoned philosophy" (191).

The notion of naturalism as a mood, a philosophical sensibility, fits my eclectic taxonomy quite well. But unlike the pragmatists at Harvard, Kuklick notes that Dewey was never able to train a school of disciples who would effectively carry his version of pragmatic naturalism forward or to other universities around the country. Dewey thought his form of naturalism was not necessarily hostile to religion in all its forms. "Dewey and his successors ruled out the supernatural, but only when they imported its values into the natural" (Kuklick 193).

10. Collins 1998, 673, has also provided a chart of the development of American philosophers from 1800 to 1935. The emphasis is on the golden years of the Harvard philosophy department as well as on the pragmatists. The chart does show the various kinds of connections that obtained between the various American philosophers during this time. My chart simply extends the process further but does not try to show the intellectual linkages as Collins does.

11. This is, needless to say, a highly eclectic typology. Some philosophers on this list, such as Robert Corrington, have devised their own maps of the naturalist tradition (Corrington 1992; 1994, 1996). The fit among the philosophers and theologians is not meant to be tight, except for the fact that all of these thinkers express a kind of naturalism and intense interest in process as an important theme in philosophical discernment. Naturalism, of course, is as difficult to define as process and just as slippery in normal and even philosophical usage. For most of the thinkers in these three families, naturalism means the opposite of supernaturalism or the postulation of some world beyond the common world of shared human assertion, action, and exhibition. This is even the case for those scholars who write as theologians, though this probably seems improbable to those readers who have not followed the intense debates about the nature of theism in the twentieth century. In fact, a philosophical theologian such as David Ray Griffin makes a strong case that his naturalistic theism is a better theology than contemporary supernaturalisms. Griffin writes, "Naturalism is usually taken to entail the claim that 'nature is all there is,' with *nature* understood as the totality of finite entities, processes, and events" (2001, 18). Hence God is ultimately defined, in terms of process theology qua naturalist philosophy, as the supreme or prime exemplar of all such entities, processes, and events; consequently, God never violates the patterns of the empirical world. What makes Griffin a theist is his claim that God, as conceptualized by process thought in the tradition of Whitehead and Hartshorne, works amid all the past, present and future emerging creatures of this or any cosmic epoch. Griffin is quite clear that Whiteheadian philosophy is a form of philosophical theology that is naturalistic to its core.

12. Of course, the other classic formulation of this principle of the process of creativity was Henry N. Wieman (1946). Wieman emphasized a fairly radical form of naturalism via a robust notion of creativity and what he called the creative event or good as contraposed to the merely created good. It was the creative event as creativity that was the highest good for Wieman.

13. Stephen David Ross explicates the principle of ontological parity by making the following set of points. First, "The principle of ontological parity is that there are no degrees of reality. All orders are real; none is more or less real" (1980, 108). This means that we can give up the search for some "really real" element or supervening order or substratum of being that will allow us to deem some thing, event, order, process, or God as the ultimately real. This is the foundation of Buchler's extremely robust naturalism and pluralism. There are only orders of orders all the way down and we cannot privilege one order more than any other. A fantasy is just as real (perhaps more real) in novels about hobbits as the world of chemical reaction in chemistry or the flat tire we discover rushing to work in our car on a Monday morning.

Second, "The principles of ontological parity and the inexhaustibility together represent the foundation of ordinal pluralism" (Ross 1980, 108). Ross argues that one reason that philosophers are forever looking for the "really real" elements of the cosmos is that they are almost all committed to a vision or understanding that the world or nature altogether is a single order. Thus, within that single order, there must be some kind of organizing principle or set of principles or something supremely real that helps the philosopher define a completely unified cosmos. Ross, here following Buchler, notes that very few philosophers have held the counterposition that the world is not the representative of a single order. According to Ross, Kant asserts in his attack on metaphysics that we can never know the world as a unified whole. (I would add a Daoist like the author of the *Liezi* to this list, and perhaps even someone like Zhu Xi, because of the unceasing nature of the flux of the cosmos, but I will return to this point slightly later in this chapter.) "The principle of inexhaustibility entails that reason cannot complete itself, and for more stringent reasons than Kant's—that the world is not a single order" (Ross 1980, 109). As Buchler taught over and over again, every order is located within other orders and orders beyond those orders, and so on forever. Ross summarizes this rejection of a really real and final order for the cosmos by stating, "An ordinal theory repudiates cosmology and asserts inexhaustibility. There is no all-encompassing order of reality" (Ross 1980, 109).

14. *Li* is often translated as "form," "pattern" or "principle." Roger Ames has convinced me through both his publications and in conversation that it would be better not to call *li* principle too quickly. Ames believes that the term "principle" carries too many Western philosophical undertones to be a good translation. Form and pattern, Ames believes, do a better job of explaining in more neutral philosophical language what someone like Zhu Xi meant. But Wm. Theodore de Bary counters that principle is precisely a fine translation of *li*, because it calls attention to the persistent aspect of moral responsibility always found in the Confucian interpretation of *li*. While appreciating Ames's point, I am more and more persuaded to follow de Bary and use "coherent principle" as the prime translation of *li*.

15. This is a highly contested claim about the ontological parity of principle and vital force in Zhu Xi's philosophy. I have defended this position before and will do so again in a later study of *daoxue*. However, I acknowledge the fact that many highly learned scholars of the Confucian tradition take the opposite view—namely, that Zhu valued principle more highly than vital force.

16. Is there a way forward that honors Whitehead's achievement while avoiding some of the more damaging criticism directed against Whitehead by scholars such as Justus Buchler, Dorothy Emmet, and Robert Neville? The most pressing site of the

conceptual problem has to do with two issues in Whitehead scholarship. The first is the nature of Whitehead's doctrine of God and the second is his commitment to the ultimate, privileged role of actual entities. I have already discussed various problems with the notion of God held by Whitehead in part 5 of *Process and Reality* and in later works such as *Adventures of Ideas* and *Modes of Thought* (Berthrong 1994, 1998a). Neville (1995c) has been one of the most persistent critics of Whitehead's failure to provide a coherent account of the nature of God. Moreover, Neville links Whitehead's inability to explain how God interacts with the world to the question of the lack of a proper Whiteheadian ontology. Moreover, Buchler and Emmet argue that there is an even more pressing problem—namely, Whitehead's desire to define the actual entity as the really real building blocks of the world. Buchler's solution to Whitehead's problem is to propose his metaphysics of natural complexes. I will follow Buchler at this point, but will expand the conversation to include Zhu Xi and Chen Chun, because I think that they can help throw more light on an expanded, global understanding of the trait of process as an important theme in speculative pluralistic and naturalist philosophies and theologies.

Two other scholars have also spent a great deal of time working on these two problems. Charles Hartshorne, albeit an independent thinker, suggested that we fix Whitehead's theory of God by abandoning Whitehead's own desire to define God as an actual occasion—that is to say, to keep God as one actual entity among all the other actual entities. What separates God from the other actual entities is that God has not yet achieved a final satisfaction and, per definition, could never actually achieve a final satisfaction in a way similar to the other actual entities, because of the particular relationship of God's conceptual and consequent natures. Hartshorne argues that the only way to make Whitehead coherent in his God-talk is to redefine God not as an actual entity but rather as a society of actual entities—God becomes a social being rather than a single actual entity. I have discussed this issue at great length in Berthrong 1998b. The other recent careful attempt to solve the problem of God's two natures is Ford 2000. Ford suggests a novel plan to save God as an actual entity. Put simply, if God cannot function effectively in the past and present, this leaves one more temporal mode open—namely, the future. Hence, Ford will define God in terms of the power of the future to have a Whiteheadian impact on the present.

17. Such a fusion of Confucian, Daoist, and contemporary Western philosophical concerns allows us to retain a profound sense of appreciation for Whitehead's focus on the role of process. However, it prescinds from the need to resolve Whitehead's complex notion of God one way or another in order to defend the role of process in the world. This version of process thought does not need to embrace the various transformations suggested by Hartshorne, Ford, or Neville.

18. As is the case with so many of the New Confucians, as with prominent Chinese philosophers of different persuasions, there is precious little good material about them in English. However, very recently two general introductions to contemporary Chinese philosophy and New Confucianism have been published in English. Taken together, these books provide an outline to the thought and historical contexts of philosophers such as Mou Zongsan and his friends and disputants. See Cheng and Bunnin (2002) and Bresciani (2001) for chapters on Mou.

19. The Confucians had their own version of the search for the essence of the tradition—namely, various accounts of the transmission of the Way (here meaning

the Confucian Way in contradistinction to other philosophical "ways"). The great scholars of the Qing dynasty school of Evidential Research also thought that they would like to return to the pristine teachings of the early sages. They sought to get behind the metaphysical encrustation of the Song and Ming philosophers, but they also discovered, as did their Protestant counterparts a few centuries later, that it was easier to think that one could find the pristine teachings of the founders than to actually do so. The greatest of the Qing scholars, such as Dai Zhen, finally realized that it was interpretation all the way down. There was nothing that could be presented as a pure essence of the tradition save for reflection on the endlessly changing patterns or principles of the vital force of *qi* 氣 (Berthrong 1998a; Elman 1984, 1990).

If there is nothing like a substantial essence to the Confucian Way, then we must ask, did someone like Feng Youlan really do something wrong if he used American neo-realism to interpret Zhu Xi? Maybe there really was something of a neo-realist strain or mood in Zhu Xi in the first place—meaning nothing more than that Zhu Xi was a realist in the sense that Zhu Xi resolutely affirmed that the world was constituted by a myriad of concrete and actual things and events. Perhaps one of the pleasures of comparative study is to shine a new light onto the material under investigation and see if the illumination reveals something that had not been known before.

Mou Zongsan is taken to be an even more extreme example of cross-cultural comparative fertilization, because Mou is so obviously a careful and wide-ranging student of Western philosophy, beginning with Whitehead and ending with Kant as his favorite Euro-American philosophers. Moreover, Mou is never shy about explaining how his interpretation of classical and neo-Confucian thought relates to the Western tradition, or to Buddhism, for that matter (Kantor 2006). Mou has been a lifelong student not only of Kant but also of the great philosophical schools of Tang Buddhism and Wei-Jin *xuanxue* 玄學 (obscure learning). An example of his range was Mou's extensive translations of Continental philosophers such as Husserl and Heidegger into Chinese in his later books so that his Chinese readers would better understand Mou's comparisons between neo-Confucian thought and Western philosophy. Actually, to read Mou with profit demands an understanding of the history of classical, early modern, and modern Western philosophy; the development of Buddhism in China; and the whole history of various schools of Chinese thought, most specifically Confucianism and Daoism.

20. Even a contemporary philosopher such as Dainian Zhang (D. Zhang 2002), who is certainly not to be identified with the New Confucian movement, chronicles over and over again the importance of the trait of process in his study of Chinese philosophical concepts. Process has and continues to play a vital role in the development of Chinese philosophical discourse.

I will illustrate Mou's argument by citing passages from a short summary of Mou's work focused on Confucianism, a summary published in the early 1960s. This is the *Special Features* (or *Traits*, if I were to follow Justus Buchler here) *of Chinese Philosophy*, first published in the 1963, with a current edition in 1994. *Special Traits/ Features* is a transcription of a set of lectures Mou gave on the outlines of Confucian philosophy and religion that he then reviewed and approved for publication. As Mou notes in a preface to a later printing of the little book, what we find here is a simple narration of his basic argument about the essential features of the Chinese philosophical tradition. Mou urges his readers to consult his long list of later major works for the substantive proof of the points he is making. I have always found this set of short lectures a useful summary of Mou's basic philosophical position on the nature of Confucian discourse, a position that he refined but did not radically transform over the last part of his long and productive life. There is now an excellent complete French translation of this small work by Ivan P. Kamenarović and Jean-Claude Pastor with an extensive introduction by Joël Thorval.

21. Mou is also no adherent of Zhu Xi, or at least not one of the common kind. Mou argued at length that Zhu Xi hijacked Confucian philosophy via the sheer genius of his vast philosophical achievement. He says that Zhu Xi really presents only a side branch of the genuine *daotong*. In fact, Mou argues that Zhu is really more in tune with Xunzi and the *Great Learning* than with Mencius and the *Zhongyong*. However, in no way does Mou deny the fact that Zhu was a great Confucian master, and one of the traits that Zhu does share with all the other Song and Ming masters is the cosmological affirmation of process. Whatever quarrels Mou has with Zhu Xi, the disagreement is not about whether or not Zhu has a robust process cosmology.

22. In their joint translation of the *Zhongyong*, published after the untimely death of Professor Hall, Hall and Ames continue to refine their field-focus model as a productive way not only of interpreting individual themes, such as the constitution of the self in early Chinese philosophy, but show how the model works as a hermeneutic tool of reading a major Confucian classic. Moreover, they make the case that a focus-field model of analysis also conduces to a processive *ars contextualis* in the case of the *Zhongyong*. Hence the dynamics of a focus-field model helps to generate the process philosophical sensibility. "The world is a field of many things and the 'things' are not discrete objects but are themselves states of becoming; they are *happenings*. . . . Processes are continuous happenings; *events* are happenings that have achieved some (always transitory) culmination" (Hall and Ames 2001, 11). Just a moment later they write, "Notions of action and reaction based upon things as externally related are not longer relevant. Instead, all such dynamics are to be understood in terms of interdependent, transactional processes" (Hall and Ames 11).

23. Zhu Xi did not believe that he needed to appeal to a theistic first principle to explain how the one becomes many and how the Supreme Polarity functions as a pivot for the process of creativity. It was not that his tradition did not have some classical theistic texts. It did in terms of the some of the earliest strata of classical poetry and history, but Zhu did not think that such appeals to a transcendent divine reality needed to be employed to provide an explanation of the transmission of the Dao. In fact, one of the most effective methods the early modern Jesuit missionaries had in introducing Christian theology into Ming China was their novel interpretation of the classical references to a high God in the canonical texts of the Confucian tradition. The Jesuits and their literati Chinese converts demonstrated that you could have a theistic reading of the early Confucian tradition and remain within the wider expanse of the Confucian Way. In the early twentieth century Whitehead employed language about God, but it was a language that was so different from the received tradition that there has been an endless debate about whether or not it can be used for the purposes of a theological reconstruction of the Western Christian religious tradition.

24. There is yet another corollary to Mou's defense of the religious dimension of the Confucian Way. Not only does religion not have to be theistic, it does not even need to be "supernatural" in any form whatsoever. The Confucian tradition, again

according to Mou, is naturalism with a profound religious dimension. The focus-field model allows for the processive interplay of natural complexes without number and without limit. One of these traits is surely the religious sense, as Kongzi said so long ago, of hearing the Dao in the morning in order to die at peace in the evening. The particular Confucian sense of religious sensibility is encapsulated in a sense of peace, rather like what Whitehead wrote about at the end of *Adventure of Ideas*, a peace informed by a profound harmonization of the interacting forces of the dynamic field as it manifests its focus again and again. This is the Supreme Polarity that is enshrined in *liyi fenshu*; in more prosaic terms, it is concern consciousness as processive and relational axiology.

25. Although I was not able to incorporate its findings in the body of the text, Thomas Metzger's massive *A Cloud across the Pacific: Essays on the Clash between Chinese and Western Political Theories* (2005) is a brilliant attempt to look at many of the comparative aspects of philosophy these days, with a focus on political theory.

APPENDIX. THE ALCHEMY OF PROCESS

1. However, as John Henderson (1998) has chronicled, the Chinese literati were just as likely to level the charge of heresy at what they deemed superstition as any medieval or early modern Christian or Muslim cleric. It was just that in the Chinese case the penalties for heresy were less rigorous as long as the heretic did not dabble in turning private speculation into direct social or political action. In short, the Chinese heretic, if a private Daoist scholar or recluse or Buddhist abbot, was much more likely to survive an encounter with the Confucian elite without any major damage to self. In fact, someone like Zhu Xi had many Daoist and Buddhist friends, some with esoteric proclivities.

2. I have written at greater length about this matter in *The Divine Deli* (1999). My argument is simple: religious pluralism has always been a fact of life, and modern religious communities ought to begin to recognize the positive aspects of this pluralism. Moreover, many modern people are cheerfully and robustly borrowing—shopping, as it were, in the many aisles of the divine deli for items from many different historical traditions in order to form their hybrid religious identities. Merely telling them that this is bad theology no longer has any impact. The genie of change is out of the bottle for good.

3. Some French scholars, such as Ferry (1995), remember the close affinities between the Nazis and aspects of the neopagan revivals in Europe—including ecological movements. However, most professional philosophers and theologians, even those interested in process, have not bothered to look into the world of the occult and magical to find allies in the search for process and transformation.

4. The respected literary critic Harold Bloom has even argued that modern American religion is basically a form of Gnosticism masquerading as Christianity. For instance, Bloom (1992) describes in fascinating detail how the Mormons and the Southern Baptists are manifestations of the same kind of semi-Gnostic American religious spirit. American religion, according to Bloom, is a religion of direct experience of the divine reality. Moreover, Americans believe that this unmediated direct experience of the divine provides salvation for the better parts of their immortal and

eternal soul. It is a startling hypothesis. New Age religion (and Wicca, for that matter), therefore, rather than being a deviant branch of American religion, is right in the mainline of the search for personal encounter with the divine reality.

5. Hanegraaff's main concern is the analysis of New Age religion in the present tense; his research is as contemporary as Shirley MacLaine. However, in order to introduce this often-scorned form of contemporary spirituality, Hanegraaff provides considerable historical material about the roots of New Age thought. He makes the case that the New Age is closely related to the Western esoteric tradition as it has come to be studied and defined in the modern history of religion research. Moreover, although the connections ought to be visible between partisans of process, change, and transformations, they often are not for a number of reasons.

6. As scholars of the Renaissance already know, when the purportedly ancient set of books known as the Hermetic Corpus arrived in Italy, there was tremendous excitement about this new discovery. In fact, Ficino was ordered to translate the Hermetic material before new texts from Plato. This is not as outlandish as it now seems. We need to remember what Ficino and his colleagues believed they held in their hands: the Hermetic Corpus was thought to represent far more ancient philosophical teachings than Plato. Hermes Trismegistus was assumed to be a teacher of what was called pristine philosophy. Perhaps this was a tradition taught to Moses and the other wise men of the ancient world. Such a discovery, had it turned out to be true, would indeed have been priceless.

7. I owe this insight about the importance of ritual as a locus of the more processive elements of the Neoplatonic philosophers to my learned student of such matters, Robert Puckett. Both Shaw (1995) and Rappe (2000) show that, at least in their theurgy, the late Neoplatonists did have a respected place for notions of transformation and process.

8. Within the circle of these four forms of modern Euro-American naturalist philosophy I include the work of George Lakoff and Mark Johnson, although their concern is expressed as a philosophy in the flesh; but what is more natural than the flesh? If pressed to place them in my typology I would define them as part of the ordinal or hermeneutic species of naturalism. With Dewey, Lakoff and Johnson are calling for a reformation of the way we deal with philosophy; and with Buchler they are naturalists. I suppose that they could also be called radical empiricists if we understand this typology in terms of William James's definition of his own thought.

9. In the modern world, the trait of process has found new champions in cosmologists such as Brian Swimme (1996), ecofeminists such as Charlene Spretnak (1991, 1999), and ecologists such as Thomas Berry (1999). These thinkers weave the notion of process, change, flux, and evolution into a tapestry that includes, at least for these four, a religious element. Moreover, this heady mix of the new cosmology, biology, and ecology finds links with what Erik Davis (1998) has called, in a book of the same title, techgnosis. The new alchemy has nothing on the fusion of New Age esotericism, neopagan revivals, and silicon-based technologies in terms of embracing change, process, and transformation as essential elementals for the alchemy of cosmic renewal. If the prophets of techgnosis and cybergrace are to be believed, a new enchantment of the world of matter is underway.

11. An interesting counterexample would be the development of rabbinic teachings about sexuality. The rabbis never taught that sexual relations, properly conducted, were evil; in fact, they were considered downright pleasant.

12.Many students have the same reaction to reading Daoist and Confucian texts. The reason for this is that there is a sense of what Hartshorne calls dual transcendence in the Daoist and Confucian sensibility. The cosmos of these two traditions is perceived as expressing the intricate intersection of the divine reality and mundane life. One of the favorite images of my students is that of the web of life that intersects with the divine elements of the cosmos. Wei-ming Tu calls this an anthroposcosmic worldview.

REFERENCES

Abu-Lughod, Janet L. *Before European Hegemony: The World System A.D. 1250–1350.* New York: Oxford University Press, 1989.

Albanese, Catherine L. *Nature Religion in America from the Algonkian Indians to the New Age.* Chicago: University of Chicago Press, 1990.

Allan, Sarah. *The Way of Water and Sprouts of Virtue.* Albany: State University of New York Press, 1997.

Ames, Roger T., Thomas P. Kasulis, and Wimal Dissanayake, eds. *Self as Image in Asian Theory and Practice.* Albany: State University of New York Press, 1998.

Ames, Roger T., and Henry Rosemont, Jr. *The Analects of Confucius: A Philosophic Translation.* New York: Ballantine Books, 1998.

Ames, Roger T. and David L. Hall. *Dao De Jing: A Philosophical Translation.* New York: Ballantine Books, 2003.

Angel, Leonard. *Enlightenment East and West.* Albany: State University of New York Press, 1994.

Angle, Stephen C. *Human Rights and Chinese Thought: A Cross-Cultural Inquiry.* Cambridge: Cambridge University Press, 2002.

Annas, Julia. "Scepticism and Value." In *Scepticism in the History of Philosophy: A Pan-American Dialogue,* ed. Richard H. Popkin. Dordrecht: Kluwer, 1996.

Annas, Julia and Jonathan Barnes. *The Modes of Scepticism: Ancient Texts and Interpretations.* Cambridge: Cambridge University Press, 1985.

Ariel, Yoav. *K'ung-Ts'ung-Tzu: The K'ung Family Masters Anthology.* Princeton, NJ: Princeton University Press, 1989.

Barzun, Jacques. *From Dawn to Decadence: 500 Years of Western Cultural Life.* New York: HarperCollins, 2000.

Bayle, Pierre. *Historical and Critical Dictionary: Selections.* Trans. Richard H. Popkin. Indianapolis: Hackett, 1991.

Behuniak, James, Jr. *Mencius on Becoming Human.* Albany: State University of New York Press, 2005.

Bellah, Robert. *Beyond Belief: Essays in Religion in a Post-traditional World*. New York: Harper & Row, 1970.

Bergson, Henri. *The Two Sources of Morality and Religion*. Trans. R. Ashley Audra and Cloudesley Brereton. New York: Henry Holt, 1935.

Berlin, Isaiah. *Concepts and Categories: Philosophical Essays*. New York: The Viking Press, 1979.

———. *The Crooked Timber of Humanity: Chapters in the History of Ideas*. New York: Vintage Books, 1992.

———. *The Roots of Romanticism*. Ed. by Henry Hardy. Princeton: Princeton University Press, 1999.

———. *Liberty*. Ed. Henry Hardy. Oxford: Oxford University Press, 2002.

Bernstein, Richard J. *Beyond Objectivism and Relativism: Science, Hermeneutics, and Praxis*. Philadelphia: University of Pennsylvania Press, 1983.

———. *The New Constellation: The Ethical-Political Horizons of Modernity/Postmodernity*. Cambridge: MIT Press, 1992.

———. *Dictatorship of Virtue: Multiculturalism and the Battle for America's Future*. New York: Alfred A. Knopf, 1994.

Berry, Thomas. *The Great Work*. New York: Bell Tower, 1999.

Berthrong, John H. "Glosses on Reality: Chu His as Interpreted by Ch'en [Chen] Ch'un [Chun]." PhD. diss., Chicago: University of Chicago, 1979.

———. *All under Heaven: Transforming Paradigms in Confucian-Christian Dialogue*. Albany: State University of New York Press, 1994.

———. *Transformations of the Confucian Way*. Boulder: Westview Press, 1998a.

———. *Concerning Creativity: A Comparison of Chu Hsi, Whitehead, and Neville*. Albany: State University of New York Press, 1998b.

———. *The Divine Deli: Religious Identity in the North American Cultural Mosaic*. Maryknoll: Orbis Books, 1999.

Berthrong, John H., and Evelyn Nagai Berthrong. *Confucianism: A Short Introduction*. Oxford: Oneworld 2000.

Birch, Charles, and John B. Cobb, Jr. *The Liberation of Life: From the Cell to the Community*. Cambridge: Cambridge University Press, 1981.

Birrell, Anne. *Chinese Mythology: An Introduction*. Baltimore: Johns Hopkins University Press, 1993.

Black, Alison Harley. *Man and Nature in the Philosophical Thought of Wang Fu-chih*. Seattle: University of Washington Press, 1989.

Bloom, Harold. *The American Religion: The Emergence of the Post-Christian Nation*. New York: Simon & Schuster, 1992.

———. *Omens of the Millennium: The Gnosis of Angels, Dreams, and Resurrection*. New York: Riverhead Books, 1996.

Bodde, Derk. 1953. "Harmony and Conflict in Chinese Philosophy." *Studies in Chinese Thought*, ed. Arthur F. Wright. Chicago: University of Chicago Press, 1953.

Bol, Peter K. *This Culture of Ours: Intellectual Transition in T'ang and Sung China.* Stanford: Stanford University Press, 1992.

Bracken, Joseph A. *The One in the Many: A Contemporary Reconstruction of the God-World Relationship.* Grand Rapids: Eerdmans, 2001.

Bresciani, Umberto. *Reinventing Confucianism: The New Confucian Movement.* Taipei: Taipei Ricci Institute for Chinese Culture, 2001.

Brooks, E. Bruce and A. Taeko Brooks. *The Original Analects: Sayings of Confucius and his Successors.* New York: Columbia University Press, 1998.

Browning, Douglas, and William T. Myers, eds. *Philosophers of Process.* New York: Fordham University Press, 1998.

Bruce, J. Percy. *Chu Hsi and His Masters: An Introduction to Chu Hsi and the Sung School of Chinese Philosophy.* New York: AMS Press, 1973. (Reprint of the 1923 Probsthain ed.)

Buchler, Justus. *Nature and Judgment.* New York: Columbia University Press, 1955.

———. *The Concept of Method.* New York: Columbia University Press, 1961.

———. *The Main of Light: On the Concept of Poetry.* New York: Oxford University Press, 1974.

———. *Toward a General Theory of Human Judgment.* 2nd ed. New York: Dover, 1979.

———. *Metaphysics of Natural Complexes.* 2nd ed, expanded ed. Albany: State University of New York Press, 1990.

Chan, Wing-tsit. *A Source Book in Chinese Philosophy.* Princeton NJ: Princeton University Press, 1963.

———. *Chu Hsi and Neo-Confucianism.* Honolulu: University of Hawaii Press, 1986.

———. *Chu Hsi: Life and Thought.* Hong Kong: Chinese University Press, 1987.

———. *Chu Hsi: New Studies.* Honolulu: University of Hawaii Press, 1989.

Chang, Carsun. *The Development of Neo-Confucian Thought.* 2 vols. New York: Bookman Associates, 1957–62.

———. *Wang Yang-ming: Idealist Philosopher of Sixteenth-Century China.* New York: St. John's University Press, 1970.

Chen Chun [Ch'en Ch'un]. *Neo-Confucian Terms Explained (The Pei-hsi tzu-I) by Ch'en Ch'un (1159–1223).* Trans. and ed. Wing-tsit Chan. New York: Columbia University Press, 1986.

Chen, Lai. *Zhu Xi zhexue yenjiu* [Studies in Zhu Xi's philosophy]. Taipei: Wenlian, 1990.

Cheng, Anne. *Histoire de la pensée chinoise.* Paris: Éditions du Seuil, 1997.

Cheng, Chung-ying [Zhongying], trans. *Tai Chen's Inquiry into Goodness.* Honolulu: East-West Center Press, 1971.

———. *New Dimensions of Confucian and Neo-Confucian Philosophy.* Albany: State University of New York Press, 1991.

Cheng, Chung-ying, and Nicholas Bunnin, eds. *Contemporary Chinese Philosophy.* Oxford: Blackwell, 2002.

Ch'ien, Edward T. *Chiao Hung and the Restructuring of Neo-Confucianism in the Late Ming*. New York: Columbia University Press, 1986.

Ching, Julia. *Confucianism and Christianity: A Comparative Study*. Tokyo: Kodansha International, 1977.

———. *The Religious Thought of Chu Hsi*. Oxford: Oxford University Press, 2000.

Chow, Kai-wing. *The Rise of Confucian Ritualism in Late Imperial China: Ethics, Classics, and Lineage Discourse*. Stanford, CA: Stanford University Press, 1995.

Chow, Kai-wing, On-cho Ng, and John B. Henderson, eds. *Imagining Boundaries: Changing Confucian Doctrines, Texts, and Hermeneutics*. Albany: State University of New York Press, 1999.

Christian, William A. *Oppositions of Religious Doctrines: A Study in the Logic of Dialogue among Religions*. New York: Herder and Herder, 1972.

———. *Doctrines of Religious Communities: A Philosophical Study*. New Haven: Yale University Press, 1987.

Chu Hsi. *The Philosophy of Human Nature*. Trans. J. Percy Bruce. New York: AMS Press, 1973 (Reprint of the 1922 Probsthain ed.)

Chu Hsi, and Lü Tsu-ch'ien. *Reflections on Things at Hand: The Neo-Confucian Anthology*. Trans. Wing-tsit Chan. New York: Columbia University Press, 1967.

———. *Chu Hsi's Family Rituals: A Twelfth-Century Chinese Manual for the Performance of Cappings, Weddings, Funerals, and Ancestral Rites*. Trans. and ed. Patricia Buckley Ebrey. Princeton NJ: Princeton University Press, 1991.

Chung, Edward Y. J. *The Korean Neo-Confucianism of Yi T'oegye and Yi Yulgok: A Reappraisal of the "Four-Seven Thesis" and Its Practical Implications for Self-Cultivation*. Albany: State University of New York Press, 1995.

Cicero. *Nature of the God, Academics*. Trans. H. Rackham. Cambridge, MA: Harvard University Press, Loeb Classical Library, 1933.

Clarke, J. J. *Oriental Enlightenment: The Encounter between Asian and Western Thought*. London: Routledge, 1997.

———. *The Tao of the West: Western Transformations of Taoist Thought*. London: Routledge, 2000.

Cobb, Jennifer. *Cybergrace: The Search for God in the Digital World*. New York: Crown, 2000.

Cobb, John B., Jr. *A Christian Natural Theology: Based on the Thought of Alfred North Whitehead*. Philadelphia: Westminster Press, 1965.

Cobb, John B., Jr., and David Ray Griffin. *Process Theology: An Introductory Exposition*. Philadelphia: Westminster Press, 1976.

Cobb, John B., Jr., and W. Widick Schroeder, eds. *Process Philosophy and Social Thought*. Chicago: Center for the Scientific Study of Religion, 1981.

Collins, Randall. *The Sociology of Philosophies: A Global Theory of Intellectual Change*. Cambridge: Harvard University Press, 1998.

———. *Macro-History*. Stanford, CA: Stanford University Press, 1999.

———. *Interaction Ritual Chains*. Princeton NJ: Princeton University Press, 2004.

A Concordance to the Liezi. Hong Kong: Commercial Press, 1996.

A Concordance to the Xunzi. Hong Kong: Commercial Press, 1996.

Confucius. *Confucius: The Analects (Lun yü)*. Trans. D. C. Lau. Hong Kong: Chinese University Press, 1992.

Corrington, Robert S. *The Community of Interpreters: On the Hermeneutics of Nature and the Bible in the American Philosophic Tradition*. Macon: Mercer University Press, 1987.

———. *Nature & Spirit: An Essay in Ecstatic Naturalism*. New York: Fordham University Press, 1992.

———. *Ecstatic Naturalism: Signs of the World*. Bloomington: Indiana University Press, 1994.

———. *Nature's Self: Our Journey from Origin to Spirit*. Lanham: Rowman and Littlefield, 1996.

Couliano, Ioan P. *Eros and Magic in the Renaissance*. Trans. Margaret Cook. Chicago: University of Chicago Press, 1987.

Creel, H. G. *Confucius and the Chinese Way*. New York: Harper and Row, 1949.

———. *What is Taoism and Other Studies in Chinese Cultural History*. Chicago: University of Chicago Press, 1970.

Csikszentmihalyi, Mark. "Confucius." In ed. David Noel Freeman and Michael J. McClymond, *The Rivers of Paradise: Moses, Buddha, Confucius, Jesus, and Muhammad as Religious Founders*. Grand Rapids: Eerdmans, 2001.

Cua, A. S. *Dimensions of Moral Creativity: Paradigms, Principles, and Ideals*. University Park: Pennsylvania State University Press, 1978.

———. *The Unity of Knowledge and Action: A Study of Wang Yang-ming's Moral Psychology*. Honolulu: University Press of Hawaii, 1982.

———. *Ethical Argumentation: A Study in Hsün Tzu's Moral Epistemology*. Honolulu: The University Press of Hawaii, 1985.

———. *Moral Vision and Tradition: Essays in Chinese Ethics*. Washington: Catholic University of America Press, 1998.

Dallmayr, Fred. *Beyond Orientalism: Essays on Cross-Cultural Encounter*. Albany: State University of New York Press, 1996.

———. *Alternative Visions: Paths in the Global Village*. Lanham MD: Rowman and Littlefield, 1998.

Damasio, Antonio. *Descartes' Error: Emotion, Reason, and the Human Brian*. New York: Putnam, 1994.

———. *The Feeling of What Happens: Body and Emotion in the Making of Consciousness*. New York: Harcourt, 1999.

———. *Looking for Spinoza: Joy, Sorrow, and the Feeling of the Brain*. New York: Harcourt, 2003.

Davaney, Sheila. *Pragmatic Historicism: A Theology for the Twenty-first Century*. Albany: State University of New York Press, 2000.

Davis, Erik. *Techgnosis: Myth, Magic, and Mysticism in the Age of Information*. New York: Harmony Books, 1998.

Dean, Thomas, ed. *Religious Pluralism and Truth: Essays on Cross-Cultural Philosophy of Religion*. Albany: State University Press of New York, 1995.

Dean, William. *American Religious Empiricism*. Albany: State University of New York Press, 1986.

———. *History Making History: The New Historicism in American Religious Thought*. Albany: State University of New York Press, 1988.

———. *The Religious Critic in American Culture*. Albany: State University of New York Press, 1994.

———. *The American Spiritual Culture: And the Invention of Jazz, Football, and the Movies*. New York: Continuum, 2002.

Dean, William, and Larry E. Axel, eds. *The Size of God: The Theology of Bernard Loomer in Context*. Macon: Mercer University Press, 1987.

de Bary, Wm. Theodore, ed. *Self and Society in Ming Thought*. New York: Columbia University Press, 1970.

———, ed. *The Unfolding of Neo-Confucianism*. New York: Columbia University Press, 1975.

———. *Neo-Confucian Orthodoxy and the Learning of the Mind-and Heart*. New York: Columbia University Press, 1981.

———. *The Liberal Tradition in China*. New York: Columbia University Press, 1983.

———. *East Asian Civilizations: A Dialogue in Five Stages*. Cambridge: Harvard University Press, 1988.

———. *The Message of the Mind in Neo-Confucianism*. New York: Columbia University Press, 1989.

———. *The Trouble with Confucianism*. Cambridge: Harvard University Press, 1991a.

———. *Learning for One's Self: Essays on the Individual in Neo-Confucian Thought*. New York: Columbia University Press, 1991b.

———, trans. *Waiting for the Dawn: A Plan for the Prince-Huang Tsung-hsi's "Ming-i-tai-fang lu."* New York: Columbia University Press, 1993.

———. *Asian Values and Human Rights: A Confucian Communitarian Perspective*. Cambridge: Harvard University Press, 1998.

de Bary, Wm. Theodore, Irene Bloom, and Richard Lufrano, eds. *Sources of Chinese Tradition*. 2 vols. 2nd ed. New York: Columbia University Press, 1999–2000.

Dewey, John. *A Common Faith*. New Haven CT: Yale University Press, 1934.

———. *Reconstruction in Philosophy*. Boston: Beacon Press, 1957.

Diggins, John Patrick. *The Promise of Pragmatism: Modernism and the Crisis of Authority*. Chicago: University of Chicago Press, 1994.

Dilworth, David. A. *Philosophy in World Perspective: A Comparative Hermeneutic of the Major Theories*. New Haven CT: Yale University Press, 1989.

Dirlik, Arif. "Confucius in the Borderlands: Global Capitalism and the Reinvention of Confucianism." *Boundary 2* (Fall 1995): 229–73, 1995.

———. "Markets, Culture, Power: The Making of a Second Cultural Revolution in China." *Asian Studies Review* 25, no. 1 (2001): 1–33, 2001.

Dubs, Homer H. *Hsüntze: The Moulder of Ancient Confucianism*. Taipei: Ch'eng-Wen Publishing Company, 1966. (Reprint of Arthur Probsthain ed., 1927.)

Dunne, George H. *Generation of Giants: The Story of the Jesuits in China in the Last Decades of the Ming Dynasty*. Notre Dame: University of Notre Dame Press, 1962.

Dworkin, Ronald, Mark Lilla, and Robert B. Silvers. *The Legacy of Isaiah Berlin*. New York: New York Review of Books, 2001.

Eber, Irene, ed. *Confucianism: The Dynamics of Tradition*. New York: Macmillan, 1986.

Ebery, Patricia Buckley. *Confucianism and Family Rituals in Imperial China: A Social History of Writing about Rites*. Princeton NJ: Princeton University Press, 1991.

Eisenstadt, S. N. *Japanese Civilization: A Comparative Study*. Chicago: University of Chicago Press, 1996.

Elman, Benjamin A. *From Philosophy to Philosophy: Intellectual and Social Aspects of Change in Late Imperial China*. Cambridge: Harvard University Press, 1984.

———. *Classicism, Politics and Kinship: The Ch'ang-Chou School of New Test Confucianism in Later Imperial China*. Berkeley and Los Angeles: University of California Press, 1990.

———. *A Cultural History of Civil Examinations in Late Imperial China*. Berkeley and Los Angeles: University of California Press, 2000.

Emmet, Dorothy. *Function, Purpose and Powers*. London: Macmillian, 1958

———. *Effectiveness of Causes*. Albany: State University of New York Press, 1985.

———. *The Passage of Nature*. Philadelphia: Temple University Press, 1992.

Empiricus, Sextus. *Outlines of Scepticism*. Ed. Julia Annas and Jonathan Barnes. Cambridge: Cambridge University Press, 2000.

Eno, Robert. *The Confucian Creation of Heaven: Philosophy and the Defense of Ritual Mastery*. Albany: State University of New York Press, 1990.

Faivre, Antoine. *Access to Western Esotericism*. Albany: State University of New York Press, 1994.

———. *Theosophy, Imagination, Tradition: Studies in Western Esotericism*. Trans. Christine Rhone. Albany: State University of New York Press, 2000.

Fang, Thomé H. *Chinese Philosophy: Its Spirit and Development*. Taipei: Linking 1981.

Fang, Zhaohui. "Metaphysics or *Xing (er) shangxue* 形 (而)上學 ? A Western Philosophical Term in Modern China." *Dao: A Journal of Philosophy* 5, no. 1 (2005): 89–107, 2005.

Faure, Bernard. *Double Exposure: Cutting Across Buddhist and Western Discourses*. Trans. Janet Lloyd. Stanford, CA: Stanford University Press, 2004.

Fehl, Noah Edward. *Rites and Propriety in Literature and Life: A Perspective for a Cultural History of Ancient China*. Hong Kong: The Chinese University of Hong Kong Press, 1971.

Fernández-Armesto, Felipe. *Millennium: A History of the Last Thousand Years*. New York: Scribner, 1995.

Ferry, Luc. *The New Ecological Order.* Trans. Carol Volk. Chicago: University of Chicago Press, 1995.

Fingarette, Herbert. *Confucius—the Secular as Sacred.* New York: Harper and Row, 1972.

Ford, Lewis S. *The Emergence of Whitehead's Metaphysics: 1925–1929.* Albany: State University of New York Press, 1984.

———. *Transforming Process Theism.* Albany: State University of New York Press, 2000.

Forke, Alfred. *The World Concept of the Chinese.* London: Arthur Probsthain, 1925.

Frank, André Gunder. *ReOrient: Global Economy in the Asian Age.* Berkeley and Los Angeles University of California Press, 1998.

French, Peter. *John Dee: The World of an Elizabethan Magus.* New York: Dorset Press, 1972.

Frisina, Warren G. *The Unity of Knowledge and Action: Toward a Nonrepresentational Theory of Knowledge.* Albany: State University of New York Press, 2002.

Fung, Yu-lan. *A History of Chinese Philosophy.* Trans Derk Bodde. 2 vols. Princeton NJ: Princeton University Press, 1952–53.

———. *A Short History of Chinese Philosophy.* Ed. Derk Bodde. New York: Macmillan, 1964.

Gardner, Daniel K. *Chu Hsi and the Ta-hsüeh: Neo-Confucian Reflection the Confucian Canon.* Cambridge: Harvard University Press, 1986.

———, trans. *Learning to Be a Sage: Selections from the Conversations of Master Chu, Arranged Topically.* Berkeley and Los Angeles: University of California Press, 1990.

Geaney, Jane. *On the Epistemology of the Senses in Early Chinese Thought.* Honolulu: University of Hawaii Press, 2002.

Gedalecia, David. "Wu Ch'eng: A Neo-Confucian of the Yüan." Ph.d. diss., Harvard University, 1971.

———. "Excursion into Substance and Function: The Development of the *T'i-yung* Paradigm in Chu Hsi." *Philosophy East & West* 24 (October 1974): 443–51, 1974.

———. *The Philosophy of Wu Ch'eng: A Neo-Confucian of the Yüan Dynasty.* Bloomington: Indiana University Press, 1999.

Ge Hong (282–343). *Baopuzi* [The master who embraces simplicity]. Sibu Beiyao Edition. Taipei: Chonghua shuju, 1966.

Girardot, Norman J. *The Victorian Translation of China: Jame Legge's Oriental Pilgrimage.* Berkeley and Los Angeles: University of California Press, 2002.

Goldin, Paul Rakita. *Rituals of the Way: The Philosophy of Xunzi.* Chicago: Open Court, 1999.

Graham, A. C. *The Book of Lieh-tzu.* London: John Murray, 1960.

———, trans. *Chuang-tzu: The Seven Inner Chapters and other writings from the book Chuang-tzu.* London: George Allen & Unwin, 1981.

———. *Reason and Spontaneity: A New Solution to the Problem of Fact and Value.* London: Curzon Press, 1985.

———. *Studies in Chinese Philosophy and Philosophical Literature*. Singapore: The Institute for East Asian Philosophy, 1986a.

———. *Yin-yang and the Nature of Correlative Thinking*. Singapore: The Institute of East Asian Philosophy, 1986b.

———. *Disputers of the Tao: Philosophical Argument in Ancient China*. La Salle: Open Court, 1989.

———. *Two Chinese Philosophers: The Metaphysics of the Brothers Ch'eng*. La Salle: Open Court, 1992a.

———. *Unreason within Reason: Essays on the Outskirts of Rationality*. La Salle: Open Court, 1992b.

Gray, John. *Isaiah Berlin*. Princeton, NJ: Princeton University Press, 1996.

Griffin, David Ray. *Reenchantment without Supernaturalism: A Process Philosophy of Religion*. Ithaca NY: Cornell University Press, 2001.

Gunn, Giles. *Thinking Across the American Grain: Ideology, Intellect, and the New Pragmatism*. Chicago: University of Chicago Press, 1992.

———. *Beyond Solidarity: Pragmatism and Difference in a Globalized World*. Chicago: University of Chicago Press, 2001.

Gunton, Colin E. *The Promise of Trinitarian Thought*. Second Edition. Edinburgh: T & T Clark, 1997.

Hagen, Kurtis. "Xunzi and the Nature of Confucian Ritual." *Journal of the American Academy of Religion* 71, no. 2 (June 2003): 371–403, 2003.

Hall, David L. *The Civilization of Experience: A Whiteheadian Theory of Culture*. New York: Fordham University Press, 1973.

———. *Eros and Irony: A Prelude to Philosophic Anarchism*. Albany: State University of New York Press, 1982a.

———. *The Uncertain Phoenix: Adventures Toward a Post-Cultural Sensibility*. New York: Fordham University Press, 1982b.

Hall, David L., and Roger T. Ames. *Thinking through Confucius*. Albany: State University of New York Press, 1987.

———. *Anticipating China: Thinking Through the Narratives of Chinese and Western Culture*. Albany: State University of New York Press, 1995.

———. *Thinking from the Han: Self, Truth, and Transcendence in Chinese and Western Culture*. Albany: State University of New York Press, 1998.

———. *The Democracy of the Dead: Dewey, Confucius, and the Hope for Democracy in China*. La Salle: Open Court, 1999.

———. *Focusing on the Familiar: A Translation and Philosophical Interpretation of the Zhongyong*. Honolulu: University of Hawaii Press, 2001.

Hanegraaff, Wouter G. *New Age Religion and Western Culture: Esotericism in the Mirror of Secular Thought*. Albany: State University of New York Press, 1998.

Hankinson, R. J. *The Sceptics*. New York: Routledge, 1998.

Hansen, Chad. *Language and Logic in Ancient China*. Ann Arbor: The University of Michigan Press, 1983.

———. *A Daoist Theory of Chinese Thought: A Philosophic Interpretation*. Oxford: Oxford University Press, 1992.

Harbsmeier, Christoph. *Science and Civilisation in China: Language and Logic*. vol. 7, part 1. Ed. Kenneth Robinson. Cambridge: Cambridge University Press, 1998.

Harkness, Deborah E. *John Dee's Conversations with Angels: Cabala, Alchemy, and the End of Nature*. Cambridge: Cambridge University Press, 1999.

Harootunian, Harry. *History's Disquiet: Modernity, Cultural Practice, and the Question of Everyday Life*. New York: Columbia University Press, 2000.

Harré, Rom and Michael Krausz. *Varieties of Relativism*. Oxford: Basil Blackwell, 1996.

Harris, James F. *Against Relativism: A Philosophical Defense of Method*. La Salle: Open Court, 1992.

Hartshorne, Charles. *The Logic of Perfection and Other Essays in Neoclassical Metaphysics*. La Salle: Open Court, 1962.

———. *The Divine Relativity: A Social Conception of God*. New Haven: Yale University Press. 1962.

———. *A Natural Theology for Our Time*. La Salle: Open Court, 1967.

———. *Creative Synthesis and Philosophic Method*. La Salle: The Open Court Publishing Company, 1970.

———. *Aquinas to Whitehead: Seven Centuries of Metaphysics of Religion*. Milwaukee: Marquette University Press, 1976.

———. *Insights & Oversights of Great Thinkers: An Evaluation of Western Philosophy*. Albany: State University of New York Press, 1983.

———. *Creativity in American Philosophy*. Albany: State University of New York Press, 1984a.

———. *Omnipotence and Other Theological Mistakes*. Albany: State University of New York Press, 1984b.

———. *The Zero Fallacy and Other Essays in Neoclassical Philosophy*. Ed. Mohammad Valady. La Salle: Open Court, 1997.

Hartshorne, Charles and William L. Reese, eds. *Philosophers Speak of God*. Chicago: University of Chicago Press. 1953.

Harvey, Graham. *Contemporary Paganism: Listening People, Speaking Earth*. New York: New York University Press, 1997.

Hauerwas, Stanley. *With the Grain of the Universe: The Church's Witness and Natural Theology*. Grand Rapids: Brazos Press, 2001.

Henderson, John B. *The Development and Decline of Chinese Cosmology*. New York: Columbia University Press, 1984.

———. *Scripture, Canon, and Commentary: A Comparison of Confucian and Western Exegesis*. Princeton NJ: Princeton University Press, 1991.

———. *The Construction of Orthodoxy and Heresy: Neo-Confucian, Islamic, Jewish and Early Christian Patterns*. Albany: State University of New York Press, 1998.

Hermanson, Jonathan R. "Human Heart, Heavenly Heart: Mystical Dimensions of Chu Hsi's Neo-Confucianism." *Journal of the American Academy of Religion* 69, no. 1 (March 2001): 103–28, 2001.

Hick, John. *An Interpretation of Religion: Human Responses to the Transcendent*. New Haven: Yale University Press, 1989.

Hinsch, Bret. *Women in Early Imperial China*. Blue Ridge Summit, PA: Rowman and Littlefield, 2002.

History of Religions. "Current Perspectives in the Study of Chinese Religions." *History of Religions* 17, nos. 3 and 4 (February-May 1978), 1978.

Hocking, William Ernest. "Chu Hsi's Theory of Knowledge." *Harvard Journal of Asiatic Studies* 1 (1936): 109–27, 1936.

Holcombe, Charles. *In the Shadow of the Han: Literati Thought and Society at the Beginning of the Southern Dynasties*. Honolulu: University of Hawaii Press, 1994.

Hong, Jun. *Zhu Xi yu Ligu [Yulgok] zhexue bijiao yanjiu* [A Comparative Study of the Philosophy of Zhu Xi and [Yi] Ligu. Beijing: Chinese Academy of Social Sciences, 2003.

Hosinski, Thomas E. *Stubborn Fact and Creative Advance: An Introduction to the Metaphysics of Alfred North Whitehead*. Lanham, Maryland: Rowman and Littlefield 1993.

Huang, Chun-chieh. *Mencian Hermeneutics: A History of Interpretations in China*. New Brunswick, NJ: Transaction, 2001.

Huang, Siu-chi. "Chang Tsai's Concept of *Ch'i*." *Philosophy East & West* 18 (October 1968): 247–60, 1968.

———. "The Moral Point of View of Chang Tsai." *Philosophy East & West* 21 (April 1971): 141–56, 1971.

———. *Lu Hsiang-shan: A Twelfth-Century Chinese Idealist Philosophy*. Westport, CT: Hyperion Press, 1977.

———. *Essentials of Neo-Confucianism: Eight Major Philosophers of the Song and Ming Periods*. Westport, CT: Greenwood Press, 1999.

Huang Tsung-hsi. *The Records of Ming Scholars*. Ed. Julia Ching with the collaboration of Chaoying Fang. Honolulu: University of Hawaii Press, 1987.

Hughes, E. R. *The Great Learning and the Mean-in-Action*. New York: Dutton , 1943.

Huntington, Samuel P. *The Clash of Civilizations and the Remaking of the World Order*. New York: Simon and Schuster, 1996.

Hutton, Ronald. *The Triumph of the Moon: A History of Modern Pagan Witchcraft*. Oxford: Oxford University Press, 1999.

Ivanhoe, Philip J. *Ethics in the Confucian Tradition: The Thought of Mencius and Wang Yang-ming*. Atlanta: Scholars Press, 1990.

———. "Confucian Moral Self Cultivation." *Journal of the American Academy of Religion* 59, no. 2 (Summer 1993): 309–22, 1993.

———, ed. *Chinese Language, Thought, and Culture: Nivison and His Critics*. La Salle: Open Court, 1996.

———. *Confucian Moral Self Cultivation*. 2nd ed. Indianapolis: Hackett Publishing Company, 2000.

Ivanhoe, Philip J., and Xiusheng Liu, eds. *Essays on the Moral Philosophy of Mengzi*. Indianapolis: Hackett, 2002.

Jackson, Carl T. *The Oriental Religions and American Thought.* Westport CT: Greenwood Press, 1981.

Jacob, Margaret C. *The Radical Enlightenment: Pantheists, Freemasons and Republicans.* London: George Allen and Unwin, 1981.

Jacobson, Nolan Pliny. *The Heart of Buddhist Philosophy.* Carbondale: Southern Illinois University Press, 1988.

Jensen, Lionel M. "The Invention of 'Confucius' and His Chinese Other, 'Kong Fuzi.' *Positions* 1, no. 2 (Fall 1993): 414–49, 1993.

———. *Manufacturing Confucianism: Chinese Traditions and Universal Civilization.* Durham: Duke University Press, 1997.

Jinkins, Michael. *Christianity, Tolerance and Pluralism: A Theological Engagement with Isaiah Berlin's Social Theory.* London: Routledge, 2004.

Johnson, Mark. *The Body in the Mind: The Bodily Basis of Meaning, Imagination, and Reason.* Chicago: University of Chicago Press, 1987.

———. *Moral Imagination: Implications of Cognitive Science for Ethics.* Chicago: University of Chicago Press, 1993.

Jonsen, Albert R., and Stephen Toulmin. *The Abuse of Casuistry: A History of Moral Reasoning.* Berkeley and Los Angeles: University of California Press, 1988.

Jullien, François. *The Propensity of Things: Towards a History of Efficacy in China.* Trans. Janet Lloyd. New York: Zone Books, 1995.

———. *Detour and Access: Strategies of Meaning in China and Greece.* Trans. Sophie Hawkes. New York: Zone Books, 2000.

———. *In Praise of Blandness: Proceeding from Chinese Thought and Aesthetics.* Trans. Paula M. Varsano. New York: Zone Books, 2004.

Kalton, Michael C., trans. *To Become a Sage: The Ten Diagrams on Sage Learning by Yi T'oegye.* New York: Columbia University Press, 1988.

Kalton, Michael C, ed. *The Four Seven Debate: An Annotated Translation of the Most Famous Controversy in Korean Neo-Confucian Thought.* Albany: State University of New York Press, 1994.

Kantor, Hans-Rudolf. "Ontological Indeterminacy and Its Soteriological Relevance: An Assessment of Mou Zongsan's (1909–1995) Interpretation of Zhiyi's (538–597) Tiantai Buddhism." *Philosophy East and West* 56, no. 1 (January 2006): 16–68, 2006.

Kasoff, Ira E. *The Thought of Chang Tsai.* Cambridge: Cambridge University Press, 1984.

Kasulis, Thomas P. *Intimacy or Integrity: Philosophy and Cultural Difference.* Honolulu, HI: University of Hawaii Press, 2002.

Kaufman, Gordon D. *In the Face of Mystery: A Constructive Theology.* Cambridge, MA: Harvard University Press, 1993.

———. *In the Beginning Creativity.* Minneapolis: Fortress Press, 2004.

———. *Jesus and Creativity.* Minneapolis: Fortress Press, 2006.

Keenan, James F., and Thomas A. Shannon, eds. *The Context of Casuistry.* Washington, D.C.: Georgetown University Press, 1995.

Kestenbaum, Victor. *The Grace and Severity of the Ideal: John Dewey and the Transcendent*. Chicago: University of Chicago Press, 2002.

Kim, Yung Sik. *The Natural Philosophy of Chu Hsi, 1130–1200*. Philadelphia: Memoirs of the American Philosophic Society, 2002.

King, Richard. *Orientalism and Religion: Postcolonial Theory, India and 'The Mystic East"*. London: Routledge, 1999.

Kirk, Kenneth E. *Conscience and its Problems: An Introduction to Casuistry*. London and New York: Longmans, Green, 1927.

Kline, T. C., III, and Philip J. Ivanhoe, eds. *Virtue, Nature, and Moral Agency in the Xunzi*. Indianapolis: Hackett, 2000.

Knoblock, John. *Xunzi: A Translation and Study of the Complete Works*. 3 vols. Stanford, CA: Stanford University Press, 1988–94.

Kohn, Livia. *Early Chinese Mysticism: Philosophy and Soteriology in the Taoist Tradition*. Princeton, NJ: Princeton University Press, 1992.

———, ed. *Daoism Handbook*. Leiden: Brill, 2000.

———. *Daoism and Chinese Culture*. Cambridge: Three Pines Press, 2001.

Kohn, Livia, and Harold D. Roth, eds. *Daoist Identity: History, Lineage, and Ritual*. Honolulu, HI: University of Hawaii Press, 2002.

Kuklick, Bruce. *The Rise of American Philosophy: Cambridge, Massachusetts 1860–1930*. New Haven: Yale University Press, 1977.

———. *Churchmen and Philosophers: From Jonathan Edwards to John Dewey*. New Haven: Yale University Press, 1985.

———. *A History of Philosophy in America 1720–2000*. Oxford: Clarendon Press, 2001.

Lach, Donald. *Asia in the Making of Europe*. 6 vols. Chicago: University of Chicago Press, 1965.

Lai, Yuen-ting. "Religious Scepticism in China." Ed. Richard A Watson and James E. Force, *The Sceptical Mode in Modern Philosophy: Essays in Honor of Richard H. Popkin*, Dordrecht: Martinus Nijhoff, 1988.

Lakoff, George. *Women, Fire, and Dangerous Things: What Categories Reveal about the Mind*. Chicago: University of Chicago Press, 1987.

———. *Moral Politics: How Liberals and Conservatives Think*. 2nd ed. Chicago: University of Chicago Press, 2002.

Lakoff, George and Mark Johnson. *Metaphors We Live By*. Chicago: University of Chicago Press, 1980.

Lakoff, George and Mark Turner. *More Than Cool Reason: A Field Guide to Poetic Metaphor*. Chicago: University of Chicago Press, 1989.

Lakoff, George and Mark Johnson. *Philosophy in the Flesh: The Embodied Mind and Its Challenge to Western Thought*. New York: Basic Books, 1999.

Lakoff, George and Rafael E. Núñez. *Where Mathematics Comes From: How the Embodied Mind Brings Mathematics into Being*. New York: Basic Books, 2000.

Lau, D. C., and Roger T. Ames, trans. *Yuan Dao: Tracing Dao to Its Source*. New York: Ballantine Books, 1998.

Ledderose, Lothar. *Ten Thousand Things: Module and Mass Production in Chinese Arts*. Princeton NJ: Princeton University Press, 2000.

Lee, Janghee. *Xunzi and Early Chinese Naturalism*. Albany: State University of New York Press, 2005.

Lehrich, Christopher I. *Language of Demons and Angels: Cornelius Agrippa's Occult Philosophy*. Leiden: Brill, 2005.

Leibniz, Gottfried Wilhelm. *Discourse on the Natural Theology of the Chinese*. Trans. Henry Rosemont and Daniel J. Cook. Honolulu: University of Hawaii Press, 1977.

Leibniz, Gottfried Wilhelm. *Writings on China*. Trans. by Daniel J. Cook and Henry Rosemont, Jr. Chicago: Open Court, 1994.

Levey, Matthew A. "Chu Hsi as a "Neo-Confucian": Chu Hsi's Critique of Heterodoxy, Heresy, and the "Confucian" Tradition." PhD. diss., Chicago: University of Chicago, 1991.

Lewis, Mark Edward. *Sanctioned Violence in Early China*. Albany: State University of New York Press, 1990.

Leys, Simon, trans. *The Analects of Confucius*. New York: W. W. Norton, 1997.

Li, Chenyang. *The Tao Encounters the West: Explorations in Comparative Philosophy*. Albany: State University of New York Press, 1999.

———, ed. *The Sage and the Second Sex: Confucianism, Ethics, and Gender*. Chicago: Open Court, 2000.

Li, Guangdi. *Zhuzi chuanshu* [The complete words of Master Zhu]. 2 vols. Taipei: She Yin Shu Yuan Yin Xing, 1977

Li, Minghui. "Li nengfuo huodong? 理 能否 活動 [Can *li*/principle move?]" *Modern Philosophy* 2005 no.2 (2005): 41–48, 2005.

Li, Qingde. *Zhuzi yulei daquan* [The classified conversations of Master Zhu]. 8 vols. Tokyo: n.p., 1973. (Copy of Japanese edition of 1668)

Liang, Qixiung. 1963. "Xunzi sixiang shuping [A critical exposition of Xunzi's thought]." *Zhexue yanjiu* 4 (1963).

———, ed. *Xunzi jianshi* [Select commentary on the *Xunzi*]. Taipei: Holo Library Publishing Society, 1974.

Liu, Dajun et al., trans. *The I Ching: Text and Annotated Translation*. Jinan: Shandong Friendship Publishing House, 1995.

Liu, Shuxian [Liu Shu-hsien] *Zhuzi zhexue sixaing de fachan yu yuancheng* [The development and completion of Master Zhu's philosophic thought]. Taipei: Student Book Company, 1982.

———. *Understanding Confucian Philosophy: Classical and Sung-Ming*. Westport CT: Praeger, 1998.

———. *Essentials of Contemporary Neo-Confucian Philosophy*. Westport CT: Praeger, 2003

Liu, Xiusheng. *Mencius, Hume and the Foundations of Ethics*. Burlington: Ashgate, 2003.

Lloyd, G. E. R. *Demystifying Mentalities.* Cambridge: Cambridge University Press, 1990.

———. *Adversaries and Authorities: Investigations into Ancient Greek and Chinese Science.* Cambridge: Cambridge University Press, 1996.

Lloyd, Geoffrey, and Nathan Sivin. *The Way and the Word: Science and Medicine in Early China and Greece.* New Haven: Yale University Press, 2002.

Lodge, David. *The British Museum Is Falling Down.* London: Penguin, 1998.

Long, A. A. *Hellenistic Philosophy: Stoics, Epicureans, Sceptics.* Berkeley and Los Angles: University of California Press, 1986.

Lynn, Richard John, Trans. *The Classic of Changes: A New Translation of the I Ching as Interpreted by Wang Bi.* New York: Columbia University Press, 1994.

Machle, Edward J. *Nature and Heaven in the Xunzi: A Study of the Tian Lun.* Albany: State University of New York Press, 1993.

MacIntyre, Alasdair. *After Virtue.* 2nd ed. Notre Dame: Notre Dame University Press, 1984.

———. *Whose Justice? Whose Rationality?* Notre Dame: Notre Dame University Press, 1988.

———. *Three Rival Versions of Moral Enquiry: Encyclopedia, Genealogy and Tradition.* Notre Dame: Notre Dame University Press, 1990.

Makeham, John. *Name and Actuality in Early Chinese Thought.* Albany: State University of New York Press, 1995.

———. "A New Hermeneutic Approach to Early Chinese Texts: The Case of the *Analects.*" *Sophia* Vol. 41, No. 1 (May 2002): 55–69, 2002

———, ed. *New Confucianism: A Critical Examination.* New York: Palgrave Macmillan, 2003a.

———. *Transmitters and Creators: Chinese Commentators and Commentaries on the Analects.* Cambridge: Harvard University Press, 2003b.

———. *Lost Soul: "Confucianism" in Contemporary Chinese Academic Discourse.* Harvard: Harvard University Asia Center, 2008.

Margolis, Joseph. *Pragmatism with Foundations: Reconciling Realism and Relativism.* Oxford: Basil Blackwell, 1986.

———. *The Truth about Relativism.* Oxford: Basil Blackwell, 1991.

———. *Interpretation Radical But Not Unruly: The New Puzzle of the Arts and History.* Berkeley and Los Angeles: University of California Press, 1995.

———. *Life without Principles: Reconciling Theory and Practice.* Oxford: Basil Blackwell, 1996.

Markhan, Ian S. *Plurality and Christian Ethics.* New York: Cambridge University Press, 1994.

Marsoobian, Armen, Kathleen Wallace, and Robert S. Corrington, eds. *Nature's Perspectives: Prospects for Ordinal Metaphysics.* Albany: State University of New York Press, 1991.

Masuzawa, Tomoko. *The Invention of Religion*. Chicago: University of Chicago Press, 2005.

McCutcheon, Russell R. *Manufacturing Religion: The Discourse of Sui Generis Religion and the Politics of Nostalgia*. New York and Oxford: Oxford University Press, 1997.

———. *Critics Not Caretakers: Redescribing the Public Study of Religion*. Albany: State University of New York Press, 2001.

Meland, Bernard E. *The Realities of Faith: The Revolution in Cultural Forms*. New York: Oxford University Press, 1962.

———. *The Secularization of Modern Cultures*. New York: Oxford University Press, 1966.

———, ed. *The Future of Empirical Theology*. Chicago: University of Chicago Press, 1969.

———. *Faith and Culture*. Carbondale: Southern Illinois University Press, 1972.

———. *Fallible Forms and Symbols: Discourses in a Theology of Culture*. Philadelphia: Fortress Press, 1976.

———. *Essays in Constructive Theology: A Process Perspective*. Ed. Perry LeFevre. Chicago: Exploration Press, 1988.

Metzger, Thomas A. *Escape from Predicament: Neo-Confucianism and China's Evolving Political Culture*. New York: Columbia University Press, 1975.

———. *A Cloud Across the Pacific: Essays on the Clash between Chinese and Western Political Theories Today*. Hong Kong: Chinese University Press, 2005.

Milbank, John. *Theology and Social Science: Beyond Secular Reason*. Oxford: Blackwell, 1993.

Milbank, John, Catherine Pickstock, and Graham Ward. *Radical Orthodoxy*. London: Routledge, 1999.

Miller, James. *Daoism: A Short Introduction*. Oxford: Oneworld, 2003.

Miller, Richard B. *Casuistry and Modern Ethics: A Poetics of Practical Reasoning*. Chicago: University of Chicago Press, 1996.

Morris, Charles. *The Pragmatic Movement in American Philosophy*. New York: George Braziller, 1970.

Mote, Frederick W. *Intellectual Foundations of China*. 2nd ed. New York: McGraw-Hill, 1989.

———. *Imperial China 900–1800*. Cambridge, MA: Harvard University Press, 1999.

Mou, Bo, ed. *Comparative Approaches to Chinese Philosophy*. Burlington: Ashgate, 2003.

Mou Zongsan. *Xindi yu Xingdi* [Mind and nature]. 3 vols. Taipei, Taiwan: Zhengjing Shuju, 1968–69.

———. *Lishi zhexue* [Philosophy of history]. Taipei: Student Book Company, 1974.

———. 1983. *Zongguo zhexue shijiu jiang* [Nineteen lectures on Chinese philosophy]. Taipei: Taiwan: Student Book Company, 1983.

———. *Yuanshan lun* [Summum bonum]. Taipei: Student Book Company, 1985.

———. *Zhongxi zhexue zhi huitong shisi jiang* [Fourteen lectures on understanding Chinese and Western philosophy]. Taipei: Student Book Company, 1990.

———. *Zhongguo Zhexue de tezhi* [Special traits/features of Chinese philosophy]. Taipei, Taiwan: Student Book Company, 1994.

Mungello, David E. *Curious Land: Jesuit Accommodation and the Origins of Sinology.* Stuttgart: Franz Steiner Verlag Wiesdbaden GMBH, 1985.

Munro, Donald J. *The Concept of Man in Early China.* Stanford: Stanford University Press, 1969.

———. *The Concept of Man in Contemporary China.* Ann Arbor: University of Michigan Press, 1977.

———. *Images of Human Nature: A Sung Portrait.* Princeton: Princeton University Press, 1988.

———. *A Chinese Ethics for the New Century: The Ch'ien Mu Lectures in History and Culture, and Other Essays on Science and Confucian Ethics.* Hong Kong: Chinese University Press, 2005.

Nauert, Charles G., Jr. *Agrippa and the Crisis of Renaissance Thought.* Urbana: University of Illinois Press, 1965.

Needham, Joseph, et al. *Science and Civilisation in China.* 8 vols. Cambridge: Cambridge University Press, 1954.

Neiman, Susan. *Evil in Modern Thought: An Alternative History of Philosophy.* Princeton, NJ: Princeton University Press, 2002.

Neville, Robert Cummings. *The High Road Around Modernism.* Albany: State University of New York Press, 1992.

———. *Eternity and Time's Flow.* Albany: State University of New York Press, 1993.

———. *Normative Cultures.* Albany: State University of New York Press, 1995a.

———. *The Cosmology of Freedom.* New Edition. Albany: State University of New York Press, 1995b.

———. *Creativity and God: A Challenge to Process Theism.* New ed. . Albany: State University of New York Press, 1995c

———. *Boston Confucianism: Portable Tradition in the Late-Modern World.* Albany: State University of New York Press, 2000.

———, ed. *The Human Condition: A Volume in the Comparative Religious Ideas Project.* Albany: State University of New York Press, 2001a.

———, ed. *Religious Truth: A Volume in the Comparative Religious Ideas Project.* Albany: State University of New York Press, 2001b.

———, ed. *Ultimate Realities: A Volume in the Comparative Religious Ideas Project.* Albany, NY: State University of New York Press, 2001c.

———. *Religion in Late Modernity.* Albany: State University of New York Press, 2002.

Ng, On-cho. *Cheng-Zhu Confucianism in the Early Qing: Li Guanddi (1642–1718) and Qing Learning.* Albany: State University of New York Press, 2001.

Nivison, David S. *The Life and Thought of Chang Hsüeh-ch'eng (1738–1801).* Stanford: Stanford University Press, 1966.

———. *The Ways of Confucianism: Investigations in Chinese Philosophy.* Ed. Bryan W. Van Norden. Chicago: Open Court, 1996.

Noble, David F. *The Religion of Technology: The Divinity of Man and the Spirit of Invention.* New York: Penguin Books, 1999.

Nylan, Michael. *Five "Confucian" Classics.* New Haven: Yale University Press, 2001.

Odin, Steve. *The Social Self in Zen and American Pragmatism.* Albany: State University of New York Press, 1996.

Papper, Jordan. *The Spirits are Drunk: Comparative Approaches to Chinese Religion.* Albany: State University of New York Press, 1995.

———. *The Deities Are Many: A Polytheistic Theology.* Albany: State University of New York Press, 2005.

Patton, Kimberly C., and Benjamin C. Ray, eds. *A Magic Still Dwells: Comparative Religion in the Postmodern Age.* Berkley and Los Angeles: University of California Press, 2000.

Pepper, Stephen C. *World Hypotheses: A Study in Evidence.* Berkeley and Los Angeles: University of California Press, 1942.

———. *A Digest of Purposive Values.* Berkeley and Los Angeles: University of California Press, 1947.

———. *The Sources of Value.* Berkeley and Los Angeles: University of California Press, 1958.

———. *Concept and Quality: A World Hypothesis.* La Salle: Open Court Publishing Company, 1966.

Pines, Yuri. *Foundations of Confucian Thought: Intellectual Life in the Chunqiu Period, 722–453 B.C.E.* Honolulu: University of Hawaii Press, 2002.

Pohl, Karl-Heinz, ed. *Chinese Thought in a Global Context: A Dialogue Between Chinese and Western Philosophic Approaches.* Leiden: Brill, 1999.

Popkin, Richard H. *Scepticism in the History of Philosophy: A Pan-American Dialogue.* Dordrecht: Kluwer 1996.

———, Ezequiel de Olaso, and Giorgio Tonelli, eds. *Scepticism in the Enlightenment.* Dordrecht: Kluwer, *1997.*

———. *The History of Scepticism: From Savonarola to Bayle.* Rev. and expan. ed. New York, 2003.

Porkert, Manfred. *The Theoretical Foundations of Chinese Medicine: Systems of Correspondence.* Cambridge: MIT Press, 1974.

Porkert, Manfred and Christian Ullmann. *Chinese Medicine.* Trans. Mark Howson. New York: William Morrow and Company, 1988.

Puett, Michael J. *The Ambivalence of Creation: Debates Concerning Innovation and Artifice in Early China.* Stanford, CA: Stanford University Press, 2001.

———. *To Become a God: Cosmology, Sacrifice, and Self-Divinization in Early China.* Cambridge: Harvard University Press, 2002.

Qian Mu. *Zhuzi xin xuean* [A new study of Master Zhu]. 5 vols. Taipei: Sanmin shuju, 1971.

Randall, John Herman, Jr. *The Role of Knowledge in Western Religion*. Boston: Starr King Press, 1958a

———. *Nature and Historical Experience*. New York: Columbia University Press, 1958b

———. *The Making of the Modern Mind*. New York: Columbia University Press, 1976.

Raphals, Lisa. *Knowing Words: Wisdom and Cunning in the Classical Traditions of China and Greece*. Ithaca: Cornell University Press, 1991.

———. *Sharing the Light: Representations of Women and Virtue in Early China*. Albany: State University of New York Press, 1998.

Rappe, Sara. *Reading Neoplatonism: Non-discursive Thinking in the Texts of Plotinus, Proclus, and Damascius*. Cambridge: Cambridge University Press, 2000.

Ren, Jiyu, ed. *Zhongguo zhexue shi* [A history of Chinese philosophy]. 4 vols. Beijing: People's Publishing House, 1979.

Rescher, Nicholas. *The Strife of Systems: An Essay on the Grounds and Implications of Philosophical Diversity*. Pittsburgh: University of Pittsburgh Press, 1985.

———. *Pluralism: Against the Demand for Consensus*. Oxford: Clarendon Press, 1003

———.*Process Metaphysics: An Introduction to Process Philosophy*. Albany: State University of New York Press, 1993.

Ricouer, Paul. *The Rule of Metaphor: Multidisciplinary studies of the creation of meaning in language*. Trans Robert Czerny with Kathleen McLaughlin and John Costello. Toronto: University of Toronto Press, 1977.

Ro, Young-chan. *The Korean Neo-Confucianism of Yi Yulgok*. Albany: State University of New York Press, 1989.

Rockefeller, Steven C. *John Dewey: Religious Faith and Democratic Humanism*. New York: Columbia University Press, 1991.

Ronan, Colin A. *The Shorter History of Science and Civilisation in China: An Abridgement of Joseph Needham's Original Text*. Cambridge: Cambridge University Press, 1978.

Roof, Wade Clark. *A Generation of Seeks: The Spiritual Journeys of the Baby Boom Generation*. New York: Harper Collins, 1994.

———. *Spiritual Marketplace: Baby Boomers and the Remaking of American Religion*. Princeton, NJ: Princeton University Press, 1999.

Rozman, Gilbert, ed. *The East Asian Region: Confucian Heritage and Its Modern Adaptation*. Princeton NJ: Princeton University Press, 1991.

Rorty, Richard. *Philosophy and the Mirror of Nature*. Princeton NJ: Princeton University Press, 1979.

———. *Consequences of Pragmatism*. Minneapolis: University of Minnesota Press, 1982.

———. *Contingency, Irony, and Solidarity*. Cambridge: Cambridge University Press 1989.

———. *Truth and Progress*. Cambridge: Cambridge University Press, 1998.

Ross, Stephen David. *Transition to an Ordinal Metaphysics*. Albany: State University of New York Press, 1980.

———. *Metaphysical Aporia and Philosophical Heresy*. Albany: State University of New York Press, 1989.

———. *The Ring of Representation*. Albany: State University of New York Press.

Roth, Harold D. *The Original Tao: Inward Training (Nei-yeh) and the Foundations of Taoist Mysticism*. New York: Columbia University Press, 1999.

Ryder, John, ed. *American Philosophic Naturalism in the Twentieth Century*. Amherst, NY: Prometheus Books, 1994.

Saley, Jay. *The Master Who Embraces Simplicity: A Study of the Philosopher Ko Hung, A. D. 283–343*. Taipei: Chinese Materials Center, 1978.

Saussy, Haun. *Great Walls of Discourse and Other Adventures in Cultural China*. Cambridge: Harvard University Press, 2001.

Schaberg, David. *A Patterned Past: Form and Thought in Early Chinese Historiography*. Cambridge: Harvard University Press, 2001.

Scharfstein, Ben-Ami. *The Philosophers: Their Lives and the Nature of Their Thought*. Oxford: Oxford University Press, 1980.

———. *The Dilemma of Context*. New York: New York University Press, 1989.

———. *A Comparative History of World Philosophy from the Upanishads to Kant*. Albany: State University of New York Press, 1998.

Schwartz, Benjamin. *The World of Thought in Ancient China*. Cambridge: Harvard University Press, 1985.

Schwartz, Vera. *The Chinese Enlightenment: Intellectuals and the Legacy of the May Fourth Movement of 1919*. Berkeley and Los Angeles: University of California Press, 1986.

Seligman, Adam. *Modernity's Wager: Authority, the Self, and Transcendence*. Princeton: Princeton University Press, 2000.

Selover, Thomas W. *Hsieh Liang-tso and the "Analects" of Confucius: Humane Learning as a Religious Quest*. New York: Oxford University Press, 2005.

Shankman, Steven, and Stephen Durrant. *The Siren and the Sage: Knowledge and Wisdom in Ancient Greece and China*. London: Cassell, 2000.

Shaw, Gregory. *Theurgy and the Soul: The Neoplatonism of Iamblichus*. University Park: Pennsylvania State University Press, 1995.

Shook, John R., ed. *Pragmatic Naturalism and Realism*. Amherst: Prometheus Books, 2003.

Shun, Kwong-loi. *Mencius and Early Chinese Thought*. Stanford: Stanford University Press, 1997.

Shun, Kwong-loi, and David B. Wong, eds. *Confucian Ethics: A Comparative Study of Self, Autonomy, and Community*. Cambridge: Cambridge University Press, 2004.

Singer, Beth J. *Ordinal Naturalism: An Introduction to the Philosophy of Justus Buchler*. Lewisberg: Bucknell University Press, 1983.

Slingerland, Edward. *Effortless Action: Wu-wei as Conceptual Metaphor and Spiritual Ideal in Early China*. New York: Oxford University Press, 2003.

Slote, Walter H., and George A. DeVos, eds. *Confucianism and the Family*. Albany: State University of New York Press, 1998.

Smart, Ninian. *Religion and the Western Mind*. Albany: State University of New York Press, 1987.

———. *Dimensions of the Sacred: An Anatomy of the World's Beliefs*. Berkeley and Los Angeles: University of California Press, 1996.

———. *World Philosophies*. London and New York: Routledge, 1999.

Smith, Kidder. "Sima Tan and the Invention of Daoism, "Legalism," *et cetera*." *Journal of Asian Studies*. Vol. 62, no. 1 (February 2003): 129–156, 2003.

Smith, Wilfred Cantwell. *Toward a World Theology: Faith and the History of Religion*. Philadelphia: Westminster Press, 1981.

———. *What is Scripture: A Comparative Approach*. Minneapolis: Fortress Press, 1993.

———. *Modern Culture from a Comparative Perspective*. Ed. John W. Burbidge. Albany: State University of New York Press, 1997.

Spence, Jonathan D. *Emperor of China: Self-Portrait of K'ang-hsi*. New York: Alfred A. Knopf 1974.

———. *The Chan's Great Continent: China in Western Minds*. New York: W. W. Norton, 1998.

Spretnak, Charlene. *States of Grace: The Recovery of Meaning in the Postmodern Age*. New York: HarperCollins, 1991.

———. *The Resurgence of the Real: Body, Nature, and Place in a Hypermodern World*. New York: Routledge, 1999.

Stalnaker, Aaron. *Overcoming Our Evil: Human Nature and Spiritual Exercises in Xunzi and Augustine*. Wessington: Georgetown University Press, 2006.

Stephens, Walter. *Demon Lovers: Witchcraft, Sex, and the Crisis of Belief*. Chicago: University of Chicago Press, 2002.

Sterckx, Roel. *The Animal and the Daemon in Early China*. Albany: State University of New York Press, 2002.

Stewart, Charles, and Rosalind Shaw, eds. *Syncretism/Anti-Syncretism: The Politics of Religious Synthesis*. London: Routledge, 1994.

Stone, Jerome A. *The Minimalist Vision of Transcendence: A Naturalist Philosophy of Religion*. Albany: State University of New York Press, 1992.

Stough, Charlotte, L. *Greek Skepticism: A Study in Epistemology*. Berkeley and Los Angeles: University of California Press, 1969.

Stout, Jeffery. *The Flight from Authority: Religion, Morality and the Quest for Autonomy*. Notre Dame: University of Norte Dame Press, 1981.

———. *Ethics after Babel: The Languages of Morals and Their Discontent*. Boston: Beacon Press, 1988.

Suchocki, Marjorie Hewitt. *God Christ Church: A Practical Guide to Process Theology*. Rev. ed. New York: Crossroad, 1992.

———. *Divinity and Diversity: A Christian Affirmation of Religious Pluralism*. Nashville, TN: Abingdon Press, 2003.

Sutin, Lawrence. *Do What Thou Wilt: A Life of Aleister Crowley*. New York: St. Martin's Press, 2000.

Swimme, Brian. *The Hidden Heart of the Cosmos*. Maryknoll, NY: Orbis Books, 1996.

Swimme, Brian, and Thomas Berry. *The Universe Story*. New York: HarperSanFrancisco, 1992.

Tan, Sor-Hoon. *Confucian Democracy: A Deweyan Reconstruction*. Albany: State University of New York Press, 2003.

Taylor, Charles. *Sources of the Self: The Making of Modern Identity*. Cambridge: Harvard University Press, 1989.

Taylor, Mark C. *The Moment of Complexity: Emerging Network Culture*. Chicago: University of Chicago Press, 2001.

Taylor, Rodney. *The Religious Dimensions of Confucianism*. Albany: State University of New York Press, 1990.

Thayer, H. S. *Meaning and Action: A Study of American Pragmatism*. Indianapolis and New York: Bobbs-Merrill, 1973.

Tillich, Paul. *Systematic Theology*. 3 vols. Chicago: University of Chicago Press, 1967.

Tillman, Hoyt Cleveland. *Utilitarian Confucianism: Ch'en Liang's Challenge to Chu Hsi*. Cambridge: Harvard University Press, 1982.

———. *Confucian Discourse and Chu Hsi's Ascendancy*. Honolulu: University of Hawaii Press, 1992a.

———. "A New Direction in Confucian Scholarship: Approaches to Examining the Differences between Neo-Confucianism and *Tao-hsüeh*." *Philosophy East & West* 42, no. 3 (July 1992): 455–74, 1992b

———. *Ch'en Liang on Public Interest and the Law*. Honolulu: University of Hawaii Press, 1994.

Toulmin, Stephen. *Cosmopolis: The Hidden Agenda of Modernity*. Chicago: University of Chicago Press, 1990.

———. *Return of Reason*. Cambridge: Harvard University Press, 2001.

Tracy, David. *Blessed Rage for Order: The New Pluralism in Theology*. New York: Seabury Press, 1975.

———. *The Analogical Imagination: Christian Theology and the Culture of Pluralism*. New York: Crossroad, 1981.

———. *Plurality and Ambiguity: Hermeneutics, Religion, Hope*. San Francisco: Harper & Row, 1987.

Tu, Ching-I, ed. *Classics and Interpretations: The Hermeneutic Traditions in Chinese Culture*. New Brunswick NJ: Transaction, 2000.

Tu, Wei-ming. Review of *Hsin-t'i yü hsing-t'i* [Mind and nature], by Mou Tsung-san. *Journal of Asian Studies* 30 (May 1971): 642–47, 1971.

———. "Reconstituting the Confucian Tradition." *Journal of Asian Studies* 33 (May 1974): 441–54, 1974.

———. *Neo-Confucian Thought in Action: Wang Yang-ming's Youth (1472–1509).* Berkeley and Los Angeles: University of California Press.

———. *Humanity and Self-Cultivation: Essays in Confucian Thought.* Berkeley: Asian Humanities Press, 1979.

———. *Confucian Thought: Self-hood as Creative Transformation.* Albany: State University of New York Press, 1985.

———. *Centrality and Commonality: An Essay on Confucian Religiousness.* Rev. ed. Albany: State University of New York Press, 1989.

———. *Way, Learning, and Politics: Essays on the Confucian Intellectual.* Albany: State University of New York Press, 1993.

———, ed. *China in Transformation.* Cambridge: Harvard University Press 1994.

Tu Wei-ming, Milan Hejtmanek, and Alan Wachman, eds. *The Confucian World Observed: A Contemporary Discussion of Confucian Humanism in East Asia.* Honolulu: University of Hawaii Press, 1992.

Tu Weiming and Mary Evelyn Tucker, eds. *Confucian Spirituality.* 2 vols. New York: Crossroad, 2003–04.

Tuan, Yi-fu. *Topophila: A Study in Environmental Perception, Attitudes, and Values.* New York: Columbia University Press, 1974.

———. *Segmented World and Self: Group Life and Individual Consciousness.* Minneapolis: University of Minnesota Press, 1982.

———. *Morality and Imagination: Paradoxes of Progress.* Madison: University of Wisconsin Press, 1989.

———. *Passing Strange and Wonderful: Aesthetics, Nature, and Culture.* Washington: Island Press, 1993.

———. *Cosmos and Hearth: A Cosmoplite's Viewpoint.* Minneapolis: University of Minnesota Press, 1996.

———. *Escapism.* Baltimore: The Johns Hopkins University Press, 1998.

Tucker, Mary Evelyn, and John Berthrong, eds. *Confucianism and Ecology: The Interrelation of Heaven, Earth, and Humans.* Cambridge: Harvard University Press, 1998.

Turner, James. *Without God, Without Creed: The Origins of Unbelief in America.* Baltimore: Johns Hopkins University Press, 1985.

van der Poel, Marc. *Cornelius Agrippa, The Humanist Theologian and his Declamations.* Leiden: Brill, 1997.

Van Norden, Bryan W. *Confucius and the Analects: New Essays.* New York: Oxford University Press, 2001.

Van Zoeren, Steven. *Poetry and Personality: Reading, Exegesis and Hermeneutics in Traditional China.* Stanford: Stanford University Press, 1991.

Verdu, Alfonso. *The Philosophy of Buddhism: A "Totalistic" Synthesis.* The Hague: Martinus Nijhoff, 1981.

Wagner, Rudolf G. *The Craft of a Chinese Commentator: Wang Bi on the Laozi.* Albany: State University of New York Press, 2000.

———. *Language, Ontology, and Political Philosophy in China: Wang Bi's Scholarly Explorations in the Dark (Xuanxue).* Albany: State University of New York Press, 2003a.

———. *A Chinese Reading of the Daodejing: Wang Bi's Commentary on the Laozi with Critical Text and Translation.* Albany: State University of New York Press, 2003b.

Waley-Cohen, Joanna. *The Sextants of Beijing: Global Currents in Chinese History.* New York: W. W. Horton, 1999.

Walker, D. P. *Spiritual and Demonic Magic from Ficino to Campanella.* London: Warburg Institute, University of London, 1958.

Wang, Aihe. *Cosmology and Political Culture in Early China.* Cambridge: Cambridge University Press, 2000.

Wardy, Robert. *Aristotle in China: Language, Categories and Translation.* Cambridge: Cambridge University Press, 2000.

Ware, James R. *Alchemy, Medicine, and the Religion in China of 320 A. D: The Nei P'ien of Ko Hung.* Cambridge: M.I.T Press, 1966.

Watson, Burton, trans. *Basic Writings of Mo Tzu, Hsün Tzu, and Han Fei Tzu.* New York: Columbia University Press, 1967.

———. *The Complete Works of Chuang Tzu.* New York: Columbia University Press, 1968.

Watson, Richard A., and James E. Force, eds. *The Sceptical Mode in Modern Philosophy: Essays in Honor of Richard H. Popkin.* Dordrecht: Martinus Nijhoff, 1988.

Watson, Walter. *The Architectonics of Meaning: Foundations of the New Pluralism.* New ed. Chicago: The University of Chicago Press, 1993.

Whitehead, Alfred North. *Science and the Modern World.* New York: Macmillan, 1925.

———. *Adventures of Ideas.* New York: Macmillan, 1933.

———. 1938.

Modes of Thought. New York: Macmillan, 1938.

———. *Process and Reality: An Essay in Cosmology.* Ed. David Ray Griffin and Donald W. Sherburne. Corrected ed. New York: The Free Press, 1978.

———. *Religion in the Making.* New York: Fordham University Press, 1996.

Wieman, Henry H. *The Source of Human Good.* Carbondale: Southern Illinois University Press, 1946.

Wiggins, James B. *In Praise of Religious Diversity.* New York: Routledge, 1996.

Wilson, Edward O. *Consilience: The Unity of Knowledge.* New York: Vintage Books, 1998.

Wilson, Thomas A. *Genealogy of the Way: The Construction and Uses of the Confucian Tradition in Late Imperial China.* Stanford, CA: Stanford University Press, 1995.

———, ed. *On Sacred Ground: Culture, Society, Politics, and the Foundation of the Cult of Confucius.* Cambridge: Harvard University Press, 2002.

Wittenborn, Allen, trans. *Further Reflections on Things at Hand: A Reader by Chu Hsi*. Lanham: University Press of America, 1991.

Wong, David B. *Moral Relativity*. Berkeley and Los Angeles: University of California Press, 1984.

Wong, Eva. *Lieh-Tzu: A Taoist Guide to Practical Living*. Boston: Shambhala Publications, 1995.

Wright, Arthur F. "A Historian's Reflections on the Taoist Tradition." *History of Religions*. Vol. 9, nos. 2 and 3 (November 1969-February 1970): 248–55, 1970.

Wu, Kuang-ming. *On Chinese Body Thinking: A Cultural Hermeneutic*. Leiden: Brill, 1997.

———. *On Metaphoring: A Cultural Hermeneutic*. Leiden: Brill, 2001.

Wurthnow, Robert. *After Heaven: Spirituality in American Since the 1950s*. Berkeley and Los Angeles: University of California Press, 1998.

Xiao Gongzhuan [Hsiao, Kung-chuan]. *A History of Chinese Political Though:, From the Beginnings to the Sixth Century A. D.* vol. 1. Trans. F. W. Mote. Princeton: Princeton University Press, 1979.

Xu Fuguan. *Zhongkuo renxing lun shi: xian-Qin pian* [A history of the Chinese theory of human nature: The Pre-Qin period]. Taipei: Commercial Press, 1975.

Yang Bojun. *Liezi jishi* [Collected commentaries on the *Liezi*]. Hong Kong: Taiping Book Company, 1965.

Yang Hsiung. *The Canon of Supreme Mystery: A Translation with Commentary of the T'ai Hsüan Ching*. Trans. and ed. by Michael Nylan. Albany: State University of New York Press, 1993.

———. *The Elemental Changes: The Ancient Chinese Companion to the "I Ching"," The T'ai Hsüan Ching" of Master Yang Hsiung*. Trans. and ed. Michael Nylan. Albany: State University of New York Press, 1994.

Yao, Xinzhong, ed. *RoutledgeCurzon Encyclopedia of Confucianism*. 2 vols. London: RoutledgeCurzon, 2003.

Yates, Frances A. *Giordano Bruno and the Hermetic Tradition*. Chicago: University of Chicago Press, 1964.

———. *The Art of Memory*. Chicago: University of Chicago Press, 1966.

———. *The Occult Philosophy in the Elizabethan Age*. London: Routledge & Kegan Paul, 1979.

———. *The Rosicrucian Enlightenment*. London: Routledge, 1986.

Yearley, Lee H. "Hsün-tzu on the Mind: His Attempted Synthesis of Confucianism and Taoism." *Journal of Asian Studies* 39, no. 3 (May 1980): 465–80, 1980.

———. *Mencius and Aquinas: Theories of Virtue and Conceptions of Courage*. Albany: State University of New York Press, 1990.

Yu, Anthony C. *Rereading the Stone: Desire and the Making of Fiction in Dream of the Red Chamber*. Princeton NJ: Princeton University Press, 1997.

———. *State and Religion in China: Historical and Textual Perspectives*. Chicago: Open Court, 2005.

Yu, David. "A Comparative Study of the Metaphysics of Chu Hsi and A. N. Whitehead." Ph.D. diss., University of Chicago, 1959.

———. 1969. "Chu Hsi's Approach to Knowledge." *Chinese Culture* (December 1969): 1–14.

Yu, Yingshi [Ying-shih]. *Zhu Xi de lishi shijei: Songdai shidafu zhenxhi wenhua de yanjiu* [Zhu Xi's historical world: research on the political culture of Song-era scholar officials]. 2 vols. Taipei: Yunchen Wenhia Gongsi, 2003.

Zhang, Dainian. *Key Concepts in Chinese Philosophy.* Trans. and ed. Edmund Ryden. New Haven CT: Yale University Press, 2002.

Zhang, Jiacai. *Quanshi yu Jiangyou: Chen Chun yu Zhuzi xue* [Interpretation and construction: Chen Chun and the study of Master Zhu]. Beijing: Zhongguo zhexue qingnian xueshu wenku, 2004.

Zhang, Liwen. *Zhu Xi sixiang yenjiu* [Studies in the thought of Zhu Xi]. Beijing: Xinhua, 1981.

Zhang Longxi. *Mighty Opposites: From Dichotomies to Differences in the Comparative Study of China.* Stanford, CA: Stanford University Press, 1998.

Zheng, Jiadong. *Mou Zongsan.* Taipei: Dongda Tushu, 2000.

Ziporyn, Brook. *Evil and/or/as the Good: Omincentrism, Intersubjectivity, and Value Paradox in Tiantai Buddhist Thought.* Cambridge: Harvard University Press, 2000.

———. *The Penumbra Unbound: The Neo-Taoist Philosophy of Guo Xiang.* Albany: State University of New York Press, 2003.

———. *Being and Ambiguity: Philosophical Experiments with Tiantai Buddhism.* Chicago: Open Court, 2004.

Zürcher, Eric. *The Buddhist Conquest of China: The Spread and Adaptation of Buddhism in Early Medieval China.* 2 vols. Leiden: Brill, 1959.

INDEX